Corsica

THE ROUGH GUIDE

There are more than one hundred Rough Guide titles
covering destinations from Amsterdam to Zimbabwe

Forthcoming titles include
Bali • California
Thailand • Venice

Rough Guide Reference Series
Classical Music • The Internet • Jazz • Opera • Rock Music • World Music

Rough Guide Phrasebooks
Czech • French • German • Greek • Hindi & Urdu • Indonesian • Italian
Mandarin Chinese • Mexican Spanish • Polish • Portuguese • Russian
Spanish • Thai • Turkish • Vietnamese

Rough Guides on the Internet
http://www.roughguides.com

Rough Guide Credits

Editor:	Vivienne Heller
Series Editor:	Mark Ellingham
Editorial:	Martin Dunford, Jonathan Buckley, Samantha Cook, Jo Mead, Amanda Tomlin, Ann-Marie Shaw, Paul Gray, Sarah Dallas, Chris Schüler, Helena Smith, Kirk Marlow, Julia Kelly (UK); Andrew Rosenberg (US)
Online Editors:	Alan Spicer (UK); Andrew Rosenberg (US)
Production:	Susanne Hillen, Andy Hilliard, Judy Pang, Link Hall, Nicola Williamson, Helen Ostick
Cartography:	Melissa Flack, David Callier
Finance:	John Fisher, Celia Crowley, Catherine Gillespie
Marketing & Publicity:	Richard Trillo, Simon Carloss, Niki Smith (UK); Jean-Marie Kelly (US)
Administration:	Tania Hummel, Alexander Mark Rogers

Acknowledgements

Many thanks to everyone who helped with this new edition, particularly Julienne Young and staff at Voyages Ilena, for generous support and expert advice during the research trips; Léon and Julien in Porto, for their hospitality and the hair-raising boat trip around Scandola; and to Martin Cradick, Su Hart and Mr Milo, for sharing their house with me while I worked on this book.

To all at Rough Guides, thanks again for a job well done, especially Vivienne Heller, for her unflagging enthusiasm and painless editing, Helen Ostick for typesetting, Sam Kirby for cartography, Nikky Twyman for proofreading, plus Narrell Leffman, Carol Pucci and Simon Lewis for Basics research.

From the previous edition, continued thanks to Theo Taylor, Jonathan Buckley, Nia Williams and Geoffrey Young.

Above all, thank you to Tracy Walker for enduring patience at the wheel, resilience in the mountains and for weathering a stormy September in southern Corsica.

This edition published June 1997 by Rough Guides Ltd, 62–70 Shorts Gardens, London WC2H 9AB.
Reprinted in September 1998.
Distributed by the Penguin Group:
Penguin Books Ltd, 27 Wrights Lane, London W8 5TZ.
Penguin Books USA Inc, 375 Hudson Street, New York 10014, USA.
Penguin Books Australia Ltd, 487 Maroondah Highway, PO Box 257, Ringwood, Victoria 3134, Australia.
Penguin Books Canada Ltd, 10 Alcorn Avenue, Toronto, Ontario, Canada M4V 1E4.
Penguin Books (NZ) Ltd, 182–190 Wairau Road, Auckland 10, New Zealand.

Printed in England by Clays Ltd, St Ives PLC.
Typography and **original design** by Jonathan Dear and The Crowd Roars.
Illustrations throughout by Edward Briant.

Corsica

THE ROUGH GUIDE

Written and researched by
David Abram and Theo Taylor

additional research by
Geoffrey Young and Nia Williams

THE ROUGH GUIDES

Help us update

We've gone to a lot of trouble to ensure that this second edition of the *Rough Guide to Corsica* is accurate and up-to-date. However, things inevitably change, and if you feel we've got it wrong or left something out, we'd like to know: any suggestions, comments or corrections would be much appreciated. We'll credit all contributions and send a copy of the next edition – or any other *Rough Guide* if you prefer – for the best correspondence.

Please mark letters "Rough Guide to Corsica" and send to:
Rough Guides, 62–70 Shorts Gardens, London WC2H 9AB or
Rough Guides, 375 Hudson St, 9th floor, New York, NY 10014.

E-mail should be sent to:
mail@roughguides.co.uk

Online updates about Rough Guide titles can be found on our website at http://www.roughguides.com

The Authors

Born in Cardiff, Wales, **David Abram** read French at Warwick University, first visiting Corsica while a student teacher in the Dordogne. After graduation, he continued to live in southern Europe, teaching English to finance trips further afield, in West Africa, Turkey and India. A masters degree in social anthropology later led him into travel writing, via a Native American reservation in Montana, and he now divides his time between working on Rough Guides and playing music at home in Bristol, UK. David is the co-author of the Rough Guides to India and Goa, and contributed to the Highlands chapter of Scotland.

Theo Taylor has long been fascinated by Corsica. As part of her degree course she lived in Bastia for a year, teaching in a lycée. During that time she developed a first-hand knowledge of all regions of the island, establishing contacts which she renewed during the eighteen months of research that went into the Rough Guide.

Readers' letters

Thanks to the many readers of the last edition who wrote to us with their comments, criticisms and suggestions. The letters of the following proved particularly useful: Brad Baker, Dr Francis Beg, Michael Brother, Jeff Cherrington, C.V. Davies, Rachel Ellison, Vincent Golding, A. Goldsmith, Alice Holden, Claire Janes, Sarah Joannes, G.M. Johnson, Denise Lawry, Charles Le Bek, Maike Lindhout, Mike and Phyllis McNiven, Selby Milner, Michael Morris, Peter Morris, Paul Norton, Ralph Ostler, Sarah Price, Anita Roberts, Valery Sanders, Hew Sandilands, Kay M. Springham and Tim Weekes.

Rough Guides

Travel Guides • Phrasebooks • Music and Reference Guides

We set out to do something different when the first Rough Guide was published in 1982. Mark Ellingham, just out of University, was travelling in Greece. He brought along the popular guides of the day, but found they were all lacking in some way. They were either strong on ruins and museums but went on for pages without mentioning a beach or taverna. Or they were so conscious of the need to save money that they lost sight of Greece's cultural and historical significance. Also, none of the books told him anything about Greece's contemporary life – its politics, its culture, its people, and how they lived.

So with no job in prospect, Mark decided to write his own guidebook, one which aimed to provide practical information that was second to none, detailing the best beaches and the hottest clubs and restaurants, while also giving hard hitting accounts of every sight, both famous and obscure, and providing up-to-the-minute information on contemporary culture. It was a guide that encouraged independent travellers to find the best of Greece, and was a great success, getting shortlisted for the Thomas Cook travel guide award, and encouraging Mark, along with three friends, to expand the series.

The Rough Guide list grew rapidly and the letters flooded in, indicating a much broader readership than had been anticipated, but one which uniformly appreciated the Rough Guides' mix of practical detail and humour, irreverence and enthusiasm. Things haven't changed. The same four friends who began the series are still the caretakers of the Rough Guide mission today: to provide the most reliable, up-to-date and entertaining information to independent-minded travellers of all ages, on all budgets.

We now publish 100 titles and have offices in London and New York. The travel guides are written and researched by a dedicated team of more than 100 authors, based in Britain, Europe, the USA and Australia. We have also created a unique series of phrasebooks to accompany the travel series, along with the acclaimed series of music guides, and a best-selling pocket guide to the Internet and World Wide Web. We also publish comprehensive travel information on our two websites: http://www.hotwired.com/rough and http://www.roughguides.com

Contents

List of Maps

MAP SYMBOLS

Motorway		Tower
Major road		Lighthouse
Minor road		Cave
Steps		Pass
Path		Escarpment
Railway		Viewpoint
Wall		Marshland
Ferry route		Tourist office
Waterway		Post office
National boundary		Bus stop
Province boundary		Parking
Chapter division boundary		Building
Airport		Church
Camping		Cemetery
General point of interest		Park
Church (regional maps)		National park
Convent/Monastery		Beach

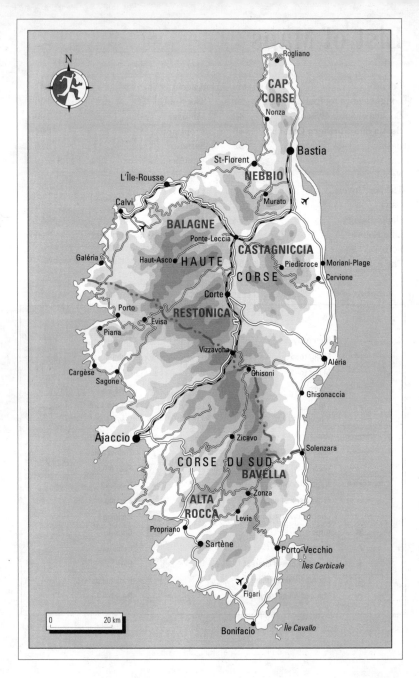

Introduction

A round one and a half million people visit Corsica each year, drawn by a climate that's mild even in winter and by some of the most astonishingly diverse landscapes in all of Europe. Nowhere in the Mediterranean has beaches finer than Corsica's perfect half-moon bays of white sand and transparent water, or seascapes more inspiring than the mighty granite cliffs of Corsica's west coast. Inland, crystalline rivers cascade from the island's central peaks, rushing through dense forests of colossal pines that have been untouched for centuries. In the north of the island, exquisite Romanesque churches overlook olive groves and ranks of vines, while to the south prehistoric statues lurk on moon-stark plains or in green valleys cloaked in aromatic maquis shrubs.

Even though the annual influx of tourists now exceeds the island's population sixfold, tourism hasn't spoilt the place. There are a few resorts, but over-development is rare and high-rise blocks non-existent, thanks largely to local resistance – sometimes violent – to the approaches of foreign speculators. Although they are obliged to import practically every consumer durable from the French mainland, many Corsicans regard themselves as a people apart, and a history of repeated invasion has only strengthened their **self-identity**. Through the Saracen raids of the Middle Ages and the periods of Spanish, Italian and French rule, the Corsicans have tenaciously held onto their heritage, and continue to preserve their **ancient culture** in the face of the modern world. Unearthly choral chants sung in the native language can still be heard in some remote regions, and a belief in the supernatural remains a potent force. A continuing preoccupation with death is attested by the mausoleums that you'll see on hillsides all over the island, while the fierce sense of family pride preserves more than a vestige of the feeling which fired the notorious vendettas of the past. The code of honour that protected the island's bandits right into the present century persists in a culture that tends to regard collaboration with the police as something shameful, and in which virtually every male carries a knife. Yet the

Corsicans' reputation for hostility to foreigners is largely unde-served. They might not be immediately approachable, but a deep hospitality is easily discovered if you make the effort – especially if you admire their island.

Where to go

Two hundred years of French rule have had limited tangible effect on Corsica, an island where Baroque churches, Genoese fortresses, fervent Catholic rituals and an indigenous language saturated with Tuscan influences show a more profound affinity with neighbouring Italy. During the long era of Italian supremacy the northeast and southwest of Corsica formed two provinces known as *Diqua dei monti* – this side of the mountains – and *Dila dei monti*, the uncontrollable side beyond. Today the French *départements* of Haute-Corse and Corse du Sud roughly coincide with these territories, and remain quite distinct in feel.

Capital of the north, **Bastia** was the principal Genoese stronghold and its fifteenth-century old town has survived almost intact. Of the island's two large towns, this is the more purely Corsican, and commerce rather than tourism is its main concern, which makes it an attractive alternative to some of the southern towns. Also relatively undisturbed, the northern **Cap Corse** harbours inviting sandy coves and coastal hamlets such as Erbalunga and Centuri-Port – friendly fishing villages that provide hotel accommodation for the few tourists who make it up here. Within a short distance of Bastia, the fertile region of the **Nebbio** contains a plethora of churches built by Pisan stoneworkers, the prime example being the cathedral of Santa Maria Assunta at the appealingly chic little port of **Saint-Florent**.

To the west of here, **L'Île-Rousse** and **Calvi**, the latter graced with an impressive citadel and fabulous sandy beach, are major targets for holidaymakers – and their hilly hinterland, the **Haute-Balagne**, offers plenty of hilltop villages to explore, as well as access to the northern reaches of the vast **Parc Naturel Régional**, an astounding area of forested valleys, gorges and peaks. The spectacular **Scandola** nature reserve, a part of the northwest coast that lies within the boundaries of the park, can be visited by boat from the tiny resort of **Porto**, from where walkers can also strike into the magnificently wild **Gorges de la Spelunca** and **Fôret d'Aitone** – where you might spot the island's delicacy, wild boar, if you keep your eyes peeled.

Climate Chart – Ajaccio

	Jan	Feb	Mar	Apr	May	June	July	Aug	Sep	Oct	Nov	Dec
Average Daily Max Temperature °C	13	14	16	18	21	25	27	28	26	22	17	14
Average Monthly Rainfall mm	76	65	53	48	50	21	10	16	50	88	97	98

Sandy beaches and rocky coves punctuate the **west coast** all the way down to **Ajaccio**, Napoléon's birthplace and Bastia's traditional rival. Its pavement cafés and palm-lined boulevards are thronged with tourists in summer, most of whom take the opportunity to sample the watersport facilities of the expansive and beautiful **Golfe d'Ajaccio**. Slightly fewer make it to nearby **Filitosa**, greatest of the many prehistoric sites scattered across this, the most heavily visited half of the island. Brash **Propriano**, the spot that has perhaps suffered most from the tourist boom, lies close to Filitosa and to stern **Sartène**, seat of the wild feudal lords who once ruled this region, and still the quintessential Corsican town.

More megalithic sites are to be found south of Sartène on the way to **Bonifacio**, a comb of ancient buildings perched atop furrowed white cliffs at the southern tip of the island. Equally popular **Porto-Vecchio** provides a springboard for excursions to the amazing beaches of the south, or alternatively to the oak forest of **Ospedale**, or even to the astounding **Col de Bavella**, where flattened pines spring from the bald granite needles. The **eastern plain** has less to boast of, but the Roman site at **Aléria** is worth a visit for its excellent museum, while to the north of Aléria lies the **Castagniccia**, a swathe of chestnut trees and alluring villages.

Corte, standing at the heart of Corsica, is the best base for exploring the stupendous mountains and gorges of the interior, with the remote valleys of the **Niolo** and **Asco** a stone's throw away. Dominating these valleys, **Monte Cinto** marks the northern edge of the island's spine of high peaks: the experienced hiker could attempt the **GR20**, an epic trail that traverses this magnificent ridge, past Monte d'Oro and Monte Renoso, as far as Monte Incudine in the south.

When to go

Whatever kind of holiday you intend to take, the **best times of year** to visit Corsica are the **late spring** and **late summer** or **early autumn**, when you're guaranteed sunshine without the stifling heat of July and August. The wild flowers carpeting the island in April and May make these delightful months to come, and autumn is just as good for scenic colour – the Castagniccia in particular is a riot of russet tones at this time of year. Beachgoers will be ensured a tan as late as October, and even if you plan a visit in the depths of winter you're unlikely to encounter much rain, though snow on the high mountains can restrict driving through the passes in January, February and March, when visibility is often obscured by mists.

Crowds are only likely to be a problem in the major resorts such as Porto-Vecchio and L'Île Rousse, especially in August, when the whole of Italy and France take their annual holiday. In the remoter areas you should book **accommodation** in advance, for the simple reason that there is rarely more than a single hotel in any village. For most of the island, however, you can rely on finding a place to stay at any time.

Part 1

The Basics

Getting There from Britain and Ireland

Flying is obviously the easiest way to reach Corsica, and you'll find a range of inexpensive deals on offer from London and Manchester. Fares inevitably vary according to the season – Easter and June to September are the peak times. The main destinations are Ajaccio, Bastia and Calvi, with some flights going to the smaller airport of Figari in the south of the island. Travelling by rail or car and ferry will usually work out more expensive than a charter flight, and is only worth considering if you want to tour mainland France on your way to Corsica.

By Plane

Air France, British Airways and TAT are the only airlines operating **scheduled flights** to Corsica from Britain, and all involve changing at either Paris or Nice on to a flight operated by a domestic carrier (Air Inter, Compagnie Corse Méditerranée, Kyrnair or TAT). Air France do a daily flight from London Heathrow to Paris Charles de Gaulle, connecting with an Air Inter flight from Orly Airport to Ajaccio, Bastia or Calvi. British Airways run a daily flight from London Heathrow to Nice, connecting with a Compagnie Corse Méditerranée flight to Calvi. Air France and British Airways also fly from Manchester to Paris and Nice daily. TAT fly out of London Heathrow to Figari, via Paris Orly.

The cheapest tickets, starting at around £260 return, are generally offered by TAT, as – unlike their competitors – both legs of the flight are on the same carrier (though British Airways handle the booking and enquiries). The least expensive Air France or British Airways fare is an **Apex** (Advance Purchase Excursion) return, costing around £290 in low season, rising to around £435 during July and August. From Manchester, Birmingham and Edinburgh the prices are slightly higher. Apex tickets must be reserved two weeks in advance and your stay must include one Saturday night. Your return date must be fixed when purchasing and there are no refunds.

Direct charter flights work out far cheaper, though it's advisable to book well in advance for July and August; at other times of the year it may be worth waiting until the last moment as the later you leave it the cheaper the price. Air 2000 fly from London Gatwick to both Calvi and Figari airports every Sunday from May to October. The other main operator is Monarch, who fly once each week to Ajaccio and Figari from Gatwick. Current costs are around £190 in high season, falling by £20 in low season, and the flying time is roughly 2hr 15min.

Tickets for charter flights are sold through specialist **agents** – bargains start at around £130 return to Calvi. There are dozens of sources, but you can most easily check what's on offer by tuning into Ceefax or visiting your local high street travel agent. Look, too, in the classified sections of the *Independent* and the *Daily Telegraph*, and in Sunday papers like the *Observer, Sunday Times* and *Sunday Independent*. If you're in London, check the back pages of listings magazine *Time Out*, the *Evening Standard* or the free travel mag *TNT*, found outside mainline train stations.

You may also want to consider a **package deal**, which takes care of flights and accommodation for an all-in price (see p.7). During slack periods at the beginning and end of the tourist season, many package companies sell off their unused seats at discount prices, advertising through the sources listed above, and these can offer exceptional bargain travel. If there seem to be no seats available at the time you wish to travel, it's often worth ringing around the package companies (see box on p.7) to see if they have any special last-minute deals.

Overland

There are numerous routes from England to the continent, and several ferries from the French mainland over to the Corsican ports (for details, see boxes on p.6). If you don't want the hassle of driving between London and Paris, you can put your car on Le Shuttle and head to France through the **Channel tunnel**, which has slashed the travelling time to Paris and Lille, from where you can pick up onward trains to Marseille, Toulon and Nice. SNCF (French Railways) also operate a motorail service that allows you to load your vehicle on a train in Calais and pick it up again in Nice, but the cost is high – £600 for a car and driver, and £105 for each additional passenger (or £52 for children). Travelling without your own car, you can opt for Eurostar's Channel tunnel service, or a slower, cheaper combination of trains and ferries to Nice, with a change in Paris. In addition, weekly buses also run direct to Nice from London Victoria.

By Rail

Much the fastest way to reach Corsica by rail is to take Eurostar's **Channel tunnel** train from London Waterloo to Paris, and then catch an onward service to one of the Mediterranean ferry ports. The journey to Nice takes eleven hours, including an hour for changing trains in Paris. You can also do the trip via Lille, thus avoiding having to cross the French capital, though this adds around an hour to the overall journey time. The standard return fare from London to Nice is £224, or £174 if you're under 26, and there are considerable reductions if you stay over a Saturday (£190 return). Bookings can be made through

Rail Agencies

British Rail International, International Rail Centre, Victoria Station, London SW1 (☎0171/834 2345).

Eurostar, EPS House, Waterloo Station, London SE1 (☎0345/303030).

Hoverspeed, Maybrook House, Queens Gardens, Dover CT17 (☎01304/240202).

Le Shuttle, PO Box 300, Folkestone, Kent CT19 (☎0990/353535).

SNCF, 179 Piccadilly, London W1 (☎0345/300003).

high street travel agents, by calling Eurostar direct, or through SNCF in London. Note, too, that there are direct connections through the Chunnel from many other British cities. The opening of the Channel tunnel has led to competitive cut-rate deals on **train and ferry/hovercraft** fares via Calais, Boulogne or Dieppe. Crossing the Channel this way works out quite a bit cheaper than using the Chunnel, but takes 5hr 30min longer. The one advantage of this route for budget travellers is that you leave London Charing Cross at 1pm and arrive in Nice at 10am the following day, thereby avoiding having to spend a night in Nice. That said, the direct Calais–Nice service only has couchettes, so you're obliged to pay a hefty £16 supplement, making the total fare from London to Nice £144 (against £190 on Eurostar).

Investing in a **train pass** is one way to reduce fares on this long haul. **EuroDomino** tickets (known as "Freedom Passes" in the UK) allow you unlimited rail travel within France (including on TGV services) for any three (£105), five (£135), or ten (£205) days in a calendar month (passengers under 26 pay £85, £110 and £175 respectively). The passes, which also entitle you to up to fifty percent reductions on train/ferry links to France, are available from accredited British Rail agents, the International Rail Centre and SNCF. Also worth considering if you plan to travel around France en route to Corsica is an **InterRail** pass, which offers one month's unlimited use of all European train services for £275 to anyone under 26 who has been a resident in Europe for at least six months. These are available through British Rail International and some travel agents, including

branches of Campus Travel and STA Travel (see box opposite).

Whichever method you choose, it's well worth **reserving** a seat (£3.70) or couchette (around £16) for your trip – something you should do well in advance in season.

By Bus

In the unlikely event that you'd want to take a coach to Corsica, there is a direct service to Nice operated by **Eurolines** (164 Buckingham Palace Rd, London SW1; ☎0990/808080), leaving once a week from London Victoria Coach Station throughout the year and three times a week from June to September. Fares are £110 return, with small reductions for under-25s and students.

Ferries from the UK to France

Of the numerous cross-Channel ferries, hovercrafts and high-speed catamarans, the most useful for **drivers** are those to France, Belgium or the Netherlands from Dover, Folkestone, Ramsgate, Newhaven, Portsmouth, Southampton, Plymouth, Felixstowe, Harwich and Hull. The fare structures are bewilderingly complex, with countless variations according to date of crossing, time of crossing and size of vehicle, but the box overleaf gives a rundown of the essential information on services and their costs – a return ticket is generally priced as two singles.

Ferries from France to Corsica

Ferries to Corsica from Marseille, Nice and Toulon (see overleaf) are run by SNCM Ferryterranée. Crossings take between seven and twelve hours on a regular ferry, or 2hr 45min–3hr 30min on the superfast NGV (Navire de Grande Vitesse). Fares on both services are the same: FF280-310 per passenger (and F235-635 for a car) from Marseille and Toulon, and F260-280 (and F210-555 for a car) from Nice. (There are also ferries from the Italian ports of Genoa, La Spezia

SNCM Addresses

Marseille: 61 bd des Dames, Marseille 13002 (☎04 91 56 30 10).

Nice: gare maritime, quai du Commerce, Nice 06000 (☎04 93 13 66 66).

Toulon: 21 & 49 av de l'Infanterie-de-Marine, Toulon 83000 (☎04 94 16 66 66).

FERRY CROSSINGS FROM BRITAIN

Route	Company	Frequency	Length of Crossing	Single Fare Car	Single Fare Passenger
Dover–Calais	Stena Sealink	6–25 daily	1hr 30min	£104–128	£24
Dover–Calais	Hoverspeed	20–24 daily	35–50min	£72–162	£25
Dover–Calais	P&O	20–25 daily	1hr 15min	£115–164	£23–28
Hull–Zeebrugge	North Sea Ferries	1 daily	14hr 30min	£70	£44
Hull–Rotterdam	North Sea Ferries	1 daily	14hr	£70	£44
Folkestone–Boulogne	Hoverspeed	6 daily	55min	£60–145	£25
Newhaven–Dieppe	Stena Sealink	2–4 daily	4hr	£94–116	£24
Plymouth–Roscoff	Brittany Ferries	1–2 daily	6hr	£114–173	£23–29
Poole–Cherbourg	Brittany Ferries	1–2 daily	4hr 30min	£68–158	£17–27
Portsmouth–Caen	Brittany Ferries	2–3 daily	5hr 45min	£68–158	£17–27
Portsmouth– Cherbourg	P&O	1–3 daily	4hr 45min	£115–164	£23–28
Portsmouth–Le Havre	P&O	2–3 daily	5hr 45min	£115–164	£23–28
Ramsgate–Dunkerque	Sally Line	5 daily	2hr 30min	£99	£20
Southampton–Cherbourg	Stena Sealink	1–2 daily	6–10hr	£151	£18–25

CROSS-CHANNEL FERRY COMPANIES

Brittany Ferries, Wharf Rd, Portsmouth PO2 (☎0990/360360).

Hoverspeed, Maybrook House, Queens Gardens, Dover CT17 (☎01304/240101).

North Sea Ferries, King George Dock, Hedon Rd, Hull HU9 (☎01482/377177).

P&O European Ferries, Channel House, Channel View Rd, Dover CT17 (☎0990/980980).

Sally Line, Argyle Centre, York St, Ramsgate CT11 (☎01843/595522); 81 Piccadilly, London W1 (☎0171/858 1127).

Stena Sealink, Charter House, Park St, Ashford TN24 (☎01233/647047), or 24hr information (☎01304/240028).

Ferry Crossings from France to Corsica

Route	Frequency	Length of Crossing	Period of Operation
Marseille–Ajaccio	3–7 weekly	11hr overnight, 4hr 30min (NGV) or 7hr daytime	year round
Marseille–Bastia	1–3 weekly	10hr overnight/daytime	year round
Marseille—Porto-Vecchio	1–3 weekly	14hr 30min overnight	June–Sept
Marseille—Propriano	1–5 weekly	12hr overnight, 9hr 30min daytime	April–Sept
Marseille–L'Île Rousse	1–3 weekly	11hr 30min overnight	June–Sept
Nice–Ajaccio	1–6 weekly	12hr overnight	year round
Nice–Bastia	1–21 weekly	6hr overnight	year round
Nice–Calvi	2–5 weekly	2hr 45min (NGV) daytime	April–Sept
Nice–L'Île Rousse	4–6 weekly	7hr overnight, 2hr 45min–5hr daytime	June–Sept
Toulon–Ajaccio	1–4 weekly	10hr overnight	April–Sept
Toulon–Bastia	1–3 weekly	8hr 30min overnight	April–Oct

Package Tour Companies in Britain

Bladon Lines, 56/58 Putney High St, London SW15 (☎0181/785 3131). *Accommodation in beach hotels and catered villas. Tennis, sailing and water-skiing included in the price. Special deals off-season.*

Corsican Affair, George House, 5–7 Humbolt Rd, London W6 (☎0171/385 8438). *Fly-drive, hotel packages, self-catering and cycling specialists.*

Corsican Places, Rutherford Business Park, Marley Lane, Battle, East Sussex (☎01424/774366). *Experienced, knowledgeable and friendly Corsica specialists, offering tailor-made packages at very reasonable prices, as well as flight-only charter fares.*

Cresta Holidays, 32 Victoria St, Altrincham WA14 (☎0161/927 7000). *Basic hotel-and-flight deals.*

French Expressions, 13 McCrone Mews, Belsize Park, London NW3 (☎0171/794 1480). *Upmarket holidays in four-star hotels, with scheduled flights. Prices start at around £1200 per person per week.*

Simply Corsica, 3 Chiswick Terrace, Acton Lane, London W4 (☎0181/995 9323). *Self-cater-ing and hotel accommodation; good value for money.*

Vacances en Campagne, Bignor, nr Pulborough, West Sussex RH20 (☎01798/869433). *Self-catering accommodation all over Corsica, from apartments and cottages to large mansions. High standards and good value for money.*

VFB Holidays, Normandy House, High St, Cheltenham GL50 (☎01242/240310). *Fly-drive family holidays with hotels and self-catering apartments. Sports facilities included in the price.*

Voyages Ilena, 7 Old Garden House, The Lanterns, Bridge Lane, London SW11 (☎0171/924 4440). *Classy hotels and self-catering accommodation in a range of beautifully located holiday homes all over Corsica; flight only, and fly-drives too. Among the oldest established and most knowledgeable operators on the island.*

Mark Warner, 20 Kensington Church St, London W8 (☎0171/393 3131). *Watersports specialists, with accommodation in upmarket beach-club-style hotels and apartments. Adults only.*

and Livorno – useful if you're doing a tour of Europe. You can contact the companies directly to reserve a space in peak season (essential with a car), or reserve places through SNCM's British agents, Southern Ferries, 179 Piccadilly, London W1 (☎0171/491 4968).

Packages

Most travel agents will be able to provide details of **packages** to Corsica, which vary from the standard travel-plus-hotel deals to more specialist trips such as walking tours. Alongside the large tour operators there exists a handful of small independent travel companies who offer pricier but more rewarding packages. Packages mostly fall into one of the following categories:

Fly-drive If you want to rent a car in Corsica, it's well worth checking with tour operators before you leave, as most deals work out much cheaper than renting on the spot.

Hotel packages These deals can be excellent value, usually featuring a good three-star hotel. All-in prices for a week's bed and breakfast in Calvi, for example, start at around £380 per person per week, rising by about £100 in high season.

Self-catering Some companies offer villa or farmhouse accommodation in combination with charter flights or fly-drives, but it's generally possible to book just the house. Accommodation prices start at £350 (or £650 peak season) per week – the shortest bookable period – for an average three-bedroomed house. Rental prices usually include insurance, water and electricity. Also available are holidays in self-catering town apartments, which tend to be slightly less expensive than the rural options.

Specialist holidays Some operators offer walking tours in Corsica, none of which come cheap; flights, accommodation, food, local transport and the services of a guide can cost up to £700 per person per week. Holidays based around watersports activities are also offered by many companies; for these, reckon on paying around £550 weekly per person.

Getting There from Ireland

No airline offers direct **flights** from Ireland to Corsica. The cheapest way is to get to either London or Paris and connect to a flight to Corsica from there. Ryanair, Aer Lingus and British Midland operate numerous daily flights **from Dublin and Cork** to both London and Paris. The cheapest fares to Paris Charles de Gaulle are generally Aer Lingus Super Apex tickets; these have to be booked seven days in advance, with a stay including a Saturday night, and cost from

IR£159; the standard return fare is IR£199. There are no direct flights **from Belfast** to Paris, but British Airways and British Midland fly to Heathrow, while Britannia Airways run to Luton for around £90 return – the cheapest service. British Airways fly daily to Paris for £140 return and British Midland also do a daily flight for around the same price. From Dublin you can slightly undercut the plane fare by getting a train ticket, but from Belfast it invariably works out cheaper to fly. For the best student/youth deals from either city, go to USIT (see box below).

Airlines and Agencies in Ireland

Aer Lingus, 40 O'Connell St, Dublin (☎01/844 4777); 46 Castle St, Belfast (☎01232/314844); 2 Academy St, Cork (☎021/327155); 136 O'Connell St, Limerick (☎061/474239).

Air Inter, 29–30 Dawson St, Dublin (☎01/677 8899).

Britannia Airways, no reservations office in Ireland – bookings from Luton Airport, Luton LU2 (☎01582/424155).

British Airways, 60 Dawson St, Dublin (☎1-800/626747); 9 Fountain Centre, College St, Belfast (☎0345/222111).

British Midland, 54 Grafton St, Dublin (☎01/798733); Suite 2, Fountain Centre, College St, Belfast (☎01232/225151).

Budget Travel, 134 Lower Baggot St, Dublin (☎01/661 1866).

Ryanair, College Park House, 20 Nassau St, Dublin (☎01/797444 or 01/770444).

Thomas Cook, 11 Donegall Place, Belfast (☎01232/240833); 118 Grafton St, Dublin (☎01/677 1721).

USIT, 19–21 Aston Quay, O'Connell Bridge, Dublin (☎01/628 9289); Fountain Centre, College St, Belfast (☎01232/324073); 33 Ferryquay St, Derry (☎01504/371888) 10–11 Market Parade, Cork (☎021/270900). *Student and youth specialists.*

Getting There from North America

From North America, Corsica is one of your more obscure European destinations. Discount travel agents – normally the mainstay of budget travellers – concentrate on high-volume routes and are unlikely to be able to ticket you beyond Paris, or perhaps Nice. By all means give it a shot, but you'll probably end up paying a published fare to Corsica.

Direct Flights

Air France is the only airline that flies all the way to Corsica (using its domestic subsidiary, Air Inter, for the final leg). However, most other transatlantic carriers have flights to Paris and can ticket you from Paris to Ajaccio or Bastia on Air Inter – the total fare might not be any more than what Air France charges, especially in winter (or even in summer, if you can find a good promotional fare to Paris). Check the box overleaf for airlines and their North American "gateway" cities.

The cheapest scheduled tickets are **Apex** tickets. These carry certain restrictions: you have to book – and pay – at least 21 days before departure and spend at least seven days abroad (maximum stay three months), and you're liable to get penalized if you change your schedule. There are also winter **Super Apex** tickets, sometimes

known as "Eurosavers" – slightly cheaper than an ordinary Apex, but limiting your stay to between 7 and 21 days. Some airlines also issue **Special Apex** tickets to those under 24, often extending the maximum stay to a year.

Fares are also heavily dependent on **season**, and are highest from around early June to the end of August, when everyone wants to travel; they drop during the "shoulder" seasons (Sept–Oct & April–May); and you'll get the best deals during the low season (Nov–March excluding Christmas). Figure on the following approximate Apex **fares** to Ajaccio, based on midweek travel (flying on weekends ordinarily adds about $50 to the return fare): New York, $716 in winter, $1009 in summer; Washington, $779/$1114; Miami, $825/$1125; Chicago, $810/$1108; Houston, $831/$1158; LA or San Francisco, $1090/$1230; Montréal or Toronto, CDN$609/$820.

Stopover Routes

If you don't mind spending a few days in Paris or London first, or if you were planning to visit other parts of France anyway, you might consider nabbing a cheap transatlantic flight through a discount travel agent and sorting out your onward travel when you get there.

Discount outlets, advertised in Sunday newspaper travel sections such as the *New York Times*, can usually do better than any Apex fare to Paris or London. They come in several forms. **Consolidators** buy up large blocks of tickets that airlines don't think they'll be able to sell at their published fares, and sell them at a discount. Besides being cheap, consolidators normally don't impose advance-purchase requirements (though in busy times you'll want to book ahead just to be sure of getting a ticket), but they do often charge very stiff fees for date changes. Also, these companies' margins are pretty tiny, so they make their money by dealing in volume – don't expect them to entertain lots of questions. **Discount agents** also wheel and deal in blocks of tickets offloaded

AIRLINES AND AGENTS IN NORTH AMERICA

AIRLINES

Only gateway cities are listed for each airline; other routings are always possible using connecting flights.

Air Canada ☎1-800/776 3000; in Canada ☎800/555 1212. *Montréal, Toronto and Vancouver to Paris and Nice.*

Air France ☎1-800/237 2747; in Canada ☎800/667 2747. *New York, Washington DC, Miami, Montréal, Toronto, Chicago, Houston, San Francisco and Los Angeles to Paris or Nice; connections to Ajaccio on Air Inter.*

American Airlines ☎1-800/433 7300. *New York, Miami, Dallas-Fort Worth, Chicago and Los Angeles to Paris.*

AOM French Airlines ☎310/338 9613. *Non-stop from Los Angeles to Paris three to five times per week.*

British Airways ☎1-800/247 9297; in Canada ☎800/668 1080. *Many North American cities to Paris and Nice (via London).*

Canadian Airlines ☎1-800/426 7000. *Montréal, Toronto and Vancouver to Paris.*

Continental Airlines ☎1-800/231 0856. *New York, Houston and Denver to Paris.*

Delta Airlines ☎1-800/241 4141; in Canada ☎800/555 1212. *Atlanta, Cincinnati and New York to Paris.*

Northwest Airlines ☎1-800/225 2525. *Los Angeles, Minneapolis and Detroit to Paris.*

PIA Pakistan International Airways ☎1-800/221 2552. *New York to Paris.*

Tower Air ☎1-800/221 2500. *Daily non-stop from New York to Paris Charles de Gaulle.*

TWA ☎1-800/892 4141. *New York, Boston, St Louis and Washington to Paris.*

United Airlines ☎1-800/538 2929. *Chicago, Washington DC, Los Angeles and San Francisco to Paris.*

US Air ☎1-800/622 1015. *Daily non-stop flights to Paris from Philadelphia.*

FLIGHT AGENTS

Airhitch ☎212/864 2000. *Standby seat broker; for a set price, they guarantee to get you on a flight as close to your preferred destination as possible, within a week.*

Air Brokers International ☎1-800/883 3273. *Consolidator.*

Council Travel ☎1-800/226 8624; email cts@ciee.org

Education Travel Center ☎1-800/7475551. *Student/youth discount agent.*

Flight Centre ☎604/739 9539. *Discount air fares from Canadian cities.*

High Adventure Travel ☎1-800/428 8735. *Nationwide student travel organization with branches (among others) in New York, San Francisco, Washington DC, Boston, Austin, Seattle, Chicago and Minneapolis. Highly recommended web site: http://www.highadv.com.*

Interworld ☎305/443 4929. *Consolidator.*

Travel Cuts ☎416/979 2406. *A student travel organization with branches all over Canada.*

---

by the airlines, but they typically offer a range of other travel-related services such as travel insurance, rail passes, youth and student ID cards, car rentals, tours and the like. These agencies tend to be most worthwhile to students and under-26s, who can often benefit from special fares and deals. Some agencies specialize in **charter flights**, which may be even cheaper than anything available on a scheduled flight, but again there's a trade-off: departure dates are fixed, withdrawal penalties are high (check the refund policy), and the plane is likely to be packed. **From Canada**, Air

Transit Holidays offers a wide selection of non-stop late spring, summer and fall flights to Paris from Vancouver and Toronto, and non-stop charters to Lyon from Toronto, and their fares are very competitive (return to Paris from Toronto $449–660, from Vancouver $759–1000). You could also try Fiesta West/Canada 3000, another Canadian charter company, which does non-stops to Paris from Vancouver and Calgary from July to September for $925.

An option well worth considering if you're on a tight budget is a **courier flight**, in which you deliver a package in exchange for a heavily dis-counted ticket. The disadvantage with these is that to get the best deals you have to book a maximum three days before departure, but if you can be this flexible you stand to save a lot of money. Standard return courier flights to Paris go for around $350, while last-minute specials can cost as little as $150. For more information, con-tact The Air Courier Association, 191 University Blvd, Suite 300, Denver, Colorado 80206 (☎303/279 3600), or consult *How to Travel Worldwide for Next to Nothing* by Kelly Monaghan ($17.50 postpaid from The Intrepid Traveler, PO Box 438, New York, NY 10034).

If you're looking to regroup somewhere in Europe before continuing on to Corsica, **London** is a good place to aim for: there are plenty of flights from there, and of course language is no problem. For advice on getting from London to Corsica, see pp.3–7. The other obvious stopover is **Paris**, where you can avail yourself of Air Inter's standard Paris–Ajaccio fare of about $114 one-way, or $228 return.

Package Tours

Corsica is way off the beaten path for most North American **tour** companies. Your choices basically come down to a couple of outfits that can arrange short-term rentals of villas ($430 and up

for a week for two people) and a couple of adventure-travel companies that do hiking trips in Corsica (about $900 for a week's trek). If you're set on going with a package tour, you might want to consider contacting a tour operator in Britain, where Corsica is a much more popular destination (see box on p.7). Alternatively, you could deal directly with Ollandini Voyages, Corsica's biggest tour operator – they're at 3 place de Gaulle, BP 304, 20176 Ajaccio, France (☎04 95 21 72 21).

Tour Operators in North America

Adventure Center, 1311 63rd St, Suite 200, Emeryville, CA 94608 (☎1-800/227 8747). *Corsican village treks ($895 for 15 days).*

Himalayan Travel, 112 Prospect St, Stamford, CT 06901 (☎1-800/225 2380). *Trekking in the Corsican interior, from $1195 for 15 days.*

Interhome, 124 Little Falls Rd, Fairfield, NJ 07004 (☎1-800/882 6864). *Short-term villa and chateau rentals.*

Vacances en Campagne, PO Box 299, Elkton, VA 22827 (☎1-800/327 6097). *Short-term rentals of châteaux and country houses, from around $430 a week.*

Getting There from Australasia

There are no direct flights from Australia or New Zealand to Corsica – the best you can do is fly direct to London, Paris or Rome and change planes there for Ajaccio or Bastia. If you qualify for student/youth discounts, it's best to book through an agent like STA (see box overleaf). Fares tend to be cheaper from mid-January to the end of February and during October and November, increasing during high season (May–Aug and Dec–Jan). Some air-lines, such as Alitalia and Air France, offer free transfer flights within Europe that can get you to Corsica. Others have competitively priced add-on fares from Paris and Rome from around A$350/NZ$420.

AIRLINES AND AGENTS IN AUSTRALIA AND NEW ZEALAND

AIRLINES

Aeroflot, 88 George St, Sydney (☎02/9233 7911). No NZ office.

Air France/Quantas, 12 Castlereagh St, Sydney (☎02/9231 1000); 2nd Floor, Dataset House, 143 Nelson St, Auckland (☎09/303 3521).

Alitalia, Orient Overseas Building, 32 Bridge St, Sydney (☎02/9247 1308); 6th Floor, Trustbank Building, 229 Queen St, Auckland (☎09/379 4457).

British Airways, 64 Castlereagh St, Sydney (☎02/9258 3300); Dilworth Building, cnr Queen & Customs streets, Auckland (☎09/3656 8690).

Cathay Pacific, Level 5, 28 O'Connell St, Sydney (local call rate ☎13 1747); 11f Arthur Andersen Tower, 205–209 Queen St, Auckland (☎09/379 0861).

Garuda, 55 Hunter St, Sydney (☎02/9334 9944); 120 Albert St, Auckland (☎09/366 1855).

JAL, Floor 14, Darling Park, 201 Sussex St, Sydney (☎02/9283 1111); Floor 12, Westpac Tower, 120 Albert St, Auckland (☎09/379 9906).

Malaysia Airlines, 16 Spring St, Sydney (local call rate ☎13 2627); Floor 12, Swanson Centre, 12–26 Swanson St, Auckland (☎09/373 2741).

Singapore Airlines, 17–19 Bridge St, Sydney (local call rate ☎13 1011); Lower Ground Floor, West Plaza Building, cnr Customs & Albert streets, Auckland (☎09/379 3209).

Thai Airways, 75–77 Pitt St, Sydney (☎02/9844 0999, or toll-free ☎1-800/422 020); Kensington Swan Building, 22 Fanshawe St, Auckland (☎09/377 3886).

AUSTRALIAN AGENTS

Anywhere Travel, 345 Anzac Parade, Kingsford, Sydney (☎02/9663 0411).

Brisbane Discount Travel, 260 Queen St, Brisbane (☎07/3229 9211).

Flight Centres, Australia: Level 11, 33 Berry St, North Sydney (☎02/9241 2422); Bourke St, Melbourne (☎03/9650 2899); Circular Quay, Sydney (☎02/241 2422); Bourke St, Melbourne (☎03/650 2899).

Northern Gateway, 22 Cavenagh St, Darwin (☎08/8941 1394).

Passport Travel, 320b Glenferrie Rd, Malvern, Melbourne (☎03/824 7183).

STA Travel, 702–732 Harris St, Ultimo, Sydney (☎02/9212 1255, or toll-free ☎1-800/637 444); 256 Flinders St, Melbourne (☎03/9654 7266).

Thomas Cook World Rail, Australia (☎1-800/422 747); New Zealand (☎09/263 7260).

NEW ZEALAND AGENTS

Budget Travel, 16 Fort St, Auckland, and at other branches around the city (☎09/366 0061, or toll free ☎0800/808 0040).

Destinations Unlimited, 3 Milford Rd, Milford, Auckland (☎09/373 4033).

Flight Centres, National Bank Towers, 205–225 Queen St, Auckland (☎09/209 6171);

Shop 1m, National Mutual Arcade, 152 Hereford St, Christchurch (☎03/379 7145); 50–52 Willis St, Wellington (☎04/472 8101).

STA Travel, Traveller's Centre, 10 High St, Auckland (☎09/309 9995); 233 Cuba St, Wellington (☎04/385 0561); 223 High St, Christchurch (☎03/379 9098); other offices in Dunedin, Palmerston North and Hamilton.

The cheapest return tickets **to London** from Sydney start at around A$1600 with Aeroflot (via Moscow), leaving twice weekly. Slightly more expensive are seats from Sydney and Auckland on Garuda (via Indonesia and Bangkok), Japan Airlines (overnighting in Tokyo), or direct on British Airways, all costing from A$1800/ NZ$2600.

Air France fly from Sydney and Auckland **to Paris** (Charles de Gaulle) via Jakarta and Singapore at least once a week from around A$2000/NZ$2200; this includes a return "side-trip" within France, which can be used to reach Nice or Marseille. Marseille and Paris can also be reached on Aeroflot's bi-weekly service from Sydney via Moscow for A$1600, and on Japan

Airlines, Malaysia Airlines, Thai Airways, Cathay Pacific and Singapore Airlines.

Qantas fly three times a week from Auckland via Sydney **to Rome**; the fare, from around A$2000/NZ$2200, allows two return "side-trips", which can get you to Nice, Marseille or Genoa. Rome can also be reached on Aeroflot's bi-weekly service from Sydney via Moscow for A$1600, and on Malaysia Airlines, Japan Airlines, Thai Airways, Cathay Pacific and Singapore Airlines.

Some **round-the-world** routings also allow Corsica as a side-trip, using a combination of airlines. Generally, six free stopovers are offered by participating carriers, with additional stopovers around $100 each in Australia and New Zealand. Fares start at A$2399/ NZ$3380. Possibilities include UA's "Globetrotter", Air New Zealand/KLM/Northwest's "World Navigator", and Qantas/ British Airway's "Global Explorer".

Red Tape and Visas

Citizens of EU countries, Japan, New Zealand, Canada and the United States do not need any sort of visa to enter France for a stay of up to ninety days. Nationals of all other countries, including Australia, must obtain a visa before arrival in Corsica – the addresses of the major French embassies and consulates are given below. Three types of visa are currently issued: a transit visa, which is valid for only three days; a short stay (court séjour) visa, valid for ninety days after date of issue; and the visa de circulation, which allows multiple stays of ninety days over three years (maximum of 180 days in any one year).

To obtain a visa you'll need an application form (available from the consulate or embassy),

French Embassies and Consulates Overseas

Opening hours for most French embassies and consulates are Mon–Fri 9am–1pm.

Australia 492 St Kilda Road, Melbourne, VIC 3001 (☎03/9820 0921); 31 Market St, Sydney, NSW 2000 (☎02/9261 5779).

Canada 42 Promenade Sussex, Ottawa, ON K1M 2C9 (☎613/789 1795); 1 place Ville Marie, Bureau 22601, Montréal, Québec, QC H3B 4S3 (☎514/878 4385); 25 rue St-Louis, Québec QC G1R 3Y8 (☎418/688 0430); 130 Bloor Street West, Suite 400, Toronto, ON M5S 1N5 (☎416/925 8041); 1201-736 Granville St, Vancouver, BC V6Z 1H9 (☎604/681 4345).

Ireland 36 Ailesbury Road, Dublin 4 (☎01/260 1666).

New Zealand 1 Willeston St, PO Box 1695, Wellington (☎04/472 0200).

UK 6a Cromwell Place, London SW7 (☎0171/838 2000); 7–11 Randolph Crescent, Edinburgh (☎0131/225 7954).

USA 4101/Reservoir Rd NW, Washington DC 20007 (☎202/944 6000); Park Square Building, Suite 750, 31 St James Ave, Boston, MA 02116 (☎617/542 7374); 737 North Michigan Ave, Olympia Centre, Suite 2020, Chicago, IL 60611 (☎312/787 5359); 10990 Wilshire Blvd, Suite 300, Los Angeles, CA 90024 (☎310/235 3200); 934 Fifth Ave, New York, NY 10021 (☎212/606 3620); 540 Bush St, San Francisco, CA 94108 (☎415/397 4330).

a passport valid for at least six months from your intended date of arrival in France, a ticket or verification of travel, and a money order or bank cheque (not a personal cheque) for A$54, with an enclosed stamped-addressed envelope.

For stays longer than ninety days you are officially supposed to apply for a Carte de Séjour, for which you'll have to show proof of income at least equal to the minimum wage. However, EU passports are rarely stamped, so there is no evidence of how long you've been in the country, and if your passport is stamped you can legitimately cross the French border, to Belgium or Germany for example, and re-enter for another ninety days.

Health and Insurance

No visitor to France requires vaccinations of any kind, and general health care in Corsica is of the highest standard. There are hospitals in all the main towns, and smaller places like Porto-Vecchio have clinics serving the surrounding area. EU nationals can take advantage of the French health services under the same terms as the residents of the island, as long as you're in possession of a form E111, application forms for which can be picked up at most major post offices. However, because the French health system provides subsidized rather than free treatment, travel insurance – covering health plus loss or theft of baggage – remains essential.

Health Problems

Under the French social security system, every hospital visit, doctor's consultation and pre-scribed medicine is charged – though in an emergency you won't be presented with the bill up front. Although all employed French people are entitled to a refund of 75–80 percent of their medical expenses, this can still leave a hefty shortfall, especially after a stay in hospital (accident victims have to pay even for the ambulance or helicopter that takes them there).

To find a **doctor**, stop at any *pharmacie* and ask for an address – we've given *pharmacie* addresses throughout the *Guide*. Consultation fees should be around 110F, and after the visit you'll be given a *Feuille de Soins* (Statement of Treatment) for later documentation of insurance claims. **Prescriptions** should be taken to a *pharmacie*, which is also equipped, and obliged, to give first aid, for a fee. The medicines you buy will have little stickers (*vignettes*) attached to them, which you must remove and stick to your *Feuille de Soins*, together with the prescription itself. In serious **emergencies** you will always be admitted to the local hospital (*centre hospitalier*), whether under your own power or by ambulance.

Insurance

Before you purchase any insurance, check what you have already – **North Americans** may find themselves covered for medical or other losses while abroad as part of a family or student policy. Many bank and charge accounts include some travel cover, and some credit cards offer insurance benefits if you use them to pay for your holiday tickets. Canadians especially are usually covered by their provincial health plans, and holders of ISIC cards are entitled (outside the USA) to be reimbursed for $3000-worth of accident coverage and sixty days of in-patient benefits up to $100 a day for the period the card is valid.

If you do want a specific travel insurance policy, there are numerous kinds to choose from: short-term combination policies covering everything from baggage loss to broken legs are the best bet and cost around $50–70 for fifteen days (depending on level of coverage), $80–105 for a month, $149–207 for two months and $510–700 for a year. One thing to bear in mind is that none of the policies currently available covers theft; they only cover loss while in the custody of an identifiable person – and even then you must make a

report to the police and get their written statement. Three companies you might try are: Access America (☎1-800/284 8300), Carefree Travel Insurance (☎1-800/323 3149) or, for Canada only, Desjardins Travel Insurance (☎1-800/463 7830).

If transiting via Britain, North Americans might consider buying a policy from a British travel agent. British policies tend to be cheaper than American ones, and routinely cover thefts – which are often excluded from the more health-based American policies.

In **Australia** and **New Zealand**, travel insurance is put together by the airlines and travel agents' organizations such as UTAG and AFTA, Cover More and Ready Plan, in conjunction with the insurance companies. Policies tend to be comparable in premium and coverage, though Ready Plan offer the best overall deals, costing A$190/NZ$220 for one month, A$270/NZ$320 for two months and A$330/NZ$400 for three months. Adventure sports are usually covered in standard policies, except mountaineering with ropes, bungy jumping and unassisted diving without an Open Water Licence. If you think you may need coverage for such activities, check the small print carefully before committing yourself. Low-cost companies in Australia and New Zealand worth telephoning for a quote include: UTAG (United Travel Agents Group), 347 Kent St, Sydney (toll-free ☎1-800/809462); AFTA (Australian Federation of Travel Agents), 144 Pacific Highway, North Sydney (☎02/956 4800); Ready Plan, 141–147 Walker St, Dandenong, Victoria (toll-free ☎1-800/337 462); Cover More, Level 9, 32 Walker St, North Sydney (☎02/9202 8000).

In **Britain**, as well as those policies offered by travel agents, consider using a specialist, low-priced firm like Columbus (17 Devonshire Square, London EC2M 4SQ; ☎0171/375 0011, fax 375 0022), Endsleigh (Cranfield House, 97–107 Southampton Row, London WC1; ☎0171/436 4451), who offer two weeks' basic cover in Europe for around £20, or Worldwide (☎0700/080 8080, fax 0132/368 366), who are even cheaper. Both have a choice of "Standard" and more expensive "Premier" coverage, the basic difference between these being the amount of compensation you're entitled to if you claim.

With all policies, for **medical treatment and drugs** keep all the bills and claim the money back later. For any **theft** (including money), register the loss immediately with the local police – without their report you won't be able to claim.

Money, Banks and Costs

French currency is the franc (abbreviated as **F** or sometimes **FF**), divided into 100 centimes. Francs come in notes of 500, 100, 50 and 20F, and there are coins of 20F, 10F, 5F, 2F, 1F, 20 centimes and 10 centimes. The exchange rate is prone to fluctuations, with the franc veering between 7F and 9F to £1, and between 3.50F and 5F to $1.

Normal **banking hours** are 9.30am to noon and 2pm to 4pm, closed on Sunday and either Monday or, less usually, Saturday. **Rates of exchange** and **commissions** vary from place to place, but as a rule of thumb, the high street banks – Crédit Agricole, Crédit Lyonnais and Société Générale – give much better value than the privately run bureaux de change around the island. Wherever you propose to change money, always shop around first, as the commission rates can vary wildly, between 20F and 50F. There is no American Express office, but you can use the credit cards at a large number of cash dispensers (see below).

Travellers' cheques, one of the safest ways of carrying your money, are available from almost any of the principal banks, whether you have an account there or not. There's usually a service charge of one percent on the amount purchased, though some go as high as five percent (your own bank may offer cheques free of charge provided you meet certain conditions). Thomas Cook, Visa and American Express, equally accepted, are the most widely recognized brands. In recent years, Thomas Cook travellers' cheques have been the best deal for British visitors to Corsica, as the Société Générale change them without charging commission provided they are in French francs.

The major **credit cards and charge cards** are usually accepted in tourist-concentrated areas, but it's best to have cash for the more remote hotels, gas stations and restaurants. Visa is the most widely recognized; American Express and Access rank considerably lower – only the Crédit Agricole bank provides facilities for Access, and many restaurants and hotels won't accept it because of the huge commissions they have to pay. You can, of course, also use your credit card to withdraw money from **automatic cash dispensers** (*distributeurs de billets*) during or outside normal banking hours. The transaction takes seconds, and the small interest fee you pay your home bank can be well worth the convenience. The one catch is that there are as yet relatively few machines in Corsica, so don't count on finding one in small towns and villages. And if you're planning to rent a car or motor bike, make sure you take a credit card along as you'll need one to fill out the mandatory deposit docket (*caution*).

Finally, it's worth noting that **Eurocheques** – formerly the cheapest and most convenient way to pay on the continent – are no longer widely accepted in Corsica, not even by the large banks.

Costs

With a cost of living higher than even the Côte d'Azur, Corsica is far from a cheap destination. Aside from the obvious fact the most commodities have to be imported by sea or air, the main reason for this is the island's economic dependence on tourism, which ensures that from June until September prices of almost everything in demand by visitors – principally rooms and restaurant meals – double or triple, allowing the locals to make enough cash during the short summer season to see them through the winter. That said, your trip need not cost you a fortune, and throughout this book we highlight ways to help you enjoy the island on a minimum budget.

Accommodation will probably constitute your main expense during your stay, particularly if you come in July and August when room tariffs soar. The majority of hotels charge 200–300F for a double room, and 200–250F for a single. As a rule of thumb, places on the coast tend to be more expensive, with the best value deals in the mountains of the interior, where there's far less seasonal price variation. Luxury places and cheap *pensions* are rarer, and where this type of accommodation exists it is listed in the guide. Staying in campsites can be a money-saver as long as you stick to the basic sites found in rural areas (around 50–100F per day) and avoid the flashy three-star complexes along the coast, which can cost almost as much as a hotel. Travelling around the island out of season you'll also find hoteliers ready to offer reductions, especially if you agree to stay for a couple of nights or more, so don't be afraid to haggle.

As for **food**, in any town you'll find restaurants with three- or four-course meals for between 75F and 100F, and the island is full of pizzerias where you can eat a filling hot meal for even less than that. Picnic fare, obviously, is less costly, particularly if you buy from small local shops or supermarkets rather than markets or specialist food outlets aimed at tourists. More sophisticated meals using takeaway salads and ready-to-heat dishes, bought in *rôtisseries* or charcuteries, can be put together without stretching the wallet too far. If you're on a tight budget, you need to beware of the expense of beer and coffee in bars, cafés and clubs – though cigarettes are thirty percent cheaper here than on the mainland. Also watch out for the cost of wine in restaurants, which can easily double your bill if you're not careful.

Public transport costs around 110F for 100km, whether you're travelling by buses or by the *micheline* train (Bastia–Ajaccio is currently around 120F). Petrol prices are amongst the highest in Europe, at just over 5F per litre for leaded and just under 5F for unleaded (approximately 25F per imperial gallon, 20F per US gallon). Car rental will set you back anything upwards of 2000F per week, depending on the season and company, and where you rent the car (rates are much higher in Corsica – see p.22). Bicycles cost about 150F per day, and motorbikes start at around 230F for a 50cc scooter.

Museums and monuments won't prove too much of a drain on your resources, for the simple reason that there are relatively few on the island. Most charge around 15F and give discounts for holders of ISIC cards or to under-26s on presentation of a passport.

Thus a **minimum daily requirement** would be around 175F per person, if camping and doing your own catering; a couple staying in budget hotels could live comfortably on about 300F per person; and, in order to have no worries at all, count on spending around 600F per day. Finally, bear in mind local attitudes to money. Living on a rock-bottom budget – camping rough, eating nothing but bread and cheese, and avoiding bars and cafés altogether – is unlikely to endear you to the locals, who love to joke about *les mangeurs des tomates* – those die-hard backpackers and camper-van tourists that are so eager to save money they miss out on one of the things Corsicans are deservedly most proud of: their wonderful cuisine.

Information and Maps

French Government Tourist Offices

Australia BNP House, 17th Floor, 12 Castlereigh St, Sydney 2000 (☎02/213 5244).

Britain 178 Piccadilly, London W1 (premium-rate line costing 45p per min: ☎0891/244123).

Canada 1 Dundas St, W Suite 2405, PO Box 8, Toronto ON M5G 1Z3 (☎416/593 4717); 1981 av McGill College, Suite 490, Montréal, QC H3A (☎514/288 4264, fax 514/845 4868).

Ireland 35 Lower Abbey St, Dublin 1 (☎01/703 4046, fax 01/874 7324).

Netherlands Prinsengracht 670, 1017 KX Amsterdam (☎20/24 75 34).

USA 444 Madison Ave, 16th Floor, New York, NY 10022 (☎212/838 7800, fax 212/838 7855); 9454 Wilshire Blvd, Suite 715, Beverly Hills, Los Angeles, CA 90212 (☎310/271 6665, fax 310/276 2835); 676 North Michigan Ave, Suite 3360, Chicago, IL 60611-2819 (☎312/337 6339).

The foreign branches of the French Government Tourist Office give away maps and glossy brochures, including lists of Corsican hotels, campsites, sports facilities and public transport services. In Corsica every major town has a tourist office (Office du Tourisme), addresses of which are detailed throughout this guide. Usually only open in summer (May–Sept), these offices give out specific local information, including free town plans, lists of leisure activities, bike hire and countless other things.

Many tourist offices also publish hotel and restaurant listings, as well as driving and walking itineraries for their areas. In mountain regions they share premises with the local hiking and climbing organizers, who can give detailed advice about the best routes to take. Map information about forest trails can be found on boards outside *maisons forestières* (forest huts) – the only one open to the public is in the Forêt d'Aitone.

In addition to the various free leaflets – and the maps in this guide – the one extra map you'll definitely want is a detailed **road map**. The Michelin yellow map series 1:200,000 (no 90) is the best map of the whole island for drivers. If you're planning to **walk or cycle**, check the three series of IGN maps: 1:100,000 (green), 1:50,000 (also green) and 1:25,000 (blue). The IGN 1:100,000 maps, the smallest-scale contoured maps available, are essential for cyclists, who tend to cycle off 1:25,000 maps in a couple of hours.

MAP OUTLETS

BRITAIN AND IRELAND

Daunt Books, 83 Marylebone High St, London W1 (☎0171/224 2295).

Easons Bookshop, 40 O'Connell St, Dublin 1 (☎01/873 3811).

Fred Hanna's Bookshop, 27–29 Nassau St, Dublin 2 (☎01/677 1255).

Hodges Figgis Bookshop, 56–58 Dawson St, Dublin 2 (☎01/677 4754).

National Map Centre, 22–24 Caxton St, London SW1 (☎0171/222 4945).

John Smith and Sons, 57–61 St Vincent St, Glasgow G2 (☎0141/221 7472).

Stanfords,* 12–14 Long Acre, London WC2 (☎0171/836 1321); 52 Grosvenor Gardens, London SW1W; 156 Regent St, London W1R.

The Travel Bookshop, 13–15 Blenheim Crescent, London W11 (☎0171/229 5260).

Waterstone's, Queens Building, 8 Royal Ave, Belfast BT1 (☎01232/247355).

* *Note*: For maps by mail or phone order, call ☎0171/836 1321.

USA AND CANADA

Book Passage, 51 Tamal Vista Drive Corte Madera, CA 94925 (☎415/927 0960).

The Complete Traveler Bookstore, 199 Madison Ave, New York, NY 10016 (☎212/685 9007); 3207 Fillmore St, San Francisco, CA 92123 (☎415/923 1511).

Elliot Bay Book Company, 101 S Main St, Seattle, WA 98104 (☎206/624 6600).

Forsyth Travel Library, 9154 W 57th St, Shawnee Mission, KS 66201 (☎1-800/367 7984).

Map Link Inc, 25 E Mason St, Santa Barbara, CA 93101 (☎805/965 4402).

Open Air Books and Maps, 25 Toronto St, Toronto, ON M5R 2C1 (☎416/363 0719).

Phileas Fogg's Books & Maps, #87 Stanford Shopping Center, Palo Alto, CA 94304 (☎1-800/233 FOGG in California; ☎1-800/533 FOGG elsewhere in US).

Rand McNally,* 444 N Michigan Ave, Chicago, IL 60611 (☎312/321 1751); 150 E 52nd St, New York, NY 10022 (☎212/758 7488); 595 Market St, San Francisco, CA 94105 (☎415/777 3131); 1201 Connecticut Ave NW, Washington, DC 20003 (☎202/223 6751).

Sierra Club Bookstore, 730 Polk St, San Francisco, CA 94109 (☎415/923 5500).

Travel Books & Language Center, 4931 Cordell Ave, Bethesda, MD 20814 (☎1-800/220 2665).

Traveler's Bookstore, 22 W 52nd St, New York, NY 10019 (☎212/664 0995).

Ulysses Travel Bookshop, 4176 St-Denis, Montréal (☎514/289 0993).

World Wide Books and Maps, 1247 Granville St, Vancouver, BC V6Z 1E4 (☎604/687 3320).

Note: For other locations, or for maps by mail order, call ☎1-800/333 0136 (ext 2111).

AUSTRALIA AND NEW ZEALAND

Bowyangs, 372 Little Burke St, Melbourne (☎03/9670 4383).

The Map Shop, 16a Peel St, Adelaide (☎08/8231 2033).

Perth Map Centre, 891 Hay St, Perth (☎09/9322 5733).

Specialty Maps, 58 Albert St, Auckland (☎09/307 2217).

Travel Bookshop, 20 Bridge St, Sydney (☎02/9241 3554).

Accommodation

At most times of the year accommodation is plentiful in the major towns and around the Corsican coast, with the exception of the eastern plain, where rooms are scarce. However, from June to August it's a good idea to book your room in advance wherever you're heading, and booking is always advised in the more remote parts of the island. August is the most problematic month, as the French and Italians take their holidays en masse at this time. The "Language" section at the back of this book should help you make your reservation, as few hoteliers or campsite managers speak any English. We've detailed a range of accommodation wherever such a range exists, but you'll find there are very few luxury places and only a couple of hostels in the whole of Corsica (at Propriano and Calvi).

Hotels

All French hotels are graded on a scale that rises to three stars, and the price of the room corresponds roughly to the number of stars, though unfortunately this system isn't very reliable in Corsica, as some hotels give themselves the stars regardless of whether they've been visited by inspectors.

Few hotels offer rooms for **under 200F**, and those that do tend to be basic, with attached showers and toilets a rarity. At the **one-star** level you can expect to pay 200–250F for a double, without an en-suite shower-toilet or bathroom. **Two-star** places charge around 250–350F for a

double including a private bathroom, and **three-star** hotels usually cost 300–450F for a double room with bathroom, and in many cases a television with satellite channels – though there are a few plush villa-hotels where the bill can rise to 600F or even higher.

Breakfast can add 30–50F per person to a bill, though there is no obligation to take it and you will nearly always do better at a café. The cost of eating **dinner** in a hotel's restaurant can be a more important factor to bear in mind when picking a place to stay. Some places insist that you take at least one full meal with them (*demi-pension*), especially in the mountains, where food is usually of a high quality.

Single rooms are only marginally cheaper than doubles, so sharing always keeps down the cost. Some hotels will provide extra beds for three or more, charging around 25 percent per bed. Note that many hotels are **open only in summer**, usually from May to September – we've indicated in the *Guide* those establishments that close for the winter. The ones that do stay open in winter often offer discounts to off-season visitors.

Ferme-Auberges and Chambres d'Hôte

Bed and breakfast accommodation doesn't yet exist in Corsica, as the notion of having a fee-paying guest in one's home runs counter to Corsican traditions of hospitality. The nearest equivalent is full-board farmhouse accommodation in one of the island's **Ferme-Auberges**, whose **chambres d'hôte** offer rural calm and the chance to sample authentic Corsican cooking. These aren't a cheap option, however, averaging out at 300F per person per day. We've included some of these in the guide, but for a full list you should contact the Maison de l'Agriculture, 19 av Noel-Franchini, 2000 Ajaccio (☎04 95 29 42 31).

Rented Houses

If you're planning to stay a week or more in any one place it might be worth considering **renting a house**. The easiest and most reliable way of finding a property is to use **Gîtes de France**, the former French Government letting service whose UK operations are now run by Brittany Ferries (enquiries ☎0990/360360), though you can still deal directly with Gîtes de France in Paris (59 rue St-Lazare, 75009; ☎01 48 70 75 75; Mon–Sat 10am–6.30pm). Call for a brochure or pick one up at a travel agent, then simply reserve a place for any number of full weeks over the phone.

Another way of finding a place is to try one of the package holiday firms listed on p.7 (though these tend to be at the upper end of the market), or to look for properties advertised in the Sunday newspapers. Finally, you can wait until you arrive in Corsica and ask any local tourist office for a list of accommodation to rent in the region – these will work out less expensive, but there's obviously the risk that nothing suitable will be on offer.

Gîtes d'Étape and Refuges

If you're planning a hiking trip you may want to make use of the network of **gîtes d'étape** and **refuges** designed exclusively for ramblers and situated at crucial stages along the main hiking trails (see p.26). The terms "gîte d'étape" and "refuge" are sometimes used interchangeably, as each offers pretty basic accommodation, but the principal difference between them is that some gîtes d'étape provide meals for around 80F, and charge around 70–80F for a night's accommodation if there's a warden in charge, which isn't always the case. At all gîtes d'étape and refuges you'll need a sleeping bag, and while some gîtes d'étape provide fairly comfortable dormitories of bunk beds as well as primitive kitchen and bathroom facilities, many refuges – especially high in the mountains – are little more than shelters, barely converted from shepherds' crofts or

ancient stone dwellings. You can usually camp in the vicinity of these refuges, if they turn out to be full up or closed – if you want to be certain of a roof over your head, check with the local tourist office before setting out.

All refuges and gîtes d'étape are marked on the large-scale IGN maps and listed in the *Walks in Corsica* book (see p.332); we've also given the addresses and telephone numbers of all gîtes d'étape in our coverage of the island's six main long-distance walks (see pp.120, 122, 177, 208, 262 and 275).

Camping

Practically every locality has at least one **campsite** to cater for the thousands of French and Italians who spend their holiday under canvas. The cheapest – around 50–60F per person per night – are usually found in deep countryside, and are very basic. On the coast especially there are superior categories of campsite, where you'll pay prices similar to those of a one-star hotel for facilities such as bars, restaurants and swimming pools. People spend their whole holiday in these places – if you plan to do the same, and particularly if you have a caravan or a big tent, it's wise to book ahead. A booklet listing all campsites in Corsica is available from the French Tourist Office (see p.18).

Lastly, a **word of caution**: never camp rough (*camping sauvage*) on anyone's land without first asking their permission. Besides the fact that it's illegal, you're liable to get a bullet flying your way. Camping on beaches is also illegal, though a lot of people do it. Wherever you camp, be careful with **fires**, as the maquis – which creeps down to the coast in many areas – burns quickly.

Getting Around

If you want to see a lot of Corsica in a fairly short time, the only way to do it is to drive, and car rental firms are found in all the main towns. This can work out expensive, but even if your budget will only stretch to a few days it's worth renting a vehicle of some kind. Bus services are adequate for linking the main towns but dwindle in the countryside. Approximate journey times and frequencies are given in "Travel details" at the end of each chapter, but bear in mind that timetables tend to change annually; you can always check schedules at a tourist office. As for the train, it's worth taking in order to admire the small part of the scenery it crosses, but not if you're in a hurry. Walking is one of the best ways of exploring the island, which has an extensive network of footpaths and forest trails.

Driving

Driving in Corsica can cause a few headaches. Once you're off the relatively smooth main roads, the twisting mountain or coastal routes offer plenty of hazards for the unwary. Corsicans delight in seeing tourists nearly pushed off the narrow tracks, but aren't so pleased when you hinder their progress by driving too slowly. Camper vans are particular targets for abuse and heavy honking. Considering the restricted breadth of most roads, it's best to ignore the jeering and take the corniche and mountain routes at a steady pace. Another reason to drive slowly are the great potholes that pit many of the roads. Roaming pigs and goats present a further problem.

Rules of the road are fairly straightforward. You drive on the right and give way to anybody coming out of a side-turning on the right, unless you see a road sign showing a red square on a white background – this means that you have priority. At traffic roundabouts the cars on the roundabout have priority. *CEDEZ LE PASSAGE* means "Give way", a *STOP* sign means come to a complete halt.

The **minimum age** to drive a car in Corsica is eighteen, and during the first year after passing your test you must not exceed 90kph (56mph). If your car is right-hand drive, you must have your headlight dip adjusted to the right before you go. Painting your headlights yellow is a courtesy rather than a requirement these days.

Speed limits are 110kph (68mph) on two-lane highways, 90kph (56mph) on other roads in non-urban areas, and 60kph (37mph) in towns. **Fines** for driving regulations are exacted on the spot, and only cash is accepted – 1300F is the minimum for speeding. There are no toll roads in Corsica.

As regards **documentation**, if you're bringing your own car, or intend to rent one, you'll need a valid driving licence. British, EC and US licences are all vaild, but the new pink EU licences are especially helpful if you come across a police officer unwilling to peruse a document in English. You must carry your car registration document and insurance papers in your vehicle. Although the international Green Card is no longer compulsory, it does provide fully comprehensive cover, so it's a good idea to get hold of one from your insurer. In Australia, international drivers' licences can be purchased from the RAC (Royal Automobile Club) offices in most major towns and cities; and from the AA (Automobile Association) in New Zealand.

Car Rental

To **rent** a car you usually need to have held a licence for over a year, though Corsican firms aren't as fussy as their British counterparts.

Car Rental Firms

Britain		**Hertz (USA)**	☎1-800/654 3001
Avis	☎0990/900500	Hertz (Canada)	☎1-800/263 0600
Budget	☎0800/181181	Holiday Autos	☎1-800/422 7737
Europcar	☎0171/834 8484		
Hertz	☎ 0990/996699	**Australasia**	
Holiday Autos	☎0990/300404	Avis	Australia ☎1-800/225533
			New Zealand ☎09/525 1982
North America		Budget	Australia ☎13-2848
Avis	☎1-800/331 1084		New Zealand ☎09/275 2220
Dollar	☎1-800/421 6868	Hertz	Australia ☎13-1918
Europe by Car	☎1-800/223 1516		New Zealand ☎09/309 0989
		Renault Eurodrive	
		Eurodrive	Australia ☎02/9299 3344

Renting a car in Corsica will generally cost in the region of £300 per week ($US490/$A60/$NZ70 per day), unless you're booking for a period of a month or more, whereas a pre-booked vehicle should cost no more than £250. In addition to the main rental firms, whose phone numbers are given in the box above (Holiday Autos' price should be unbeatable), you might consider a **fly-drive** deal from a tour operator or an airline (see p.7. Should you want to take a chance with a local Corsican company, you'll find them at the airports, the main towns and the resorts – we've detailed the most useful ones throughout the *Guide*.

If you **break down**, your only option is to hail a passing car and get them to take you to the nearest garage, so check that the cost of repairs is covered by your rental agreement, or – if you're in your own vehicle – consider taking out extra insurance cover to meet this eventuality. If you have an accident or break-in you should make a report to the local police (and keep a copy) in order to make an insurance claim; in the event of an accident you are also obliged to complete a *constat à l'aimable* (jointly agreed statement), which your car insurers or rental company should give you. As for **fuel**, note that in remote country areas – such as Cap Corse and the interior – fuel stations are especially scarce, so remember to fill up in the towns. Unleaded fuel (*sans plomb*) is available everywhere.

Bicycles

Cycling is a popular sport in Corsica, and you'll see many teams of cyclists streaming along the

mountain roads. Corsicans are used to parties of cyclists clogging the roads, and will go out of their way to make room for you, while hotels are quite obliging about looking after your bike, even to the point of allowing it into your room. However, as a way of getting around the island cycling is only to be considered if you're in good shape.

If you want to **bring your bike** from home, flying is by far the easiest way – most airlines will charge just £10 for transporting the machine, provided you pack it in the prescribed way. Car ferries carry bicycles for free, but the French railway SNCF charges a flat fee of 150F for transporting your bike, which cannot be taken on the train you're travelling on; usually there's a three- or four-day time lag between your arrival at a given place and your bike's arrival. If you are taking your own bike from the UK, it's a good idea to join the **Cyclists' Touring Club**, which will suggest routes and supply advice to members; they also run a particularly good insurance scheme. The cost of membership is £25 a year (£12.50 for students, the unemployed and under-12s), and their address is Cotterell House, 68 Meadrow, Godalming, Surrey GU7 3HS (☎01483/417217).

In view of the toughness of the terrain (and the relative scarcity of shops supplying spares for touring bikes), you might prefer to **rent a bike** for a short trip from one of the main towns and tourist resorts, where you'll find plenty of outlets – we've listed many of them in the *Guide*. One day's rental of a mountain bike (*vélo tous terrains* or *vtt*) should cost around 100–180F, with a 500–1500F deposit.

Driving Vocabulary

to park the car	*garer la voiture*	puncture	*la crevaison*
car park	*le parking*	to inflate	*gonfler*
no parking	*defense de stationner*	battery	*la batterie*
		plugs	*bougies*
fuel station	*la station-service*	to break down	*tomber en panne*
fuel	*l'essence/le super*	petrol can	*le bidon*
fill it up	*faire le plein*	insurance	*l'assurance*
oil	*l'huile*	traffic lights	*les feux*
air line	*une ligne à air*	red light	*le feu rouge*
tyre	*le pneu*	green light	*le feu vert*
wheel	*la roue*		

Cycling Vocabulary

to adjust	*ajuster*	handlebars	*le guidon*
axle	*l'axe*	inner tube	*la chambre à l'air*
ball-bearing	*le roulement à billes*	loose	*dévissé*
battery	*la pile*	to lower	*baisser*
bent	*tordu*	mudguard	*le garde-boue*
bicycle	*le vélo*	pannier	*le pannier*
bottom bracket	*le logement du pédalier*	pedal	*la pédale*
		pump	*la pompe*
brake cable	*le cable*	rack	*la porte-bagages*
brakes	*les freins*	to raise	*relever*
broken	*cassé*	to repair	*réparer*
bulb	*l'ampoule*	saddle	*la selle*
chain	*la chaîne*	spanner	*la clef*
frame	*le cadre*	to straighten	*rédresser*
gears	*les vitesses*	stuck	*coincé*
grease	*la graisse*	tight	*serré*

Motorcyles

Corsica is perfect **motorcycle** terrain, and during the summer its roads are teeming with tourers (most of them from Germany). If you've come without your own vehicle or can't afford to rent a car, you might consider **renting a bike**. This used to be relatively inexpensive compared to car hire, but today's high insurance premiums have pushed most of the smaller operators out of business, and forced prices to often prohibitive levels. Even so, it's well worth splashing out on a bike for at least a couple of days – the sense of freedom is hard to beat.

Bikes can be rented at various towns and resorts around the island, and the choice of vehicles on offer is pretty standard; only the prices vary. Cheapest of all, at around 200–230F per day, is a 500cc moped. While these are fine for nipping to and from the beach, they tend to struggle on the hills, which effectively writes off most of the island except the eastern plain. For a trip into the interior or around the coast, you'll need at least a Vespa-style 80cc scooter, preferably a new one. Starting at around 280F per day, these can comfortably carry a rider and pillion passenger on level ground, and will make it over the even the highest mountain passes if you're riding solo. Trials-style 125cc bikes are also widely available, though they cost upwards of 350F per day; anything larger than that will set you back more than 400F.

In addition to the daily rental rate, you'll need to leave a hefty **deposit** (*caution*) of around 4000F. Rather than accept a cheque or cash, most companies these days prefer to swipe a credit card through their machine and keep the docket as security, tearing it up if you return the bike in a satisfactory condition.

Motorcyle Rental Companies

Bastia Plaisance Service Location, Port Toga (☎04 95 31 49 01).

Calvi Location Ambrosini, rue R-Villa-Antoine (☎04 95 65 02 13).

Ajaccio Locacorse, 10 rue Bévérini (☎04 95 20 71 20); Corse Évasion, Montée St-Jean (☎04 95 20 52 05); BMS Location, Port Tino Rossi (☎04 95 21 33 75).

Propriano TCC Sarl, 25 rue Général-de-Gaulle (☎04 95 76 15 32); Location Valinco, 25 av Napoléon (☎04 95 76 11 84).

Bonifacio Corse Moto Services, quai Nova (☎04 95 73 15 16).

Porto-Vecchio Garage Legrand, route de Bonifacio (☎04 95 70 15 84); Corse Moto Service, Yamaha Garage, route de Bastia (☎04 95 70 45 51); Suzuki Garage, route du Port-de-Plaisance (☎04 95 70 36 05).

Corte Scoot-Air Location, place Paoli (☎04 95 46 01 85).

Rental vehicles take some rough treatment, so check yours thoroughly before you ride off to make sure the brakes, lights and horn work. It's also a good idea to make a note of any scratches or bumps with the owner present. The cost of rental should include a helmet, and covers third-party insurance, but not damage incurred to the vehicle in any accident – another reason to ride defensively. Crash your bike, and you'll almost certainly have to foot the bill. Theft is another problem – every year, rented scooters are stolen from car parks above beaches. For this reason, owners should issue you with a strong D-lock (anti-vol) or chain, which you fasten around the front wheel. This, however, will at best only act as a deterrent, so be sure to use the steering lock as well each time you park up. If the bike does get stolen, notify the rental company and local police immediately. In theory, the company should be covered by their insurance for theft, but check this before you leave their office; some insist on retaining most or all of your deposit if a bike disappears.

Buses and Trains

Buses are Corsica's main public transport service, covering many areas that the train doesn't reach. The main routes are Bastia–Ajaccio (direct), Bastia–Porto-Vecchio (stopping at Ghisonaccia), Bastia–Calvi (stopping at L'Île Rousse), Ajaccio–Bonifacio (stopping at Propriano and Sartène), Calvi–Porto (direct) and Porto–Ajaccio (stopping at Cargèse). In rural areas the timetable is constructed to suit working and school hours, which means there's often just one bus a day in any direction, departing at a dauntingly early hour. Many services are also suspended, or dras-

tically scaled down, during the winter. We've referred to bus schedules throughout this book, but it's always a good idea to check departure times at the local tourist office or gare routière before you set off. Full summaries of all bus services on the island also appear in the "Travel details" listed at the end of each chapter.

Corsica's diminutive **train**, the *micheline* or *trinighellu* (little train), crosses the mountains from Ajaccio to Bastia via Corte, with a subsidiary line running from Ponte Leccia, north of Corte, to Calvi. The train follows a rattling precarious route across the island and is far slower than the bus (the 100km from Ajaccio to Bastia takes 4hr, as opposed to 3hr by bus) – due largely to delays caused by cows and goats roaming onto the lines, and by the driver having a chat with the "officials" posted at each station. **Tickets** cost about the same as the buses, ie 100F per 100km. If you can provide proof that you're a student you get a discount on all tickets, and often if you're travelling to or from the university town of Corte you don't even need a card.

Hiking

Hiking is without doubt the best way to explore Corsica's amazing interior and remote stretches of coast, and there are nearly 1000km of marked trails to help you do just that. Ranging from two-week routes over the mountainous spine of the island to leisurely half-day ambles across cool forests and stream valleys, these are maintained by the Parc Naturel Régional de Corse and municipal councils, and cater for all levels of ability.

Never underestimate the **dangers** of walking in wilderness areas. Every year lives are lost on the mountains, usually because the walkers fail to observe a few golden rules. First and foremost, be preared for sudden and dramatic changes of **weather**, particularly at altitude. Snow falls are common from late October until early June, and during the summer violent storms frequently descend on exposed ridges and peaks, driving hikers off the mountain or into refuges, sometimes for days on end. So take along adequate **clothing**: a sturdy pair of purpose-made boots with plenty of ankle support is essential (nearly every walk in Corsica involves crossing streams and boulder-strewn ground at some point), as are warm clothes and a waterproof coat. You should also be equipped for the heat, with a sunhat and high-factor sun cream – sunstroke, caused by prolonged dehydration and exposure to strong sunlight, is no joke if it hits you three or four hours from the nearest refuge.

Also indispensable are a **compass** and detailed **map** of the route. IGN publish the best contour maps for hikers (see p.18), but you can save a lot of money if you buy the Parc Naturel Régional's excellent **topo-guides**, which contain the sections of the IGN maps pertaining to specific trails, plus a detailed description of the route (in French), along with lots of other useful information. Costing around 90F, they're sold at most good bookshops and large tourist offices on the island, and are essential if you're considering one of the long-distance footpaths outlined below.

Many walks are best attempted from early spring through to late summer, principally to profit from the long daylight hours and avoid the mists and snow that descend over the hills in winter. From June until September, an early start is essential so as to arrive at the end of your walk before the afternoon heat becomes too unbearable.

Hiking Trails

Of the six main long-distance hiking trails in Corsica, the most famous is the **GR20** (covered on p.120), which crosses the island diagonally from Calenzana in the northwest to Conça in the southeast. Normally completed in ten to twelve days, it takes in the cream of Corsica's mountain scenery, with innumerable opportunities for side-trips to the surrounding peaks. However, the relentless series of arduous ascents and descents mean it's only suitable for experienced, fit and well-equipped hikers.

If you're keen to hike for a week or more but don't feel up to tackling the GR20, try one of the five other long-distance routes established by the Parc Naturel Régional. Designed to take in the most scenic and unspoilt corners of the island, these are consistently varied and well marked, and have the additional attraction of **gîtes d'étape** (see p.21) at the ends of most stages, where you can enjoy a hot shower, clean dormitory bed and self-catering facilities for around 80F; most also provide four-course evening meals on request, for a supplement of around 75F. This means you can hike without the burden of a heavy backpack, carrying only a change of clothing, plus food and water for a day.

The five routes are covered in the Parc Naturel Régional's topo-guide, *Corse: Entre Mer et Montagne*, but we've included reviews of each in the part of the *Guide* section where the path begins, giving an outline of the route, advice on accommodation and details of how to get to the trailhead by public transport. If you're deciding on which footpath to follow, check out these accounts before investing in maps or the topo-guide: **Mare e Monti**, from Calenzana to Cargèse in ten days, p.122; **Mare a Mare Nord**, Moriani to Cargèse via Corte in nine to ten days, p.275; **Mare a Mare Centre**, Ghisonaccia to Ajaccio in seven days, p.262; **Mare e Monti Sud**, Porticcio to Propriano in five days, p.177; and **Mare a Mare Sud**, Propriano to Porto-Vecchio in six days, p.208.

In addition to the long-distance paths, the Parc Naturel Régional has established a network of easier trails designed for day hikes. Known as **sentiers de pays**, these are waymarked, and a series of glossy leaflets (sold at park information counters and tourist offices throughout the island) indicate the route on black-and-white reproductions of the relevant IGN map. Once again, the *Guide* section features accounts of those we consider most worthwhile.

The descriptions of **walks and hikes** featured in this book are intended for reference only, to help you select and plan your route. Although we've gone to great lengths to ensure that the accounts are correct in every respect, we strongly recommend you take along the relevant IGN map or topo-guide – and ideally one of the walking guides listed in "Books" on p.331 – without which you may well lose the trail.

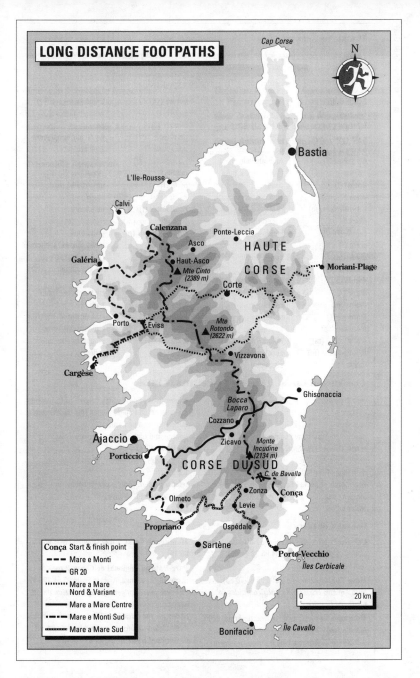

LONG DISTANCE FOOTPATHS

Cap Corse

N

Bastia

L'Ile-Rousse

Calvi

Calenzana

Asco

Ponte-Leccia

HAUTE

Galéria

Haut-Asco
▲ Mte Cinto
(2389 m)

CORSE

Moriani-Plage

Corte

Porto

Evisa

Mte
Rotondo
(2622 m) ▲

Cargèse

Vizzavona

Ghisonaccia

Bocca
Laparo

Cozzano

Ajaccio

Zicavo

Monte
Incudine
(2134 m) ▲

Porticcio

CORSE DU SUD

C. de Bavella

Olmeto

Zonza

Conça

Levie

Propriano

Ospédale

Sartène

Porto-Vecchio
Îles Cerbicale

Conça Start & finish point
- - - Mare e Monti
-·- GR 20
······· Mare a Mare
        Nord & Variant
——— Mare a Mare Centre
-··- Mare e Monti Sud
······· Mare a Mare Sud

0   20 km

Bonifacio   Île Cavallo

HIKING VOCABULARY

The following list is intended primarily as an aid to translating the Parc Naturel Régional's topo-guides, but it should also come in useful when asking directions.

(vb) = verb; (m) = masculine noun; (f) = feminine noun; (adj) = adjective; * = Corsican word

balisé (adj)	waymarked	*longer* (vb)	to follow (eg a river)
belvédère (m)	view point	*météo* (f)	weather forecast
bifurquer (à gauche/ à droite) (vb)	to bear (left/right)	*montée* (f)	ascent
boussole (f)	compass	*névé* (m)	patch of eternal snow
bergeries (f)	high-altitude shepherds' huts	*passerelle suspendue (f)*	rope bridge
*bocca**(f)	pass	*pente* (f)	slope
chemin (muletier) (m)	(mulepackers') path	*piste* (f)	unsurfaced road
cascade (m)	waterfall	*raide* (adj)	steep
courbe(f)	bend	*randonnée* (f)/ *randonneur* (m)	hike/hiker
crête (f)	ridge	*ravitaillement* (m)	provisions
défilé (m)	gorge, ravine	*refuge* (m)	bothy, hikers' shelter
descente (f)	descent	*rive (gauche/ droite)* (f)	(left/right) bank (of a stream or river)
ébouli (m)	boulder choke	*ruisseau* (m)	stream
étape (f)	stage (of a hike)	*sac à dos* (m)	rucksack, backpack
fleuve (m)	river	*sentier* (m)	path
fontaine (f)	spring	*sommet* (m)	summit (of a mountain)
franchir (vb)	to cross		
gîte d'étape (m)	hikers' hostel	*torrent* (m)	mountain stream
hébergement (m)	accommodation	*vallée* (f)	valley
lacets	zigzags		

Checklist of Useful Items for Low-Altitude Hikes

map/topo-guide
compass
day sack
lightweight waterproof coat
warm, fleece-style sweater
money pouch
a change of clothes
head torch or pocket flashlight
sleeping bag
water bottle

blister pads and/or surgical spirit, with plasters
slippers or light sports shoes (for the evenings)
corkscrew and pen knife
sunhat and high-factor suncream
pocket dictionary
plastic bags (for keeping things dry in your backpack)
telephone card (public phone booths in Corsica don't take small change)

Useful Contacts

Corsica Loisirs Aventure, rue Notre-Dame-de-Lourdes, 20200 Bastia (☎04 95 32 54 34). *Guided group expeditions.*

Move, 20214 Calenzana (☎04 95 62 70 83). *Small group trips with qualified guides in northern Corsica.*

Muntagne Corse, 2 av de la Grande-Armé, 2000 Ajaccio (☎04 95 20 53 14). *Among the island's oldest-established walking holiday company.*

Muntagnoli Corsi, 20122 Quenza (☎04 95 78 65 19).

Parc Naturel Régional de Corse, 2 rue Sergeant-Casalonga, Ajaccio (☎04 95 51 79 10). *The best source of general information on all aspects of hiking in Corsica; and you can phone for the latest weather bulletins. It's also a good place to buy maps and leaflets for all the marked trails in Corsica.*

Also featured throughout the book are descriptions of good walks and hikes not included in Parc Naturel literature. While many of these are gentle strolls between villages, some are hard climbs up the island's highest peaks, requiring experience and confidence at altitude. Before setting out on any such route, check the weather forecast and ensure you are properly equipped; an **ice axe** or snow poles can be extremely useful on some ascents where sheltered gullies hold patches of eternal snow.

Eating and Drinking

Corsican cuisine is not delicate, but its hearty rich stews and seafood dishes can provide some exceptional meals. Wherever you go you'll be offered a range of charcuterie (cured ham and smoked sausages) and, as you'd expect on a Mediterranean island, you'll find plenty of oysters, mussels, lobster and prawns on the menu. Freshwater fish and game also feature prominently, with such specialities as blackbird paté and roast kid appearing on special occasions. Snack food is primarily French, with Italian influence almost as evident (ie pizzas), and there's a wide choice of restaurants to cater for the tourist population. Menus are always in French, occasionally with translations, and you'll find some classic French dishes featured alongside the regional food.

Breakfast and Snacks

A croissant, pain au chocolat (a chocolate-filled croissant) or a sandwich with hot chocolate or coffee is the standard **breakfast**, which is best taken in a bar or café – you'll pay through the nose in any hotel.

At **lunchtime** you may find cafés offering a *plat du jour* (chef's daily special) at between 55F and 75F for a limited or no-choice menu. The croque-monsieur or croque-madame (variations on the toasted cheese sandwich) is on sale in cafés and street stands, along with *frites*, crêpes, *galettes* (wholewheat savoury pancakes), *gauffres* (waffles), *glaces* (ice creams), slices of pizza and all kinds of fresh sandwiches. Cafés in the mountains will make you up a *casse-croûte*, a large sandwich often filled with a generous slice of *lonzu* (cured ham) or local *saucisson*.

For **picnics**, local shops and occasional supermarkets can provide you with almost anything you need from fruit to pâté, and a visit to a *rôtisserie* or charcuterie is always rewarding. Cooked meat, ready-made dishes, cheese, quiches and assorted salads can all be bought by weight from the latter, or you can ask for *une tranche* (a slice), *une barquette* (a carton) or *une part* (a portion).

Salons de thé, though few and far between, serve brunches, salads and the like as well as cakes and ice cream and a wide selection of teas. They tend to be a good deal pricier than cafés as you pay for the swish decor. Pâtisseries do wonderful cakes and local sweet delicacies such as chestnut cake and *fiadone* (see box p.36), as well as some savoury snacks like pizza and *tartelettes* (mini-quiches) and *canistrelli* (shortbread-style biscuits).

Full-Scale Meals

You'll find a sprinkling of excellent restaurants scattered about the island, with the best generally in the villages. Fine fish restaurants pre-dominate on the coast, as you'd expect, and inland you can get excellent trout at cosy auberges, where local game will also be on offer (for more on Corsican dishes, see below and p.35–36). Otherwise, there's an abundance of pizzerias and crêperies for those on a budget, and many of these places also often offer a wider choice of dishes than their name would suggest – regional cuisine, salads and pasta might all feature on the menu.

For country restaurants it's a good idea to reserve a table, though in most towns and resorts you won't need to bother. In many places you may have problems finding something open after 10pm, though in the larger tourist resorts there's always something open in summer. Don't forget that hotel restaurants are usually open to non-residents, and are often good value.

Prices are posted outside the restaurant, and usually the least expensive option is the **menu fixe**, where the number of courses has already been determined and the choice is limited. These revolve around standard dishes such as steak and chips (*steack frites*), chicken and chips (*poulet frites*), or fried fish of some kind (*friture du golfe* is common), and cost an average 80–100F. The *plat du jour*, often a regional dish, might well be featured on the *menu fixe*, but for unlimited access to the chef's specialities you'll have to go **à la carte**, when you can expect to pay upwards of 80F for the main course. In Corsica, as in the rest of France, any salad (sometimes vegetables too) comes separate from the main dish, and you will be offered coffee, which is also charged extra, to finish off the meal. Fish, incidentally, is sold by weight; the price quoted represents the cost per 100g, so check how much it will come to before the waiter disappears with it into the kitchen or you could get a nasty shock when your bill arrives.

Desserts in Corsica, as in many Mediterranean countries, are something of a disappointment, with crème caramel, chocolate mousse or a piece of fruit the standard offerings. If you crave something sweet, check out the nearest pâtis-serie or ice-cream parlour. It's perfectly normal for diners to finish a main meal in one restaurant and retire to a café-pâtisserie for desert.

Service compris or *s.c.* means the **service charge** is included. *Service non compris, s.n.c.,* means that it isn't and you need to calculate an additional fifteen percent. **Wine** (*vin*) or a **drink** (*boisson*) is unlikely to be included, though occasionally it is thrown in with cheaper menus. When ordering wine, ask for *un quart* (0.25 litre), *un demi-litre* (0.5 litre), *une carafe* (a litre) or *un pichet* (a jug). You'll normally be given the house wine unless you specify otherwise; if you're worried about the cost just ask for *vin ordinaire*.

Vegetarians will have problems in Corsican restaurants, as many dishes are meat-based. A good idea is to have a variety of starters that include salads and crudités, or resort to the pizza and pasta places. Remember the following: *Je suis végétarien(ne). Est-ce qu'il y a quelques plats sans viande?* (I'm a vegetarian. Are there any non-meat dishes?).

Corsican Specialities

The unique flavour of Corsican cooking comes from the maquis herbs and plants – thyme, marjoram, basil, fennel and rosemary – enhanced by olive oil and spices, especially in the south of the island, where flavours are less subtle than in the north.

You'll find the best **charcuterie** in the north, where pork is smoked and cured in the cold cellars of the village houses – it's particularly tasty in the **Castagniccia**, where wild pigs feed on the **chestnuts** which were once the staple diet of the region's inhabitants. Here you can also taste chestnut fritters (*fritelli a gaju frescu*) and chestnut cake (*pulenta*) sprinkled with sugar or eau de vie. **Brocciu**, a soft *fromage frais* made with ewe's milk, is found everywhere on the island, forming the basis for many dishes, including omelettes stuffed with *brocciu* and mint, and *cannelloni al brocciu*. *Suppa Corsa* is another delicious meatless choice; the precise recipe varies from region to region, but it's always packed with beans and garlic. *Fromage Corse* is also very good – a unique hard **cheese** made in the sheep-rearing Niolo and Asco regions, where *cabrettu a l'istrettu* (kid stew) is also a speciality.

Game – mainly stews of hare and wild boar but also roast woodcock, partridge and wood pigeon – features throughout the island's mountain and forested regions. Here blackbirds (*merles*) are made into a fragrant pâté, and **eel and trout** are fished from the unpolluted rivers. Red mullet (*rouget*), sea bream (*loup de mer*) and a great variety of **shellfish** is offered along the coast – the best crayfish (*langouste*) comes from around the Golfe de St-Florent, whereas

FOOD AND DISHES

Basic Terms

Pain	Bread	*Poivre*	Pepper	*Verre*	Glass
Beurre	Butter	*Sel*	Salt	*Fourchette*	Fork
Oeufs	Eggs	*Sucre*	Sugar	*Couteau*	Knife
Lait	Milk	*Vinaigre*	Vinegar	*Cuillère*	Spoon
Huile	Oil	*Bouteille*	Bottle	*Table*	Table

Snacks

Un sandwich/	**A sandwich ...**	**Crêpe ...**	**Pancake ...**
une baguette ...		*au sucre*	with sugar
jambon	with ham	*au citron*	with lemon
fromage	with cheese	*au miel*	with honey
saucisson	with sausage	*à la confiture*	with jam
à l'ail	with garlic	*aux œufs*	with eggs
au poivre	with pepper	*à la crème de*	with chestnut purée
pâté (de cam-	with pâté (country-	*marrons*	
pagne)	style)	**Other Fillings/**	
Croque-monsieur	Grilled cheese and	**Salads**	
	ham sandwich	*Anchois*	Anchovy
Croque-madame	Grilled cheese and	*Andouillette*	Tripe sausage
	bacon, sausage,	*Boudin*	Black pudding
	chicken or an egg	*Cœurs de palmiers*	Hearts of palm
		Épis de maïs	Corn on the cob
Oeufs ...	**Eggs ...**	*Fonds d'artichauts*	Artichoke hearts
au plat	Fried	*Hareng*	Herring
à la coque	Boiled	*Langue*	Tongue
durs	Hard-boiled	*Poulet*	Chicken
brouillés	Scrambled	*Thon*	Tuna
Omelette ...	**Omelette ...**	**And Some Terms**	
nature	plain	*Chauffé*	Heated
aux fines herbes au	with herbs	*Cuit*	Cooked
fromage	with cheese	*Cru*	Raw
Salade de ...	**Salad of ...**	*Emballé*	Wrapped
tomates	tomatoes	*A emporter*	Takeaway
betteraves	beets	*Fumé*	Smoked
concombres	cucumber	*Salé*	Salted/spicy
carottes rapées	grated carrots	*Sucré*	Sweet

Soups (soupes) and Starters (hors d' uvres)

Bisque	Shellfish soup	*Velouté*	Thick soup, usually
Bouillabaisse	Marseillais fish soup		fish or poultry
Bouillon	Broth or stock		
Bourride	Thick fish soup	**Starters**	
Consommé	Clear soup	*Assiette anglaise*	Plate of cold meats
Pistou	Parmesan, basil and	*Crudités*	Raw vegetables with
	garlic paste added		dressings
	to soup	*Hors d'œuvres*	Combination of the
Potage	Thick vegetable	*variés*	above, plus
	soup		smoked or mari-
Rouille	Red pepper, garlic		nated fish
	and saffron may-		
	onnaise served		
	with fish soup		

Fish (poisson), Seafood (fruits de mer) and Shellfish (crustaces or coquillages)

Anchois	Anchovies	*Daurade*	Sea bream	*Louvine,*	Similar to
Anguilles	Eels	*Éperlan*	Smelt or	*loubine*	sea bass
Barbue	Brill		whitebait	*Maquereau*	Mackerel
Bigourneau	Periwinkle	*Escargots*	Snails	*Merlan*	Whiting
Brème	Bream	*Flétan*	Halibut	*Moules (ma-*	Mussels
Cabillaud	Cod	*Friture*	Assorted	*rinière)*	(with shal-
Calmar	Squid		fried fish		lots in
Carrelet	Plaice	*Gambas*	King prawns		white wine
Claire	Type of	*Hareng*	Herring		sauce)
	oyster	*Homard*	Lobster	*Oursin*	Sea urchin
Colin	Hake	*Huîtres*	Oysters	*Palourdes*	Clams
Congre	Conger eel	*Langouste*	Spiny lobster	*Praires*	Small clams
Coques	Cockles	*Langoustines*	Saltwater	*Raie*	Skate
Coquilles St-	Scallops		crayfish	*Rouget*	Red mullet
Jacques			(scampi)	*Saumon*	Salmon
Crabe	Crab	*Limande*	Lemon sole	*Sole*	Sole
Crevettes	Shrimp	*Lotte*	Burbot	*Thon*	Tuna
grises		*Lotte de mer*	Monkfish	*Truite*	Trout
Crevettes	Prawns	*Loup de mer*	Sea bass	*Turbot*	Turbot
roses					

Fish Terms

Aïoli	Garlic mayonnaise served with salt cod and other fish	*Fumé*	Smoked
		Fumet	Fish stock
		Gigot de mer	Large fish baked whole
Béarnaise	Sauce of egg yolks, white wine, shal- lots and vinegar	*Grillé*	Grilled
		Hollandaise	Butter and vinegar sauce
Beignets	Fritters	*A la meunière*	In a butter, lemon and parsley sauce
Darne	Fillet or steak		
La douzaine	A dozen		
Frit	Fried	*Mousse, mousseline*	Mousse
Friture	Deep-fried small fish	*Quenelles*	Light dumplings

Meat (viande) and Poultry (volaille)

Agneau (de présalé)	Lamb (grazed on salt marshes)	*Foie*	Liver
		Foie gras	Fattened (duck/ goose) liver
Andouille, andouillette	Tripe sausage		
		Gigot (d'agneau)	Leg (of lamb)
Bœuf	Beef	*Grillade*	Grilled meat
Bifteck	Steak	*Hâchis*	Chopped meat or mince hamburger
Boudin blanc	Sausage of white meats		
		Langue	Tongue
Boudin noir	Black pudding	*Lapin, lapereau*	Rabbit, young rabbit
Caille	Quail	*Lard, lardons*	Bacon, diced bacon
Canard	Duck	*Lièvre*	Hare
Caneton	Duckling	*Merguez*	Spicy, red sausage
Contrefilet	Sirloin roast	*Mouton*	Mutton
Coquelet	Cockerel	*Museau de veau*	Calf's muzzle
Dinde, dindon	Turkey	*Oie*	Goose
Entrecôte	Ribsteak	*Os*	Bone
Faux filet	Sirloin steak	*Porc*	Pork

Poulet	Chicken	*Steack*	Steak
Poussin	Baby chicken	*Tête de veau*	Calf's head (in jelly)
Ris	Sweetbreads	*Tournedos*	Thick slices of fillet
Rognons	Kidneys	*Tripes*	Tripe
Rognons blancs	Testicles	*Veau*	Veal
Sanglier	Wild boar	*Venaison*	Venison

Meat and Poultry Dishes . . .

Bœuf bourguignon	Beef stew with Burgundy, onions and mushrooms	*Coq au vin*	Chicken cooked until it falls off the bone with wine, onions, and mushrooms
Canard à l'orange	Roast duck with an orange-and-wine sauce	*Steak au poivre (vert/rouge)*	Steak in a black (green/red) peppercorn sauce
Cassoulet	A casserole of beans and meat	*Steak tartare*	Raw chopped beef, topped with a raw egg yolk

. . . and Terms

Blanquette, daube, estouffade, hocheôt, navarin and ragoût	All are types of stew
Aile	Wing
Carré	Best end of neck, chop or cutlet
Civit	Game stew
Confit	Meat preserve
Côte	Chop, cutlet or rib
Cou	Neck
Cuisse	Thigh or leg
Épaule	Shoulder
Médaillon	Round piece
Pavé	Thick slice
En croûte	In pastry
Farci	Stuffed
Au feu de bois	Cooked over wood
Au four	Fire-baked
Garni	With vegetables
Gésier	Gizzard
Grillé	Grilled
Magret de canard	Duck breast
Marmite	Casserole
Mijoté	Stewed
Museau	Muzzle
Rôti	Roast
Sauté	Lightly cooked in butter

For steaks:

Bleu	Almost raw
Saignant	Rare
À point	Medium
Bien cuit	Well done
Très bien cuit	Very well cooked
Brochette	Kebab

Garnishes and sauces:

Beurre blanc	Sauce of white wine and shallots, with butter
Chasseur	White wine, mushrooms and shallots
Diable	Strong mustard seasoning
Forestière	With bacon and mushroom
Fricassée	Rich, creamy sauce
Mornay	Cheese sauce
Pays d'Auge	Cream and cider
Piquante	Gherkins or capers, vinegar and shallots
Provençale	Tomatoes, garlic, olive oil and herbs

Fruit (fruit) and Nuts (noix)

Abricot	Apricot	*Brugnon, nectarine*	Nectarine
Amandes	Almonds	*Cacahouète*	Peanut
Ananas	Pineapple	*Cassis*	Blackcurrants
Banane	Banana		

Cérises	Cherries
Citron	Lemon
Citron vert	Lime
Figues	Figs

Fraises (de bois)	Strawberries (wild)	*Myrtilles*	Bilberries	*Prune*	Plum
Framboises	Raspberries	*Noisette*	Hazelnut	*Pruneau*	Prune
Fruit de la passion	Passion fruit	*Noix*	Nuts	*Raisins*	Grapes
Groseilles	Redcurrants and gooseberries	*Orange* *Pample-mousse*	Orange Grapefruit	**Terms:**	
		Pêche (blanche)	(White) peach	*Beignets*	Fritters
				Compôte de	Stewed ...
				Coulis	Sauce
Mangue	Mango	*Pistache*	Pistachio	*Flambé*	Set aflame in alcohol
Marrons	Chestnuts	*Poire*	Pear		
Melon	Melon	*Pomme*	Apple	*Frappé*	Iced

Vegetables (légumes), Herbs (herbes) and Spices (épices)

Ail	Garlic	*Endive*	Chicory	*Petits pois*	Peas
Algue	Seaweed	*Épinards*	Spinach	*Piment*	Pimento
Anis	Aniseed	*Estragon*	Tarragon	*Pois chiche*	Chick peas
Artichaut	Artichoke	*Fenouil*	Fennel	*Pois mange-tout*	Snow peas
Asperges	Asparagus	*Flageolet*	White beans		
Avocat	Avocado	*Gingembre*	Ginger	*Pignons*	Pine nuts
Basilic	Basil	*Haricots*	Beans	*Poireau*	Leek
Betterave	Beetroot	*verts*	string	*Poivron (vert, rouge)*	Sweet pepper (green, red)
Carotte	Carrot		(french)		
Céleri	Celery	*rouges*	kidney	*Pommes (de terre)*	Potatoes
Champignons, cèpes, chanterelles	Mushrooms of various kinds	*beurres* *Laurier*	butter Bay leaf	*Primeurs*	Spring vegetables
Chou (rouge)	(Red) cabbage	*Lentilles* *Maïs*	Lentils Corn	*Radis*	Radishes
Choufleur	Cauliflower	*Menthe*	Mint	*Riz*	Rice
Ciboulettes	Chives	*Moutarde*	Mustard	*Safran*	Saffron
Concombre	Cucumber	*Oignon*	Onion	*Salade verte*	Green salad
Cornichon	Gherkin	*Pâte*	Pasta or pastry	*Sarrasin* *Tomate*	Buckwheat Tomato
Échalotes	Shallots	*Persil*	Parsley	*Truffes*	Truffles

Dishes and Terms

Beignet	Fritter
Farci	Stuffed
Gratiné	Browned with cheese or butter
Jardinière	With mixed diced vegetables
A la parisienne	Sautéed in butter (potatoes); with white wine sauce and shallots

Parmentier	With potatoes
Sauté	Lightly fried in butter
A la vapeur	Steamed
Je suis végétarien(ne). Il y a quelques plats sans viande?	I'm a vegetarian. Are there any non-meat dishes?

Desserts (desserts or entremets) and Pastries (pâtisserie)

Bombe	A moulded ice-cream dessert
Brioche	Sweet, high-yeast breakfast roll
Charlotte	Custard and fruit in lining of almond fingers

Crème Chantilly	Vanilla-flavoured and sweetened whipped cream
Crème fraîche	Sour cream
Crème pâtissière	Thick eggy pastry-filling

Crêpes suzettes	Thin pancakes with orange juice and liqueur	*Petits fours*	Bite-sized cakes/ pastries
Fromage blanc	Cream cheese	*Poires Belle Hélène*	Pears and ice cream in chocolate sauce
Glace	Ice cream	*Yaourt, yogourt*	Yoghurt
Ile flottante/ œufs à la neige	Soft meringues floating on custard		
Macarons	Macaroons	**Terms**	
Madeleine	Small sponge cake	*Barquette*	Small boat-shaped flan
Marrons Mont Blanc	Chestnut purée and cream on a rum-soaked sponge cake	*Bavarois*	Refers to the mould, could be a mousse or custard
Mousse au chocolat	Chocolate mousse	*Coupe*	A serving of ice cream
Palmiers	Caramelized puff pastries	*Crêpes*	Pancakes
Parfait	Frozen mousse, sometimes ice-cream	*Galettes*	Buckwheat pancakes
		Gênoise	Rich sponge cake
		Sablé	Shortbread biscuit
Petit Suisse	A smooth mixture of cream and curds	*Savarin*	A filled, ring-shaped cake
		Tarte	Tart
		Tartelette Sarrasin	Small tart

And one final note: always call the waiter or waitress *Monsieur* or *Madame* (*Mademoiselle* if a young woman), never *Garçon*, no matter what you've been taught in school.

CORSICAN DISHES

Starters

Cannelloni al brocciu	Pasta stuffed with *brocciu* and mint with tomato sauce	*Suppa di pesce/ soupe de poisson*	Fish soup served with toast and garlic
Omelette al brocciu	Omelette filled with *brocciu*	*Suppa Corsa/ soupe Corse*	Vegetable soup with beans

Charcuterie

Coppa	Smoked pork shoulder	*Lonzu*	Smoked pork fillet
Figatellu	Pork liver sausage	*Prisuttu*	Cured ham

Main Courses

Aziminu	Rich, heavily spiced, garlicky fish stew	*Stifatu*	A roll of stuffed meats – goat, lamb and sometimes blackbird – served with grated cheese
Bianchetti	Little fish fried in batter		
Cabrettu a l'istrettu	Strongly spiced kid stew		
Formaghju di porcu	Pork brawn seasoned with onion, garlic, pepper and maquis herbs	*Tianu di cingale/sanglier en daube*	Wild boar stew with potatoes
Fritelle di gaju frescu	Fritters made with chestnut flour and *brocciu*	*Tianu d'agnellu*	Lamb stew
		Tianu di fave	Pork and bean stew
Lasagne di cignale	Wild boar lasagne	*Tianu di pisi*	Onions, carrots, peas and tomato stew
Pivarunata	Peppery beef and potato stew with pimentos	*Tripette*	Tripe in tomato sauce

Cheese and Puddings

Brocciu	Soft white cheese made with curds	*Canistrelli*	Soft shortbread-type biscuits made with white wine and honey
Fromage Corse	Uniquely flavoured indigenous hard cheese	*Fiadone*	Tart filled with *brocciu*
		Fritelli/ beignets	Small doughnuts, sometimes made with chestnut flour

oysters (*huîtres*) are a speciality of the eastern plain.

Many of the dishes listed above are only found in authentic Corsican places, but you'll always find one or two specialities on the menu of a standard restaurant. The French translation is given where the name will usually appear in French on the menu.

Drinking

Cafés and bars line the streets and squares of Corsica's towns and tourist resorts, and these are where you'll likely do most of your drinking, whether as a prelude to food (*apéritif*) or as a sequel (*digestif*). Bars tend to be dark, functional places, whereas cafés are more open, often featuring a terrace where you can sit and watch life pass by. Every bar or café displays a price list with progressively increasing prices for drinks at the bar, at the table or on the terrace.

Wine (*vin*) is the regular drink, with rosé the type produced in greatest volume in Corsica. *Vin de table* is generally drinkable and always inexpensive; restaurant mark-ups for quality wines, on the other hand, can be very high for a country where wine is so plentiful. In bars, you normally buy by the glass, and just ask for *un rouge, un blanc* or *un rosé; un pichet* gets you a quarter-litre jug.

Of the local products, you should be sure to try the **Santa Barba** or **Fiumicicoli** wines of the Sartène area, which come in both red and rosé, and the **Patrimonio**, a robust white wine from Cap Corse. The favoured aperitifs are the sweet muscat produced on Cap Corse, and the drink known as **Cap Corse**, a fortified wine flavoured with herbs and quinine.

Belgian and German brands account for most of the **beer** you'll find. Draught beer (*bière à la pression*) is the cheapest alcoholic drink after

wine – ask for a *demi* (defined as 25cl). Bottled beer is exceptionally cheap in supermarkets.

Strong alcohol is drunk right through the day, the most popular drink being strong aniseed-based *pastis*, especially the local brand, **Casanis**. Brandies and eaux de vie are always available – the latter comes in a variety of flavours, such as *prune* (plum) and *cerise* (cherry), and is usually distilled locally in the villages. In many small restaurants and bars you'll be offered these free. You may also be offered **Cedratine** and **Myrthe**, which are locally made sickly sweet liqueurs.

On the **soft drink** front, you can buy cartons of unsweetened fruit juice in supermarkets, though in cafés the bottled nectars such as *jus d'abricot* (apricot) and *jus de poire* (pear) still hold sway. Some cafés serve tiny glasses of fresh orange and lemon juice (*orange/citron pressé*); otherwise it's the standard fizzy cans. Bottles of **mineral water** (*eau minérale*) and spring water (*eau de source*) – either sparkling (*pétillante*) or flat (*plate*) – abound. Note that tap water (*eau du robinet*) is particularly good quality in Corsica, coming from the fresh mountain streams.

Coffee is invariably *espresso* and very strong. *Un café* or *un express* is black, *un crème* is white, *un café au lait* (served at breakfast) is *espresso* in a large cup or bowl filled up with hot milk. Ordinary tea (*thé*) is Liptons' tea-bag tea nine times out of ten; to have milk with it, ask for *un peu de lait frais*. Herb teas (*infusions*) are served in every café and can be a refreshing alternative. The more common ones are *vervaine* (verbena), *tilleul* (lime blossom) and *tisane* (camomile). **Chocolat chaud** – hot chocolate – unlike tea, can be had in any café.

Post, Phones and Media

Operator Numbers and Phone Codes

To call **Corsica from abroad**, dial ☎00 33 plus the nine-digit number (omit the first 0).

To call **abroad from Corsica**, the country codes are as follows:

Britain ☎44

Ireland ☎353

USA and Canada ☎1

Australia ☎61

New Zealand ☎64

To speak to the **operator**, dial ☎10; the **international operator** is ☎19 33 11.

Post offices – postes or PTTs – are generally open Monday to Friday 9am to noon and 2 to 5pm, plus 9am to noon on Saturday. However, don't depend on these hours: in the major towns you might find the main office open through the day, whilst opening and closing times vary enormously in the villages.

Mail Services

You can have letters sent to you by **Poste Restante** at any main post office on the island. The addresses of the principal offices are: cours Napoléon, Ajaccio 20000, and av Maréchal-Sebastiani, Bastia 20200. To collect mail you'll need a passport, and should expect to pay a charge of a few francs. If you're expecting mail, it's worth asking the clerk to check under all your names, as filing systems tend to be erratic. The quickest international service for **sending letters** is by *aérogramme*, sold at all post offices. You can get ordinary **stamps** (*timbres*) at any *tabac* (tobacconist). If you're sending **parcels** abroad, try to check prices in the various leaflets available: small *postes* may need reminding of the huge reductions for printed papers and books, for example.

Telephones

You can make domestic and international phone calls from any box (*cabine*), which these days only take **phone cards** (*télécartes*), obtainable for 40F and 100F from post offices and some *tabacs*. Coin-only boxes are only found in out-of-the-way bars, cafés and villages, and take 1F, 5F and 10F pieces. For **calls within Corsica**, whatever the distance, you should dial all eight digits of the number, and all ten for **calls within France**; for **international calls**, dial 19, wait for a tone, and then dial the country code (see box above), then the subscriber number minus its initial 0.

An alternative to dialling internationally from a *cabine* is to use the booths at main post offices, where you pay after making the call. If you do this, make sure you count your units, which are clearly displayed – mistakes can made in calculating the bill. To make a reverse-charge call to a number abroad, phone the international operator.

Newspapers and Magazines

The Corsican newspapers with the widest circulations are the two **local dailies**: Corse-Matin, printed by Nice-Matin, and Le Corse-Provencal, which is more of a tabloid. These usually feature reports of gruesome shootings or hold-ups, which tend to be given greater prominence than news of the wider world, and are useful for listings. Of the **national dailies** Le Monde (daily except Mon) is the most intellectual and respected, with no concessions to entertainment (such as pictures), but written in an orthodox French that is probably the easiest to understand. *Libération* (daily except Mon), is moderately left wing and colloquial, with good selective coverage; *L'Humanité* is the Communist Party newspaper, with a constantly diminishing readership. All the other nationals are firmly on the Right. British newspapers and the *International Herald Tribune* are intermittently available in the larger resorts, and in Ajaccio and Bastia.

Weeklies, on the *Newsweek/Time* model, include the wide-ranging, Left-leaning *Le Nouvel-Observateur* and its Rightist counterweight, *L'Express*. The best and funniest investigative journalism is in *Le Canard Enchaîné*, but it's almost incomprehensible to non-natives. Corsican nationalists are represented by the weekly political magazine *Aritti*, with articles in French and Corsican, and there's also a general-interest Corsican monthly called *Kyrn*, which has some articles in Corsican.

TV and Radio

You get both **French and Italian television** in Corsica. French is slightly better quality, featuring a range of programmes from trashy quiz shows to intellectual discussions about wine. The third channel – **FR3** – features Corsican regional programmes, with a local news bulletin every lunchtime and evening and a sporadic schedule of documentaries. Italian television is less widely available; the RAI channels are the best, featuring documentaries and good news coverage. Many hotels also have **satellite** channels, which include at least one English-speaking station.

There are a few local **radio** stations in Corsica, many of them broadcasting within a tiny area. The best of these is Bastia's RCFM (Radio Corse Frequenza Mora; 103FM), broadcasting in French and Corsican and playing a good variety of music, including the traditional folk music and modern Corsican bands.

Business Hours and Public Holidays

Basic hours of business are 8am till noon and 2 till 6pm; almost everything in Corsica – shops, museums, tourist offices, most banks – closes for a couple of hours at midday. In remote parts of the island lunch breaks tend to be lengthier and opening times less reliable. Food shops all over the island often don't open until midway through the afternoon, closing around 7.30pm or 8pm, just before the evening meal.

The standard **closing days** are Sunday and Monday, and in small places you'll find everything except the odd *boulangerie* shut on both days. **Museums** are not very generous with their hours, tending to open around 10am, close at noon until 2pm or 3pm, and then run through until 5pm or 6pm – opening hours from mid-May to mid-September are generally slightly longer than during the rest of the year. Museum closing days are usually Monday or Tuesday, sometimes both. Most churches are open all day; if you come across one that's locked, you can ask for the key at the local mairie (town hall).

Public Holidays

There are twelve national holidays (*jours fériés*), when most shops and businesses, though not museums and restaurants, are closed.

January 1

Easter Sunday

Easter Monday

Ascension Day (forty days after Easter)

Pentecost (seventh Sunday after Easter, plus the Monday)

May 1 May Day/Labour Day

May 8 Victory in Europe Day

July 14 Bastille Day

August 15 Assumption of the Virgin Mary

November 1 All Saints' Day

November 11 Armistice Day

December 25

Festivals and Events

Aside from the nationally celebrated **religious festivals**, such as the Assumption of the Virgin Mary, local saints' days are celebrated in Corsican towns throughout the year, and often include fireworks and processions. Many events are music- and arts-based affairs, with outdoor concerts and film festivals boosting the local tourist industry. There are also a few local **country fairs** where you can hear traditional Corsican singing and purchase regional specialities.

Of the innumerable Catholic feast days the most fervent are the **Easter** celebrations, almost invariably featuring a parade across town bearing a statue of the Virgin or of Christ, followed by Mass and a street party with fireworks and music. Many of these rituals also include a procession called a *granitola*, an ancient rite whereby a line of penitents forms a spiral as it moves through the town. The most intense of all Corsican religious ceremonies is the **Catenacciu** in Sartène, an Easter procession led by a penitent who drags a cross through the streets in imitation of Christ's walk to Golgotha.

Of the island's plethora of **folk festivals**, one that is definitely worth attending is the September *Santa di u Niolu* in Casamaccioli, a riotous event involving much drinking, singing and gambling. Corte's Ghjurnate di u Populu Corsu summer festival brings together nationalist separatists from all over Europe for a week of concerts and political speeches. Mediterranean folk **music festivals** take place at various locations throughout the summer, and there's a two-week jazz festival at Calvi every June.

The box below gives a rundown on the main annual events, with cross-references to the places in the *Guide* where you'll find more details.

Calendar of Events

March 18 – **Ajaccio** *Notre-Dame-de-la-Miséricorde* (see p.163).

Good Friday – **Erbalunga** *La Cerca* (see p.69); **Sartène** *U Catenacciu* (see p.230); **Calvi** *La Granitola* (see p.107).

March (first fortnight) – **Bastia** English film festival (see p.60).

May 3 – **Bastia** *Le Christ Noir* (see p.60).

June 2 – **Bastia**, **Ajaccio** and **Calvi** *St-Erasme* Fishermen's festival celebrated with a mass and firework displays in the harbour.

June (third week) – **Calvi** Jazz festival (see p.108).

July – **Corte** *Ghjurnate di u Populu Corsu* Folk music festival.

August – **Ajaccio** *Fêtes Napoléoniennes* Son et lumière in the Jardin du Casone.

August – **Calvi** *Citadella in Festa* (see p.108).

August 15 – **Bastia** and **Ajaccio** *L'Assomption*.

September – **Calvi** *Rencontres Polyphoniques* (see p.69).

September 8 – **Lavasina** *Notre-Dame-de-Lavasina* (see p.68).

September 8–10 – **Casamaccioli** *Santa di u Niolu* (see p.294).

Nov (third week) – **Bastia** Mediterranean film festival (see p.60).

Trouble and the Police

Emergency Numbers

Ambulance ☎15
Police ☎17
Fire service ☎18

Consulates in Marseille

Canada ☎04 91 37 19 37
Britain ☎04 91 53 43 32
Ireland ☎04 91 54 92 29
Netherlands ☎04 91 25 66 64
USA ☎04 91 54 92 00

Despite Corsica's reputation for violence and extremist politics, you are unlikely to encounter any trouble during your stay on the island, provided you keep within the law and avoid confrontations with the locals. Petty crime is minimal, though it makes sense to keep a close eye on your valuables in the crowded tourist resorts. If you should get robbed, hand over the money promptly and start dialling the cancellation numbers for your travellers' cheques and credit cards. Vehicles are rarely stolen, but tape players and luggage left in cars are more vulnerable to thieves. Try not to leave any valuables in sight, and make sure you have insurance.

There are two main types of French police (popularly known as *les flics*): the **Police Nationale** and the **Gendarmerie Nationale**. For all practical purposes, they are indistinguishable; if you need to report a theft, or other incident, you can go to either. A noticeable presence in Corsica are the **CRS** (*Compagnies Républicaines de Sécurité*), a mobile force of heavies posted here to handle demonstrations and the terrorist threat, with whom you should have no contact unless you inadvertently get caught up in a riot.

The police have the right to demand identification from any citizen, so if you want to avoid all possible hassle, make sure you're able to produce your passport or something equally incontrovertible. For driving violations such as speeding, the police also have the right to impose on-

the-spot fines. Should you be arrested on any charge, you have the right to contact your nearest consulate, which is likely to be in Marseille (see box above). People caught smuggling or possessing **drugs**, even a few grammes of marijuana, are liable to find themselves in jail, and the consulate will not be sympathetic.

Sexual and Racial Harassment

Women are less likely to experience **sexual harassment** in Corsica than in mainland France or Italy. Men do tend to stare, but they rarely approach or pass audible comment. An inbuilt "respect" for the opposite sex means that men will never take advantage of a situation – if a woman is in any trouble she can rely on a Corsican (male or female) to help out. It's not unusual to be offered a drink in a bar, and accepting doesn't leave you open to any harassment – rather it's a case of people not liking to see you paying as a guest in their country. Walking around at night is usually safe, especially in mountain villages and major towns. You're more likely to encounter trouble from foreigners in tourist resorts.

You may, as a woman, be warned about *les Arabes*, a standard instance of French **racism**. If you are Middle Eastern or black your chances of avoiding unpleasantness are unfortunately slim. Empty hotels claiming to be full, police demanding your papers and sometimes abusive treatment from ordinary people are all commonplace.

Disabled Travellers

France has no exceptional record for providing facilities for disabled travellers, and Corsica lags far behind other regions in this respect. Accessible hotels do exist in the major resorts, and ramps or other forms of access are gradually being added to museums, but the situation is far from satisfactory. The organizations listed below can provide various forms of useful information.

TRAVELLING WITH A DISABILITY: USEFUL CONTACTS

FRANCE

APF (Association des Paralysés de France), 17–21 bd Auguste-Blanqui, 75013 Paris (☎01 40 78 69 00). *A national organization with regional offices all over France, which can provide lists of accessible accommodation.*

CNFLRH (Comité National Française de Liaison pour la Réadaption des Handicapés), 236bis rue Tolbiac, 15013 Paris (☎01 53 80 66 66). *Information service for disabled travellers, with details of accessible accommodation, holiday centres, etc. Also distributes various useful guides, including one to Corsica.*

BRITAIN AND IRELAND

Access Project 33, Blackwall Lane, London SE10 (☎0181/858 2375). *Information service giving details of disabled facilities throughout the world.*

Holiday Care Service, 2nd Floor, Imperial Building, Victoria Rd, Horley, Surrey RH6 7PZ (☎01293/774535). *Information on all aspects of travel.*

RADAR (The Royal Association for Disability and Rehabilitation), 12 City Forum, 250 City Rd, London EC1V (☎0171/250 3222, Minicom 0171/250 4119). *A good source of advice on holidays and travel.*

TRIPSCOPE, The Courtyard, Evelyn Rd, London W4 5JL (☎0181/994 9294). *Phone-in travel information and advice service.*

USA AND CANADA

Mobility International USA, PO Box 10767, Eugene, OR 97440 (voice and TDD ☎503/343 1248). *Information, access guides, tours and exchange programme. Annual membership $20.*

Travel Information Service, Moss Rehabilitation Hospital, 1200 West Tabor Rd, Philadelphia, PA 19141 (☎215/456 9600). *Telephone information and referral service.*

Twin Peaks Press, Box 129, Vancouver, WA 98666 (☎206/694 2462 or 1-800/637 2256). *Publisher of the* Directory of Travel Agencies for the Disabled ($19.95), *listing more than 370 agencies worldwide;* Travel for the Disabled ($19.95); *the* Directory of Accessible Van Rentals ($9.95); *and* Wheelchair Vagabond ($14.95), *loaded with personal tips.*

AUSTRALIA AND NEW ZEALAND

ACROD (Australian Council for Rehabilitation of the Disabled), PO Box 60, Curtin ACT 2605 (☎06/682 4333); 55 Charles St, Ryde (☎02/9809 4488). *Provides lists of travel agencies and tour operators for people with disabilities.*

Disabled Persons Assembly, PO Box 10, 138 The Terrace, Wellington (☎04/472 2626). *Organization with details of tour operators and travel agencies for people with disabilities.*

Directory

BEACHES are public property within 5m of the high-tide mark; it's illegal to camp on them, however. Some beaches are protected areas, where you are prohibited from climbing on the dunes; and beware of goats – an aggressive hazard in many spots.

CHILDREN are adored in Corsica and welcome in bars and restaurants. Hotels charge a small supplement for an extra bed or cot. Bus and train travel is free for the under-4s, half-fare for 4–12s.

CIGARETTES are the only consumer items cheaper than in mainland France, selling at 6F per packet.

CONTRACEPTIVES Condoms (*preservatifs*) are prominently displayed on pharmacy counters, and there's an increasing number of dispensing machines in public places. You need a prescription for the Pill (*la Pilule*).

DIVING Clubs all over Corsica supply equipment and instruction for around 500F per day. At least bring a snorkel, as the sea is the clearest in the Med and packed with colourful fish.

ELECTRICITY is 220v, using plugs with two round pins.

LAUNDRY Self-service laundries in Corsica are extremely rare. *Pressing* services in Bastia and Ajaccio will do laundry for a high price and hotels will do it for around 50F per load. You could discreetly do your own in your hotel room, though technically it's forbidden to wash clothes in hotels.

LEFT LUGGAGE *Consignes* are found in the ports and train stations, charging around 10–25F per item per day.

PHOTOGRAPHIC FILM is expensive in Corsica, so bring as much as you'll need.

RIDING Former mule tracks converted into riding trails provide plenty of possibilities for trekking. Long-distance rides, with accommodation provided along the way, are organized by the Association Regionale pour le Tourisme Équestre, 20230 San Nicolao (☎04 95 38 56 70). Expect to pay between 400–600F per day.

SKIING Although skiing is possible in the mountains, don't be fooled by tourist office advertising – snow is minimal and the prepared slopes are less than impressive. For information on cross-country skiing (*ski à fond*), contact Muntagne Corse in Liberta, Parc Bilello, Immeuble Girolata, av Napoleon-III, 2000 Ajaccio (☎04 95 23 17 42), or the Comité Régional Corse de Ski, 34 bd Paoli, 20200 Bastia (☎04 95 32 01 94).

TIME French summertime begins on March 28 and finishes on September 26, and is therefore an hour ahead of Britain for most of the year, except in October when times are the same. It's six hours ahead of Eastern Standard Time, nine hours ahead of Pacific Standard Time.

TOILETS Toilets, usually found at the back of bars, can be primitive hole-in-the-floor affairs, tending to lack paper. Outside public toilets are nonexistent.

The Guide

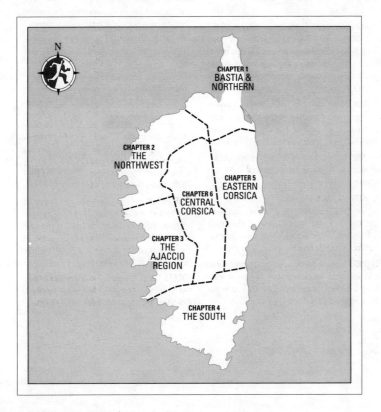

Chapter 1

Bastia and northern Corsica

B astia, nowadays capital of the *département* of Haute-Corse, was the capital of the entire island under Genoa's colonial administration, and it was the Genoese who laid the foundations of northern Corsica's prosperity by encouraging the planting of vines, olives, chestnut trees and other more experimental crops – there's a village called Sparagaghjiu (Asparagus) in the hills above St-Florent. The long-term result of this development was that the peasant farmers of the north tended to be not just better off than their southern counterparts, but also politically more ambitious. Thus, when Pascal Paoli recruited his rebel armies it was on this region's downtrodden rich that he concentrated his efforts, rather than on the downtrodden poor of the south. Even today there's a palpable difference in the political climate of the island's two halves, with northerners tending to see themselves as more radical, energetic and enterprising.

A thriving freight and passenger port, **Bastia** is the point of arrival for many visitors, and it can be a rather depressing experience at first, with industrial sprawl on the way into town from the airport, high-rise blocks stacked up the hillsides above town, and no decent beaches. Yet, while Bastia lacks the appeal of sleek Ajaccio, this is the town to visit if you want to get to grips with modern Corsica, for a quarter of the island's population lives and works here and in the immediate surroundings. Moreover, despite suffering considerable damage in World War II, the city has retained its Italian character, especially around the **Vieux Port**, a horseshoe of vertiginous buildings dominated by the towers of the Église St-Jean-Baptiste and bulk of the Genoese citadel.

The nearest beaches are to the south along the unremarkable stretch of coast known as **La Marana**, which adjoins the **Étang de Biguglia**, a huge lagoon that's a haven for migrating birds, and the beautiful Pisan church of **La Canonica**. To the north of Bastia, a single road follows the shore of the long rocky peninsula of **Cap Corse**,

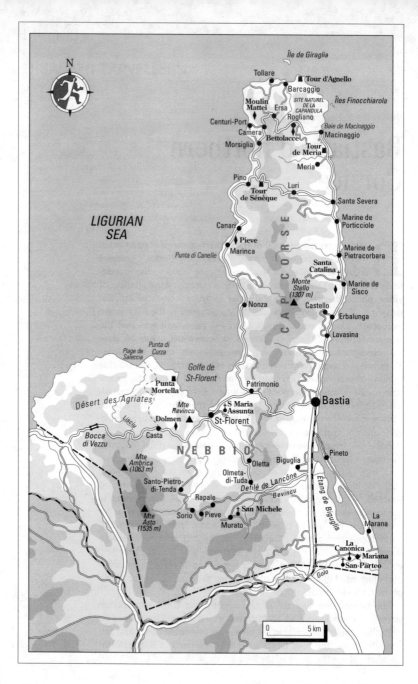

giving access to some exceptionally beautiful and unspoilt stretches
of coast, as well as a string of diminutive ports, of which **Erbalunga**
and **Centuri-Port** are the pick. At the base of the cape's finger, on
the western side, lies **St-Florent**, a smart sailing centre and fishing
village with most of the north's accommodation outside the capital.
The hinterland of St-Florent, the **Nebbio**, is famed for the wines produced near **Patrimonio**, for dramatically sited upland villages such
as **Oletta** and **Santo Pietro di Tenda**, and for the finest Romanesque
churches on the island – Santa Maria Assunta, on the outskirts of St-
Florent, and the chapel of San Michele, near Murato. West of St-
Florent lies the uninhabited **Désert des Agriates**, a vast semi-barren
expanse covered in massive clumps of rock, stands of cactus and the
ruins of ancient stone dwellings. The coast here is generally wild and
inaccessible, though the beaches of **Saleccia** and **Loto** are amongst
the finest in Corsica.

Public transport in the region is generally better than elsewhere
on the island, but that isn't saying much. Corsica's train, the *micheline*, threads south from Bastia a little way, passing the Étang de
Biguglia, but doesn't serve anywhere else covered in this chapter.
Buses aren't common, but you can get one up into Cap Corse or the
Nebbio at certain times of the week, and daily to St-Florent, while
during the summer services run along the north coast to Calvi, skirting the southern fringes of the Désert des Agriates.

Bastia

Paradoxically, the dominant tone of Corsica's most successful commercial town, **BASTIA**, is one of charismatic dereliction, as the city's
industrial zone is spread onto the lowlands to the south, leaving the
centre of town with plenty of aged charm. This charm might not be
too apparent from the vast **place St-Nicolas** and the two boulevards
parallel to it, which, though flanked by faded Art Deco shop fronts,
are choked with expensive cars and busy shoppers. But to the south
of here lies the old quarter known as the **Terra Vecchia**, a tightly
packed network of haphazard streets, flamboyant Baroque churches
and lofty tenements, their crumbling golden-grey walls set against a
backdrop of maquis-covered hills. **Terra Nova**, the historic district

on the opposite side of the old port from Terra Vecchia, is a tidier zone that's now Bastia's yuppie quarter, housing the island's top-flight architects, doctors and lawyers.

Young upper-crust Bastiais always used to be sent to Italian universities for their education, a traffic that has had a marked effect on the city's tradition of professional success and on its cultural life – it's here that you'll find Corsica's only purpose-built theatre. Modelled on Milan's La Scala, it was regularly visited by the great Italian opera stars, and nowadays, even though some of the gloss has gone, the place fills up for occasional concerts by touring companies from Italy, or for one of Bastia's film festivals. Nothing packs in the crowds quite like the recurrent nationalist rallies, however, for Bastia is something of a centre for dissidence. Discontent with the way the city is run is a constant feature of life here, as highlighted in 1989 when Bastia's civil servants rioted over the mysterious disappearance of local government funds – the disturbances culminated soon after with the razing of the local tax office by a nationalist-terrorist bomb. Highly politicized and busily self-sufficient, Bastia may make few concessions to tourism, but its grittiness makes it a more genuine introduction to Corsica than its long-time rival on the west coast.

A brief history of Bastia

In the twelfth century, when Corsica was under Pisan control, wine was exported to the Italian mainland from **Porto Cardo**, forerunner of Bastia's **Vieux Port**. Moorish raids made the area too vulnerable to inhabit, however, and it wasn't until the Genoese ascendancy that the port began to thrive. At first the Genoese governed from the former Roman base at Biguglia, to the south, but in 1372, when the fort was burned down by Corsican rebels, the Genoese governor abandoned the malarial site in favour of Porto Cardo, a spot close to Genoa and within easy trading distance of the fertile regions of the eastern plain, Balagne and Cap Corse. Before the end of the decade the governor, Leonello Lomellino, had built the *bastiglia* (dungeon) which gave the town its name; ramparts were constructed high on the escarpment above the port, and Genoese families, attracted by offers of free building land, began to settle within the fortifications in an area which became **Terra Nova**.

The sixteenth century saw the rise of a new class of merchants and artisans, who settled around the harbour on the site of Porto Cardo, the area now known as **Terra Vecchia**. The boom lasted until 1730, when Bastia was raided by an army of four thousand peasants, following similar attacks on Aléria and the Balagne settlements. Provoked to desperation by the corrupt despotism of the Genoese republic, the *paesani* went on the rampage for three days, annihilating most of the population of Terra Vecchia, who lacked the protection of the upper-class inhabitants of Terra Nova. Peace was final-

ly restored by the intervention of the bishop of Aléria, but the Bastia
remaining Genoese merchants promptly left for the safer ports of
Bonifacio and Calvi, and Bastia went into decline.

During the **War of Independence** Bastia became a battleground.
Pascal Paoli coveted the town for its strong position facing Italy, but
it took two attempts and the efforts of the British fleet to take the
town – the second assault was led by Nelson and Hood, who, though
outnumbered by two to one, overcame the defenders in a long and
difficult siege. In 1794, in the wake of this vistory, Bastia became
home for English viceroy Sir Gilbert Elliot, who lived here for the two
years of the Anglo-Corsican alliance. Bastia's hour of glory was
short-lived, however, as the French finally gained full control of
Corsica in 1796, and the island was divided into two *départements*.

Despite the fact that in 1811 Napoleon appointed Ajaccio capital
of the island, initiating a rivalry between the two towns which exists
to this day, Bastia soon established a stronger trading position with
mainland France. The **Nouveau Port**, created in 1862 to cope with
the increasing traffic with France and Italy, became the mainstay of
the local economy, exporting chiefly agricultural products from Cap
Corse, Balagne and the eastern plain. During World War II Bastia's
economic prominence made it an obvious target, and it was the only
town on Corsica to be severely bombed. A German division based
here caused much of the destruction, but it was the Americans who
caused the most damage, launching an attack as the people came out
to celebrate their liberation. Many buildings were destroyed, including much of the old governor's palace, and the consequences of the
bombing can still be seen in Terra Vecchia.

Today Bastia's population has grown to fifty thousand, with the
long-standing industries of freight handling and small-scale manufacture providing most of the employment, augmented by the burgeoning bureaucracies of local government. The city has also
become a hotbed of nationalist activity, with more than its fair share
of political assassinations and bombings in recent years; among
these was the explosion in July 1996 in the Vieux Port, which killed
a prominent Cuncolta leader. However, the worst tragedy since the
war occurred on May 5, 1992, when a stand in the Furiani stadium,
home of Corsica's top football team, Sporting Club de Bastia (SCB),
collapsed during a European Cup tie with arch rivals Olympic de
Marseille (OM). Seventeen supporters died in the disaster and more
than 1300 were injured. Those responsible have yet to be brought to
book, while the issue of compensation for the victims has become
embroiled in scandal and protracted legal cases.

Arrival and information

Bastia's Poretta **airport** is 16km south of town, just off the Route
Nationale; shuttle buses (*navettes*) into the centre coincide with
flights, dropping passengers at the north side of the main square,

BASTIA AND NORTHERN CORSICA

place St-Nicolas, for 42F. The **train station** (gare SNCF; ☎04 95 32 80 60) is five minutes' walk west of here along the av Maréchal-Sébastiani, and has a pricy *consigne* where you can leave luggage for 26F per article. **Ferries** arrive at the **Nouveau Port**, a short way north of the town centre, whose terminal building, the gare maritime, harbours a Crédit Agricole exchange counter (July–Sept 11am–5pm), and a left-luggage room (daily 8–11.30am & 2–7.30pm; 10F per article). **Buses** from Ajaccio and Porto Vecchio stop opposite the post office (PTT) on av Maréchal-Sébastiani, whereas those coming from Calvi pull in outside the train station. Local suburban services, and those from Cap Corse, work out of the bus station behind the Hôtel de Ville, two minutes' north of the square. There are two large **car parks**, one underground beneath place St-Nicolas, and one in the citadel, on the right as you enter the main town from the south.

The **tourist office** is at the north end of place St-Nicolas (June–Sept daily 8am–8pm; Oct–May Mon–Sat 8am–6pm, Sun & holidays 8am–noon & 2–5pm; ☎04 95 31 00 89). Although the staff won't fall over themselves to help you, they can provide useful **bus timetables** for services from Bastia, and free, fold-up **maps** of Corsica.

For information on **changing money**, see "Listings" on p.61.

Accommodation

Bastia's passenger port receives twice as many visitors as Ajaccio's, but few linger in the city, preferring to head straight off to quieter corners of the island. This may in part explain the relative shortage of **hotel rooms**. Choice is particularly limited at the bottom end of the scale, so if you're on a tight budget think twice about spending a night here. Most of the classier places line the road to Cap Corse north of the port; the more basic ones are found in the centre of town, within striking distance of place St-Nicolas. Wherever you plan to stay, it's advisable to reserve a day or so in advance by telephone.

There is also a handful of **campsites** located outside the town, all accessible by bus. The most convenient if you're relying on public transport is *Les Orangers*.

Hotels

L'Alivi, route du Cap, Ville Pietrabugno (☎04 95 31 61 85, fax 04 95 31 03 95). Large, swish, seaside three-star, 3km north of the city, with a pool, car park and private access by elevator to the beach. Among Bastia's top hotels. ⑥.

Central, 3 rue Miot (☎04 95 31 71 26). Recently renovated hotel just off the south side of place St-Nicolas. Clean, comfortable, very central, and by far the best economy deal in the city. Their pricier options have air-con and en-suite bathrooms; the rest share toilets. ②–③.

Forum, 20 bd Paoli (☎04 95 31 02 53, fax 04 95 31 26 41). Cosy and attractively chic, with spacious rooms, bar and relaxing terrace on enclosed courtyard. ④–⑤.

L'Imperial, 2 bd Paoli (☎04 95 31 06 94, fax 04 95 34 13 76). Slightly over-priced two-star on the south side of town. Recently redecorated, but its rooms are on the small side. ③.

Napoléon, 43 bd Paoli (☎04 95 31 60 30, fax 04 95 31 77 83). Plush two-star with tiny rooms (few with air-con). Central and efficient. ④–⑤.

Pietracap, 20 route de San-Martino, Pietranera (☎04 95 31 64 63). Luxury hotel with swimming pool, 4km from the centre, on hillside with great views. Closed winter. ⑥.

Posta-Vecchia, quai des Martyrs-de-la-Libération (☎04 95 32 32 38, fax 04 95 32 14 05). Large, chic hotel (the only one in the Vieux Port) with wonder-ful views across the sea from (pricier) front-side rooms. ④–⑤.

Riviera, 1 rue du Nouveau-Port (☎04 95 31 07 16, fax 04 95 34 17 39). Well-established and comfortable, with good-sized, clean and airy rooms (some overlooking the harbour). Very popular, so book ahead June–Sept. ④.

Sud Hôtel, av de la Libération, Lupino (☎04 95 30 20 61, fax 04 95 30 53 85). Charming, recently renovated place on the south edge of town (1km along air-port road, and west off RN193), with own car park, sociable patio and friend-ly owners. Good value. ③.

L'Univers, 3 av Maréchal-Sebastiani (☎04 95 31 03 38, fax 04 95 31 19 41). Variously priced rooms in an old tenement opposite the post office. Their no-frills cheaper options are dingy, but the air-con rooms upstairs are comfortable enough. Handy for the bus and train stations. ②–③.

Les Voyageurs, 9 av Maréchal-Sebastiani (☎04 95 31 08 97). In the touristy part of town and well situated for buses and trains, but dowdy, airless and dark. ②–③.

Campsites

Esperenza, Plage du Pinède, route de Pineto (☎04 95 36 15 09). About 11km south of Bastia, beyond *San Damiano* (see below) and with fewer facilities. Hourly buses in summer from the gare routière.

Les Orangers, Miomo, 4km north along the route to Cap Corse (☎04 95 33 24 09). Shady, attractive site near the sea; the half-hourly bus to Erbalunga will drop you here.

San Damiano, Pineto, 10km south of Bastia (☎04 95 33 68 02). Huge, spa-cious 200-place site with excellent facilities; take the road to the left across the bridge at Furiani roundabout. Buses as for the *Esperenza*. April–Oct.

The town

Bastia is not a large town, and all its sights can easily be seen in a day without the use of a car. The spacious **place St-Nicolas** is the obvi-ous place to get your bearings: open to the sea and lined with shady trees and cafés, it's the main focus of town life. Running parallel to it on the landward side are **boulevard Paoli** and **rue César Campinchi**, the two main shopping streets, but all Bastia's historic sights lie with-in **Terra Vecchia**, the old quarter immediately south of place St-Nicolas, and **Terra Nova**, the area surrounding the **Citadelle**. Tucked away below the imposing, honey-coloured bastion is the much-photographed **Vieux Port**, with its boat-choked marina and crumbling eighteenth-century tenement buildings. By contrast, the **Nouveau Port** area, north of the *place*, is bland and modern, with lit-tle of interest other than restaurants and bars.

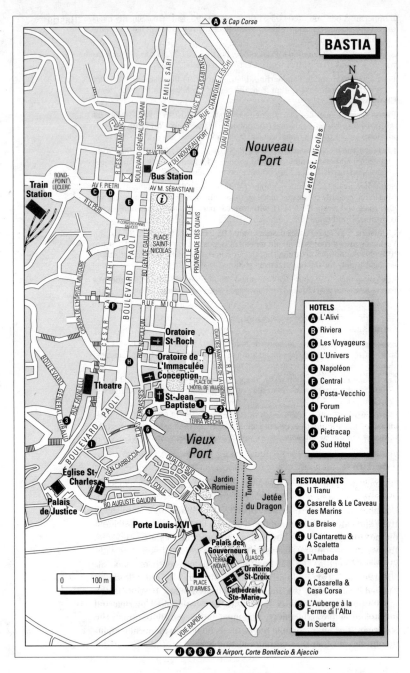

BASTIA

N

Nouveau
Port

Jetée St. Nicolas

AV. EMILE SARI

R. COMM. LUCE DE CASABIANCA

RUE CHANOINE LESCHI

QUAI DU FANGO

R. DU NOUVEAU PORT

Ⓑ

SQ.
ST-VICTOR

BOULEVARD GÉNÉRAL GRAZIANI

R. CÉSAR CAMPINCHI

Bus Station

ROND-
POINT
LECLERC

**Train
Station**

AV. F. PIETRI

Ⓒ Ⓓ

R. CÉSAR

AV. M. SÉBASTIANI

Ⓔ

ⓘ

R. CONVENTIONNEL SALICETI

PLACE
SAINT-
NICOLAS

VOIE RAPIDE

PROMENADE DES QUAIS

BOULEVARD PAOLI

BD GÉNÉRAL DE GAULLE

CHEMIN DE L'HÔPITAL MILITAIRE

R. CÉSAR CAMPINCHI

RUE MIOT

Ⓕ

BOULEVARD

RUE NAPOLÉON

**Oratoire
St-Roch**

**Oratoire de
L'Immaculée
Conception**

Ⓖ

QUAI DES MARTYRS DE LA LIBÉRATION

VOIE RAPIDE

Ⓗ

PLACE DE
L'HÔTEL DE VILLEROY

Theatre

RUE FAVALELLI

**St-Jean
Baptiste**

TERRASSES

❶

❷

Ⓘ

❸

❹

❺

TERRA VECCHIA

❻

RUE NAPOLÉON

*Vieux
Port*

BOULEVARD PAOLI

BD GÉNÉRAL GIRAUD

R. GEN. CARBUCCIA

**Église St-
Charles**

QUAI DU SUD

R. DU COLLE

Jardin
Romieu

Tunnel

**Palais
de Justice**

BD AUGUSTE GAUDIN

Jetée
du Dragon

Porte Louis-XVI

**Palais des
Gouverneurs**

PL.
GUASCO

TERRA
NOVA

❼

**Oratoire
St-Croix**

P

PLACE
D'ARMES

**Cathédrale
Ste-Marie**

| 0 | 100 m |

VOIE RAPIDE

HOTELS

Ⓐ L'Alivi
Ⓑ Riviera
Ⓒ Les Voyageurs
Ⓓ L'Univers
Ⓔ Napoléon
Ⓕ Central
Ⓖ Posta-Vecchio
Ⓗ Forum
Ⓘ L'Impérial
Ⓙ Pietracap
Ⓚ Sud Hôtel

RESTAURANTS

❶ U Tianu
❷ Casarella & Le Caveau
des Marins
❸ La Braise
❹ U Cantarettu &
A Scaletta
❺ L'Ambada
❻ Le Zagora
❼ A Casarella &
Casa Corsa
❽ L'Auberge à la
Ferme di l'Altu
❾ In Suerta

Place St-Nicolas

The most pleasant spot to soak up Bastia's Mediterranean atmosphere is **place St-Nicolas**. Lined by palms and leafy plane trees, the long rectangular square is the social hub of the town: during the evening, with the Nouveau Port's gigantic white ferry boats forming a surreal backdrop, its cafés fill up with snappily dressed young Bastiais on their way home from work, while pensioners take leisurely promenades under the trees. Apart from the faintly camp marble statue of Napoléon in Roman emperor's garb, the square's only real sight is wonderful Art Deco façade of the **Maison Mattei**, on the northwest side. This old-established wine merchants (July & Aug open till 10pm), sells liqueurs from all over the island, including the famous local quinine-based aperitif, Cap Corse.

Terra Vecchia

From place St-Nicolas the main route south into **Terra Vecchia** is **rue Napoléon**, a narrow street with some ancient offbeat shops and a pair of sumptuously decorated chapels on its east side. The first of these, the **Oratoire de St-Roch**, is a Genoese Baroque extravagance, built in 1604 and reflecting the wealth of the rising bourgeoisie. Particularly remarkable are its walls, which are covered with finely carved wooden panelling. The chapel also possesses a magnificent **organ** decorated with gilt and wooden sculpture; hardly altered since it was built in 1750, it's played on religious festivals and in special concerts.

A little further along stands the **Oratoire de L'Immaculée Conception**, built in 1611 as the showplace of the Genoese in Corsica, who used it for state occasions such as the inauguration of the governor. In later years, the English viceroy, Sir Gilbert Eliot, held parliamentary sessions here during the brief Anglo-Corsican alliance. Overlooking a pebble mosaic of a sun, the austere façade belies the flamboyant **interior**, where crimson velvet draperies, a gilt and marble ceiling, frescoes and crystal chandeliers create the ambience of an opera house. The unusually narrow nave terminates at an elaborate polychromatic marble altar, over which hangs an unimpressive copy of Murillo's *Immaculate Conception*. On the left stands a **statue of the Virgin**, which, on December 8, is paraded through the streets to the church of St-Jean-Baptiste. The sacristy houses a tiny **museum** (daily 9am–6pm; free) of minor religious works, of which the wooden statue of Erasmus, patron saint of fishers, dating from 1788, is most arresting.

If you cut back through the narrow steps beside the Oratoire de St-Roch, a two-minute walk will bring you to **place de l'Hôtel-de-Ville**, commonly known as place du Marché because of the half-hearted **market** that takes place here each morning. At the south end of the square is the **Église St-Jean-Baptiste**, an immense ochre edifice that dominates the Vieux Port. Its twin campaniles are Bastia's distinguishing feature, but the interior is less than impressive – built in 1636, the church was restored in the eighteenth century in a hideous Rococo overkill of multicoloured marble. Decorating the walls are a few unremarkable Italian paintings from Napoléon's uncle, Cardinal Fesch, an avid collector of Renaissance art (see p.167).

Around the church extends the oldest part of Bastia, an oppressively secretive zone of dark alleys, vaulted passageways and seven-storey houses locked in isolation from the rest of town. Hidden among them, on the rue Castagno, is one of Corsica's few remaining synagogues, the **Beth Meir**. A plaque on its wall alludes to the anti-Semitism that was rife in Bastia during World War II, after which all but a handful of the town's Jewish population left. Since then, families of Moroccan immigrants have moved in to take their place as the district's much-disparaged underclass, lending a distinctly North African feel to this former Jewish ghetto.

By turning right outside the Église St-Jean-Baptiste and following rue St-Jean you'll come to **rue Général-Carbuccia**, the heart of Terra Vecchia. Pascal Paoli once lived here, at no. 7, and Balzac stayed briefly at no. 23 when his ship got stuck in Corsica on the way to Sardinia. Set in a small square at the end of the road is the **Église St-Charles**, an august Jesuit chapel whose wide steps provide an evening meeting place for locals; opposite stands the **Maison de Caraffa**, an elegant house with a strikingly graceful balcony.

The **Vieux Port** is the most appealing part of town: soaring houses seem to bend inwards towards the water, peeling plaster and boat hulls glint in the sun, while the south side remains in the shadow of the great rock that supports the citadel. Site of the original Porto Cardo, the Vieux Port later bustled with Genoese traders, but since the building of the ferry terminal and commercial docks it has become a backwater, deserted by day, when the clinking of a few fishing boats echoes around the harbour. It's livelier at night, with the glow and noise from the harbourside bars and restaurants. These continue round the north end of the port along the wide **quai des Martyrs-de-la-Libération**, where live bands clank out pop classics for the tourists in summer.

The best view of the Vieux Port is from the **Jetée du Dragon**, the quay that juts out under the citadel. To build it, engineers had to destroy a giant lion-shaped rock known as the Leone, which formerly blocked the entrance to the harbour, and which featured in the foreground of many nineteenth-century engravings of Bastia. To reach the citadel from the quai des Martyrs, you can walk through the **Jardin Romieu**, an eighteenth-century terraced garden adorning the cliff on this side of the harbour. Despite the elegantly sweeping stone steps, the gardens are dusty and unremarkable and are a notorious hang-out for dubious characters – certainly not the spot for a picnic.

Terra Nova

The military and administrative core of old Bastia, **Terra Nova** (or
the **Citadelle**) lords it over the old port from its perch atop a sheer-
sided rocky promontory. Beautifully restored over the past couple of
decades, the quarter has a distinct air of affluence, and its lofty apartments and neatly colour-washed houses are now largely the preserve
of Bastia's yuppies. The area is focused on **place du Donjon**, which
gets its name from the squat round tower that formed the nucleus of
the town's fortifications and was used by the Genoese to incarcerate
Corsican patriots – Sampiero Corso was held in the dungeon for four
years in the early sixteenth century. Next to the tower a strategically
placed terrace **bar** commands a magnificent view which, on a clear
day, extends across the Tyrranean Sea to the Tuscan island of Elba.

Facing the bar is the impressive fourteenth-century **Palais des
Gouverneurs**, Terra Nova's most prominent landmark. With its great
round tower, arcaded inner courtyard and pristine peach-coloured
paintwork, this building has a distinctly Moorish feel. During the
Genoese heyday, the governor and the local bishop lived here with an
entourage of seventy horsemen, entertaining foreign dignitaries and
hosting massive parties. When the French transferred the capital to
Ajaccio, it became a prison, and was then destroyed during Nelson's
attack of 1794. The subsequent rebuilding was not the last, as parts
of it were blown up by the Americans in 1943, and today the restor-
ers are trying to regain something of the building's former grandeur.

Part of the palace is given over to the **Musée d'Éthnographie
Corse** (daily June 9am–6.30pm, July–Aug 9am–8pm, Sept–May
9am–noon & 2–6pm; last entry 45min before closing time; 15F),
which presents the history of Corsica from prehistoric times to the
present day. Its dusty vaulted chambers contain a motley collection
of exhibits from rare rock specimens to Pascal Paoli memorabilia, an
array that at first sight seems rather tired yet does include a handful
of fascinating historical titbits.

In amongst the geological specimens in the first room on the
ground floor are some rare minerals, including the unique greenish
ring-patterned diorite found in Ste-Lucie-de-Tallano, and a sample of
the orangey-brown sulphurous arsenic which the Germans used to
make gas bombs in World War I. The next *salle* houses archeological
finds and some of the few remaining Roman artefacts left in Corsica.
Among these is a diminutive **sarcophagus** decorated with hunting
scenes. Thought to have belonged to a child, it was discovered in
Bastelicaccia, near Ajaccio, where it was being used as a horses' drinking trough. From here, the exhibition proceeds chronologically, illus-
trating the island's history with old maps, engravings and indecipher-
able documents, along with cases relating to key figures such as
Sampiero, King Théodore and Nelson. On your way around, look out
for Napoléon's uncannily realistic death mask, and for the original **flag
of Independence**, an emblem of obscure origins (see box overleaf).

The Moor's Head

You can't travel far in Corsica without coming across the island's ubiquitous national symbol, the **Moor's head**. Depicting the profile of a young black male with a white scarf, or *banneau*, tied behind his head, this enigmatic image crops up everywhere, from car stickers to key rings, postcards to football pennants. Yet its origins are obscure, shrouded in a mixture of myth and historical fact.

The first concrete associations of the Moor's head with Corsica date from the early seventeenth century, when it featured on German maps of the island. This inspired Théodore von Neuhof to use the image on the single silver coin he had minted to mark his short reign as king of Corsica. Not until November 24, 1762, however, was it declared the official symbol of Corsican Independence, at the instigation of Pascal Paoli.

The choice of the Moor's head seems somewhat strange, given the fact the symbol was known to have originally come from Spain and was at one time synonymous with the threat of colonial rule. It first came to the region on the battle standards of the kings of Aragon, who ruled neighbouring Sardinia following the expulsion of the Saracens during the Crusades. Indeed, the white *banneau*, which on Aragon standards was drawn covering the eyes rather than the forehead, is believed to symbolize the defeat of the Muslims and their forced conversion to Christianity, while the Aragon arms of Sardinia featured four heads – one for each of the four victorious battles against the Saracens fought on the island.

The association of the Moor's head emblem with the defeat of the Saracens during the Middle Ages finds echoes in an old Corsican legend. In the story, a young woman named Diana from Aléria, on the east coast, was abducted by Moorish pirates and taken to Grenada. However, her fiancé, Paoli, managed to free her and, after crossing the Sierra Nevada, return safely to Corsica. The king of Grenada, Mohammed Abdul Allah, was furious at being outwitted by a peasant and instructed his top general, Mansour ben Ismail, to recapture the fugitives dead or alive. After landing at Piana on the west coast, the Moors are then said to have raped and pillaged their way across the mountains to Aléria, where they were engaged, and eventually defeated by, a courageous Corsican army. In the course of the battle, Paoli avenged Diana's abduction by slaying Mansour and parading his disembodied head at the end of a stick around the entire island – whence the now famous image.

In more recent times, the Moor's head has been appropriated by the nationalist movement as the unofficial emblem of the Corsican Independence struggle. Wherever you find a French *tricolore*, you're almost certain to see a black-and-white Moor's head flag flying provocatively nearby.

The final room on the ground floor houses an exhibition on daily life in different regions of Corsica, giving some idea of the harsh realities of existence on the land. Chestnut flour mills, farm instruments, olive presses and life-size mannequins of shepherds from the remote Niolo region provide the bulk of the display – explicating practices that are still continued in some regions of the island.

Most visits to the museum wind up with a guided tour (price included in admission fee) of the recently renovated Genoese **dun-**

geons below the governor's palace. Although of little interest in themselves, the damp stone chambers are well worth a look if you can follow the French commentary, which describes in gruesome detail the conditions endured by the 350 or more innmates encarcerated here, many of them chained for days on end to the wet walls. Particularly poignant is the cell in which resistance fighters were held and tortured by the Nazis during World War II; one actually cut out his own tongue rather than divulge the whereabouts of his comrades.

On the terrace of the museum stands the conning tower of the submarine **Casabianca**, which played a major part in the liberation of Corsica from the Germans by ferrying weapons and ammunitions from Algeria. The sub was named after twelve-year-old Giocante de Casabianca, who died at Aboukir in 1798 when he refused to leave his father's ship after it had been attacked by Nelson's fleet – giving Felicia Hemans her inspiration for the poem beginning, "The boy stood on the burning deck".

Back in place du Donjon, if you cross the square and follow rue Notre-Dame you come out at the **Église Ste-Marie**. Built in 1458 and overhauled in the seventeenth century, it was the cathedral of Bastia until 1801, when the bishopric was transferred to Ajaccio. The over-restored façade is an ugly shade of peach, and there's nothing of interest inside except a small silver statue of the Virgin, which is carried through Terra Nova and Terra Vecchia on August 15, the Festival of the Assumption. Virtually next door, in rue de l'Evêché, stands the **Oratoire Ste-Croix**, a sixteenth-century church decorated in Louis XV style, all rich blue paint and gilt scrollwork. It houses another holy item, the **Christ des Miracles**, a blackened oak crucifix which in 1428 was discovered floating in the sea surrounded by a luminous haze. A festival celebrating the miracle takes place in Bastia on May 3.

Beyond the church, the narrow streets open out to the tiny **place Guasco**, a delightful square at the heart of the citadel that typifies the exclusivity of Terra Nova. A few benches offer the chance of a rest before descending into the fray.

The beaches

Crowded with schoolchildren in the summer, the pebbly **town beach** in Bastia is only worth visiting if you're desperate for a swim. To reach it, turn left at the flower shop on the main road south out of town, just beyond the citadel. A better alternative is to head 1km further along the same road to the long beach of **L'Arinella** at Montesoro, the beginning of a sandy shore that extends along the whole east coast. A **bus** to L'Arinella leaves from outside *Café Riche* on bd Paoli every twenty minutes; get off at the last stop and cross the railway line to the sea. There are a couple of sailing and windsurfing clubs here, plus a bar.

Bastia

Leaving Bastia in the other direction, you will find sandy beaches about a kilometre along the road to **Cap Corse**, but these are rather polluted and the sea tends to be choppy.

Eating, drinking and nightlife

Lively place St-Nicolas, packed with cafés, is the place to be during the day, particularly between noon and 3pm when the rest of town is deserted. For a more sedate atmosphere, head along bd Paoli and rue Campinchi, which are lined with chichi salons de thé offering elaborate creamy confections, local chestnut cake and doughnuts. Late-night clubbers can revive themselves with an early coffee and a pain au chocolat at one of the three cafés in place de l'Hôtel-de-Ville, which open at 4.30am for the market traders. You'll find that most cafés serve croque-monsieurs at exorbitant prices, but for better-value **snacks** try the offbeat retro **kiosks** on place St-Nicolas, which sell hot dogs, crêpes, *paninis* and tasty *casse-croûtes* for a few francs. Numerous **pizza vans** are scattered about town until about 9pm (there's usually one outside the train station), evidence of a strong Italian influence that's also apparent in the predominance of pizzerias and pasta places crammed into the narrow backstreets behind the quai des Martyrs. The town also boasts some excellent yet inexpensive **restaurants** serving Corsican specialities such as wild boar and charcuterie, and fish is inevitably prominent: the posh places on the quai des Martyrs do the best *aziminu*, a Corsican version of bouillabaisse. Most of the good restaurants are to be found around the Vieux Port and on the quai des Martyrs, with a sprinkling in the citadel. The establishments listed below are open daily unless specified.

Drinking is serious business in Bastia. The **Casanis** pastis factory is on the outskirts of town in Lupino, and this is indisputably the town's drink – order a "Casa" and you'll fit in well. There are many bars and cafés all over town, varying from the stark, bright bars of Terra Vecchia that are the haunt of old men, to the elegant, dimly lit cafés on place St-Nicolas, where you can sip hot chocolate on low leather seats. The best place to buy wine is *Grand Vin Corse* at 24 rue Campinchi; the obliging proprietor will fill up plastic bottles of muscat from the barrels for you, at 5F per litre.

Bastia doesn't offer much in the way of **nightlife**. There are a couple of cinemas, a good theatre and a good central club. The best source of information about all events is the daily local paper *Corse Matin*, produced in Nice.

Bars and cafés

Bar Corsica, 2 rue Spinola. Tucked away behind the Vieux Port, this is the place to hear traditional Corsican singing.

Café Napoléon, 16 bd Général-de-Gaulle. Recently refurbished, elegant café, famous for its surly waiter, a character straight out of *Asterix*.

Café Riche, 29 bd Paoli. Busy café that's a centre for gambling, next door to the first betting shop in Corsica.

L'Escale, 12 rue Luce-de-Casabianca. Spacious bar opposite the Nouveau Port, boasting the only pool tables in town.

L'Impériale, 6 bd Général-de-Gaulle. Busy café at the centre of place St-Nicolas. The only place selling cigarettes late at night, hence the tide of people throughout the small hours.

Le Pigalle, Vieux Port. Serves the cheapest beer *à la pression* in Bastia.

Le Pub Assunta, 5 place Fontaine-Neuve. Large, lively bar with a snooker table on its mezzanine floor and a terrace opening onto the old quarter. A good selection of draught beers, and live music nights with local bands on Thursdays.

Restaurants

L'Ambada, Vieux Port. Deservedly popular pizzeria on the lively north side of the harbour, opposite the citadel, serving inexpensive set menus 70–85F. Plenty of fresh seafood options, plus regional dishes, salads and pasta. Closed Sat & Sun lunchtimes.

L'Auberge à la Ferme di l'Altu, hauteurs de Tintorajo, Furiani (☎04 95 33 37 67). Highly reputed, rustic-style Corsican speciality restaurant, 6km south of town on a hillside overlooking the coast. Hard to find, but worth the effort. To get there, follow the RN193 until you reach the watersports shop *Nauticorse*, then turn right; it's signposted from the Tintorajo crossroads further up the hill. Moderate to expensive. Closed Sun evening & Mon.

La Braise, 7 bd Hyacinte-de-Montrea (☎04 95 31 36 97). Authentic Corsican pizzeria, whose succulent meat dishes and pizzas, cooked over wood grills with maquis herbs, have made its owner something of a local celebrity. Bank on around 100F for the full works. Closed Sun & Aug.

U Cantarettu, Vieux Port. Corsican lasagne and sublime pizzas. A nightly concert of popular Corsican ballads courtesy of the owner. Moderate.

Casa Corsa, 1 quai des Martyrs. The freshest fish, and regional specialities such as *fiadone*, a kind of eggy cake, served indoors or alfresco on the quayside.

A Casarella, 6 rue Ste-Croix (☎04 95 32 02 32). Innovative Corsican-French cuisine served on a terrace with a fine view over the Vieux Port. Try their *casgiate* (nuggets of fresh cheese baked in the oven) or the rarely prepared *storzappretti* (a Bastiais speciality traditionally dished up to priests on Sun). Moderate to expensive. Closed Sat & Sun lunchtimes.

Le Caveau du Marin, 4 quai des Martyrs. Welcoming little place decked out like a fishing hut, sharks' teeth and all. Seafood pasta a speciality. Moderate.

Chez Gino Raugi, rue Capanelle, off bd Graziani, at the north end of place St-Nicolas. Arguably Corsica's greatest ice-cream maker, from an illustrious line of local *glaciers*. In winter, they also do a legendary chickpea tart to take away.

In Suerta, villa Agostini, Suerta, 5km along the road to St-Florent (☎01 95 33 37 87). Traditional peasant food (hearty lamb stews, soups, pasta and an excellent *cannelloni al brocciu*), as well as more adventuous seafood dishes (mussels cooked in oranges), served in a homely environment, with views over the Étang de Biguglia. Not a great choice of dishes, but still among the best restaurants in the area. Around 120F for a four-course meal (without wine). Closed Mon & Oct.

A Scaletta, Vieux Port. Entrance on the steps leading from the port to Église St-Jean-Baptiste. Fresh fish, served on a precarious balcony overlooking the boats. Generous Corsican speciality menu at 75F, with a good range of inexpensive à la carte options, and, if you're lucky, eau de vie on the house.

U Tianu, 4 rue Monsigneur-Rigo. Famous, characterful nationalist hang-out down a narrow lane off quai des Martyrs. Excellent charcuterie and a different menu every day, featuring local dishes such as blackbird pâté and hare and olive stew. If you eat in only one restaurant in Bastia, it should be this. Moderate.

Le Zagora, Vieux Port. French-style Moroccan restaurant with tables in a tastefully ethnic interior or on a tiny balcony overlooking the harbour. Try their delicious tagines, veal with plums and almonds, or chicken in olive sauce, washed down with mint tea. Inexpensive.

Nightlife

What there is of Bastia's nightlife centres around the bars, cafés and restaurants of the Vieux Port and place St-Nicolas. A couple of discos and cinemas add some variety to an evening, but you'll have to search hard for a crowded venue, as the preferred entertainment of Bastiais seems to be a quiet night in front of the television.

If there is a concert in Bastia it will almost certainly be held in the theatre in place Favalelli (box office Mon–Sat 9am–noon; tickets 100–150F), west of rue César-Campinchi. Concerts of traditional Corsican singing and nationalist rallies are also regular events at the theatre and at the Chambre de Commerce off place de l'Hôtel-de-Ville – check out the fly posters scattered around town.

Of Bastia's two cinemas, the triple-screen *Regent*, at 13 rue César-Campinchi, shows new films, always dubbed, whereas the *Studio*, in nearby rue Miséricorde, is a small outfit showing mostly subtitled art films. The week-long Festival du Film et des Cultures Méditerranéennes takes place in the third week of November at the cinemas and the theatre, showcasing films, backed up by exhibitions, from all parts of the Mediterranean region. There's also a British film festival in the first two weeks in March, featuring fairly recent releases with French subtitles.

Nightclubs are few and far between. In the centre of town, the best is the long-established *St Nicolas*, underneath the *place* at 14 bd Général-de-Gaulle, whose music is more varied than the usual endless Europop. Out of town, *L'Apocalypse*, 10km along the La Marana stretch south of Bastia, is *the* disco to be seen at, but it attracts a mainly teenage crowd, and you'll need a car to get there. Entry is free and drinks extortionate at both, which keep going till dawn (closed Mon & Tues).

Summer firework displays are a regular occurrence, with the most spectacular show happening in place St-Nicolas on Bastille Day (July 14), when street parties are held all over town. A solemn procession heralds the Fête de l'Assomption, or le Quinze-Aout (Aug 15), after which the Vieux Port becomes overrun by revellers. Other annual events include the Fête du Christ Noir on May 3 (see p.57), a regatta in June and the Foire de Bastia in July, which has stalls – mainly promoting local businesses – and live music in the evenings.

Listings

Airlines Air France, 6 av Émile-Sari (☎04 95 32 10 29 or 04 95 54 54 95); Air Inter, 6 av Émile-Sari (☎04 95 31 79 79). Both companies also have branches at Poretta airport.

Airport enquiries ☎04 95 54 54 54.

Banks and exchange Most of the main banks and automatic cash dispensers are on place St-Nicolas, at the bottom of bd Paoli, and on rue César-Campinchi. The main branch of the Société Générale (best for changing Thomas Cook travellers' cheques) is at the bottom of the square on rue Miot. American Express travellers' cheques are best changed at Crédit Agricole, who have a foreign exchange counter in the arrivals hall of the gare maritime in the Nouveau Port. One place to avoid is the Change at 15 av Maréchal-Sebastiani, opposite the post office (July & Aug Mon–Sat 9am–7pm), which charges a very stiff commission fee.

Bicycle and motorbike rental Locacycles, behind the Palais de Justice (☎04 95 32 30 64), rent bicycles by the day or for longer periods. The only place in Bastia offering motorbike rental is Plaisance Service Location, Port Toga, at the north side of the Nouveau Port (☎04 95 31 49 01), which has bikes from 50 to 400cc. Rates start at 230F per day.

Bookshops The best-stocked bookshop and stationer is L'Île aux Livres, at the top of rue César-Campinchi, which has a great selection of titles on Corsica, plus music on CD and cassette.

Bus information The tourist office at the top of place St-Nicolas keeps timetables of all services to and from Bastia, and can advise about services in other areas of the island.

Car rental Avis (Ollandini), 40 bd Paoli (☎04 95 32 57 30), airport (☎04 95 36 03 56); Hertz, square St-Victor (☎04 95 31 14 24), airport (☎04 95 30 05 15); Europcar, 1 rue du Nouveau-Port (☎04 95 31 59 26), airport (☎04 95 30 09 50).

Hospital Centre Hôpitalier de Falconaja, rue Imperiale, Lupino (☎04 95 55 11 11).

Laundry Pressing, 4 rue César-Campinchi, does laundry and dry cleaning; the only self-service laundry is in Lupino, way out in the industrial zone.

Left luggage In the arrivals hall of the gare maritime at the Nouveau Port (daily 8–11.30am & 2–7.30pm; 10F per article), or at the train station (26F per article).

Pharmacies Plenty on bd Paoli, or try Ricci-Luciani, at the top of place St-Nicolas, near the tourist office (8.30am–12.15pm & 2.30–7pm). In an emergency, call ☎ 04 95 31 99 17.

Post office The central post office is on av Maréchal-Sebastiani, between the train station and place St-Nicolas.

Taxis There is a taxi rank at the south end of place St-Nicolas (☎04 95 34 07 00).

Travel agents Corse Eurotours, 14 rue César Campinchi (☎04 95 32 52 22); Corse Voyages, 2 av Émile-Sari (☎04 95 34 12 59).

Water and adventure sports Corse Loisirs Aventures, 3 rue Notre-Dame-de-Lourdes (☎04 95 32 54 34), and Planete Corse, "Villa Henri", Impasse Campanelle (☎04 95 37 85), offer guided adventure holidays, with options in hiking, mountain biking, white-water rafting, skiing and kayaking. For diving, the best outfit in Bastia is the Club Plongé Bastiais, Villa Capulla, Strada di Onda (☎04 95 33 31 28), who offer courses at various levels, and day trips for experienced divers out of the Vieux Port. You'll need a medical certificate and insurance, and the cost of a dive is 180F, or less if you have your own equipment.

Moving on from Bastia

As Corsica's busiest passenger ferry port, with road and rail connections to most parts of the island, Bastia is the north's main transport hub, and if you're travelling without the luxury of your own vehicle you're bound at some stage to pass through here. Obtaining information about departure times and points can sometimes be difficult, mainly because most services are run by private companies with offices scattered across town. The only place that keeps up-to-date timetables for all public transport services operating out of Bastia is the tourist office on place St-Nicolas, where you can also get advice about onward journeys from other parts of the island, and towns and cities on the continent.

By plane

Bastia's Poretta **airport**, 16km south of town, is served by direct flights from London (Gatwick and Stansted), and several major French cities; a full list of destinations appears on p.95. The cheapest way to get there from the town centre is on the beige-and-blue shuttle bus, or *navette*, which departs seven times daily from the Leclerc roundabout, in front of the train station. For precise times of the service, which costs 42F each way, call ☎04 95 31 06 65.

By ferry

Regular car and passenger **ferries** operate all year round between Bastia and the French ports of Nice and Marseille, with a less frequent service to Toulon. Also served are the Italian ports of Genoa, La Spezia and Livorno, plus Piombino from July to mid-September. In summer be sure to reserve a place, especially if travelling by car; vehicle supplements on all services during high season are around 280F. The fares quoted below apply to a single foot passenger travelling in July and August; children can normally travel for half the adult fare. Tickets are sold through the ferry operators' offices listed below, and at travel agents across the city (see "Listings", p.61).

Corsica Ferries, 7 bd Général-de-Gaulle (☎04 95 32 95 95, fax 04 95 32 14 71), or at the gare maritime (☎04 95 32 95 94, fax 04 95 32 95 55). To Genoa (May, June & Sept 1–2 daily, July & Aug 1–3 daily; 6hr; 200F); La Spezia (April 3 weekly, May–Sept 1–2 daily; 3hr 45min; 180F); Livorno (March–May 2–3 weekly, June & Sept 6 weekly, July & Aug 1–2 daily; 4hr; 180F).

Corsica Marittima, 15 bd Général-de-Gaulle (☎04 95 32 69 04, fax 04 95 32 69 09). To Genoa (July & Aug daily; 5hr; 200F); Livorno (April–early Sept 1–2 weekly; 3hr 30min; 200F).

Mobylines, Sarl Colonna D'Istria & Fils, rue Commandant, Luce de Casablanca, Bastia (☎04 95 31 46 29, fax 04 95 32 17 94). To Genoa (April to mid-Sept 2–4 weekly; 6hr; 190F); Livorno (April to mid-June 2–5 weekly, mid-June to Sept 1–2 daily; 4hr; 180F); Piombino (July to mid-Sept daily; 3hr 30min; 180F).

SNCM, Nouveau Port, BP 57 (☎04 95 54 66 88, fax 04 95 54 66 69). To Nice (July & Aug 1–3 daily, May, June & Sept 3 weekly, rest of year 1 weekly; 4hr 30min–6hr; 280F); Marseille (July & Aug 2 weekly, Sept 3 weekly, rest of year

By train

Corsica's famous narrow-gauge train, the **micheline**, terminates in Bastia, and there are regular services from the town to stations along both branches of the line. During the summer (July 1–Sept 23), four trains run each day between Bastia and Ajaccio, via Corte, while for the rest of the year (Sept 24–June 30), only two services operate Monday to Saturday, with an additional two trains on Sunday. The schedule for the line connecting Bastia, L'Île Rousse and Calvi remains the same all year round, with two services running per day. Timetables (*horaires*) are available from the train station and tourist office. For information, call ☎04 95 32 80 60.

By bus

Bastia is better connected by bus than any other town on the island, but finding out when and from where the services depart can be problematic. Roughly speaking, buses to smaller, rural destinations – including Patrimonio, Nonza, Cap Corse, Nebbio and St-Florent – tend to operate out of the gare routière, at the north end of place St-Nicolas behind the Hôtel de Ville, whereas services to the main towns start from less obvious spots. For **Ajaccio** (via Corte), **Bonifacio** and **Porto-Vecchio**, you pick up the bus from the roadside opposite the main post office on av Maréchal-Sébastiani. Services for **Corte** only, and **Calvi** (via **L'Île Rousse**), depart from outside the train station.

For a complete rundown of destinations reachable by bus from Bastia, see "Travel details" on p.95. Exact departure times are best checked at the tourist office or by telephoning the bus company direct on the following numbers: Rapides Bleus (for Ajaccio, Porto-Vecchio and Bonifacio), ☎04 95 31 03 79; Transports Micheli (for Cap Corse), ☎04 95 35 61 08; Autocars Santini (for St-Florent), ☎04 95 37 02 98; Transport Saladini (for Macinaggio), ☎04 95 35 43 88; Les Beaux Voyages (for Calvi), ☎04 95 65 15 02; Autocars Cortenais (for Corte), ☎04 95 46 02 12.

Tickets for all services are available on the bus from the driver.

South of Bastia

It's easy to be put off by the industrial sprawl **south of Bastia**, but amidst the built-up areas there are some hidden sights ideal for a half-day excursion. At the Furiani junction, about 3km along the N193, you can turn off the main road to follow the stretch of coast known as **La Marana**, where holiday villages and villas back a sandy beach lined with pine woods. Between this strand and the N193 lies

the Étang de Biguglia, a wildlife-rich lagoon named after the ancient capital of Corsica, now an unremarkable village on the slopes above the main road. The lagoon stretches as far as the Roman site of **Mariana**, 25km south of Bastia, where you can see the remains of a twelfth-century basilica and the superb **Pisan church** of La Canonica.

There is no public transport direct to Mariana. **Buses**, which leave from opposite the Bastia gare routière at 11.30am and 6pm in summer, take you along La Marana as far as Pineto. From here it's a good 3km walk to the Roman site.

La Marana and the Étang de Biguglia

Traditionally the summer haunt of prosperous Bastia families, the 16km littoral known as **La Marana** (pronounced "mar*an*") is the beginning of the sandy stretch that continues more-or-less uninterrupted all the way down to Porto-Vecchio in the south. Largely the preserve of joggers and windsurfers, the beach offers shady pine woods, restaurants and bars, and even though the sea is quite polluted due to boat traffic and the proximity to Italy, it makes an agreeable excursion from Bastia when the heat gets too much.

All this part of the coast is divided into holiday residences or sections of beach attached to bars, the latter freely open to the public. Try **A Pagoda**, about 5km along the road: popular with the young crowd, this has a disco and a large open-air bar. Another good spot is **Pineto**, the furthest beach along the road and therefore the least crowded in the summer, where the bus terminates.

Fed by the rivers Bevinco and Golo, the **Étang de Biguglia** is the largest lagoon in Corsica and one of its best **birdlife** sites, thanks largely to the reed beds bordering the water. Of the birds that nest in the reeds, various species of warblers are most common – in summer you'll find reed warblers at the southern end of the lagoon, as well as moustached warblers and cetti warblers, with their distinctive loud repetitive cry. In winter Biguglia is a stop-off point for migrating grey herons, kingfishers, great crested grebes, little grebes, water rails and various species of duck, such as the spectacular red-crested pochard, immediately identifiable by its red bill, red feet and a bright-red head.

Mariana

The Roman town of **Mariana**, just south of Étang de Biguglia, can be approached by taking the turning for the airport, 16km along the N193, or the more scenic coastal route through La Marana.

Founded in 93 BC as a military colony, Mariana had become a Christian centre by the fourth century, when its basilica was built. The settlement was damaged severely by the Vandals and Ostrogoths in the fifth and sixth centuries, and by the time of the Genoese occupation Mariana had become so waterlogged and malarial that it had to be abandoned. The **houses**, **baths** and **basilica** are now too ruined to be of great interest, but the square **baptistry** has a remarkable mosaic floor decorated with dancing dolphins and fish looped around a bearded Neptune – Christianized pagan images representing the Four Rivers of Paradise.

Adjacent to Mariana stands the church of Santa Maria Assunta, commonly known as **La Canonica**. Built in 1119 close to the old capital of Biguglia, it is the finest of around three hundred churches built by the Pisans in their effort to evangelize the island. Modelled on a Roman basilica, the perfectly proportioned edifice is decorated outside with Corinthian capitals plundered from the main Mariana site and with plates of Cap Corse marble, their delicate pink and yellow ochre hues fusing to stunning effect. The interior has been recently restored in a very plain style, and is used for concerts and for Mass on religious festivals.

About 300m to the south of La Canonica stands **San Parteo**, built in the eleventh and twelfth centuries over the site of a pagan burial ground. A smaller edifice than La Canonica, the church also displays some elegant arcading and fine sculpture – on the south side, the door lintel is supported by two writhing beasts reaching to a central tree, a motif of Oriental origins.

Cap Corse

Until Napoléon III had a coach road built around **Cap Corse** in the nineteenth century, the promontory was effectively cut off from the rest of the island, relying on Italian maritime traffic for its income – hence its distinctive Tuscan dialect. Ruled by feudal lords who retained substantial independence from the island's governors, it maintained a peaceful existence that greatly influenced the character of the Capicursini, or **Cap Corsins**. For all the changes brought by the modern world, Cap Corse still feels like a separate country.

Forty kilometres long and only fifteen across, the cape is divided by a spine of mountains called the Serra, which peaks at **Cima di e Folicce**, 1324m above sea level. The coast on the **east side** of this divide is characterized by tiny ports or *marines*, tucked into gently sloping river-mouths, alongside coves that become sandier as you go further north. The villages of the **western coast** are sited on rugged cliffs, high above the rough sea and tiny rocky inlets that can be glimpsed from the corniche road. Cap Corse remains virtually untainted by tourism: wild flowers grow in profusion on the mountainsides in spring, goats graze freely, fishing villages are quiet and traditional, and many of the inland slopes are occupied by vineyards, producing the fragrant **wine** that's one of the cape's major exports. It's only in the last twenty years or so that hotels have appeared, with the highest concentration at **Macinaggio** and **Centuri-Port**, on either side of the northern tip. Unfortunately, though, much of the once verdant countryside has been blackened by fire (see p.80).

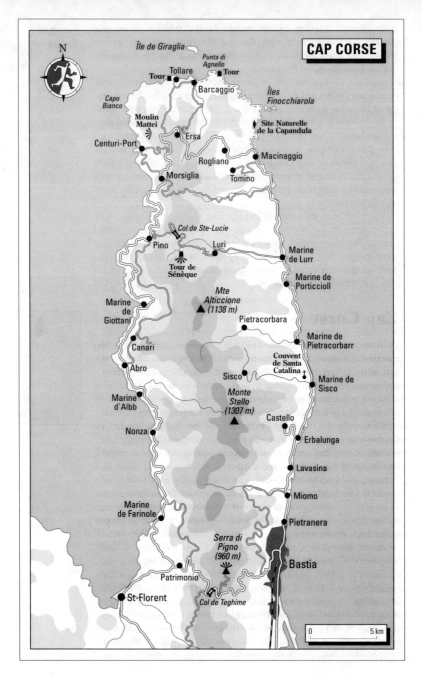

CAP CORSE

N

Île de Giraglia

Punta di
Agnello

Tollare   Tour
Tour
Barcaggio

Capo   Îles
Bianco   Finocchiarola

Moulin
Mattei   Site Naturelle
Ersa   de la Capandula

Centuri-Port

Rogliano   Macinaggio

Morsiglia

Tomino

Col de Ste-Lucie

Pino   Luri   Marine
de Lurr

Tour de
Sénèque   Marine de
Porticcioll

Mte
Alticcione   Marine de
(1138 m)   Pietracorbara   Pietracorbarr

Marine
de   Couvent
Giottani   de Santa
Catalina   Marine de
Canari   Sisco   Sisco

Abro

Monte
Stello
Marine   (1307 m)   Castello
d`Albb

Nonza   Erbalunga

Lavasina

Miomo

Marine   Pietranera
de Farinole

Serra di
Pigno
(960 m)   Bastia

Patrimonio

St-Florent
Col de Teghime

0   5 km

Many people tackle the 100km corniche in a one-day tour from Bastia. A less arduous alternative is to cut across the peninsula at Santa Severa, thereby getting a taste of the interior and a look at the spectacular **Tour de Sénèque**, where, according to popular legend, the Roman poet-philosopher Seneca spent his exiled years. Best of all, of course, would be to spend a few days here. If you're driving, bear in mind that fuel stations are few and far between, so fill up in Bastia. For those without transport, a **circular tour bus** operates daily from Bastia all year round. There's also a regular bus to **Erbalunga**, a placid fishing village 10km north of Bastia, where the buildings, ending in one of the ruined lookout **towers** for which the cape is famous (see p.69), rise directly from the sea.

Even more conspicuous than these towers are the **convents, churches** and in particular **Romanesque chapels** scattered over the cape; it was on Cap Corse that some of the first Christian centres in Corsica were created, and this was the only region of the island where the Franciscan movement had any real influence. Elaborate marble **mausoleums** are also a common feature often occupying lonely places on the inland hill-slopes and standing out strikingly white in a sea of green maquis.

A brief history of Cap Corse

Inhabited by various ancient civilizations – the Phoenicians, Greeks and Romans were all here – Cap Corse became significant in the tenth century, when the da Massa lords came over from Pisa and established fiefdoms across the region. By the following century Genoese settlers were being drawn to the cape's vineyards, and after Genoa's trouncing of Pisa at the Battle of Meloria in 1284, the feudal lords of Cap Corse became important – if intermittent – allies of the island's new rulers. Two local families shared most of the cape from this time – the da Mare clan held the north whilst the da Gentile ruled the south, a situation that lasted into the late eighteenth century, when the French gained control of the island.

Although subject to the Genoese, the lords of Cap Corse were allowed a certain autonomy: largely ignored by the rest of the island, and well positioned for trading with the French and Tuscan ports, they were able to control their profits to a greater extent than their compatriots in the south. By the seventeenth century, Cap Corse was economically more successful than any other region in Corsica, but **piracy** was a huge problem for the cape's tiny ports, which is why the coast is dotted with some thirty fortified towers, built as refuges for the local villagers in times of trouble (see p.89). The late eighteenth and early nineteenth centuries saw an upsurge in emigration from the cape, as a shortage of agricultural land (brought about by a sharp rise in population) forced thousands of *capicursini* to seek their fortunes in the colonies of South America and the Caribbean. Many of the emigrants grew rich on gold prospecting and coffee or sugar planting, and in time returned home to live in large villas, or *palazzi*, erected on their ancestral land. Known as "les maisons d'Américains", these ostentatious country mansions, with their colonial-style colonnades and arches, lend a distinctively Central or South American feel to villages such as Rogliano, Morsiglia and Pino. Most are still in use, and during the summer welcome families from Puerto Rico or Venezuela, where Corsican colonies still exist – indeed, one former Venezuelan president was a Corsican.

Today, though wine continues to be a major export and nationalist politicians are promoting exploitation of the indigenous cedrat fruit, from which a liqueur and jam are made locally, tourism has become the only way to make real money. So far, however, it has been slow to develop on the cape, and there are few spots where concrete spoils the view.

The eastern cape

The **eastern coast** of the cape progresses from tightly packed villas immediately outside Bastia to desolate *marines* such as **Pietracorbara** in the north, via fishing villages such as **Porticciolo** and **Erbalunga**. The D80, which follows the coast all the way around Cap Corse as far as St-Florent, is mostly built up within a short radius of Bastia (about the first 5km), so it's a good idea to leave the main road at the roundabout a couple of kilometres out of town, taking the turn-off signposted as the "Route de la Corniche". This loop bypasses the worst of the developed strip and gives a good panorama from the mountains.

San Martino di Lota to Lavasina

Three kilometres along the corniche you pass through the terraced village of **SAN MARTINO DI LOTA**, no longer a pristine place but giving a tremendous view, which on clear days takes in the islands of Monte Cristo and Elba. The winding road rejoins the coast at **MIOMO**, a conspicuously wealthy village of posh villas and private beaches. By the small pebbly public beach stands the southernmost **Genoese tower** of the coast, an enormous squat construction with a ridged turreted top.

LAVASINA, a further 3km up the coast, grew up around a sanctuary created in the sixteenth century by one Danesi, who was given a painting of the Virgin which he donated to the sanctuary in lieu of payment for some merchandise. It became a place of pilgrimage in 1675, when a nun called Marie-Agnès, having disembarked from a boat to take shelter from a storm, prayed at the sanctuary and was promptly cured of her paralysis of the legs. Within two years the **Église Notre-Dame-des-Graces** had been built to house the miraculous painting. An ugly rectangular grey clock tower, surmounted by a stiff statue of the Virgin, was added to the large pink building in the nineteenth century and effectively ruined the classical lines of the church. Inside, however, you might as well take a look at the famous **Madonne de Lavasina**, which hangs above the great black-and-white altar. The painting, a melancholy work from the school of the Umbrian artist Pietro Perugino, is still believed to perform miracles and is the focus of a **festival** on September 8, involving a candlelit procession on the beach and a midnight Mass.

Erbalunga and around

Built along a rocky promontory 3km north of Lavasina, the small honey-pot port of **ERBALUNGA** is the highlight of the east coast, with its aged, pale buildings stacked like crooked boxes behind a small harbour and ruined Genoese watchtower. A little colony of French artists lived here in the 1920s, perhaps drawn by the fact that the ancestors of the poet Paul Valéry came from here, and the village has drawn a steady stream of admirers ever since. It gets a fair number of tourists throughout the year, and come summer it's transformed into a veritable cultural enclave, with concerts and arty events adding a spark to local nightlife.

A port since the time of the Phoenicians, Erbalunga was once a more important trading centre than Bastia or Ajaccio. With the increasing exportation of wine and olive oil, in the eleventh century it became the capital of an independent village state, ruled by the da Gentile family, who lived in the palazzo that dominates **place de Gaulle**. Its ascendancy came to an end in the 1550s, when long-running conflicts within the da Gentile camp finally broke the family's hold on this part of the cape, and in 1557 French troops destroyed the port, reducing the fifteenth-century tower to the ruined state it's in today.

Erbalunga is famous for its **Good Friday procession** known as the **Cerca** (Search), which has evolved from an ancient fertility rite. Starting at Église St-Érasme, at the entrance to the village, a procession of hooded penitents covers a distance of 14km, passing through the hamlets of Pozzo, Poretto and Silgaggia in the mountains and picking up people on the way. At nightfall, back in Erbalunga, the penitents form a spiral known as the *Granitola* (Snail); candles held high, they move to place de Gaulle and the spiral unwinds, while a separate part of the procession forms the shape of the cross.

The village is closed to vehicles, but there's a **car park** on the left-hand side of the main road from Bastia, where the regular **bus** from place St-Nicolas stops. From here you walk down to the harbour through place de Gaulle, where the mairie and the *palazzo* Gentile stand side by side. On the harbour, a couple of **bars** shaded by an enormous chestnut tree look out across the water to the tower. The one **hotel**, the *Castel' Brando* (☎04 95 30 10 30, fax 04 95 33 98 18; April to mid-Oct; ⑨), is among the most stylish on the island. Sited at the entrance to the square, it's an elegant old stone-floored *palazzo* crammed with period furniture and surrounded by mature palm trees, with a pool and plenty of parking space. It doesn't have a restaurant, so for a proper **meal** you have to head for the harbour. The pick of the places here has to be *U Fragnu*, down the lane leading north from the harbour (☎04 95 33 93 23; June–Sept). With its aptly named terrace, *Le Pied dans l'Eau*, lapped by waves, this old converted olive mill has plenty of character, and its set menus of predominantly Corsican specialities (100–150F including wine) offer reasonable value for money. Otherwise – not to be confused with the pizzeria of the same name – try the slightly less expensive *L'Esquinade – Chez Antoine*, under the plane trees behind on the harbour front (☎04 95 33 22 73), or *Le Pirate*, close by, which has been here for years and serves mainly fresh seafood.

Monte Stello

The starting point for the climb up **Monte Stello** (1307m), the second-highest peak on Cap Corse (the highest is neighbouring Cima di e Folicce, 1324m), is the medieval hamlet of **Pozzo**, 3km from Erbalunga and 1km from Castello. In Pozzo's square, a sign marked "Monte Stello 3h" points the way through the houses into the maquis, where the trail starts off clearly marked by arrows and daubs of blue paint. Behind the village you'll come to a stream which you cross and then scramble up the slope onto a wide terrace wall. From here there are fine views of the dark slopes rolling down to the sea, and the schist roofs of Pozzo and Poretto set amongst olive trees and blackberry bushes.

Ten minutes' walk up the slope you come to a deserted stone cottage, just beyond which you cross a stone wall, and then take the right track where the road forks. At the next fork continue bearing right and then, just before you reach another abandoned building, turn left. After thirty minutes you'll come to the meeting of four paths – bear left here and follow the red painted arrows into the deep valley. Another fifteen minutes will bring you to a fork, where you continue along the higher track, which passes a bubbling spring – a good place to stop for a breather and a drink. The narrow path through the valley is marked by piles of stones, which are easy to lose sight of if you're not concentrating.

Another five minutes and you'll come to a marshy patch of scrub; here you head straight up the mountainside between two piles of stones set amid the undergrowth. Skirting to the left of a prominent rocky outcrop, you'll come to the **Col de Santa Maria**, where you get a breathtaking view over the cape to the gulf of St-Florent and beyond to the Désert des Agriates. As you cross this ridge, the rocky sprawl of Monte Stello appears to the right. A few minutes down to the right you'll see white paint marks leading on towards the summit. After ten minutes, you'll come to a large rock with an arrow and "500m" painted on it, marking the final ascent – here you have a choice of the easier path to the left, or the steep climb which veers up to the right, again marked with white paint. At the top, after a total of about three hours' walking, you're rewarded with a stupendous view of the cape and, if it's not too misty, south to the highest mountain peaks of Corsica, among them Monte Cinto, Monte Renoso, Monte Incudine and Rotondo.

The thirteenth-century castle at **CASTELLO**, one of the many bases of the da Gentile family, stands 2km inland from Erbalunga, beyond the hamlet of Mausoleo. This ghostly village, dominated by the now ruined castle, was the scene of a family feud that lasted a hundred years and split the da Gentile family into two factions. The strife began in 1450, when the lady of the castle, known simply as *La Sposetta* (The Little Wife), began an affair with one Guelfuccio, cousin of her husband Vinciguerra da Gentile. On discovery of this deception Vinciguerra stabbed his errant wife to death, chased his cousin out of the castle and stormed off to settle with his brother in nearby Erbalunga. Here he built a new castle, which was wrecked in 1556 by the French, supported by members of the Castello branch of the da Gentile clan. Quick to retaliate, the Erbalunga side of the family, supported by the Genoese, launched an attack against Castello, an action resulting in the total devastation of the port when the French struck back the following year. *La Sposetta* is generally thought to haunt Castello – presumably she also drops in on the da Gentile family's house, built in 1602 at the entrance to the hamlet.

Fifteen minutes' walk south of the village along the road to Silgaggia, you come to the well-preserved little chapel of **Notre-Dame-des-Neiges**, which dates from the tenth century and houses the oldest known **frescoes** in Corsica. Dating from 1386, they depict several saints, including Christopher, Catherine and possibly George.

From Erbalunga to Tomino

Beyond Erbalunga the landscape takes on a more desolate aspect and the road gives an ever clearer view of the rocky coast. After 6km you reach **Sisco**, a *commune* made up of several hamlets scattered over the mountainside and the tiny seaside village of **MARINE DE SISCO**. This last comprises a small sandy beach, a cluster of restaurants and hotels, making it a pleasant stopover. If you decide to stay, the best place is *Hôtel de la Marine*, the first hotel you come to on the right (☎05 95 35 21 04; Easter–Sept; ③), which consists of rooms in terraced chalets that open onto a quiet garden behind the beach. There's no restaurant, but breakfast is served on the stone-floored verandah of the main house. If this place is full, try the swisher *U Pozzu*, opposite (☎05 95 35 21 17, fax 05 95 35 27 19; ④); it's a bit bland, as is their restaurant, but the rooms are comfortable enough, and the welcoming proprietress speaks fluent English. By far the best value in the village are the four simply furnished rooms, all with en-suite WCs, available for half board at the *Auberge A Stalla Sischese*, 200m along the road leading inland from *U Pozzu* (☎05 95 35 26 34; May–Oct; ⑤). Their restaurant is also excellent for an authentic slap-up Corsican **meal**, featuring carefully prepared local specialities (*ravioli au brocciu*, *ratatouille* and *fiadone*) in unpretentious surroundings for around 100F per head.

There are two churches in Sisco worth visiting. The most striking is **San Michele**, a beautiful Romanesque chapel, which can be reached from **CHIOSO**, the *commune*'s principal hamlet, 7km via the D32 which leads off from the coast road at the centre of the *marine*. Just beyond the large, unremarkable Église St-Martin, take the right-hand track signposted to San Michele, and after a couple of minutes you'll see a rocky track leading uphill on the left; you can leave the car here and climb the last 2km to San Michele. The elegant chapel, built in 1030 by Pisan masons, occupies a spectacular windswept hillside overlooking the Marine de Sisco, with Pietracorbara a misty ridge of buildings stretching to the north. On September 29, the Festival of St Michael brings pilgrims up from the surrounding hamlets to celebrate Mass here.

Back on the main coast road, the huge **Couvent de Santa Catalina** stands on a hillside high above the corniche, about 500m beyond Marine de Sisco. The convent is now an old people's home, but you can visit the church, which is reached by taking a left off the main road, along a hairpin bend that doubles back to the building. (Ignore the turning next to the large stone statue of St Catherine, some 200m before, which leads to a dead end.) Built in the twelfth century, the graceless church, overshadowed by an ugly tower, was enlarged in the fifteenth century, when the hulking buttresses were added and the entrance widened to receive the pilgrims who came to see its famous relics. Including a piece of the clay from which Adam was made, an almond from Paradise, and one of Enoch's fingers, the relics were enshrined here in the thirteenth century by fishermen who, caught in a storm off Cap Corse, vowed to bring their holy cargo to the first church they came across if they were saved. This happened to be Santa Catalina; unfortunately, the relics are now kept in the mairie at Chioso and are not accessible to visitors. Perhaps the most impressive feature of the church's bare interior is the round crypt, dating from the 1200s and based – like nearly all round churches – on the Holy Sepulchre in Jerusalem.

Heading north, you'll soon come to **PIETRACORBARA**, where's there's a beach and a couple of pizzerias, but it's a less alluring spot for a picnic and a bathe than **PORTICCIOLO**, a further 7km on. The village is attractively small and crumbling, with a tiny mooring for fishing boats jutting into the green sea and a white sandy beach that you're pretty much guaranteed to have to yourself.

At the little *marine* of **SANTA SEVERA**, 2km further, there's the opportunity to cut across the cape to visit Luri and the Tour de Sénèque (see p.79). The village also has a few hotels, but as it does-n't ooze character you're better off waiting until you get to Macinaggio (see opposite).

MERIA, a collection of pastel-shaded cottages surrounding a well-preserved tower, lies 6km beyond Santa Severa. From here it's another 2km to the little *commune* of **Tomino** (Tuminu), dubbed "the cradle of Christianity in Corsica" because the island's earliest Christians hid in caves here during the Saracen raids of the sixth century. Sited on a windy rocky spur 2km south of Macinaggio, it was once a serious rival to commercial Rogliano (see p.76), producing an excellent muscat wine. These days the village is virtually deserted, but the view is worth the steep climb. Following the unsignposted hairpin road, on foot or by car, which emerges on the left just before you enter the village of Macinaggio, you'll soon come to the crest of the hill, where a Baroque chapel and a Genoese tower face each other across the road before a scattering of houses. In the near distance you can see the Îles Finocchiarola and the Tuscan island of Capraia across the vast expanse of deep-blue sea.

The northern cape

Macinaggio, northern terminus of the road along the east side of the cape, is also the largest settlement due north of Bastia, offering a spread of hotels and restaurants, as well as a fuel station. The only **bus** service to this somewhat isolated resort runs in summer from Bastia three times a week. The land between Macinaggio and **Barcaggio**, at the very tip of Corsica, forms part of a protected zone called the **Site Naturelle de la Capandula**, and is a wonderful area to explore on foot, boasting some glorious **beaches**. Known as the "holy promontory" in Roman times because of its Christian settlements, the tip of the cape also has many ruined chapels, such as **Santa Maria**, near Macinaggio. Inland, the eight hamlets of **Rogliano**, spectacularly spread out over the slopes 5km from Macinaggio, were for a few centuries the fief of the da Mare family, whose castles and towers lie scattered over the hills. On the western side of the northern tip, the chief focus of interest is **Centuri-Port**, where the colourful horseshoe-shaped harbour holds several hotels.

Macinaggio

A port since Roman times, well-sheltered **MACINAGGIO** was developed by the Genoese in 1620 for the export of olive oil and wine to the Italian peninsula, and in later years played its part in the wider history of the island. Pascal Paoli landed here in 1790 after his exile in England, whereupon he kissed the ground and uttered the words "O ma patrie, je t'ai quitté esclave, je te retrouve libre" ("Oh my country, I left you as a slave, I rediscover you a free man") – a plaque commemorating the event adorns the wall above the ship chandlers. Napoléon also stopped here on his way to Bastia as he fled from the Paolists in 1793, and in 1869 the Empress Eugénie was forced by a storm to disembark here on her way back from the opening of the Suez Canal, before taking refuge in Rogliano – the road from Macinaggio to Rogliano has been called the "Chemin de l'Impératrice" ever since. There's not much of an historic patina to the place nowadays, but with its boat-jammed marina, its line of colourful seafront awnings and its definitive end-of-the-world feel, Macinaggio has a certain intrinsic appeal. In addition, its proximity to some of the best beaches on Corsica makes it irresistible.

The best place to **stay** is the *Hôtel des Îles*, a renovated old building opposite the marina (☎04 94 35 43 02, fax 04 95 35 47 05; ③), which also has a good restaurant. The tiny rooms at the front overlook the port but get noisy at night, being above the most popular bar in the resort, so if you're a light sleeper ask for a room around the back of the building. Otherwise your best bet is *U Libecciu*, situated behind the marina, on the road that leads north off the D80 road to Rogliano (☎04 95 35 43 22; May–Sept, with obligatory half board July & Aug; ④); it's a modern building with no view to speak of, but the rooms are spacious and the restaurant is excellent. *U Ricordu*, on the south side of the road to Rogliano (☎04 95 35 40 20, fax 04 95 35 41 88; March–Dec; ④–⑤, with obligatory ⑤ half board Aug), is along the same lines as the *U Libecciu*, and has a swimming pool and a sauna. Macinaggio's only **campsite**, *U Stazzu*, lies 1km north of the harbour and is signposted from the Rogliano road (☎04 95 35 43 76; May–Oct). The ground is hard, but there's ample shade and easy access to the nearby beach.

Besides the hotel **restaurants** above, you could try the *Pizzeria San Columbu*, at the end of the port facing out to sea, which does a passable seafood pizza, or, for a gourmet Corsican meal, *Les Îles*, one of a string of places with tables under awnings on the quayside, which does good fresh fish dishes, cocktails and ice creams. Set menus start at 100F, so count on around 150F for a four-course meal with wine.

Site Naturelle de la Capandula

Macinaggio's town beach is seaweed-strewn and dirty, but you can get to some stunning stretches of white sand and clear sea by following the track at the north end of the marina to the **Site Naturelle de la Capandula**. Covering 377 hectares of windswept maquis and pristine coast between Macinaggio and Bracaggio, the reserve, which encompasses the deserted Îles Finocchiarola and the Île de la Giraglia, can only be crossed on foot, via a coastal path that takes you through some of the most spellbinding scenery on the island.

Although Capandula is off limits to motor vehicles, it is possible to drive the 2km from Macinaggio to the **Baie de Tamarone**, whose deep clear waters make this a good place for diving and snorkelling. The car park here also marks the start of the popular **coastal walk** through the reserve, known as the "Sentier des Douaniers" after the Genoese customs officials who originally cut the path. Clearly marked with yellow splashes of paint, it winds via a series of exquisite coves and ruined watchtowers all the way to Barcaggio – a return trip of around four hours. Note that there are no springs along the way, so carry plenty of drinking water. For the less adventurous, there's a shorter circular route (1hr 30min–2hr), which begins at the Baie de Tamarone and takes in most of Capandula's highlights. From the car park, follow the Sentier des Douaniers along the line of the bay and around the headland to a second beach, **Plage des Îles**.

The sprinkling of barren islets offshore are known as the **Îles Finocchiorola**, after the wild fennel that grows in abundance over the rocks in the area. Hundreds of gulls and cormorants haunt this strip of coast, which, during March and June, is a stop-off for migrating **birds** from North Africa. If you're here at this time, look out for the elusive Audouin's gull, with its distinctive red bill encircled by a black band. Only 2500 pairs still survive in the Mediterranean, and they are a protected species here. Other types you might expect to see are the more common herring gull, large with grey upper parts, black wing tips and a yellow bill; the black-headed Mediterranean gull; and perhaps a Manx shearwater or Cory's shearwater. Though similar in appearance to gulls, these last two brown-backed species are distinguished by the way they glide low over the sea with straight, stiff wings. The islets are a nature reserve, only visitable between March and August, and fires and camping are strictly forbidden. **Boat excursions** run in July and August from the marina in Macinaggio; tickets cost 60F. The round trip includes a stop on the largest islet so that enthusiasts can do a spot of birdwatching.

Half an hour after leaving the Baie de Tamarone, you arrive at a stunning arc of turquoise sea known as the **Rade de Santa Maria**, site of an isolated Romanesque chapel. Raised on the foundations of a sixth-century church, the **Chapelle Santa Maria** comprises a tenth-century and a twelfth-century chapel merged into one, hence the two discrepant apses.

This bay's other distinctive landmark is the the huge **Tour Chiapelle**. Dramatically cleft in half and entirely surrounded by water, the ruined three-storeyed building was one of three *torri* built on the northern tip of the cape by the Genoese in the sixteenth century (the others are at Tollare and Barcaggio) as lookout posts against the increasingly troublesome Moorish pirates (see p.89). As Macinaggio grew in importance, the towers were also used by health and customs officers, who controlled the maritime traffic with Genoa. Pascal Paoli established his garrison here in 1761, having failed in his attempt to take Macinaggio, and contemplated building a rival port. Six years later, to undermine Genoa's position in the area, Paoli sent two hundred men under the command of Achille Murati to capture the neighbouring island of Capraia, which had belonged to Genoa since 1507. Murati's relatively easy victory marked the beginning of the downfall of the Genoese in Corsica.

If you turn south from the Chapelle Santa Maria and follow the track past a vine-covered hillside for around thirty minutes, you'll eventually arrive back at the Baie de Tamarone. Note that this circular walk can also be done in a clockwise direction by turning left out of the Tamarone car park instead of right at the start of the hike, and following the track inland to the chapel, and thence around the coast.

Rogliano

A cluster of schist-tiled hamlets scattered in a lush valley below the jagged grey crags of Monte Poggio make up the *commune* of **Rogliano** (Ruglianu), 7km up a series of hairpin bends from Macinaggio. This is one of the oldest and most picturesque settlements in Corsica. The constituent hamlets – Bettolacce, Olivo, Magna, Soprana, Vignale, Sottana and Campiano – were the base of the da Mare lords from the twelfth to the sixteenth centuries, and the ruins of their convents, towers and castles are distributed among them. However, the village's name, derived from the Latin *Pagus Aurelianus*, dates from the Roman era when Rogliano presided over a busy trade with the Italian coast, while the oldest vines on the hillside are known to be of Carthaginian origin.

The easternmost and largest hamlet, **BETTOLACCE**, is dominated by the privately owned **Tour Franceschi**, an enormous round tower in remarkable condition. It also boasts a **post office** and an excellent hotel, the *Auberge Sant'Agnellu*, opposite the pleasantly proportioned church of Sant'Agnellu (☎/fax 04 95 35 40 59; mid-April to Oct, with obligatory half board July & Aug; ③–④), which has large, comfortable rooms with televisions and a magnificent restaurant terrace overlooking the valley. At 90F, the set menu of mainly Corsican specialities represents good value, and the views are superb.

Isolated in the valley some 500m beneath Bettolacce stands the ruined sixteenth-century **Église St-Côme-et-St-Damien**, accessible via the path leading opposite *Auberge Sant'Agnellu*. A curious rectangular bell tower stands separated from the nave, which is the oldest part of the church. **VIGNALE**, the hamlet above Bettolacce, is dominated by the crumbling ruins of the **Castello di San Colombano**, from which there's a magnificent view across the valley to Macinaggio. The castle was built in the twelfth century and became known as "U Castelacciu" (The Bad Castle) in the sixteenth when Giacomo Santa da Mare abandoned the Genoese cause, switched his allegiances to Sampiero Corso and defected to the Franco-Turkish army. In 1553 the Genoese retaliated by destroying the castle, which was later restored then burned down in 1947.

From here a track leads 300m to **OLIVO** and the **Couvent St-Francois**, an imposing vine-covered building straight out of a Gothic romance. The convent and adjoining church, surmounted by a spindly clock tower, were built in 1520 by the Franciscans, who also restored them in 1711. They are now private property and closed to the public.

Barcaggio and around

To get to the very tip of Corsica, continue west along the D80 for about 5km (slowing down for goats on your way), until you reach

Ersa, where the D253 twists off northwards to **BARCAGGIO**, giving breathtaking views of the Île de la Giraglia surrounded by pale-green sea.

Barcaggio is tiny – just a jetty, a couple of restaurants and a dozen houses built from the greenish local schist – but the setting is sublime and the **beach** one of the finest in Corsica. Curving east of the village to a headland crowned by a Genoese watchtower, it is set against a backdrop of austere, maquis-covered hills that are oddly reminiscent of the Scottish Highlands. You can leave your vehicle in the village **car park** (also a park for camper vans), from where a track leads through the dunes to a crystalline sea. The *La Giraglia* hotel (☎04 95 35 60 54, fax 04 95 35 65 92; April–Oct; ⑨), occupies a fantastic location at the north end of the village overlooking the tiny harbour (rooms 25 & 26 have the best views), though it's expensive for what it offers and doesn't accept credit cards. Nor does it have a restaurant, so if you fancy a **meal** your only option is *U Pescadore*, an ugly prefab hut on the jetty, which serves pricy fresh seafood dishes.

The northern extremity of Corsica is marked by the **Île de la Giraglia**, a green islet covered with wild leeks a metre high. Surmounted by a lighthouse, it also has a sixteenth-century Genoese tower adorning its rocky slopes.

About 2km west of Barcaggio lies **TOLLARE**, a neglected little coastal village of squat grey cottages huddled behind and a tiny pebble beach. Apart from the handful of holidaymakers who rent houses in the summer, hardly anyone ventures out here, but you can park up and pitch your tent on a patch of council-owned grass.

Centuri

From Tollare, a potholed road loops back up the valley to re-join the D80, close to the turn-off for Barcaggio. If you continue west on the main road you'll go over the **Col de Serra** (365m); for a fantastic **view**, walk from the col up to **Moulin Mattei**, the round building with the coloured tiled roof on the hill above the road. Some considerate soul has installed a stone picnic table in the lee of this former windmill (restored by the Maison Mattei as tasting place for their famous aperitif, Cap Corse), from whose terrace you can admire an impressive panorama along the peninsula's north and west coasts.

Once over the col you soon come to **CAMERA**, the first hamlet of the *commune* of **Centuri** (pronounced "Chen*t*ori"), where the bizarre cylindrical turrets of the **Chateau de Bellavista** peer from the woods beneath the road. One of many so-called "Maisons d'Américains" in this area, the castle (closed to the public) was built in the nineteenth cenutry for Count Leonetto Cipriani, a mercenary in the service of the Duke of Tuscany who later became a close friend of Napóleon. The smaller hamlet of **Canelle**, overlooking Centuri-Port and accessible from Camera along the road heading north or on foot from the port, is renowned for its enormous fig trees, whose drooping branches overhang the houses and shadow the road.

When Boswell arrived here from England in 1765, the former Roman settlement of **CENTURI-PORT** was a tiny fishing village, recommended to him for its peaceful detachment from the dangerous turmoil of the rest of Corsica. Not much has changed since Boswell's time: Centuri-Port exudes tranquillity despite an influx of summer residents, several of them artists who come to paint the fishing boats in the slightly prettified harbour, where the grey stone wall is highlighted by the green serpentine roofs of the encircling cottages, restaurants and bars. The twenty or so boats are evidence of the village's still thriving fishing industry, and lobster potting provides an important income for its handful of permanent residents. The only drawback with the settlement from the tourists' point of view is that the small pebble **beach** to the south is disappointingly grubby and not ideal for sunbathing.

Practicalities

Centuri-Port has more **hotels** than anywhere else on Cap Corse. The best value among them is the *Hôtel-Restaurant du Pêcheur*, the pink building in the harbour (☎04 95 35 60 14; April–Oct; ③), which is also the most pleasant and fills up quickly in high season; its rooms are agreeably cool, with thick stone walls and green shutters, and it has a popular **restaurant**. The *Vieux Moulin*, in a prime location behind the harbour on the right as you enter the village (☎04 95 35 60 15; ③), has a marvellous terrace, but the rooms are rather stuffy and the obligatory 150F menu is not up to much. The *Hôtel La Jetée*, at the far end of the jetty (☎04 95 35 64 47; ②), is well situated and has a good fish restaurant; its rooms are pretty ordinary and don't have sea views, but they're the cheapest in the village during high season. Otherwise you have the *Hôtel A Marinara*, a small welcoming hotel situated behind *du Pêcheur* (☎04 95 35 62 95; obligatory half board; ⑤), also with a restaurant; and the *Centuri*, an ugly four-storey modern block next door to the *Marinara* (☎04 95 35 61 70, fax 04 95 35 64 20; ④), pitched primarily at Italian visitors. For **campers** there's *Camping l'Isolettu*, 400m south along the D35 (☎04 95 35 63 63; May–Oct), an uninviting option but unfortunately the only choice in the vicinity. Centuri-Port has a **supermarket** which sells newspapers, and a **bread van** comes at ten o'clock every morning and stops outside the *Vieux Moulin*.

The western cape

South of Centuri the corniche cuts through villages stacked up the cliffsides above small *marines* that are often masked from the road by rocky outcrops. At **Pino** you can take a detour inland to see the

Tour de Sénèque, while further south **Canari** offers another remark-able Romanesque church. Just a few kilometres north of St-Florent lies **Nonza**, perhaps the most spectacular of all the cape villages, perched on the edge of the cliffside above a black sandy beach.

Morsiglia

The change of scenery south of Centuri is striking and sudden: gen-tle green slopes give way to chalky cliffs that plunge down from the high corniche road, deep indents punctuate the coast and the sea is a dark peacock-feather blue.

After 6km the three towers of **MORSIGLIA** (Mursiglia) come into view: six of these enormous structures were originally built here to defend against Moorish pirates in the sixteenth century (see p.89). A few kilometres further lies the **Golfe d'Aliso**, a small cove where the sea has an incredible depth and colour, and the red sand makes a dazzling contrast. There's access to the shore from the road, though not much room to park.

Tour de Sénèque

A short distance north of Pino (see overleaf), a turn-off in the direc-tion of Luri will take you winding through pine woods to the Col de Ste-Lucie. If you take the steep turning on the right at the pass, then head along a badly potholed lane through the forest, you'll soon come to an abandoned school, above which looms the **Tour de Sénèque**. Set atop a pinnacle of black rock, the impressively for-bidding tower was built in the fifteenth century by the da Mare fam-ily, on the spot where Seneca is said to have lived from 41 to 49 AD, having been exiled for offending Emperor Claudius and accused of seducing the emperor's niece. His rampant misconduct didn't stop there. During his exile, Seneca reputedly once came down from his rock in an attempt to ravage the Corsican women, for which he was attacked with nettles – hence the profusion of the plants around the base of the tower. Whilst here he wrote a few bitter verses about the place:

> Oh Corsica whom rocks terrific bound
> Where nature spreads her wildest deserts round
> In vain revolving seasons cheer thy soil
> Nor ripening fruits, nor waving harvests smile.

It's a thirty-minute climb through the woods to the tower – well worth the effort for the views, which extend to both coasts of the cape and over the Monte Stello massif. To pick up the trail, follow the motorable dirt track from the deserted school towards the radio transmitter above you in the woods, then bear left along the path that peels from it after about five minutes. From here, it's a stiff ten-minute climb through the trees to the top, with the last 20m or so over exposed rocks.

Bush Fires and the Bovine Connection

Each year, between ten- and twenty-thousand hectares of land are devastated by fire in Corsica (one-fifth of the total surface area burned annually in France). All kinds of people have been blamed for starting the blazes – from lone pyromaniacs to cigarette-butt-chucking tourists – but the real culprits have only recently been singled out: cows, or more accurately, their owners.

The link between the annual infernos and the skinny cattle roaming the island's interior leads back to Brussels and the European Union's Common Agricultural Policy. In the late 1970s, the EU, attempting to reduce its milk lakes and butter mountains, introduced grants for dairy farmers to convert to beef and veal. Although they had never in fact produced much milk, the Corsicans responded by developing a sudden passion for cattle husbandry: within twenty years, the number of cows on the island nearly tripled from 29,000 to 80,000, bringing in a shower of lucrative **subsidies** from Brussels. Ironically, few of the recipients of EU money actually own any land – proof that you possess cattle is enough to secure entitlement. The cows, meanwhile, wander freely across communal areas of maquis, which the *faux éleveurs*, or "fake cattlemen" (also dubbed "the subsidy hunters"), routinely burn so that fresh shoots of grass will grow to feed their neglected animals. This technique has been used by pastoralists for centuries to provide food for cattle in long, dry summers, but their careful control of the fires meant that the amount of land damage was always sustainable.

That local cattle owners are behind the majority of bush fires has long been common knowledge in Corsica. However, it took a Fire Service study to bring the issue into the open. Dividing the island into blocks of four-hundred hectares, the *pompiers* kept detailed records of all fires reported and cross-referenced their findings with livestock ownership statistics. Soon patterns emerged, and it became possible to predict to within eighty percent of certainty when, where and in what weather conditions fires were most likely to occur.

In September 1994, when the bureaucrats in Brussels finally got wind of what was happening in Corsica, all EU aid to the island was suspended. The effects of the move were dramatic: bush fires fell to one-tenth of the normal level that summer. Solving the problem in the long term, however, may be more difficult. EU subsidies bring in large sums of money for cattle owners, and any threat to their livelihood is bound to come up against stiff resistance. Nor is it only the farmers who benefit from the fires, but also builders (who restore damaged houses), foresters (to replant the trees) and, of course, firemen (who welcome the overtime pay). Combine the financial disincentive with the customary Corsican mistrust of outside interference, and the future for the maquis looks black indeed.

Luri

Passing over the Col de Ste-Lucie, you soon come to the *commune* of **Luri**, an unexceptional place surrounded by a delightful landscape of lemon trees and vineyards. At **PIAZZA**, Luri's central hamlet, you might take a look at **Église St-Pierre**. Dating from the seventeenth century, it houses a late sixteenth-century painting that represents the life of St Peter against a background showing the local castles in the fifteenth century – the one on the left is the Tour des Motti, a precursor of the Tour de Sénèque, and on the right is the Castello di San Colombano, at Rogliano (see p.76).

A good place to stay near Luri is *Chez Alain et Marie–Thé Gabelle*, at La Tour "Li Fundali", Spergane (☎04 95 35 06 15; ③, optional half board ④), a wonderfully unpretentious inn tucked away in a high nook at the foot of a ruined Genoese tower, with great views over the valley. To get there from Piazza, take the lane that turns right out of the hamlet by the post office, and follow the signs for Spergane, 3km further up the hill.

Pino

A sense of the tropics pervades the air at **PINO** (Pinu), some 2km south of the turning for Luri. Palm trees grow up the cliff, and the houses, coloured pale pink, orange and yellow, feature turreted roofs and verandahs. The grander ones are "maisons d'Américains", one of which built by Antoine Liccioni, who, like many of his generation, left the village vowing not to return until he was rich. Liccioni struck lucky, discovering seams of gold in both Venezuela and Brazil, and when he died it is said he owned half of Guyana. You could stop in the village for a drink under the shade of the chestnuts and plane trees, or follow the steep road from just outside the village down to the *marine*, where a fifteenth-century **Franciscan convent** lies half-hidden amongst a jungle of bamboo. Although its outward appearance is grim, try to get inside for a look at the faded fifteenth-century frescoes above the entrance, featuring the Virgin flanked by saints Francis and Bernard. If the convent is locked, ask for the key at Église Ste-Marie, in the centre of the village.

Canari and around

South of Pino the high corniche road winds past rocky inlets for several kilometres through Barretali and **Marine de Giottani**, where there's a small pebbly beach. Some 5km further, you come to **Canari**, a large *commune* with a couple of notable churches, served in summer by twice-weekly buses from Bastia (depart gare routière Tues & Fri 5.30pm).

Right on the main road in Canari's chief hamlet, **MARINCA**, stands the Romanesque **Santa Maria Assunta**. Built at the end of the twelfth century, it's attractive chiefly for the quirky sculpture that decorates the cornice beneath the roof – weird mask-like faces alongside strange beasts and stylized patterns. The gloomy Baroque **Église St-François**, formerly attached to a Franciscan monastery, is situated a little way up the road in **PIEVE**. The highlight here is a fifteenth-century gilded panel of St Michael, on the left as you enter; a panel from the same altarpiece is set into the sacristy cupboard door. Also of interest is the sixteenth-century *Assumption of the Virgin* on the right of the nave, above the tomb of Vittoria da Gentile, who died in 1590 at a convent, no longer in existence, in Canari.

From here it's a gentle fifteen-minute walk along a marked path up to **EMISA** and the tiny fifteenth-century **Chapelle Ste-Catherine**, which houses two faded panels from that period. Alternatively, you could descend to the tiny *marine* of Canari, where the **restaurant** *U Scogliu* (☎04 95 37 80 06; April to mid-Oct), overlooking the rocks, serves some of the tastiest fish on Cap Corse. The chef only does à la carte dishes, and a four-course meal with wine will set you back around 200F per head.

South of Marinca, the road cuts across a sheer mountainside horrendously disfigured by the workings of an **asbestos mine**, whose closure in 1966 resulted in the dumping of untold quantities of toxic dust on the surrounding beaches. The mine has also been blamed for the premature deaths of many ex-employees.

Nonza

Set high on a black rocky pinnacle that plunges vertically into the sea, the village of **NONZA** is one of the highlights of the Cap Corse shoreline. The village was formerly the main stronghold of the da Gentile family, and the remains of the **fortress** are still standing on the furthest rocks of the overhanging cliff. Nonza has a shady square, behind which you twist your way through stone-tiled houses and bougainvillea bushes to reach the ruined fortress and the more impressive green **watchtower** nearby. In 1768 the tower, one of the few on the island built in Paoli's time and not by the Genoese, witnessed one of the greatest con tricks in military history. The French, having succeeded in taking over all of Cap Corse, closed in on the Nonza garrison, which was under the command of one Captain Casella. Fearing that Casella's tenacity would lead them to their deaths, the Corsican troops absconded, leaving him to defend the tower single-handed. This he did, using a system of cables to maintain constant fire from a line of muskets and a single cannon, until the disheartened French offered a truce. Old Casella demanded that his army be allowed to parade out in dignity, and duly emerged alone and on crutches, brandishing his pistol, to the amazement of the besieging army.

Nonza is also famous for **Julia**, patron saint of Corsica, who was martyred here in the fifth century. The story goes that she had been sold into slavery at Carthage and was being taken by ship to Gaul when the slavers docked here. A pagan festival was in progress, and when Julia refused to participate she was raped, tortured and crucified; the gruesome legend relates that her breasts were then cut off and thrown onto a stone, from which sprang two springs, now enshrined in a chapel by the beach. To get there follow the sign on the right-hand side of the road before you enter the square, which points to the **Fontaine de Ste-Julie**, down by the rocks.

Reached by a flight of six hundred steps, the long grey **beach**, with a thick line of white surf bordering the dark sea, is thus coloured as a result of pollution from the asbestos mine up the coast. This may not inspire confidence, but the villagers insist it's safe these days (they take their own kids there in the summer), and from the bottom you do get the best view of the tower, which looks as if it's about to topple over into the sea. You can **stay** in Nonza at *Auberge Patrizi* (☎04 95 37 82 16; ④), run from the big peach-coloured restaurant in the square opposite the church. Made up of two village houses (the one with rooms to let is five minutes' walk down the track towards the beach), the *Auberge* is an old-fashioned place where half-board is obligatory, but the food is good and plentiful. The shady **café** under the plane trees on the other side of the road is another good place for a pit stop, serving a range of light snacks in addition to drinks.

The Nebbio

Named after the thick mists that sweep across it in the spring and autumn, the **Nebbio** (Nebbiu) has for centuries been one of the most fertile parts of Corsica, producing honey, chestnuts and some of the island's finest wine. Officially, the region includes the barren **Désert des Agriates**, further west, but essentially Nebbio comprises the amphitheatre of rippled hills, vineyards and cultivated valleys that converge on St-Florent, a region nicknamed "A Conca d'Oro" (the Golden Shell) by Pascal Paoli because it encompassed all the wealth of the region. Nourished by the headwaters of the **Aliso river**, its many beautiful villages, perched on pale-green bluffs of schist that jut from the gently sloping sides of the basin, are swathed in greenery, with finger-thin bell towers pointing from their midst. In spite of their proximity of the coast, tourism has made little impact on these scattered settlements, which remain largely dependent on agriculture and EU subsidies. The one major development in recent times has been the shift to **viticulture**: some of the wines produced around the *commune* of **Patrimonio** rival those of Sartène, and *caves* offering wine tastings (*dégustations*) are a feature of the whole region.

The Nebbio's chief town and best base is **St-Florent**, at the base of Cap Corse, a bishopric until 1790 and now a chic coastal resort. It remains the Nebbio's chief town and best base, while villages such as **Olmeta-di-Tuda** and **Oletta**, being close to Bastia, are lively and well-populated places, especially in the summer when families move up to the cooler mountains from the city. The two most notable historic sites in this part of the island are the Pisan church of **Santa Maria Assunta**, just outside St-Florent, and the diminutive **San Michele de Murato**, close to the chapels strewn across the valley between **Rapale** and **Santo Pietro di Tenda**.

The principal form of **public transport** serving the Nebbio is the twice-daily bus from Bastia to St-Florent (depart gare routière June–Sept daily 10.30am & 5pm). In addition, less frequent services run to Murato (depart Palais de Justice May–Oct Mon–Fri 6.30pm), Olmeta di Tuda (depart gare routière daily 6pm) and St Pietro di Tenda (depart gare routière Mon, Wed & Fri 4pm).

St-Florent

Viewed from across the bay, **ST-FLORENT** (San Fiurenzu) appears as a bright line against the black tidal wave of the Tenda hills, the pale ancient houses seeming to rise straight out of the sea, overlooked by a squat circular citadel. It's a relaxing town, blessed with a decent beach and a good number of restaurants, but the key to its success is the **marina**, which by luring the yacht-owning classes has made St-Florent something of a low-key St-Tropez. Yet, for all the attentions of the rich and famous, the place remains relatively unspoilt for the time being, and its position next to the Désert des Agriates lends it a pleasant air of isolation.

In Roman times a town called **Cersunam** existed on the site where the Santa Maria Assunta stands today, a kilometre east of the present village. Few traces remain of the settlement, which in the

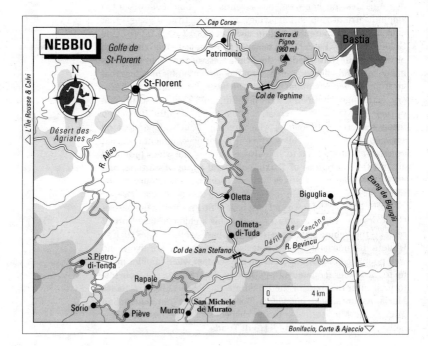

mid-fifteenth century was eclipsed by the port that developed around the new Genoese citadel. St-Florent proceeded to prosper as one of Genoa's strongholds, largely through the export of olive oil produced in its fertile hinterland, but later went into decline as its population – ravaged by malaria, Moorish pirates, and continual battles between the Corsicans, the French and the Genoese in the mid-sixteenth century – dwindled to 65. The town was also fought over during the struggles for independence in 1769; and it was from here that Paoli set off for London in 1796, never to return.

St-Florent is tiny and you won't find a great deal to see, but there are lots of cafés in which to sit and do nothing. **Place des Portes**, the centre of town life, has tables facing the sea in the shade of plane trees, and in the evening it fills with strollers and nonchalant boules players. In **rue du Centre**, which runs west off the square, parallel to the seafront and marina, you'll find some restaurants, shops and wine-tasting places – be sure to sample the sweet, maquis-scented muscat made around here. To reach the **citadel**, climb to the end of rue du Centre and pass through the large wire gate – it looks like private property but is accessible to the public. Unique in Corsica for its circular shape, the citadel, or *torrioni*, was built in 1439 for the Genoese governors, but was bombarded by Nelson's fleet in 1794 and is now a tumbledown construction full of pigeons. It does, however, give a beautiful view of the hills of the Nebbio and the mountains of Cap Corse disappearing into mists up the coast. At sunset you should move back down to the seafront, when the rocks glow with a fiery light.

The nearest **beach**, Plage de la Roya, is a windy stretch of sand and mud flats to the west of the village, fine for windsurfers but less than ideal for bathing as the sea is rather murky due to sewage from the town. To get there, cross the bridge to the south of place des Portes, taking a right turn through the car park. A better option is the nameless beach that lies a further 2km southwest along the main road – at the beach it becomes the D81. Here the sea is much clearer and you get a fantastic view of the town, with its dark backdrop of undulating mountains.

Practicalities

Buses run from Bastia's gare routière to St-Florent twice daily, leaving at 10.30am and 5.30pm between June and September, and at 11am and 6pm during the rest of the year (except Oct–May Wed & Sat, when they leave at noon & 5.30pm), pull into the village car park, behind the marina. This is also the departure point for the return buses to Bastia, which from June to September leave at 7am and 2pm, and at 6.50am and 1.30pm from October until May. The journey takes one hour. Bus times vary a little from year to year, but can be checked at the **tourist office**, at the top of the village

(Mon–Fri 9am–noon & 2–6pm, Sat 9am–noon; ☎04 95 37 06 04). This place also hands out free **maps** of St-Florent and its environs, as well as the usual range of glossy leaflets on the area. The **post office** next door will change travellers' cheques (for a 1.2 percent commission) if they are in French francs or dollars, but not if they are in sterling. Both the Société Générale and Crédit Agricole **banks**, off place des Portes (Mon–Fri 9–11.45am & 2–4.30pm), have bureau de change counters and hole-in-the-wall cash dispensers that accept Visa cards.

Les Halles de St-Florent, on the bridge, is the best **supermarket** for miles, and is open on Sundays in the summer. There's a **pharmacy** two minutes up the small unmarked road leading east off place des Portes towards the Santa Maria Assunta cathedral. You'll find a cluster of **telephones** in the marina car park in front of the square.

To explore the beaches of the Désert des Agriates, you can hire a **boat** from Corse Plaisance, on the bridge overlooking the marina next to the supermarket (☎04 95 37 19 28). **Motorcycles** are available for rent from Sun Folies, on Plage de la Roya (☎04 95 37 04 18).

Accommodation

St-Florent is a popular resort and **hotels** fill up quickly, especially at the height of summer when prior booking is essential. *Hôtel Europe*, slap on place des Portes (☎04 95 37 00 33; ④), is the most attractive option – an old-fashioned place in a prime location with comfortable rooms (ask for one facing the sea) and a lively local bar downstairs. *Hôtel du Centre*, 100m up the main street from the *Europe* (☎04 95 37 00 68; ④), is a good fall-back, whose modest but clean rooms have en-suite showers and toilets. A more homely option is *Chez Gisèle et Pière*, 9 route de la Plage d'Ozo (☎04 95 37 13 14; ②–③), which offers cosy accommodation in a family house, 100m from the beach. This place is particularly good value and thus often full, so reserve as far in advance as possible.

A fair number of **campsites** are dotted about the coast, most of them large two-star places in the pine trees behind the beach, packed in August and closed out of season. Closest to town is *Camping U Pezzu*, route de la Plage d'Ozo (☎04 95 37 01 65), 3km west on the small road that backs the beach. The three-star *Camping Kalliste*, 2km further on the same road (☎04 95 37 03 08), is larger and marginally posher, with its own beachside bar and restaurant.

Eating and drinking

St-Florent is renowned for its crayfish (*langouste*) and red mullet, but be careful when choosing your **restaurant** – the tourist places displaying menus in every language along the quayside tend to be mediocre. A reasonably priced place for excellent fish and Corsican specialities, such as stews and rich game dishes, is the cavernous

Cabistan, in rue du Centre, with a huge fish tank facing the street; they have a commendable set menu at 80F, and plenty of delicious Italian dishes. More expensive is *La Marinuccia*, at the far end of the same street below the citadel, which serves the best fish in St-Florent and boasts a terrace jutting out into the sea. For classy Corsican cuisine, *Ind'e Lucia (Chez Lucie)*, also off the the square below the citadel, is hard to beat. Among their regular specialities are wild boar terrine and rabbit stew, served indoors or on the terrace. Main courses here are not cheap (best value is the 100F set menu), but carafes of quality local wine cost just 20F. If you're on a tighter budget, try *A Marina (Chez César)*, on the harbour front, which serves up no-nonsense pizzas *au feu de bois*, lasagnes, copious salads and several filling pasta options for a very reasonable 50F.

The *Europe* is the most popular café in place des Portes. *Bar du Passage*, opposite, attracts a younger clientele, partly on account of its jukebox, but *Bar de Col d'Amphore*, on the north side, has stylish 1930s decor and is the place to pose in.

Around St-Florent

The area around St-Florent offers plenty of opportunities for short excursions: the cathedral of **Santa Maria Assunta** is only a fifteen-minute walk from the town centre; also within walking distance are the **Tour de Mortella** and the creepy **Dolmen de Monte Recincu**; and the wonderful beach of **Saleccia** can easily be reached by boat.

Santa Maria Assunta

Situated in a lonely spot a kilometre east of St-Florent on the original site of the Roman settlement of Nebbium, **Santa Maria Assunta** – the so-called "Cathedral of the Nebbio" – is a fine example of Pisan Romanesque architecture, rivalled only by La Canonica at Mariana, its exact contemporary (see p.65). To reach it, head down the road running due east off place des Portes. In summer the cathedral is left open all day, but in winter you have to ask for the key at the tourist office.

Deprived of its bell tower, which was knocked down in the nineteenth century, and set among pastures next door to a farmyard, the cathedral has a distinctly barn-like appearance. Built of warm yellow limestone, it's a superlatively elegant barn, though, and a close look soon reveals an unexpected wealth of harmonious detail: gracefully symmetrical blind arcades decorate the western façade, and at the entrance twisting serpents and wild animals adorn the pilasters on either side of the door.

The interior, too, is deceptively simple. Carved shells, foliage and animals adorn the capitals of the pillars dividing the nave where, immediately to the right, you'll see a glass case containing the mummified figure of **St Flor**, a Roman soldier martyred in the third century for his Christian beliefs. Found among the catacombs of Rome with a vial of blood signifying martyrdom, the soldier's remains were donated by Pope Clement XIV to the Bishop of the Nebbio in 1771, and a gilded wooden statue stands as a further commemoration in the apse. The spacious nave also holds the tomb of **General Antoine Gentili**, a supporter of Pascal Paoli during the struggles for independence.

Dolmen de Monte Recincu

A visit to the **Dolmen de Monte Recincu**, a large stone tomb in the maquis on the edge of the Désert des Agriates, makes a pleasant half-hour walk from St-Florent. To get there, walk to the end of the beach – just beyond, on the left, a track leads off to the dolmen.

This megalithic tomb, made up of three roughly hewn stone slabs, is popularly known as the **Casa di u Lurcu** (House of the Ogre), after a gigantic creature with the head of a man and a wolf-like body that allegedly used to terrorize the locals by sucking the blood of their cattle. One day, so the legend goes, the people decided to strike back. Gauging the monster's shoe size from his footprints, they made him some huge boots, which they filled with tar and left by his drinking place. Duly ensnared, the *Lurcu* tried to bribe the villagers with a special recipe for *brocciu*, a Corsican cheese, but the people suspected a trap and threw him into a ditch and buried him. Though it's not clear exactly when the stones were placed here, the legend dates them around 1500 BC.

Tour de Mortella

The ruined **Tour de Mortella**, isolated on the coast 7km west of St-Florent, is the most impressive piece of Genoese architecture hereabouts. Built around 1520 as an anti-piracy measure, the tower soon fell into disuse due to its inaccessibility, but was rediscovered by English soldiers two hundred years later. The English made use of it during the wars of Independence, and later employed it as a model for towers raised back home in preparation for Napoléon's expected invasion (see box opposite).

You reach the tower on foot by following a track that leads off from the end of the beach (past the left turn to the dolmen). At first the track gently climbs past villas and houses before cutting through some woods; after half an hour you'll come to a gate with a sign reading "Anse de Fornali" – go through the gate and follow the path straight onto the sea, from where a narrow track leads along the rocks to the tower.

A tour of inland Nebbio

St-Florent may attract the bulk visitors to the Nebbio, but the picturesque **villages** of its **hinterland** form the real heart of the region. Backed by a wall of sheer granite mountains, they cling to the sides of the spectacular **Aliso basin**, overlooking a vista of undulating vineyards that tumble to a deep cobalt-blue sea. Graffiti scrawled

Pirates and Watchtowers

Crowning rocky promontories and clifftops from Cap Corse to Bonifacio, the 91 crumbling Genoese watchtowers that punctuate the Corsican coast have become emblematic of the island's picture-postcard tranquillity. Yet they date from an era when these shores were among the most troubled in Europe. During the early fifteenth century, some five hundred years after the Moors had been ousted from the interior, Saracen **pirates** from North Africa began to menace the coastal villages, decending suddenly from the sea and making off with any valuables – including people – that could be shipped back to the Barbary States whence they came.

Held for ransom or sold as slaves, captured Christians were prime plunder for the pirates, and hundreds of islanders were abducted each year. Some did eventually return to their homelands, though not to resettle. Taking advantage of a law that allowed a slave to claim his freedom if he converted to Islam, former captives would set themselves up as traders in their new countries or, more often, turn to piracy as a means to amass a fortune. For some reason, the latter vocation appealed particularly to Corsicans: records show that, of the ten thousand or so pirates operating out of Algiers in the mid-sixteenth century, some six thousand were from the island, and it is a little-known fact that most of the raids on Corsica during the Genoese era were perpetrated by former natives. Among these were such notorious figures as Mammi Pasha, the scourge of his birthplace, Cap Corse, and Piero Paolo Tavera, better known as Hassan Corso, one of two Corsicans who actually rose to become kings, or deys, of Algiers.

Pirate raids became so common by the end of the fifteenth century that many Corsicans left the coast altogether, retreating to villages in the hills. To protect those that remained, as well as their threatened maritime trade, the Genoese erected a chain of **watchtowers**, or *torri*, at strategic points on the island. Comprising one or two storeys, these squat round towers measured 12–15m in diameter, with a single doorway 5m off the ground reached by a removable ladder. They were paid for by local villagers and staffed by watchmen, or *torregiani*, whose job it was to signal the approach of any unexpected ships by lighting a fire on the crenellated rampart at the top of the tower. In this way, it was possible to alert the entire island in a single hour.

Piracy more or less died out by the end of Genoese rule, but the *torri* remained in use long after, proving particularly effective during the Anglo-Corsican invasions of the late eighteenth century. The British were so impressed with the system that they erected similar structures along the south coast of England and Ireland to warn of attacks by the French. Named after the first Genoese watchtower ever built in Corsica – on the Pointe de Mortella, protecting the port of St-Florent and the Nebbio – these **Martello towers** were later used as lookout posts in World War II. The one overlooking the mouth of the River Liffy in Dublin has even become a world-famous landmark, immortalized as the setting for the first chapter of James Joyce's *Ulysses*.

over any exposed rock face reminds you that this is a staunchly nationalist area; the Nebbio witnessed some of the fiercest fighting during the wars of Independence against the French in the eighteenth century, and the spirit of resistance has never diminished.

The Nebbio

Strung together by the winding D62, the villages of inland Nebbio can be visited in an easy day's drive from St-Florent. Aside from a handful of churches and **statue-menhirs**, they harbour few sights, but the constantly changing views make this round trip one of the most rewarding forays from the coast. Most people follow a loop from St-Florent, climbing the **Col de Teghime** and dropping down through **Oletta** to the **Col de San Stefano**, then up to **Murato**, and down again to **Santo Pietro di Tenda** before heading back to St-Florent. If you're driving into the Nebbio from Bastia, you can join this loop at Col de Teghime or Col de San Stefano, the latter approached by the dramatic **Défilé de Lancone**; driving from St-Florent, the circuit may be shortened by taking the road straight up to Oletta. The Bastia–St-Florent bus follows the direct route over the Col de Teghime, not stopping along the way.

Patrimonio

Leaving St-Florent by the Bastia road, the first village you come to, after 6km, is **PATRIMONIO**, centre of the first Corsican wine region to gain *appellation contrôlée* status. Apart from the famous local muscat, which can be sampled in the village or at one of the *caves* along the route from St-Florent, Patrimonio's chief asset is the sixteenth-century **Église St-Martin**, occupying its own little hillock and visible for miles around. The colour of burnt sienna, it stands out vividly against the rich green vineyards, but the interior was effectively ruined in the nineteenth century, when an elaborately painted ceiling and overdone marble altar were installed.

In a small clearing 200m south of the church, reached via the lane that drops sharply downhill from the crossroads, stands a two-metre tall **statue-menhir** known as *U Nativu*, a late megalithic piece dating from 800–900 BC. The only limestone menhir ever discovered in Corsica, it was ploughed up in four fragments by a local farmer in 1964, restored and placed here under a small shelter. A carved T-shape on its front represents a breastbone, and two uncannily life-like eyebrows and a chin can also be made out.

Patrimonio's only other claim to fame is its annual open-air **guitar festival**, held in the last week of July, when performers and music aficionados from all over Europe converge on the village.

The one commendable place to **stay** in the area is *U Casome* (☎04 95 37 14 46, fax 04 95 37 17 15; ④), a large hotel in the village with huge rooms and great views over the Nebbio; coming from St-Florent, continue on the D81 for 250m past the turning for the church in Patrimonio, then follow the sign off the hairpin bend to the hotel. It doesn't have a **restaurant**, but during July and August you can eat fine Corsican cuisine at the nearby *Jardin du Menhir* (☎04 95 37 01 11), which serves 130F set menus in its shady garden.

Col de Teghime to Oletta

From Patrimonio the road climbs in a series of sharp switchbacks to the **Col de Teghime** (548m), from where it's possible to see the coastlines of both sides of the cape (when it's not swathed in fog). A stunning panorama of St-Florent and Patrimonio spreads out to the west, while to the east you'll see Bastia, with the glistening Étang de Biguglia stretching south. It's not unusual for the weather to be entirely different on either side. For an even better view, follow the Bastia road for another kilometre and turn left onto the D338, which leads to the **Serra di Pigno**, a gentle climb of about 45 minutes – a massive television antenna marks the summit.

The road south of the Col de Teghime will bring you after 10km to **OLETTA**, where faded multicoloured houses are stacked haphazardly against each other up the hill, and vegetation springs from cracks in the walls. The eighteenth-century **Église St-André**, in the centre of the village, has an ancient relief of the Creation (symbolized by a tree of life) embedded in its recently renovated façade, a relic from the church that occupied the site in the twelfth century. Inside there's a graceful triptych dating from 1534, portraying the Virgin and Child flanked by saints John the Baptist and Reparata. This used to reside in a local peasant's house until the Madonna allegedly called out to the mother of the household to warn her that her baby's cot had caught fire. Thereafter the triptych was transferred to the church, and has been venerated as miraculous ever since.

The **square** outside the church witnessed one of the more gruesome episodes in the Paolist insurrections of the eighteenth century, when a daring rebel plan to seize Oletta from the French backfired. Eager to make an example of his Corsican prisoners, the French commander condemned the rebels to a horrible death. After having their fingers crushed in a metal vice, they were led naked to the square carrying torches of flaming wax, and forced to plead forgiveness. The executioner then tore out their arms and kidneys, gashed open their thighs, and finally tied them face upwards on a cartwheel, where they were left to die.

If you can keep this grizzly episode out of your mind and choose to **stay** in Oletta, try *A Maggina*, at the entrance to the village (☎04 95 39 01 01; ②), which has cosy en-suite rooms with superb views over the Nebbio to the sea. Their **restaurant**, whose terrace also enjoys a fine panorama, is worth a stop too, serving a good selection of local dishes such as duck and olives, roast lamb and veal *sauté*; their set menus range from 110F to 140F, including wine.

Olmeta-di-Tuda to Murato

If you continue along the D82 you come to the hamlet of **OLMETA-DI-TUDA**, which rises abruptly from the rocky slopes. Huge elm trees dominate the foreground, and the distant peaks of Monte Astu create a forbidding backdrop.

A further 3km along, the crossroads at the **Col de San Stefano** (349m) marks the entrance to the **Défilé de Lancone**, an exhilarating, precipitous descent that hits the main coast road 9km south of Bastia. Hewn out of the black rock, with nationalist graffiti adorning the rock face at every lurching bend, the road winds far above the River Bevinco, from whose bed the serpentine for the church of San Michele de Murato was quarried. The Défilé is a road to be treated with respect – numerous little shrines along the way testify to the fatal smashes that have occurred here.

If you continue along the D5 instead of taking the Défilé, you'll soon pass the Pisan church of **San Michele de Murato**, which sits gracefully on a grassy ledge high above the hazy mountainous landscapes of the Nebbio. Built around 1280, this late Romanesque building is notable for its asymmetrical patterning of dark-green serpentine and off-white marble, a jazzy counterpoint to the simple lines of the single-naved church, though these were damaged in the late nineteenth century when the disproportionate bell tower was added. Outside, there's some sophisticated carving on the arches of the blind arcades and immediately beneath the roof, depicting gargoyles, wild beasts and human figures – look out for a relief on the north wall, showing an ashamed Eve reaching out to take the huge apple proffered by the serpent. Within the church you'll find less to catch the eye, though there's a faded fifteenth-century *Annunciation* frescoed on the arch of the apse. The church is always open to visitors.

The village of **MURATO**, a short distance beyond the church, has a good, inexpensive **restaurant**, *Le Monastère*, which serves delicious roast kid and lamb in maquis herbs at tables on a grassy terrace overlooking the village. Murato is also renowned for its crusty round bread (*miches*) and plaited loaves (*scaccies* and *scacettes*), which you can buy in the boulangerie just down the road from *Le Monastère*. If you feel like splashing out on a gourmet meal, head for *Ferme-Auberge Campu di Monte*, a wonderful farmhouse restaurant perched on the mountain on the outskirts of the village (June 28–Sept 15 daily; rest of year Fri & Sat evening & Sun lunchtime only; ☎04 95 37 64 39). At around 200F per head for the full works, it's not cheap, but the views are great and the food sublime, with traditional veal stews and fresh trout among their specialities. Finding the place is something of a challenge: turn left at the *Victor Bar* in the village, and follow the road down to the river at the bottom of the valley; shortly after the bridge, an unsurfaced track (indicated with a sign for the auberge) turns right off the road, heading 1.5km to the farm.

On from Murato

To continue the Nebbio tour, backtrack to the D162, which hugs the side of the Tenda massif as it runs west, snaking through villages built precariously on the lip of a shadowy forested valley. At **RAPALE**, a tiny ancient hamlet with castle-like houses built of schist stone, you can see the Romanesque chapel of **San Cesareo**, a green-and-white ruin hidden in the woods south above the village – it's a fifteen-minute walk.

Back on the main road, another 2km will bring you to **PIEVE**. Set on a plinth in front of the church in the heart of this village are three well-preserved **stone menhirs**. Carved in the same minimalist style as the monolith at Patrimonio (see p.90), the 3000-year-old family group gazes out across the Aliso basin to the forbidding wall of cloud-fringed peaks to the west.

From Pieve, the road twists through valleys along the River Aliso through Sorio and on to **Santo Pietro di Tenda**, an attractive red stone settlement spread out under the shadow of the Mount Asto massif (1535m). An ancient chronicle recalls that a fierce battle took place on the mountain above the village sometime in the tenth or eleventh century, when four thousand Moors were killed by a combined army of Spanish and Corsican troops, led by the Count of Barcelona. This defeat heralded the end of Muslim occupation of the island in the medieval era, but no traces of the momentous battle have ever come to light. These days the village's main point of interest is the tall Baroque **Église St-Jean**, joined by a bell tower to the contemporaneous Chapelle Ste-Croix. The latter is closed to the public, but inside the church you'll find the most lavish decor in the Nebbio – elaborate trompe l'œil painting on the walls and a gloomy seventeenth-century *Descent from the Cross* above the altar, which has a wooden tabernacle displaying some fine marquetry on its pedestal.

If you follow the road for 12km until it joins the D81, another 7km takes you to St-Florent.

The Désert des Agriates

Bordered by 35km of wild and rugged coastline, the **Désert des Agriates** is a vast area of uninhabited land, a rocky moonscape interspersed with clumps of cacti and maquis-shrouded hills. The desert's limits extend eastwards to Golfe de St-Florent, stretch west to the mouth of the Ostriconi River and down as far south as San Pietro di Tenda. Although it might appear inhospitable, the desert has a long agricultural history, as its name implies – *agriates* means "cultivated fields". During the time of the Genoese, it was a veritable breadbasket: the Italian occupiers even levied a special wheat tax on local farmers (most of whom came from Cap Corse) to prevent any build-up of funds that might have financed an insurrection in the area. Every winter until the early years of this century, shepherds from the mountains of Niolo and Asco would move down with their flocks to the desert for the annual bartering of goats' and ewes' cheese, which they exchanged for olive oil and wheat cultivated on the Agriates. The grain was stockpiled in square stone storage huts known as *pagliaghju* or *paillers*, about twenty groups of which still exist and are nowadays used by hunters for shelter.

In the course of the eighteenth and nineteenth centuries, fires and soil erosion reduced the region to desert, and it was a total wilderness by the 1970s, when numerous crackpot schemes to redevelop the area were mooted. These included a proposal to convert it into a test zone for atomic weapons, and a plan to transform the entire coast into a purpose-built Club-Med-style tourist complex, complete with concrete holiday villages and a giant marina. In order to block these schemes, the government gradually acquired the Agriates from its various owners (among them the Rothschild family), designating it a protected site. Wildlife, however, remains under threat, not least from trigger-happy hunters. Various ecologically sound projects are currently under discussion, such as plans to introduce controlled breeding of the Agriates's **wild boar**, the purest type on the island due to the isolation of the area, but now endangered by illegal hunting. Other rare species, such as the huge orange-and-brown Jason butterfly, are also under threat of extinction, largely due to the fires that increasingly devastate the maquis (in September 1992, 3000 hectares went up in smoke in a single day, fanned by a mistral blowing onshore at 150km/hr). The maquis also harbours many species of rare birds, including bee-eaters, red-backed shrikes and various kinds of warbler.

Marked footpaths are being established around the coast of the desert, but it remains a difficult area to penetrate by motor vehicle. Only one of its many beautiful **beaches** is accessible by car. **Plage de Saleccia**, 10km west along the coast from St-Florent by the Punta di Curza, is among the most exquisite beaches in Corsica. A glistening stretch of silver sand lapped by translucent green sea, it's so photogenic it was used in the film *The Longest Day*. To get there, head 12km west of St-Florent, passing through the hamlet of **CASTA**. A short way beyond the hamlet you reach the *Hôtel Le Relais de Saleccia* (see below), from where a very rough dirt track drops down into the desert. Before venturing any further, enquire at the hotel about the state of the track, which even when it's in good condition can only be attempted by 4WD vehicles and motorcycles. After 11km of relentless ruts, the *piste* passes Corsica's most remote campsite, *U Paradisu*, and ends at a car park. This is a great base from which to explore the desert on foot, with paths leading in both directions up the coast. Head east around the maquis-covered headland for an hour and you'll arrive at the sheltered cove of **Plage de Loto**. A short way beyond here lies the **Punta di Martello**, crowned by the most famous of the island's Genoese watchtowers (see p.89).

Practicalities

There's just one major road in the desert, the D81, which cuts across its south side and passes through the **Bocca di Vezzu** (312m), a mountain pass where fabulous views extend across to the Nebbio. Any of the buses running between Calvi or L'Île Rousse and Bastia

will drop you at Casta, where *Le Relais de Saleccia* (☎04 95 37 14
60; Easter–Sept; ④) is the only **hotel** in the area. Run by a welcoming young couple, the hotel, which boasts a fine view of Monte Genova and the surrounding desert, has only five rooms (three of them with terraces). A meal at their small restaurant will set you back a little under 100F. **Mountain bikes** (*vtt*) can also be rented from here for the trip to Saleccia, costing 70F for a full day.

Campers should press on along the track from the hotel to Saleccia, where the *U Paradisu* **campsite** overlooks the beach from the brow of a shady hill (☎04 95 37 82 51; May–Oct). The ground is stony, but they have a bar, restaurant and café, and even change travellers' cheques.

For **information** about the area, visit the Syndicat Mixte Agriate, in Santo Pietro di Tenda (Mon–Fri 9am–noon & 2–4pm; ☎04 95 37 72 51), or the tourist office in St-Florent (see p.85).

Travel details

FLIGHTS
Bastia to: London (March–Oct 2–4 weekly; 1hr 40min); Lyon (April–Sept 5 weekly; 1hr); Marseille (April–Oct 3–4 daily; 45min); Nice (April–Oct 3–4 daily; 45min); Paris (April–Oct 3–4 daily; 1hr 35min).

TRAINS
Bastia to: Ajaccio (2–4 daily; 3hr 40min); Algajola (2 daily; 2hr 40min); Aregno-Plage (2 daily; 2hr 40min); Belgodere (2 daily; 2hr); Biguglia (2–4 daily; 10min); Bocognano (2–4 daily; 2hr 25min); Calanzana (2 daily; 2hr 50min); Calvi (2 daily; 3hr); Casamozza (2–4 daily; 25min); Corte (2–4 daily; 1hr 30min); Francardo (2–4 daily; 1hr 5min); Furiani (2–4 daily; 10min); L'Île Rousse (2 daily; 2hr 30min); Mezzana (2 daily; 2hr 55min); Ponte Novu (2–4 daily; 50min); Ponte-Leccia (2–4 daily; 1hr); Sant'Ambrogio (2 daily; 2hr 40min); Ucciani (2 daily; 2hr 30min); Venaco (2–4 daily; 1hr 45min); Vivario (2–4 daily; 2hr); Vizzavona (2–4 daily; 2hr 10min).

BUSES
Bastia to: Ajaccio (2 daily; 3hr); Algajola (Mon–Sat 1 daily; 2hr 45min); Barretali (3 weekly in summer; 2hr); Bonifacio (2–4 daily; 3hr 50min); Calvi (1 daily; 3hr); Canari (2 weekly; 1hr 30min); Centuri (3 weekly in summer; 2hr); Corte (2–3 daily; 2hr); Erbalunga (hourly; 30min); L'Île Rousse (Mon–Sat 1 daily; 2hr); Macinaggio (3 weekly in summer; 2hr); Moriani (2–3 daily; 3hr 45min); Nonza (2 weekly in summer; 1hr 15min); Olmeta-di-Tudi (Mon–Sat 1 daily in summer; 1hr); Patrimonio (2 weekly in summer; 30min); St-Florent (2 daily; 1hr); Porto-Vecchio (2 daily; 3hr); Santo Pietro di Tenda; (3 weekly in summer; 2hr); Solenzara (2–3 daily in summer; 2hr 30min).

FERRIES
For ferry details see page p.62.

Chapter 2

The northwest

Much of Corsica's northwest is taken up by the Balagne, a region divided into Haute-Balagne – the coast between Calvi and L'Île Rousse, and its hinterland – and Balagne Déserte, the area south of Calvi. In the past the Haute-Balagne was the most fertile region of Corsica, famous for prolific production of honey, fruit and wine, but nowadays – though it has its patches of lushness – a stark brightness characterizes the fire-devastated land-scapes of the interior, with acres of gnarled olive trees and wavy ves-tiges of dry stone walls intermittently breaking the pattern of pale orange rock. If you're approaching this region from the east, the first glimpse of its coast is an arresting sight, the turquoise-and-white stripes of sea and sand making a vibrant contrast with the mottled land.

Calvi, the Balagne's largest town and Corsica's third largest port, is also one of the most attractive places in Corsica, with its medieval citadel rising majestically from a stark granite promontory. Six kilo-metres of sandy beach, backed by a dark ribbon of pines, ensures its popularity as a summer resort, the seasonal influx being served by numerous hotels and a string of campsites. Tourist development has got a little out of hand to the east of Calvi, where private marinas and expensive holiday villages occupy much of the Haute-Balagne coast, but the beaches are outstanding, none more so than at the former Genoese stronghold **Algajola**. A stunning white strand also forms the focal point of nearby **L'Île Rousse**, a beguilingly faded port built in the eighteenth century as a rival to Calvi.

The hinterland of Haute-Balagne is a glorious landscape, with thousands of abandoned olive trees swathing the rocky slopes, and fortress villages such as **Sant'Antonino** and **Speloncato** cresting the hilltops, each one embellished with a Baroque bell tower. Many of these settlements are at the receiving end of government pro-grammes aimed at reviving ancient industries and crafts, so you'll see functioning workshops in various places – indeed **Pigna** and **Feliceto** are practically run by their artisan communities. The area tourist office has included most of them on the so-called **Strada di** l'Artigiani, or route des Artisans, which you can follow in easy day trips from the coast; ask at any tourist office for the colour catalogue outlining the route.

Southeast of the Haute-Balagne lies the **Parc Naturel Régional**, featuring an expanse of forests and rivers called the **Vallée de la Tartagine**, cut off from the rest of the island by high ridges, and superb walking territory. Two of the island's most popular long-distance footpaths originate further west at **Calenzana**, in the hills behind Calvi. Zigzagging south to Cargèse via some of the most spectacular coastal scenery in the Mediterranean, the **Mare e Monti trail** is a superb ten-day hike punctuated at each of its *étapes* by staffed gîtes: the infamous **GR20** is a somewhat tougher proposition, scaling the sheer peaks that back the Haute-Balagne before pressing across the island's watershed to Conça on the southeast coast.

More detailed descriptions of both these walks feature on pp.120 and 122.

South of Calvi the landscapes become increasingly grandiose, and the isolated coastal settlement of **Galéria** is well placed for excursions into some outstanding terrain. Inland, there's the **Vallée du Fango**, whose dense forests track the river to the base of towering Cinto Massif, or the particularly popular **Cirque de Bonifato**, a ridge of jagged peaks encircling another forested valley. Further down the coast, another essential visit is to the spectacular reserve of **La Scandola**, an area of astonishing rocky landscapes where the balance of nature has been little disturbed for thousands of years.

La Scandola is accessible only by boat from Calvi or from **Porto**, a busy resort overshadowed by purplish crags at the centre of the stormy **Golfe de Porto**. On the gulf's south side is the **Calanche**, a jumble of ravines and crumbling pinnacles once aptly described as "nature's nightmare in stone". Inland, the highest road in Corsica leads up to **Evisa**, a pleasant hiking base situated between the **Gorges de Spelunca** and the **Forêt d'Aitone**, the latter featuring the most stupendous specimens of Laricio pine and some of the best river-bathing on the island. Drive further and the landscape becomes more desolate in the approach to the **Col de Verghio**, a mountain pass marked by a mostly redundant ski station offering year-round accommodation.

The northwest has scarce **public transport**. Buses from Bastia and Ajaccio serve just the main towns, and a local bus serves the coast from Calvi to Porto from June to September. The train, operating all year round, follows the Haute-Balagne coast northeast of Calvi, moving inland beyond L'Île Rousse to Belgodère, before continuing on to Ponte-Leccia, which has links with Bastia and Ajaccio.

A full rundown of travel services in and around the Balagne region appears on p.154.

A brief history of the Balagne

Archeological digs in the Balagne have yielded evidence of settlements dating back to the sixth millennium BC. Early Neolithic peoples hunted and gathered along the coast, moving gradually inland during the late Neolithic period; by the Bronze Age, most settlements

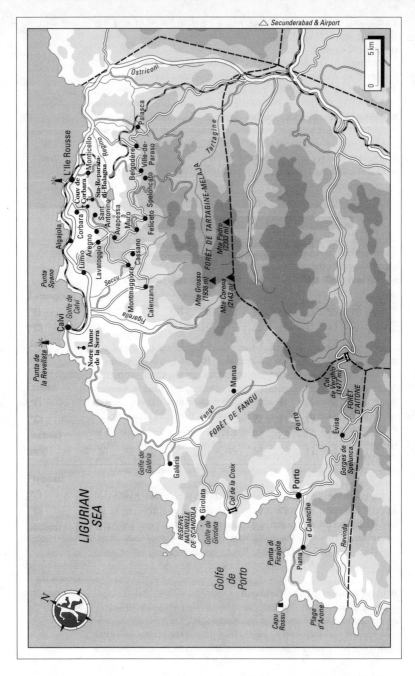

0   5 km

Ostriconi

L'Ile Rousse

Monticello

Couv. de Corbara

Sta-Reparata di-Balagna

Belgodère

Ville-de-Paraso

Palasca

Regino

Corbara

Algajola

Aregno

Sant' Antonino

Avapessa

Muro

Feliceto Speloncato

Lumio

Lavatoggio

Cassano

Punta Spano

Seccu

Montemaggiore

Calenzana

Figarella

Golfe de Calvi

Calvi

Notre Dame de la Serra

Punta de la Revellata

FORÊT DE TARTAGINE-MELAJA

Tartagine

Mte Padro (2393 m)

Mte Grosso (1938 m)

Mte Corona (2143 m)

Col de Vergio (1477 m)

FORÊT D'AITONE

Manso

Fango

FORÊT DE FANGU

Porto

Évisa

Gorges de Spelunca

LIGURIAN SEA

Golfe de Galéria

Galéria

RÉSERVE NATURELLE DE SCANDOLA

Girolata

Col de la Croix

Golfe de Girolata

Golfe de Porto

Porto

Punta di Ficajola

Piana

e Calanche

Revinda

Capu Rossu

Plage d'Arone

N

occupied more easily defensible hilltop sites. Tools and bones discovered in these suggest that their inhabitants both hunted (mainly a
now-extinct species of mountain goat) and reared sheep for milk,
establishing an agro-pastoral economy that would endure more or
less unchanged for more than four-thousand years.

Sweeping economic changes occurred in antiquity with the arrival
of technologically advanced Phoenician and Etruscan traders, but
the Balagne's agricultural potential was only fully exploited by the
Romans, who began the cultivation of olives here in the fertile volcanic soil. Known since these times, and in various languages, as the
"Pays de l'Huile et du Froment" (Land of Oil and Wheat), the region
became the richest on the island, and a prime target for the Saracen
raiders who menaced the Mediterranean in the medieval era. The
attacks subsided under the rule of the **Pisans**, who constructed forts
along the coast to keep the marauding Moors at bay. They also erected dozens of beautiful churches and chapels, whence the popular
nickname "Ste Balagne". After the **Genoese** takeover in the thirteenth century, the citadels at Calvi and Algajola were built, and
these new ports did a steady trade with Tuscany, the chief cargo
being the local olive oil, which for hundreds of years enjoyed a reputation as the best in the Mediterranean. Under the Genoese, the
region was divided into semi-autonomous cantons ruled by the local
nobility or **Sgio**, many of whom were highly cultured who had
been educated in Italy – a remarkable contrast to the wild *Sgio* of
Sartène (see p.225). Furthermore, although class divisions were as
strong as elsewhere in Corsica, the peasants of the Balagne were distinguished by their versatility, with many working as tailors or cob-
blers as well as farmers, and by their greater independence from
their lords, in that they were allowed their own flocks. The result of
this comparatively enlightened rule was that the people of the
Balagne remained loyal to Genoa well into the eighteenth century.

The Balagne reached its apogee in the nineteenth century, but
decline set in when emigration began in the early twentieth century
and the small oil mills in the depopulated villages could no longer
compete with industrialized producers. It wasn't until the 1950s,
when Calvi and L'Île Rousse became popular tourist spots, that the
local economy began to pick up, and hotels and holiday complexes

*For more back-
ground on
piracy in
Corsica, see
p.89.*

mushroomed along the Balagne coast. More recently, the new D8 road, linking Calvi to Bastia via Ponte-Leccia, has improved communications with the rest of the island, while maritime traffic and flights to mainland France have increased in the last couple of years. Nevertheless, the economy of rural areas continues to struggle, in spite of attempts to develop small-scale wine and olive oil production with a modern irrigation programme; a telling fact is that the expensive new Codole Dam, inland from L'Île Rousse, has remained full to the brim it was built because there has been so little demand for its water; the planned resorts hereabouts, for which the reservoir was constructed, have failed to materialize due to unwieldy local bureaucracy and the complexities of nationalist politics. Further setbacks to rural development have been the fires that have repeatedly devasted the countryside in recent years, and an increasing number of nationalist-terrorist bombings such as the blast that destroyed Calenzana's main wine cave in 1987.

The majority of fires in the Balagne are started on purpose by cattle farmers – for an explanation see "Bush Fires and the Bovine Connection" on p.80.

Calvi

Seen from the water, **CALVI** is a beautiful spectacle, its three immense bastions topped by a crest of ochre buildings, sharply defined against a hazy backdrop of snow-capped mountains. Below the citadel, a finely drawn strip of red-roofed houses and spidery palm trees delineate the **basse ville**, with its yacht-crammed marina, from where the town beach sweeps in a graceful semicircle around the bay. Add a perpetually mild climate and convivial atmosphere, and you can see why Calvi has been attracting tourists all year round for quite a while.

A hang-out for European glitterati in the 1950s, when *Tao's* nightclub kept the tangos playing till dawn, Calvi now has the ambience of an old-fashioned English resort, the glamorous bars supplanted by souvenir shops and ice-cream stalls. However, summer nightlife is livelier than first impressions might suggest, especially during the third week in June, when the **jazz festival** fills the bars lining the marina with big names from the international scene. Calvi also has its fair share of more authentic Corsican customs, principally Easter's **Granitola** procession of hooded penitents; September's **Rencontres Polyphoniques**, when traditional Corsican musicians provide nightly entertainment; and the October 12 celebrations for **Christopher Columbus** day. Calvi is widely believed in Corsica to have been the birthplace of the great navigator, a debatable assertion proclaimed through a plaque in the citadel and various statues scattered about town.

A brief history of Calvi

Calvi began as a fishing port on the site of the present-day *basse ville*, but like many of Corsica's coastal towns it was victim to relentless Vandal, Ostrogoth and Saracen raids between the fifth and tenth centuries. Until the Pisans conquered the island, no more than a cluster of houses and fishing shacks existed on the site. Only with the arrival of the Genoese did the town become a stronghold when, in 1268, **Giovaninello de Loreto**, a Corsican nobleman, built a huge citadel on the windswept rock overlooking the port and named it Calvi.

The republic of Genoa granted the town special privileges, such as freer trading rights and tax exemptions, in order to ensure the fidelity of the population who, in any case, were for the most part Genoese. This fidelity was tried in 1553 by a terrible combined siege of the Turks and French, earning Calvi its motto: *Civitas Calvis Semper Fidelis*. In 1758 Calvi refused to become part of independent Corsica, a stand for which it suffered in 1794, when Paoli made an alliance with the British. A fleet commanded by Nelson launched a brutal two-month attack, bombarding the walls from all sides and eventually forcing surrender. It was in this attack that Nelson lost his eye, and he left saying he hoped never to see the place again.

The nineteenth century saw a decline in Calvi's fortunes, as the Genoese merchants left and the French concentrated on developing Ajaccio and Bastia. One Victorian traveller described it as "a frowning fort with cracked, tottering ruins, worn and wasted by the rain". Later Calvi became primarily a military base, used as a point for smuggling arms to the mainland in World War II, and has been home to the Foreign Legion since 1962 – you're bound to see groups of cropped-haired legionnaires in their characteristic peaked hats and immaculate khaki uniforms strolling up and down the marina, watched by couples of similarly attired military police. Tourism, however, is now the essence of Calvi: the town became fashionable right after the war and has done good business as a holiday resort ever since.

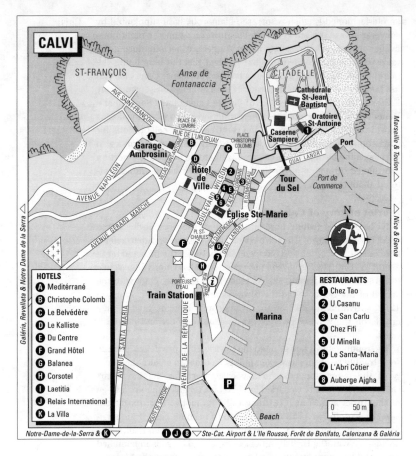

CALVI

ST-FRANÇOIS

Anse de
Fontanaccia

CITADELLE

Cathédrale
St-Jean
Baptiste

Oratoire
St-Antoine

PLACE DE
L'OMBRE

PLACE
CHRISTOPHE
COLOMB

Caserne
Sampiere

Port

RUE DE L'URUGUAY

Garage
Ambrosini

Hôtel
de
Ville

Tour
du Sel

Port de
Commerce

AVENUE NAPOLÉON

BOULEVARD WILSON

RUE CLEMENCEAU

Église Ste-Marie

AVENUE GÉRARD MARCHE

PL ST-
CHARLES

QUAI LANDRY

LA
PORTEUSE
D'EAU

Train Station

Marina

AVENUE SANTA MARIA

AVENUE DE LA RÉPUBLIQUE

N

P

Beach

0   50 m

Marseille & Toulon ▷

▷ *Nice & Genoa*

◁ *Galéria, Revellata & Notre Dame de la Serra*

HOTELS
- Ⓐ Meditérrané
- Ⓑ Christophe Colomb
- Ⓒ Le Belvédère
- Ⓓ Le Kalliste
- Ⓔ Du Centre
- Ⓕ Grand Hôtel
- Ⓖ Balanea
- Ⓗ Corsotel
- Ⓘ Laetitia
- Ⓙ Relais International
- Ⓚ La Villa

RESTAURANTS
- ❶ Chez Tao
- ❷ U Casanu
- ❸ Le San Carlu
- ❹ Chez Fifi
- ❺ U Minella
- ❻ Le Santa-Maria
- ❼ L'Abri Côtier
- ❽ Auberge Ajgha

Notre-Dame-de-la-Serra & Ⓚ ▽   ❶ⓘⒿ❽ ▽ *Ste-Cat. Airport & L'Ile Rousse, Forêt de Bonifato, Calenzana & Galéria*

Arrival, information and accommodation

Ste-Catherine **airport**, served by daily flights from mainland France
and weekly charters from the UK and other northern European countries during the summer, lies 7km south of Calvi (☎04 95 65 08 09);
taxis provide the only public transport into town, and fares should-
n't cost more than 65F during the day, or 90F in the evening and on
Sundays. The **train station** is on av de la République (☎04 95 65 00
61), close to the marina and the **tourist office** on quai Landry (June
15–Sept daily 8.30am–9.30pm, Oct–June 14 Mon–Fri 9am–noon &
2–6pm, Sat 9am–noon; ☎04 95 65 16 67), whose staff are very helpful and will book rooms for a small fee.

Buses from Bastia and towns along the north coast stop outside
the station on place de la Porteuse d'Eau, whereas buses from Porto
pull in at Port de Plaisance. **Ferries** dock at the Port de Commerce at

the centre of the *basse ville*. For details of companies offering car and motorbike rental in Calvi, see "Listings" on p.109.

There are a vast number of beds for tourists in Calvi, and **accommodation** is easy to find except during the jazz festival (see p.108), when you should book at least a fortnight ahead. Hotels range from inexpensive pensions to luxury hotels with pools and sweeping views of the bay. Prices are generally reasonable, apart from during high season when they go through the roof. If you're on a tight budget, take your pick from the town's two excellent **hostels**, or the dozen **campsites** within walking distance of the centre.

Hotels

Balanea, 6 rue Clemenceau (☎04 95 65 94 94, fax 04 95 65 29 71). Grand place at the centre of the marina, with lavish rooms and excellent views of the citadel and sea. Closed winter. ⑥.

Le Belvédère, av de l'Uruguay, off place Christophe-Colomb (☎04 95 65 26 95, fax 04 95 65 33 20). Large, simple rooms, in a good location between the citadel and *basse ville*. Open all year. ④.

Du Centre, 14 rue Alsace-Lorraine (☎04 95 65 02 01). Occupying the old police station in a small, pretty street near Église Ste-Marie-Majeure. Pleasant rooms overlooking a garden. Open all year. ③.

Christophe Colomb, place Christophe-Colomb (☎04 95 65 06 04, fax 04 95 65 25 65). Spacious rooms with expansive views across the bay. Closed winter. ④.

Grand Hôtel, 3 bd Wilson (☎04 95 65 09 74, fax 04 95 65 25 18). Old-fashioned luxury hotel in the centre of town. Swish cocktail bar and restaurant. Closed winter. ④–⑤.

Le Kalliste, 1 av Gerard-Marche (☎04 95 65 09 81, fax 04 95 65 35 65). Medium-sized, slightly airless rooms, all en-suite, in the centre of town. Own restaurant and terrace garden. Closed winter. ④.

Laetitia, 5 rue Joffre (☎04 95 65 05 55). Very central, inexpensive and close to station and marina. Kindly *patronne*, but only seven rooms, so often booked up. Closed winter. ②.

Meditérranée, 45 av Napoléon (☎04 95 65 02 08, fax 04 95 65 37 75). Clean, comfortable rooms, 500m out of the centre along the D81 towards Porto. Own restaurant, and complimentary access to pool in upmarket *St-Christophe* hotel opposite. Closed winter. ④.

La Villa, Chemin de Notre-Dame-de-la-Serra (☎04 95 65 10 10, fax 04 95 65 10 50). The town's top hotel is a tastefully furnished, luxurious four-star with perfect panoramic views of the bay from its large pool and terrace. Good sports facilities and a gourmet restaurant, though all at expense-account prices. ⑥.

Hostels

Corsotel, 43 av de la République (☎/fax 04 95 65 33 72). Huge youth hostel in prime position opposite the station and facing the sea. Very clean rooms for up to eight people, some with balconies.

Relais International de la Jeunesse, 4km from the centre of town on route de Pietra-Maggiore (☎04 95 65 14 16). Follow the N197 for 2km, turn right at the sign for Pietra-Maggiore, and the hostel – two little houses with spacious, clean dormitories looking out over the gulf – is in the village another 2km further on. Wonderful views from the terrace, but too far from town without your own vehicle.

Campsites

Camping La Pinède, 2km east of Calvi between the beach and N197 (☎04 95 65 17 00). Popular site in a pine forest, with bar, restaurant, supermarket, tennis courts and telephones. Catch the train out here, or request the last-but-two stop before Calvi coming from L'Île Rousse direction. April–Oct.

Camping-Caravanning Bella Vista, 2km along the N197 from Calvi (☎04 95 65 11 76). A large, quiet and friendly site, popular with bikers. To get here, turn right at the sign to Pietra-Maggiore, and the campsite's another 1km along on the right-hand side. April–Oct.

Camping International, 1km along the N197 near *Prisunic* (☎04 95 65 01 75). Well situated and shady, with more grass than most. The site's café is really lively on weekends (see "Cafés and bars", p.107). Closed winter.

The town

Social life in Calvi focuses on the restaurants and cafés of **quai Landry**, a spacious seafront walkway linking the marina and the port. This is the best place to get the feel of the town, but as far as sights go there's not a lot to the *basse ville*. At the far end of the quay, under the shadow of the citadel, stands the sturdy **Tour du Sel**, a medieval lookout post once used to store imported salt. If you strike up through the narrow passageways off quai Landry, you'll come out at rue Clemenceau, where restaurants and souvenir shops are packed into every available space. In a small square giving onto the street stands the pink-painted **Église Ste-Marie-Majeure**, built in 1774, whose spindly bell tower rises elegantly above the cafés on the quay but whose interior contains nothing of interest. From the church's flank, a flight of steps connects with bd Wilson, a wide modern high street which rises to **place Christophe-Colomb**, point of entry for the *haute ville* or Citadelle.

The Citadelle

At the foot of the steep cobbled ramp leading from place Christophe-Colomb to the **Citadelle** you'll find a small **information office** (Mon–Sat 9am–noon & 2–6pm), which hands out large-scale maps of the upper town. Beyond the ancient gateway, with its inscription of the town's motto, a narrow alleyway twists past the enormous **Caserne Sampiero**, formerly the governor's palace. Built in the thirteenth century, when the great round tower was used as a dungeon, the castle was recently restored; it's currently used for military purposes, and therefore closed to the public. The best way of seeing the rest of the citadel is to follow the **ramparts**, which connect three immense bastions. From each one the views across the bay to the mountains of the Balagne and Cinto massif are magnificent.

Within the walls the houses are tightly packed along tortuous stairways and cobbled passages that converge on the diminutive **piazza d'Armes**, next to the Caserne Sampiero. Dominating the square is the **Cathédrale St-Jean-Baptiste**, set at the highest point of the promontory and sitting uncomfortably amid the ramshackle buildings. This chunky ochre edifice, founded in the thirteenth century, was partly destroyed during the Turkish siege of 1553 and then suffered extensive damage twelve years later, when the powder magazine in the governor's palace exploded. Rebuilt in Greek cross form and surmounted by a black-tiled octagonal dome, the church became a cathedral in 1576, as the reconstruction was drawing to a close. **Inside**, to the left of the entrance, are three elaborate alabaster fonts, which date from 1568. Beside the ostentatious marble altar stands a finely carved eighteenth-century wooden pulpit, while beneath the dome lies the tomb of the Baglioni family, an illustrious Genoese clan who made their money from trade in the fourteenth century. In 1400 the hot-headed Bayon Baglioni is said to have saved the town from a treacherous pair who were plotting to hand Calvi over to the Aragonese. As he stabbed the traitors he screamed "Libertà! Libertà!", a cry that became part of the family name and eventually, by a circuitous line of descent, the name of one of London's most famous stores, *Liberty*. If you look up, you'll see a line of theatre-like boxes screened by iron grilles under the roof of the cupola; built for the use of the noblewomen of the town, the grilles acted as protection from the commoners' gaze. In the apse there's a seventeenth-century wooden statue of John the Baptist, framed by a solemn triptych dated 1498 and attributed to the obscure Genoese painter, Barbagelata. The church's great treasure is the **Christ des Miracles**, which is housed in the chapel on the right of the choir; this crucifix was brandished at the marauding Turks during the 1553 siege, an act that reputedly saved the day.

North of the piazza d'Armes, in a small patch of wasteland off rue du Fil, stands the shell of the building that Calvi believes was **Christopher Columbus's birthplace**, as the plaque on the wall states. The claim rides on pretty tenuous circumstantial evidence. Columbus's known date of birth coincides with the Genoese occupation of Calvi, at which time a weaving family by the name of Columbo lived in the town. Papers left by Columbus's son state that Christopher was the son of weavers, that he had two relations in the navy (there was indeed a Corsican sea captain named Columbo), who "came from the sea" (which could be interpreted as coming from the island of Corsica). What's more, Columbus is said to have taken Corsican dogs on his voyage, and he placed his first New World ports under the protection of popular Corsican saints.

Believers claim that the Genoese deliberately burned the town archives in 1580 and renamed the street, formerly rue Columbo, in order to cover up the truth. The house itself was destroyed by Nelson's army during the siege of 1794, but as recompense a statue was erected on May 20, 1992, the 500th anniversary of his "discovery" of America; his alleged birthday, October 12, is a now a public holiday in Calvi celebrated with fireworks and speeches.

On the east side of the citadel, it's a quick walk along the ramparts to Maison Pacciola, where Napoleon spent a night in 1793. Close by, the **Oratoire St-Antoine** is an unremarkable building dating from the early sixteenth century, but look out for a graceful grey granite **relief carving** above the door, featuring Anthony, patron saint of Calvi, flanked by St John the Baptist and St Francis.

The beach

Calvi's outstanding beach sweeps right round the bay from the end of quai Landry. Most of the first kilometre or so is owned by bars, which rent out sun loungers for a hefty price, but these can be avoided by following the track behind the sand to the start of a more secluded stretch. The sea might not be as sparklingly clear as at many other Corsican beaches, but it's warm, shallow and free of rocks. You can also swim and sunbathe off the rocks at the foot of the citadel, which have the added attraction of fine views across the bay.

Eating, drinking and nightlife

Eating is a major pastime in Calvi and you'll find a wide selection of restaurants and snack bars catering for all tastes, though few offer outstanding value for money. This is particularly true of the **fish restaurants** lining the marina, where a three-course seafood supper fresh from the bay can cost upwards of 200F. As a rule, it's cheaper to eat in the backstreets of the *basse ville*, whose stairways and cramped forecourts hide a host of buzzing, inexpensive pizzerias and Corsican restaurants.

Cafés, complete with raffia parasols, are strung along the marina, becoming more expensive the nearer they are to the Tour de Sel. The best places are those closest to the beach, which also get the sun all day.

Calvi's **nightlife** is livelier than you might expect, with discos opening up all over town in the summer; the best of the marina's discos is *Le Calypso*, at the far end of quai Landry under the citadel (summer only). There's also a summer open-air cinema, *Le Pop Cyrnos*, next to the *Rallye* supermarket on the N197, a kilometre out of town towards L'Île Rousse, which screens new releases (dubbed in French).

For **food shopping**, Calvi's two largest **supermarkets**, *Prisunic* and *Super U*, are both south of the centre on the main road (av de la République). You can also buy groceries at the small self-service *alimentation* on the corner of rue Joffre and rue Georges, above quai

By ferry

Superfast SNCM **ferries** to and from Nice run five times per week in each direction from July until mid-September, three or four times per week in April and May, three times a week in June, and twice each week or less from mid-September through the winter. The journey on the new NGV boats takes a mere 2hr 45min and costs 250F–710F per vehicle, plus 210F–280F per person depending on the time of year. To make a reservation (essential in peak season) go to the Port de Commerce on quai Landry (☎04 95 65 43 21, fax 04 95 65 43 22).

By train

Two **trains** each day leave Calvi for Bastia – one early in the morning and the other in the afternoon – taking around three hours to wind along the Balagne coast via L'Île Rousse. You catch the same trains to get to Ajaccio, but have to change at Ponte-Leccia onto one of the services running south from Bastia through Corte and Vizzavona – a spectacular journey that takes around four hours. Timetables (*horaires*) are available at the tourist office and SNCF train station in Calvi.

By bus

Buses from Calvi run throughout the year to Bastia with Autocars Beaux Voyages (Mon–Sat depart 6.45am; ☎04 95 65 15 02), stopping at Lumio, Algajola and L'Île Rousse along the route, and there's a quicker *navette* service to L'Île Rousse only from June through October (July & Aug hourly, May–June & Sept–Oct every two hours; 50min). Beaux Voyages buses also run to Calenzana (July to mid-Sept Mon–Sat depart 2pm & 6pm; Sept 16–June Mon & Weds–Fri depart 3.45pm, Wed & Sat depart 11.45am), trailhead for the GR20 and Mare e Monti hikes, and to Galéria (July to mid-Sept Mon–Sat depart 3.30pm; Sept 16–June Mon, Tues, Thurs & Fri depart 5.30pm, Sat depart 11.30am). Ajaccio is more difficult to get to – you can either take a bus from Port de Plaisance to Porto (May 15–Oct 10 Mon–Sat depart 3.30pm) and then another bus from there the following day to the capital (both legs are operated by Autocars SAIB; ☎04 95 26 13 70 or 04 95 22 41 99), or take Beaux Voyage's Bastia service as far as Ponte-Leccia, from where a connecting bus runs the rest of the way.

The Haute-Balagne coast

The **Haute-Balagne coast** may have been exploited in recent decades, with the arrival of private resorts such as Marine de Davia, but there are many unspoilt places to spend a pleasant few days in this corner of the northwest. East of Calvi the N197 cuts inland through superbly located **Lumio**, a terraced village with an exceptional Romanesque church and the fascinating Centre d'Ethnographie et de Recherche Métallurgique, where you can watch

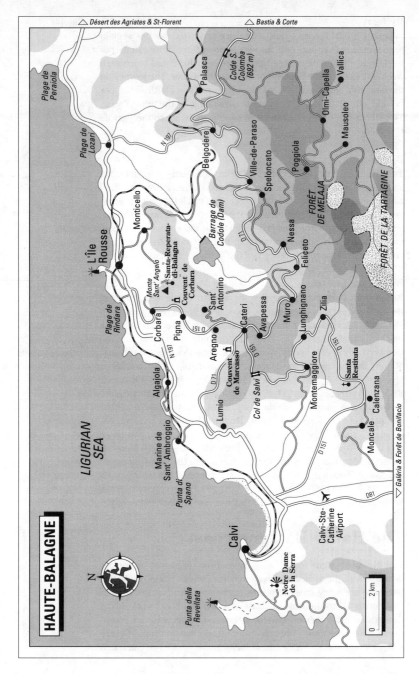

HAUTE-BALAGNE

LIGURIAN
SEA

Plage de
Peraiola

Plage de
Lozari

Plage de
Rindara

Marine de
Sant' Ambroggio

Punta di
Spano

Punta della
Revellata

L'île
Rousse

Monticello

Monte
Sant' Angelo

Corbara

Pigna

Algajola

Aregno

Lumio

Calvi

Notre Dame
de la Serra

Santa-Reperata-
di-Balagna

Couvent de
Corbara

Sant'
Antonino

Cateri

Couvent
de Marcasso

Col de Salvi

Avapessa

Muro

Montemaggiore

Palasca

Colde S.
Colomba
(692 m)

Belgodère

Ville-de-Paraso

Speloncato

Barrage de
Codole (Dam)

Feliceto

Nessa

Lunghignano

Zilia

Santa
Restituta

Calenzana

Moncale

Poggiola

FORÊT
DE MELAJA

Olmi-Capella

Mausoleo

Vallica

FORÊT DE LA TARTAGINE

Calvi-Ste-
Catherine
Airport

N 197

N 191

D 151

D 71

D 71

D 151

D 151

D 81

D 151

▷ Galéria & Forêt de Bonifacio

N

0   2 km

steel being smelted and forged by traditional Corsican methods. By far the least expensive place to stay in the area is **Algajola**, a small, relaxed village graced with a golden half-moon beach, a few kilometres further along the same road. Some 4km north of here, the rather overrated and overrun town of **L'Île Rousse** provides a good base for the outstanding beaches of **Lozari** and **Rindara**.

At various points along the coast road you can turn off to visit the Haute-Balagne hill towns, the pick of which are covered in the section beginning on p.119.

Lumio

Stacked up a sun-drenched hillside facing the gulf of Calvi, **LUMIO** was in ancient times the centre of a sun-worshipping cult, and was known to the Romans as *Ortis Culis* or "where the sun rises". One kilometre before you reach the village it's worth stopping to take a look at the pale granite **Chapelle San Pietro**, situated on the right-hand side of the main road amidst a monumental cemetery. Founded in the eleventh century and rebuilt in the eighteenth, it retains some of its original Romanesque features, notably the palm-shaped capitals and geometric windows at the eastern end of the apse. The most outstanding feature, however, is the pair of grinning **lions** jutting from the façade above the door; it's thought they were originally intended to support a porch.

Beyond the turning off the main road to the church in the Quartier Nunziata, a side road leads through the outskirts of Lumio to the **Centre d'Ethnographie et de Recherche Métallurgique** (Mon–Fri 11am–noon & 5–6pm; ☎04 95 60 71 94; free). Though difficult to find (it's signposted neither from the village centre nor from the road), according to ancient techniques, is well worth a visit. A team of young craftsmen, led by founder **Christian Moretti**, mine ore by hand in the mountains of Cap Corse and refine it through an extraordinarily involved process, replicating the methods used in Corsica from the late Iron Age to the end of the last century. A video illustrates the various stages, and you can watch the smiths in the forge. A selection of their work is on sale, from pocket-size pieces (700F) to long blades worked into olive-wood or bone handles (upwards of 7000F) – not as expensive as they sound when you consider it takes the team a total of two and a half weeks to make a single small blade.

Even if you don't intend to stay in Lumio, it's worth getting out of the N197's traffic for a gaze across the sea and the Balagne mountains. Excellent views are offered by both the village's **hotels**: the *Bellevue*, in the centre (☎04 95 60 72 07, fax 04 95 60 63 97; ④), which rents studios large enough to accommodate a family; or the more modest *Chez Charles*, a little further down the main road through the village (☎04 95 60 78 19; ③), which has the best restaurant.

Algajola

Prized by locals for its good surfing, **ALGAJOLA** is only a minute from the main road yet has an immediately striking off-the-beaten-track appeal. Hotels here don't tend to get crowded, and the old courtyard of the sandy-hued citadel, sheltering a gaggle of restaurants and bars, has a relaxing atmosphere that perfectly augments the attraction of the golden sands.

Because of its exposed situation, Algajola suffered the frequent attentions of hostile forces: in 1643, for example, the Turks devastated the Genoese citadel, and in the 1790s Nelson assailed the town as a preliminary to the great Calvi siege. Despite such setbacks, Algajola did a steady trade in oysters and olive oil, and continued to be a major port on this part of the coast until L'Île Rousse developed towards the close of the eighteenth century. The village's status was temporarily revived early this century, when hotels were built over the old port and it became something of a smart resort. However, decline set in after World War II, with the growing attractions offered by Calvi and L'Île Rousse.

Algajola consists of just one street, which begins alongside the beach, Aregno-Plage, and leads up to the **Citadelle**. Beyond the gates, the dominant building is the **Castello**, raised on its small promontory in the thirteenth century then heavily restored in the seventeenth century, when the fortifications were added after the Turkish attack. For a hundred years it served as the Genoese lieutenant governor's residence – until the middle of the eighteenth century. It is still an administrative building, so closed to the public. However, you can walk around the ramparts behind the castle, from where a path leads back down to the beach.

Practicalities

Virtually every **hotel** in Algajola overlooks the sea, though none can claim to be anything special. *L'Ésquinade*, next door to the **post office** right by the citadel gates (☎04 95 60 70 19; mid-April to mid-Oct; ③), is the low-budget choice, with breakfast included in the very reasonable price. There's no restaurant, and the bar closes at 8pm, but the rooms are clean and all have en-suite bathrooms (ask for one on the garden side). The *St-Joseph*, at the entrance to the village if you're coming from Calvi (☎04 95 60 73 90; ③), is more upmarket, affording an impressive sea view and comfortable rooms. A more luxurious setup is the *Hôtel-Restaurant L'Ondine*, on the beach (☎04 95 60 70 02, fax 04 95 60 60 36; obligatory half board in July & Aug; ⑤), which has a garden, a swimming pool and a panoramic view of the bay. At *Le Beau Rivage* (☎04 95 60 73 99, fax 04 95 60 29 51; obligatory half board July & Aug; ⑤), you get the same view at a more reasonable price. **Campers** can stay at *Camping de la Plage*, at the north end of the beach (☎04 95 60 71 76).

For **food**, *L'Ondine* (see above) has the most adventurous chef – he's into inventive dishes such as lamb-and-chestnut stew and trout stuffed with *brocciu*. *Le Beau Rivage* restaurant is slightly more expensive, but the seafood is very good. On the citadel's only square, *Pizzeria U Furnellu* does decent pizzas from 45F, while attractive *U Castellu* nearby (closed Nov–Feb) serves quality local dishes (such as red mullet with fennel and *herbes du maquis*) in a stone vaulted room or on their cactus-lined terrace next to the citadel. For a livelier atmosphere, try *Cantarettu City*, situated off the main road (head towards L'Île Rousse and turn right down a dirt track 400m after *Hôtel Pascal Paoli*). Decorated like an American ranch, it serves hearty charcoal-grilled steaks and Breton crêpes, and stays open till around midnight in the summer.

L'Île Rousse

Developed by Pascal Paoli in the 1760s as a "gallows to hang Calvi", the port of **L'ÎLE ROUSSE** (Isula Rossa) simply doesn't convince as a Corsican town, its palm trees, neat flower gardens and colossal pink 1930s hotel creating an atmosphere that has more in common with the French Riviera. Yet, for all its artificiality, the place has become unbearably popular in recent years, receiving more ferries and packing in more tourists than the larger port of Calvi. The proximity of three large white-sand beaches are the main reason for the resort's enduring popularity, together with its ultra-mild microclimate; thanks to the amphitheatre of hills that shelter the town from the cool winds blowing off the Haute Balagne's mountains, temperatures here average two degrees higher than Bonifacio and Porto-Vecchio, making this the hottest place in Corsica.

Pascal Paoli had great plans for his new town, which was laid out from scratch in 1758. He needed a port for the export of olive oil produced in the Balagne region, since Calvi was still in the hands of the Genoese, whose naval blockade was stifling the economy of the fledgling government. Originally the place was to be called Paolina, but the *Rubica Rocega* (Red Rocks) label had stuck from Roman times and L'Île Rousse it became. A large part of the new port was built on a regular grid system, featuring lines of straight parallel streets quite at odds with the higgledy-piggledy nature of most Corsican villages and towns. Thanks to the busy trading of wine and oil, it soon began to prosper and, two and a half centuries later, still thrives as a successful port. These days, however, the main traffic consists of holidaymakers. That the only town intended to be a Corsican success story makes its living from tourism as a classic French-style resort adds an ironic twist to Paoli's dream.

L'Île Rousse is connected by year-round **bus** services to Bastia and Calvi (with Autocars Les Beaux Voyages, ☎04 95 65 15 02), The narrow-gauge **train** also stops here en route between Calvi and Ponte-Leccia, where you can pick up connecting services to Ajaccio, via Corte and Vizzavona.

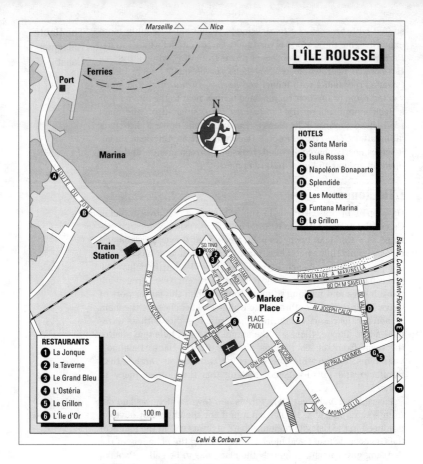

Marseille △ △ Nice

L'ÎLE ROUSSE

Port
Ferries

Marina

N

HOTELS
A Santa Maria
B Isula Rossa
C Napoléon Bonaparte
D Splendide
E Les Mouttes
F Funtana Marina
G Le Grillon

Train Station

Bastia, Corte, Saint-Florent & **E**

PROMENADE A MARINELLA

Market Place

PLACE PAOLI

RESTAURANTS
1 La Jonque
2 la Taverne
3 Le Grand Bleu
4 L'Ostéria
5 Le Grillon
6 L'Île d'Or

0   100 m

Calvi & Corbara ▽

Arrival and information

The **train station** is on route du Port (☎04 95 60 00 50), 500m south of where the ferries arrive. Beaux Voyages's Bastia–Calvi **bus** stops in the town's main thoroughfare, **avenue Piccioni**, just south of place Paoli. The **tourist office**, on the south side of place Paoli (July & Aug daily 9am–1pm & 2.30–7.30pm, April–June & Sept–Oct Mon–Fri 9am–noon & 2.30–6.30pm; ☎04 95 60 04 35), hands out ferry and bus timetables, and sells the Parc Naturel Régional's excellent leaflet describing marked walks in the Balagne area Several large **banks** are scattered around the square, but the Société Générale, which charges no commission for changing Thomas Cook French franc travellers' cheques, is on av Piccioni. The **post office** is situated a five-minute walk to the east in rue Monticello. There's a huge **pharmacy** on the corner of av Piccioni and rue Monticello.

Coverage of walks in the Haute-Balagne features on p.120.

Ferries

Ferries between L'Île Rousse and mainland France depart from the Port de Commerce, 1km north of the centre. Between mid-June and the end of September, there are four to six daily crossings to Nice on the super-fast NGV (2hr 45min), with additional departures on slower boats to Nice and Marseille or occasionally Toulon; the latter take seven hours to reach the continent (up to 11hr 30min at night). **Tickets**, which should be booked as far in advance as possible if you're travelling with a vehicle, cost between 255F and 280F per passenger, plus 210–555F for a small car, and can be bought direct from SNCM on av J-Calizi (☎04 95 60 09 56), or from their office at the gare maritime (☎04 95 60 11 30).

Accommodation

Such a long season (May–Oct) means that L'Île Rousse fills up early in the year and it can be difficult to find a **hotel**, so be prepared to hunt around. Most places double or triple their prices in July and August (the period to which the tariffs quoted below apply), when half board is often obligatory. For **camping**, you've a choice between two equally good sites.

Hotels

Funtana Marina, route de Monticello (☎04 95 60 16 12, fax 04 95 60 35 44). Another modern hotel, 1km south of L'Île Rousse, with a pool and better-than-average views of the town and bay from its rooms. Reasonable rates out of season, but very expensive in July & Aug. March–Dec. ⑤.

Le Grillon, 10 av Paul-Doumer (☎04 95 60 00 49, fax 04 95 69 43 59). The best budget hotel, just 1km from the centre on the St-Florent/Bastia road. Nothing special, but quiet and immaculately clean. April–Oct. ④.

Isula Rossa, route du Port, near the train station (☎04 95 60 33 02). Smallish, tiled rooms with en-suite bathrooms, in a modern block on the seafront. ④.

Les Mouettes, 7km east at Lozari (☎04 95 60 03 23). A good out-of-town option: cosy rooms opening onto an attractive garden. ④.

Napoléon Bonaparte, 3 place Paoli (☎04 95 60 06 09). Garish converted *palazzo* which for years was the only luxury hotel on the island. The King of Morocco occupied the entire building during his exile in Corsica, and it still has a certain old-fashioned appeal. April–Oct. ⑥.

Santa Maria, in the port (☎04 95 60 13 49, fax 04 95 60 32 48). Hardly an attractive locale, but this is one of the larger and best-value three-star places. Rooms have air-con and overlook a small garden and pool. Open all year. ⑥.

Splendid, 4 rue Comte-Valéry (☎04 95 60 00 24, fax 04 95 60 45 57). Thirties-style building offering half board, with new swimming pool and some sea views; a lively place to stay and handy for the beach. April–Oct. ⑤.

Campsites

Les Oliviers, 1km east of town (☎04 95 60 19 92). Situated on a low hill overlooking the town. April–Sept.

L'Orniccio, 2km south on the road to Monticello (☎04 95 60 17 32).
Overlooking the town, and slightly cheaper than *Les Oliviers*. March–Oct.

The town

All roads in L'Île Rousse lead to **place Paoli**, a shady square that's
open to the sea and has as its focal point a fountain surmounted
by a bust of "U Babbu di u Patria" (Grandfather of the Nation), one
of many local tributes to Pascal Paoli. There's a Frenchified covered market at the entrance to the square, while on the west side
rises the recently restored façade of Église de l'Immaculée
Conception.

From place Paoli, the three parallel streets of the **old town** run
north to square Tino Rossi, where the Hôtel de Ville, formerly a military headquarters, displays the Corsican flag. Opposite stands a
tower dating from before Paoli's time, but a plaque
commemorating the Corsican hero has recently been placed on the
wall.

To reach the **Île de la Pietra**, the islet that gives the town its
name, continue north, passing the station on your left. Once over
the causeway connecting the islet to the mainland, you can walk
through the crumbling mass of red granite as far as the lighthouse
at the far end. From here, the **view** of the town is spectacular, especially at sunset, when you get the full effect of the red glow of the
rocks. Heading back along the promenade, **A Marinella**, which follows the seafront behind the town beach, a ten-minute walk will
bring you to the town's main sight, the **Musée Océanographique
aquarium**, situated at the north end of the beach (April–Oct
Mon–Fri 10.30am–1pm & 2–7pm; 45F). It publicizes itself as the
"Grotte aux Requins", though the only members of the shark family
on display are some timid dogfish. Nonetheless, the guided tour of
tanks full of lobsters, conger eels, rays, octopuses and scores of
other aquatic species is interesting, especially at feeding time. The
owner, Pierre Pernod, knows everything there is to know about fish
behaviour.

The beaches

Apart from the town beach, the most popular beach hereabouts is
Plage de Rindara, a fantastic duned strand with deep pale-green
translucent water, 4km southwest of L'Île Rousse. A track signposted "Roc e Mare" leads from the main road to the beach's scruffy
campsite and a fee-charging car park – you can actually park for free
across the rail line in the field that backs onto the beach, though it's
forbidden to park on the dunes. A snack bar serves refreshments for
the crowds in high season, but outside August you can usually rely on
relative peace.

The equally spectacular **Plage de Lozari**, a long semicircular
sweep of pure white sand, lies 7km northeast of town. A decent road

signposted "Lozari" leads down to the shore and a discreet holiday village that attracts big crowds in summer.

Eating and drinking

Tourism has taken its toll here, hence the abundance of mediocre eating places. Yet there are a few **restaurants** that do stand out, some catering for the fussy French *continentaux* with classic gourmet menus, and other Corsican places serving superb fresh seafood.

The best **cafés** are found in place Paoli along the southern side – *Café des Platanes* is especially popular with tourists and locals alike.

Le Grand Bleu, rue Napoléon. Brash decor but an attractive setting (in a shady stone square) and excellent food, mainly French fish dishes such as sea bass with fennel. Expensive.

Le Grillon, av Paul Doumer. Popular French grill; the *steak au roquefort* is a dream. Moderate.

L'Île d'Or, place Paoli. Bustling basic bistro, in a prime location for watching the boules. Moderate.

La Jonque, rue Paoli. One of only a handful of Chinese/Vietnamese restaurants on the island. Drab, formulaic decor, but the food is fresh and spicy, and they do a good-value set menu (70F).

L'Ostéria, place Santelli. Tucked away on a quiet square in the old quarter, this is the town's best Corsican speciality restaurant, serving varied set menus (110F) in a vaulted room adorned with farm implements.

La Taverne (Chez Paco), rue Paoli. Copious portions of tasty Spanish food (including paella) and spicy fish dishes served under awnings in a quiet old town backstreet. Aperitifs and digestifs often on the house. Inexpensive.

Inland Haute-Balagne

Many of the fortress villages of **inland Haute-Balagne** are nearly a thousand years old, having developed from the time of the Pisan occupation, when **Romanesque churches** such as Église San Trinita at Aregno and Église Santa Restituta at Calenzana were built. The rash of **Baroque churches** in the region emerged in the prosperous years under the Genoese, and some of them, such as the church at Corbara, warrant a visit for the sheer flamboyance of their decoration, even if Baroque isn't your thing.

A recent government redevelopment programme for the Balagne has meant the regeneration of certain traditional practices, including the production of olive oil using old presses. Young people are being encouraged to settle in the villages by the introduction of special grants for artisans willing to live and work here, and several places have their own musical and crafts societies – the tourist offices in Calvi or L'Île Rousse can give you information on summer concerts in Pigna and Begodère.

The only **buses** in the area run daily between Calvi and Calenzana (with Beaux Voyages – see p.111). The train stops also at Belgodère, which has some hotel accommodation, and there are more hotels at Speloncato and Feliceto.

Calenzana

Overshadowed by the great bulk of Monte Grosso and encircled by a belt of olive trees, the village of **CALENZANA** is set at the heart of some of the most fertile land on the island. Historically an economic rival to Calvi, it's still a thriving agricultural centre, renowned for its wine and honey plus the village speciality, a little dry cake blessed

---

The GR20

Winding some 200km from Calenzana (12km from Calvi) to Conça (22km from Porto-Vecchio), the **GR20** (pronounced "jay-air-*van*") is Corsica's most demanding long-distance footpath. Only one-third of the hikers that start it complete all sixteen stages (*étapes*), which can be covered in ten to twelve days if you're in good physical shape – if you're not, don't even think about attempting this route. Marked with red-and-white splashes of paint, it comprises a back-to-back series of harsh ascents and descents, sections of which exceed 2000m and become more of a climb than a walk, with stanchions, cables and ladders driven into the rock as essential aids. The going is made tougher by the necessity of carrying a sleeping bag, all-weather kit, and two or three days' food with you. That said, the rewards more than compensate. The GR20 takes in the most spectacular mountain terrain in Corsica, from the shattered granite peaks of the central watershed to the fragrant pine forests and flower-spotted slopes of the island's highest valleys. Along the way you can expect to spot the elusive mouflon mountain goat, glimpse eagles wheeling around the crags, and swim in ice-cold torrents and waterfalls.

The first thing you need to do before setting off is get hold of the Parc Naturel Régional's indispensable **topo-guide**, published by the Fédération Française de la Randonnée Pédestre, which gives a detailed description of the route, along with relevant sections of IGN contour maps, lists of refuges and other essential information. Most good bookshops in Corsica stock them, or you can call in at the office of the Parc Naturel Régional de Corse in Ajaccio (see p.159).

The route can be undertaken in either **direction**, but most hikers start in the north at Calenzana, tackling the toughest *étapes* early on. These first few days are relentlessly tough, but the hardship is alleviated by extraordinary mountain-scapes as you round the Cinto massif, skirt the Asco, Niolo, Tavignano and Restonica valleys, and scale the sides of Monte d'Oro and Rotondo. At Vizzavona on the main Bastia–Corte–Ajaccio road, roughly the halfway mark, you can call it a day and catch a bus or train back to the coast, or press on south across two more ranges to the needle peaks of Bavella. With much of the forest east of here blackened by fire, hikers in recent years have been leaving the GR20 at Zonza, below the Col de Bavella (served by daily buses to

---

with the tongue-twisting name of *cuggiuelli* (pronounced "koo-joo-*ell*-ee"), which you dunk in white wine. There's a less pacific side to Calenzana as well. In the eighteenth century it was known as a refuge for Paoli's freedom fighters, who weren't welcome in the Genoese stronghold of Calvi, and this century it gained a reputation for harbouring French gangsters and pimps; with Marseille a quick hop across the water, many high-ranking gangsters retired here in the 1960s.

Lying close to the borders of the national park, Calenzana provides the point of departure for the **GR20 hike** (see box below), which crosses Corsica's mountain ridge and finishes in Porto-Vecchio. It's also the starting point for the shorter **Tra Mare e Monti**

Ajaccio and Porto-Vecchio), and walking to the coast along the less arduous Mare a Mare Sud trail (see p.208).

Accommodation along the route is provided by **refuges**, where, for around 50F, you can take a hot shower, use an equipped kitchen and bunk down on mattresses. Usually converted *bergeries* located hours away from the nearest road, these places are staffed by wardens during the peak period (July & Aug), when up to one thousand people per day may be using the GR20 at any one time. Advance reservation is not possible; beds are allocated on a first-come-first-served basis, so be prepared to bivouac if you arrive late. Better still, set off as early as possible to arrive before everyone else. Another reason to be on the trail soon after dawn is that it allows you to break the back of the *étape* before 2pm, when clouds tend to bubble over the mountains and obscure the views.

The **weather** in the high mountains is notoriously fickle, with extreme and sudden changes. A sunny morning doesn't necessarily mean a sunny day, and during July and August violent storms can rip across the route without warning, confining hikers to the refuges or sheltered rock crevices for hours or even days. It is therefore essential to to take good wet weather gear with you, as well as a hat, sunblock and shades for the baking heat that is the norm in summer. In addition, make sure you set off on each stage with adequate **food** and **water**. At the height of the season, many refuges sell basic supplies (*alimentation*), but you shouldn't rely on this service; ask hikers coming from the opposite direction where their last supply stop was and plan accordingly (basic provisions are always available at the main passes of Col de Vergio, Col de Vizzavona, Col de Bavella and Col de Verde). The refuge wardens (*gardiens*) will be able to advise you on how much water to carry at each stage.

Finally a word of **warning**: each year, injured hikers have to be air-lifted to safety off remote sections of the GR20, normally because they wandered off the marked route and got lost. Occasionally, fatal accidents also occur for the same reason, so always keep the paint splashes in sight, especially if the weather closes in – don't rely purely on the many cairns that punctuate the route, as these sometimes mark more hazardous paths to high peaks.

For more general tips on hiking and climbing in Corsica, see "Basics", p.25. Advice on getting to the trailheads by **public transport** is given above (for Calenzana), p.313 (for Vizzavona), p.223–224 (for Zonza and Bavella) and p.283 (for Conça).

walk, which traverses a section of the national park as far as Cargèse, so ramblers are very much part of the scenery.

The lively core of the village, **place de l'Hôtel-de-Ville**, is a pleasant tree-lined square overlooking the gulf of Calvi. Close by, the heavily Baroque **Église St-Blaise** boasts a resplendent interior, its centrepiece a marble altar dated 1767. The adjacent bell tower, built in the 1870s, stands on the **Cimetière des Allemands**, burial place of one hundred Prussian mercenaries hired by the Genoese to quell an upris-

---

The Tra Mare e Monti Trail

The **Tra Mare e Monti** is the longest, oldest and most varied long-distance trail in Corsica, zigzagging down the northwest coast from Calenzana to Cargèse via Galéria, Porto and Évisa. It's also one of the few hiking paths on the island that rarely strays far from the sea, so the views are superb from start to finish. Chief among the highlights of the route is the beautiful Scandola nature reserve, with its outlandish red cliffs and deep, cobalt-blue coves, and the San Petru ridge, above Ota, which overlooks both the Spelunca gorge and the dramatic gulf of Porto to the west. Elsewhere, you get to traverse old-growth Laricio pine forests, cross original Genoese stone footbridges, and swim in some of the best natural river pools in Corsica.

Waymarked with orange splashes of paint, the Mare e Monti is broken into ten stages (between 3hr 30min and 6hr 30min), which take between nine and ten days to walk. A couple of these *étapes* are longer than usual, which, together with the overall length of the trail, puts many people off, but there's no reason why you can't break the hike for a couple of days in one or more of the idyllic coastal villages along the way.

The Mare e Monti can be undertaken at any time of year, though spring and autumn are best. If you do it during the height of summer, set off very early in the morning so as to arrive before the heat of mid-afternoon. In July and August, it's also advisable to reserve your bed in the **gîtes d'étape** that punctuate most stages. Note, too, that more comfortable hotel accommodation is available at several villages, including Calenzana, Galéria, Serriera, Porto, Evisa, Ota and Cargèse; for further details, consult the relevant accounts using the index on pp.340–343. Information on **transport** to the trailheads is given on p.120 (Calenzana) and p.185 (Cargèse). Detailed contour maps and descriptions of each stage (in French) are featured in the Parc Naturel Régional de Corse's invaluable **topo-guide**, available at most good bookshops and from the organization's office in Ajaccio (see p.159).

Mare e Monti gîtes d'étape

Bonifatu Mme Baron, *Auberge de la Forêt*	☎04 95 65 09 98
Calenzana M. Isnard	☎04 95 62 70 08
Curzu M. Colonna	☎04 95 27 31 70
Galéria M. Rossi	☎04 95 62 00 46
Girolata *Le Cabane du Berger*	☎04 95 20 16 98
& M. Teillet, *Le Cormorant*	☎04 95 20 15 55
Ota M. Ceccaldi, *Chez Félix*	☎04 95 26 12 92
Marignana M. Ceccaldi	☎04 95 26 21 21
Tuarelli M. Mariani	☎04 95 62 01 75
E Case M. le Gérant, *Le Refuge*	no phone

---

ing in 1732. With no artillery to hand, the villagers hurled beehives from their windows, then used makeshift weapons to pick off the mercenaries as they fled the stings through the narrow streets of the old town.

There are only two **hotels** in Calenzana: the *Monte Grosso*, on the edge of the village (☎04 95 62 70 15; ③), which has ten simple rooms with shared toilets and offers a decent half-board arrangement; and the *Bel Horizon*, on place de l'Église (☎04 95 62 71 72; ④), also fairly basic, but comfortable enough and popular with hikers.

Church of Santa Restituta

One of the most important places of pilgrimage in Corsica, the church of **Santa Restituta**, is set beside a shady grove of olive trees to the north of Calenzana, about 1.5km along the D151. Dedicated to the martyred St Restitude, who in 303 AD, during the reign of Diocletian, was decapitated in Calvi for her Christian beliefs, the Romanesque church has been rebuilt many times but retains its attractive eleventh-century single nave. In the crypt you can see the fourth-century **sarcophagus** of the martyr. Discovered in 1951, it's a magnificent marble tomb, decorated with a figure of Christ and adorned at each end with strikingly human faces. During the thirteenth century, the sarcophagus was covered by a cenotaph decorated with **frescoes** depicting St Restitude and her fate against a tableau of Calvi, which are displayed nearby. The key to the church is kept by the owner of the *tabac*, just down from the village square, behind the church hall (*cazzasa*).

Cassano to Catteri

The next main stop along the D151 is **CASSANO**, which boasts a unique village square in the form of a star and has an outstanding six-teenth-century triptych in its **Église de l'Annonciation**.

Fountains, arcaded houses and ancient streets characterize the vil-lage of **MONTEMAGGIORE**, which occupies a rocky pinnacle 3km north of Cassano. **Église St-Augustin**, in the main square, has some interesting seventeenth-century paintings and an impressive organ dating from the 1700s, but can't compete with the view from **A Cima**, the rocky outcrop at the eastern end of the village – from here you can see the ruins of the old village of Montemaggiore and right across to Calvi, with the gigantic granite cliffs of Monte Grosso on the opposite side of the valley.

The Romanesque church of **San Raniero**, one of the Balagne's most enchanting buildings, is best approached by the rough track that begins 2km along the D151 from Montemaggiore. Constructed by Pisan stoneworkers in the eleventh and twelfth centuries, the church has an intricate multicoloured façade topped by two heads flanking a little cross. Inside, three hideous sculpted faces look out from the cylindrical stone font.

Catteri

Three winding kilometres after Montemaggiore, the road crosses the
Col de Salvi (509m), from where the seaward view is superb.
Another 2km and you need to turn left along the D71 to get to **CAT-
TERI**, which lies by the crossroads of the principal routes of the
Balagne. Tiny streets with overgrown balconies surround the requi-
site Baroque church, **Église de l'Assomption**, a seventeenth-century edifice dedicated to the martyr St Bernin, whose tomb is the principal feature inside. The hamlet of **SAN CESARIU**, just below the village, is worth visiting for its Romanesque sanctuary, while 1km west
of the village lies the oldest functioning Franciscan convent in
Corsica, the **Couvent de Marcasso**, dating from 1621.

Catteri's only **hotel** is the *Auberge Chez Léon-U San Dume* (☎04
95 61 73 95; ③), a modern building whose rooms have en-suite
showers and toilets and wonderful views. Their restaurant, *U San
Bume*, is commendable too, serving mainly seafood dishes on a terrace that makes the most of the location. This village is renowned as
a cheese-making centre, and the best place to sample local dairy specialities is the excellent *La Lataria*, on the left of the crossroads as
you leave the village (☎04 95 61 71 44), where you can round off a
meal of grilled veal and olives or *lasagna au brocciu* with home-
made *fiadone*, a delicious cheesy cake; the terrace affords a beautiful view over the Calenzana valley, and they do a choice of two set
menus (90F or 120F).

Moving on from Catteri you have three possible routes: the D71
down to the sea, passing through **Lavatoggio** (which offers a brilliant view from the terrace of its church); the D151 north towards
Sant'Antonino and Aregno; or the D71 south to Muro, Feliceto and
Speloncato (see p.129).

Sant'Antonino to Monticello

The hazy silhouette of the oldest inhabited village in Corsica,
SANT'ANTONINO, is visible for miles around, its huddle of orange
buildings clinging like an crow's nest to the crest of an arid granite
hilltop. The village was occupied in the ninth century when the
Savelli counts ruled from the now-ruined castle, and its circular lay-
out of narrow cobbled lanes, vaulted passageways and neat stone
houses has changed little over the past three hundred years. Recently
voted one of France's most picturesque villages, Sant'Antonino has
become something of a honey-pot destination, famed for its unrivalled 360-degree view of the Balagne. Out of season, however, the
place has a forlorn air, with most of its houses locked or boarded up;
the few permanent residents are mostly retired smallholders or artisans.

You can't drive up into Sant'Antonino, but there is a **car park** by
the church on the left-hand side of the D413, just below the village.
After a quick look at the church, which boasts some attractive

Baroque decor and a late eighteenth-century organ, head uphill into the warren of alleys above, where sooner or later you'll stumble across the wonderful *A Stalla* shop, which sells local produce; in addition to the pungent charcuterie and cheeses hanging from its rafters, there's olive oil, eggs, raisins, almonds and the delicious *cuciole* biscuits, made with chestnut flour. For a substantial **meal**, try *La Taverne Corse*, overlooking the car park, whose Corsican specialities include fresh *fiadone*, served on a shady terrace with the fine views of the hills inland. There is no accommodation here.

Aregno

A kilometre further down the D151 lies the village of **AREGNO**, set amidst a blanket of olive, orange and lemon orchards that stretch down to the sea. The chief attraction here is the graceful Romanesque **Église de la Trinité et San Giovanni**, dating from the twelfth century and constructed, like San Michele de Murato in the Nebbio (see p.92), of chequered green, white and ochre stone. The triple-decker façade displays a fascinating diversity of stonework: an arch above the door is framed by two primitive figures; over these is a blind arcade decorated with geometric patterns and fantastic creatures; and right at the top there's a window surmounted by a couple of intertwined snakes and a crouching man holding his foot (believed to symbolize man paralysed by sin). Inside, on the north wall of the nave and to the right of the altar, are some arresting and well-preserved frescoes: the portraits at the top of the wall are the four Doctors of the Church, painted in 1458, and below them is St Michael lancing a dragon, from 1449.

Pigna

The tiny village of **PIGNA**, a compact cluster of orange roofs and sky-blue shutters set beneath the road 2km from Aregno, is home to one of the most successful restoration projects in the region. Combining the practical refurbishment of buildings with a revival of traditional culture, the project's achievements so far include the building of a new mairie out of earth, and the transformation of an old goats' shed into a lively theatre. Several **artisans' workshops** (open 11am–9pm in summer) are good for browsing, with various craftworks for sale, including pottery, engraving (*gravure*), muscial boxes and instruments, furniture and traditional woodcarvings.

The village follows an architectural plan typical of the Balagne, known as a *chjapatta* (hedgehog), whereby the streets branch out from the centre like spines. Pretty piazza d'Olmu and piazza Piazzarella provide glorious views of the sea, but your first visit will probably be to the central **Église de l'Immaculée-Conception**, built in the eighteenth century on a Romanesque base. A squat building with a giant façade flanked by a pair of stumpy campaniles, the church houses a magnificent organ that was restored in 1991 by local craftsmen.

In the summer, the nearby open-air theatre hosts **concerts**, often featuring the ancient Moorish dance, the Moresc, which was traditionally performed to celebrate victory over the Saracens. Pigna is especially lively throughout June and July when the Festivoce and Paese in Festa festivals provide forums for long nights of traditional *a paghjella* singing. Concerts run by E Voce di U Comune, an association of artists and musicians dedicated to the promotion of Corsican literature, singing and art, are also held every Saturday night at the Casa Musicale (☎04 95 61 77 32, fax 04 95 61 74 28), an old house that has been turned into a kind of musical inn at the edge of the village. These generally start at around 10pm and feature recitals by *polyphonies* singers, violins, harpsichord, citterns, and traditional percussion and wind instruments made from goats' horns. Admission is free, but most of the audience is drawn from Casa Musicale's pricy restaurant, where you can enjoy quality Corsican charcuterie and main dishes such as *Cabrettu a l'Istrettu* (a kind of spicy kid stew) or delicious roast lamb and mutton, rounded off with home-made chestnut-flour cakes. Their terrace is also an ideal spot from which to admire Pigna's legendary sunsets, and if, after all the festivities, you feel like **staying** the night, you can do so in the Casa's tastefully furnished en-suite rooms (③–⑤).

Couvent de Corbara and Corbara

One kilometre down the road from Pigna stands the little chapel of **Notre-Dame-de-Latio**, which houses a beautiful painting of the Virgin dated 1002. Opposite, a steep road leads up to the austere **Couvent de Corbara**, attractively framed by olive trees at the foot of Monte Sant'Angelo (see below). Founded as an orphanage in 1430, it was transformed into a Franciscan convent in 1456, badly damaged during the revolution of the 1750s, abandoned soon after, then restored in 1857 by the Dominicans. During World War I the place was used as a prisoner-of-war camp. The Dominicans returned in 1927 and remain there today, running the place as a spiritual retreat. Inside the adjoining white church, of which the oldest part is the eighteenth-century **choir**, you can see the **tombs** of the Savelli family (see p.128) bearing the family arms – two lions holding a rose.

A mule track behind the convent leads to the summit of Monte Sant'Angelo (560m), a stiff one-hour walk that requires proper boots. From the top you can see for miles across the Balagne and over the Désert des Agriates to the west coast of Cap Corse – on extremely clear days, it's possible to see the Alps. You can descend either by the same route, or by heading south to Sant'Antonino or east to Santa Reparata di Balagna.

Fanning out over the Colline de Monte Guido, 2km beyond the convent road and 2km inland from the coast road, **CORBARA** is a strange mixture – a quintessential Balagne town with a distinctly

Moorish appearance thanks to its bleached flat-roofed houses and narrow vaulted passageways. Capital of the Balagne before the Genoese took over and founded the citadel at Calvi, Corbara boasts the largest of the Balagne parish churches, the **Église de l'Annonciation**, a glitzy Baroque edifice built in 1685. Inside, the most overblown feature is the enormous swirling main altar flanked by two cloud-borne angels, which was constructed from Carrara marble brought over in the 1750s. The painted panels and carved furniture in the sacristy date from the fifteenth century and are relics of the church that occupied this site before the present structure. Two doors down from the church stands a grand house bearing the arms of the Franceschini family, who owned the village from the ninth to the nineteenth centuries. Known as the **Casa di Turchi**, it was built by Marthe ("Davia") Franceschini while she was married to the Sultan of Morocco (see box below).

Inland Haute-Balagne

Davia Franceschini: Queen of the Moors

Corbara's Casa di Turchi is associated with the extraordinary story of **Davia Franceschini**, a member of the local ruling family who, in the late eighteenth century, rose to become Queen of Morocco. According to the local version of events, Davia was the daughter of a poor charcoal-burner and his wife who decided to seek their fortune on the mainland. Shortly before leaving Corsica, the girl came across a destitute old woman, half-dead with cold and hunger, to whom she gave food. The beggar returned the kindness by giving her a talisman, "La Main de Fatma", which he said would bring luck on her journey. In the event, the voyage to Marseille turned into a disaster as a storm broke the mast of the boat and swept it south to the Moorish coast, where the passengers were promptly imprisoned. It was at this point that the talisman came to Davia's aid: struck by the beauty of both the object and its wearer, the jailer took the young Corsican woman to meet his sultan, who immediately recognized the pendant hanging around her neck. It had belonged to a long-lost sister who had run away years ago to escape an arranged marriage with an ugly old merchant, never to been seen or heard of again. The sultan was smitten with Davia and they were married soon after. Her family was allowed to return to Corbara, where they lived in a grand house on the square.

This epic, however, is more fairy story than historical truth. In fact, the real Davia did not come from, and never even visited, Corsica. Born Marthe Franceschini in Tunis, she was the daughter of a couple abducted from Corbara by pirates in 1754 – an all-too-common occurrence at the time. Mother and child were both freed, only to fall into the hands of pirates a second time, and ended up in the Marrakech slave market. Eventually, Marthe, or **Daouia Lalla** as she was later known, entered the Sultan of Morocco's harem and grew to become the ruler's favourite and most influential wife. After her death in the plague of Larache in 1799, her story was taken up and embellished by writers of exotic Oriental fiction, whence the more colourful Cinderella-syle yarn still spun by locals in Corbara's village bar.

More background on the pirate raids on Corsica appears on p.89.

Occupying a rocky pinnacle below the village, the craggy ruin of U
Forte was once seat of the Savelli clan, the former overlords of this
region. Founded in 1292 by Aldruvando, a vassal who had rebelled
against Count Arrigho Savelli, the castle was completed in 1375 by
Savelli's son, Mannone Savelli de Guido. When the castle was dis-
mantled by the Genoese in the early sixteenth century, following a
battle between the feudal lords and the republic, Savelli de Guido's
descendants restored the nearby **Castel de Guido**, a fort founded in
816 by Guido de Sabelli, who was made Count of the Balagne by the
pope after a victory against the Saracens. Here the Savellis ruled in
an uneasy coexistence with the Genoese for two hundred years.
Then, in 1798, this castle too was wrecked, on the orders of a political adversary of the Savelli family, one of whom was Paoli's chief
administrator for the new town of L'Île Rousse.

Santa Reparata di Balagna and Monticello

From Corbara you can head back inland by the D263, which climbs
up the side of the Regino valley for 3km before reaching **SANTA
REPARATA DI BALAGNA**, a terraced village of ancient crumbling
buildings and arcaded streets that give you spectacular glimpses of
the sea. The best viewpoint is the terrace of Santa Reparata, from
where L'Île Rousse occupies the foreground against a magnificent
crest of mountains. The church was built over a Pisan chapel and
retains the eleventh-century apse, though the façade dates from
1590.

*Details of
accommoda-
tion around
Monticello
appear in the
l'Île Rousse
listings on
p.117.*

Four kilometres higher up the D263 lies **MONTICELLO**, fief of
the great warlord Giudice della Rocca, whose thirteenth-century
Castel d'Ortica sits on a rocky hillock to the north of the village, surrounded by a belt of olive trees. In the centre of the village, the sole
sight is the imposing **Maison Malaspina**, formerly owned by descendants of Pascal Paoli's sister, and yet another house in which
Napoléon once spent a few days.

Catteri to Feliceto

To the south of Catteri the D71 swings through a region that's
received a lot of government money to attempt to reverse the
effects of the Balagne's recent dramatic depopulation. Smaller-
scale initiatives are in place too, as you'll see at **AVAPESSA**, whose
ancient watermill produces an olive oil that you can sample at
L'Alivu, a restaurant set up by a community of young people trying to revive the local economy. Gîtes have also been opened in the
vicinity – the mairie in the village square has full details (☎04 95
61 74 10).

The next village along the route is **MURO**, once a hive of artisans,
blacksmiths, silk weavers and carters. Nowadays it's part of the programme to revive old industries in the region, hence the two olive oil
mills straddling the river are working once again.

The village's three churches provide further evidence of the former prosperity of this once thriving community. An elegant bell tower and an imposing façade decorated wth statues distinguish the eighteenth-century **Église de l'Annonciation**, on the right as you enter the village. Inside, the usual profusion of marble surrounds a **Crucifix des Miracles**, which in 1730 allegedly started bleeding during Mass and now attracts a steady trickle of penitents and pilgrims. The church opposite, **Santa Croce**, is much older, dating from the fourteenth century, and even more ancient is nearby **San Giovanni**, a partly ruined eleventh-century church, one of the oldest in Corsica.

Glass and olive oil are the chief products at **FELICETO** (Filicetu), a village scattered over the banks of the River Regino, 2km east of Muro. The village is also famous for the purity of its water – a couple of sources 200m west of the village provide a refreshing halt along the way. The inevitable Baroque church is **Église St-Nicolas**, its crypt containing the lavish tombs of local bigwigs; the next-door **Chapelle St-Roch** has a beautiful seventeenth-century wooden statue of Roch, patron saint of shepherds and horsemen, in a chapel beside the altar. If you're in the mood for a brisk walk, the building known as the **Falconaghja** (Eagle's Nest) is an hour's climb along the footpath on the left as you leave the village heading north. A mayor of the village constructed this in the last century so he could keep an eye on his citizens with a telescope; later it became a hide-out for passing outlaws, hence the alternative name *Maison des Bandits*.

In the village centre you'll find one of the few **hotels** in these parts, the *Mare e Monti* (☎04 95 63 70 20, fax 04 95 63 02 01; May–Sept; ④), an enormous fifteenth-century building with a faded façade and plain stone-floored interior. Its rooms are of modest size and have good views over the valley, but the adjacent restaurant lacks character. A better place to **eat** is *U Mulinu* (☎04 95 61 73 23; June–Sept daily except Tues), a restored olive oil mill at the eastern end of the village. Thanks to its eccentric owner and fine Corsican cooking, this place is renowned throughout France and gets booked out weeks in advance during the summer, though it's worth phoning ahead to see if they have a table free. Set menus start at around 160F, which includes an aperitif, a choice of desserts and as much of the house wine as you can drink.

Speloncato and Belgodère

Named after the caves and cavities that riddle the rocky prominence on which it sits, **SPELONCATO**, 6km from Feliceto and 33km east of Calvi, is one of the most appealing Balagne villages. A tight cluster of terracotta-red roofs crouched in the shadow of the Monte Grosso massif, it's dominated by the ruins of an eleventh-century fortress, while the core of the place is the delightfully compact market square, **place de la Libération**. Opposite its café stands the massive **hotel** *Spelunca* (☎04 95 61 50 38, fax 04 95 61 53 14;

Speloncato marks the start of a twisting mountain road into the Tartagine Valley, covered on p.131.

> **The Speloncato "Eclipse"**
>
> The best known of Speloncato's many caves is the **Pietra Tafonata** (literally "pierced stone"), a barrel-shaped grotto 2km up the mountain from the village. Open at both ends, the eight-metre tunnel has for centuries been used by shepherds for shelter, and may have been enlarged by prehitoric hunters, whose remains archeologists have unearthed amid the detritus littering the cave floor. It is also responsible for an extraordinary "eclipse" that takes place here twice each year. At precisely 6pm on April 8 and September 8, the sun sets behind the ridge to the west of the village, only to reappear moments later as its rays shine through the Pietra Tafonta, briefly illuminating the square.

May–Sept; ③), former residence of Cardinal Savelli, an eighteenth-century papal minister whose corruption earned him the nickname *Il Cane Corso* (The Corsican Dog); its owner loves to brag about the many stars that have stayed here, among them Isabelle Adjani and Gerard Depardieu. The hotel doesn't have a restaurant, but you can **eat** well at the *Auberge de Domalto* (☎04 95 61 50 97), just below the village off the D71, which serves careful and imaginative cuisine in a stylish eighteenth-century house. Their set menu costs around 130F, and advance reservation is essential.

BELGODÈRE, fourteen winding kilometres northeast of Speloncato, lies at the junction of the main inland routes and provides a possible base for the beaches around L'Île Rousse (see p.118), 15km northwest. The main Calvi–Ponte Leccia train also stops here, though the distance between the station and the village is too great to be covered on foot, and there are no taxis on hand. You can **stay** at *Hôtel Niobel*, in the centre of the village (☎04 95 61 34 00, fax 04 95 61 35 85; May–Sept; ④), a modern but cosy hotel with a good **restaurant**, whose large windows offer breathtaking views of the Balagne coast. Local specialities here include lambs' liver and veal stew, and most credit cards are accepted.

There are a couple of churches in and around the village worth a look: **Église St-Thomas** dates from the sixteenth century and houses a magnificent painted panel of the Virgin and Child; the **Oratoire de la Madonuccia**, 500m from the square along the Speloncato road, harbours Corsica's oldest statue of the Madonna, placed here in 1387 to seal a reconciliation between Speloncato and the rival villages of San Columbano. Legend has it that the site was chosen because two bullocks who were transporting it between the opposing settlements stopped here and refused to move, which local people took to be a sign. Once you've checked the chapel out, you could walk up to **Château Malaspina**, a nineteenth-century fort, accessible by a stone stairway that starts nearby.

Quite a lively spot by Balagne standards, Belgodère hosts two **music festivals**: the Festival de Musique Classique de Lozari in April, and Rencontres Musicales Aostu in Musica in August.

The Giunssani

The Giunssani is a spectacularly isolated part of the Balagne, enclosed by Monte Grosso (1938m) and Monte Padro (2393m), the northernmost high peaks of Corsica's mountainous spine. Rising in the cirque of Monte Corona, just south of Monte Grosso, the **River Tartagine** flows through its heart, fed on its northern flank by tributaries whose ravines are overlooked by four high-altitude villages and a scattering of more remote hamlets. Swathed in deep-green chestnut and oak forest, these are exquisitely picturesque but see surprisingly few visitors considering their proximity to the coast; most people who come here do so only for a day to take advantage of the **hiking trails** that thread around the lush sides and floor of the valley.

There are two **approaches** to the region. The first is via the D63, which begins about 500m south of Speloncato, climbs up a high open route to the windswept Bocca di a Battaglia pass, and then plunges south, coming to a dead end in the base of the valley. The other route is along the D963, which branches off the N197 6km east of Belgodère, then drops down into the Tartagine valley from the Bocca Campana pass. If you're visiting the area as a day trip from the coast, you could travel in on one road and out on the other, completing a loop that strings together the main settlements.

Following this route in an anticlockwise direction, the first place you'll come to is **PIOGGIOLA**, a crown of yellow buildings nestled in a fold of hundred-year-old chestnut trees at an altitude of 1000m – which makes it one of the highest villages in Corsica. **Accommodation** is available in the ten-roomed *Auberge l'Aghjola*, situated on the right as you leave the village (☎04 95 61 90 48; obligatory half board; ⑤). It's somewhat overpriced, but the owners have managed to preserve some of the building's original rustic feel and the food in their **restaurant** downstairs (open to non-residents by reservation) is excellent, with local game and other mountain specialities providing the staple fare. A much less expensive place to stay is *A Pasturellu*, a little further down the hill on the right (☎04 95 61 91 45; ③). Popular with hikers, the rooms are simple, with small en-suite showers and toilets on the corridor, but the elderly *patronne* is very friendly; this is also one of the few places in the Balagne that offers single occupancy rates (①).

Beyond Pioggiola the road divides, one branch of the D963 descending to the region's principal village, **OLMI-CAPELLA**, a cluster of sharp red roofs and mellow stone overlooking the Tartagine. In past centuries, many of the inhabitants of this village used to make their living as itnerant traders, selling top-quality Giunssani olive oil and leather shoes throughout the island; apparently their customers regarded them as *unti e fini* (unctuous and fine) – as much, presumably, for their slippery salesmen tactics and slick attire as their good manners and greasy mule packs. There's nowhere to stay here, but you can **eat** definitive Giunssani cooking

Walks in the Giunssani

Cut off by two of the highest motorable passes on the island, the Giunssani is a walker's and mountain biker's paradise, with an extensive network of well-marked and well-maintained trails leading through hectares of pristine pine, chestnut and oak forest. The Parc Naturel Régional has produced a leaflet entitled *Giunssani: Oasis de Verdure*, detailing the routes on a monochrome section of the area IGN map, which you should pick up at a tourist office before attempting any of the trails outlined below.

Eight different **round walks** are featured in the leaflet, marked every 10m or so with splashes of orange paint. For a day hike, try the five-hour route from Olmi-Capella to Vallica, which takes in a water mill, a Genoese bridge and bathing spots along the Tartagine River; or the five-hour loop from Pioggiola to Forcili and back, which skirts the cirque below Monte Tolu before dropping down to the Bocca di a Scoperta pass above Mausoleo. This latter hike can be extended by an hour to take in the San Parteo peak (1680m); an unmarked mountain path scales the east flank of the cirque and follows the ridge to the summit, from where you follow the spine of another ridge west to rejoin the waymarked trail to Mausoleo. The maison forestière marks the start of another great five-hour loop that hugs the true right bank of the Tartagine then climbs up to Mausoleo, before winding up the awsome Melaja valley. After crossing the stream, you follow the path down until it meets the D963, which you keep to for the remaining 45 minutes back to the maison forestière.

In addition to these relatively easy *sentiers du pays*, Giunssani offers several more challenging hiking trails that give access to the high ridges and peaks surrounding the basin. Affording superb panoramic views of the Balagne, the most popular of these is the six-hour climb up the Tartagine valley to the **Refuge d'Ortu di Piobbu**, springboard for the ascents of Monte Corona and Capu a u Dente, and an important étape on the GR20 (see p.120), for which you'll need to carry all-weather gear, a sleeping bag, and a day's food and water. To pick up the equally demanding trails to **Col de la Tartagine** (1852m), 15km southwest, and **Col de L'Ondella** (1845m), 10km south, follow the waymarks from the maison forestière along the south side of the river until you reach signposts indicating the way. The routes to both these passes are ancient transhumance arteries used by shepherds and traders to reach the pastures of the west coast and upper Asco valley. They're fairly straightforward, though you definitely need to take IGN **topo-map** 25-4149, as well as adequate clothing and supplies.

at the *Auberge La Tornadia*, 2km east of the village in the direction of Pioggiola (☎04 95 61 90 83; April–Oct), frequented as much by locals as visitors. Specialities include roast suckling lamb, fresh pasta made with chestnut flour and, during the autumn, wild forest mushroom sauces; their home-baked biscuits and cakes are great too. Expect to pay 120–160F per person.

Carry on 3km further east and you'll come to **VALLICA**, a sleepy place swamped in greenery and overshadowed by Monte Padro on the other side of the valley. There's little of note in the village other than the nineteenth-century church, a new helipad, a supermarket, bakery, and the tiny **museum** in the mairie (June–Sept Mon–Sat 10am–noon & 2–5pm), which exhibits traditional farm implements and various ancient tools uncovered in the region. Apart from the spectacular views, the best reason to pause here is the excellent *U Piattu Spartu* **restaurant** (☎04 95 61 92 76), tucked away behind the church in a tranquil old house. The mustachioed proprietor-chef prepares a different menu each day, mostly with ingredients straight from the garden or surrounding forest; his single set menu costs 120F, excluding wine – good value considering the superb location and quality of cuisine.

The other branch of the D963 from Pioggiola descends to a junction for the ancient village of **MAUSOLEO**, the last of the Tartagine quartet, which boasts a fifteenth-century church containing an olive-wood statue of John the Baptist. Past the Mausoleo turning, the D963 twists through the spectacular gorges of the River Melaja to the banks of the Tartagine, terminating at the maison forestière and the **Fôret de la Tartagine-Melaja**. For a brief taste of the forest, you can follow various short marked paths from here; the principal major hikes are detailed in the box opposite.

South of Calvi

From Calvi, two routes run south down to **Galéria**, a tiny fishing settlement and summer resort situated about 25km down the coast. If speed is your main concern, the inland D251/D51 is the better option, a well-maintained road that cuts through the **Balagne Déserte**, a region of deep-red rocks and shiny green maquis. This is one of the most sparsely populated corners of the island, largely due to the ravages of Muslim pirates in the fourteenth and fifteenth centuries, who burned some ninety villages to the ground and carried off their inhabitants as slaves to ports of North Africa; later, a succession of plagues took their toll, while fierce fighting with the Genoese during Paoli's war of independence ensured the area's terminal decline by wiping out virtually all of its few remaining menfolk.

The D51 separates from the D251 about 10km out of Calvi at **Suare**, from where the latter road continues to the **Cirque de Bonifato**, a luscious forest of Laricio pines and evergreen oaks bordering some of the highest mountains in Corsica. The alternative route to Galéria is the D81, a hair-raising corniche bordered by gigantic boulders that looks down on a rock-strewn deep-purple sea. This road rejoins the D51 at the Cinque Arcate bridge, where a right turn brings you to Galéria and a left leads to the **Vallée du Fango**, one of the least-traversed areas of Corsica, worth visiting for its dramatic combination of deep-green forests and barren ground scattered with great orange rocks. To the southwest of Galéria stretches a peninsula whose tip is protected as the **Réserve Naturel de**

South of
Calvi

Scandola, a wildlife-rich seascape that can be viewed only by boat (for details of trips, see p.138).

Public transport along this route is limited to Autocars Beaux Voyages's mini-bus from Calvi to Galéria (July–Sept 15 Mon–Sat; ☎04 95 65 11 35), and Autocars SAIB's service between Calvi and Porto (May 15–Oct 10 Mon–Sat daily in Aug; ☎04 95 22 41 99). Cycles and scooters can also be rented from Calvi (see p.109) and Porto (see p.141), though these are more expensive than those available in Ajaccio. If you have the time, however, the best way to explore this beautiful stretch of coast is on foot, via the Tra Mare e Monti long-distance **footpath**, which runs from Calenzana, just south of Calvi, to Galéria, Porto and across the hills to Cargèse. For a fuller description of the trail, see p.122.

Cirque de Bonifato

An immense basin of forested land encircled by a ring of orange crags, the **Cirque de Bonifato** is a 20km drive along the D251 southeast of Calvi, plus a further 8km on foot. The adjacent forests of Calenzana and Bonifato are magnificent hiking terrain, and the best place to start exploring them is the maison forestière, a foresters' hut located in the heart of the woodland where the road ends. If you just want to take a look around, leave the car in the nearby car park and retrace your approach as far as the **Chaos de Bocca Rezza**, a viewing point on the north side of the road, less than 1km away. From here you can see across the forest as far as the immense granite pinnacles enclosing the cirque to the east. If you're going to tackle anything more ambitious, you'll probably want to check into the large *Auberge de la Forêt*, by the car park (☎04 95 22 09 98; April–Oct; ③, optional half board ④); catering mainly for hikers and backpackers, it also offers dorm beds in more basic gîte accommodation (①, optional half board ②). You can also camp or bivouac here for 30F, which includes hot showers.

The most obvious walk is the one up to **Spasimata** (1190m), a row of disused dry stone huts in the core of the cirque, marking the spot where shepherds once rested on their journey down to Calenzana. It's a relatively easy-going five-hour hike from the auberge, initially following the forest trail that skirts the nearby waterfall and then tracks the River Figarella, which courses through great hollowed-out slabs of pink granite. After thirty minutes you'll come to the confluence of the rivers Melaja and Figarella, from where a path marked with red and white paint ascends to Spasimata, a route that crosses several streams and intersects with the GR20 mountain trail at the top. Here you'll find the *Refuge du Carozzu*, the only refuge in the vicinity.

*For more on
the GR20, see
p.120.*

Galéria

Isolated at the edge of a scalded landscape of deep-red rocks and straggly eucalyptus trees, **GALÉRIA** is believed to have been first settled by the Phoenicians in the sixth century BC, possibly even before the rise of Aléria on the east coast (see p.264). Numerous Roman artefacts found in the vicinity – including fragments of a Roman anchor discovered by divers here during summer of 1992 – have also helped archeologists identify this as the site of ancient Kalaris, named on Ptolemy's map of the Mediterranean and a key port in classical times. Later, the anopheles mosquito ruled supreme, ensuring that the village remained malaria-ridden until the advent of DDT in the 1930s. More recently, Galéria has turned its relatively remote location to profit, becoming a popular summer resort and sailing centre. Its handful of hotels and restaurants back onto a jetty and surround a small semicircle of sand spreading from the foot of a Genoese tower, while 500m north out of the village lies Plage de Riciniccia, a vast red-shingled cove that's been adopted by nudists.

South of Calvi

Practicalities

Galéria's **tourist office** is at Maison a Torra, a hut located 4km away from the village, at the junction of the D81 and D351 by the Cinque Arcate bridge (June–Sept daily 9am–noon & 2–6pm; ☎04 95 62 02

The Galéria to Girolata Hike

The hike from **Galéria to Girolata**, a tiny fishing village at the east edge of the Scandola reserve that can only be reached on foot or by boat (see p.138), is the fourth and most spellbinding stage of the ten-day Mare e Monti trail. Winding from sea level up the Tavulaghu ravine and over the Capu Licchia ridge (700m) to the Gulf of Porto, the route takes in some of the wildest scenery on the west coast, including the red volcanic crags of Scandola and the sugar-loaf Capu Rossu cliffs, 6km south across a deep-blue bay. You can do this hike at any time of year, though spring and autumn are best; if you attempt it in high summer, set off early in the morning, as much of the path is exposed.

The trail, waymarked with orange splashes of paint, is signposted from Galéria's gîte, from where you turn left, cross a small bridge and, 200m later, turn left again along the path that veers south through the maquis. After passing a small reservoir, the footpath climbs the Tavulaghu, crossing from one side of the stream bed to the other as it makes for the head of the valley. The going gets tougher towards the top, with the trail zigzagging through dense vegetation and evergreen oak forest to the ridge, reached after three hours. From here the views are breathtaking as you follow the rocky spine due west, ascending to a maximum height of 784m before dropping down to the **Bocca di Fuata pass** (4hr 40min). A easy trail strikes downhill from the col to a fork, where you bear right and wind along the base of the Cavone ravine to Girolata village, visible below. For details of **accommodation** in Girolata, see p.139.

Return by the same route (6hr 20min) or else follow the Mare e Monti trail for another hour and a quarter until it reaches the D81 at **Col de la Croix**, from where you can hitch back to Galéria. **Buses** also stop here at 9am en route between Porto and Calvi (April 15–Oct 10 Mon–Sat, daily in Aug; Autocars SAIB ☎04 95 26 13 70).

27). The office carries useful information for hikers, including a list of mountain gîtes d'étapes, and sells route leaflets and topo-maps of the area. A **bus** stops at this junction twice daily: at 10.20am coming from Porto and 3.50pm from Calvi.

The village has plenty of places to **stay**, ranging from dormitory accommodation for walkers to swish self-catering chalets. There are also couple of small hotels 1km east of the village in the lower Fango valley (see below), and a well-equipped **campsite**, *Les Deux Torrents* (☎04 95 62 00 67; June–Sept), 5km north on the Calvi road. Most of the mid-range places offer optional half board and have adequate **restaurants**, but the most popular place to eat is the *Loup de Mer*, on the beach, which specializes in lobster and other locally caught seafood. It's prices are reasonable, with set menus starting at 70F, and they serve a range of crêpes and pizzas, indoors or on a breezy rear terrace that overlooks the bay. Alternatively, try the unpretentious *Auberge* restaurant up in the village, whose menus are less imaginative but better value for money; this is also a good place to splash out on lobster and crayfish (order a day in advance).

Auberge Galéris, just behind the *Filosorma* (☎04 95 62 02 89). Half a dozen modest rooms with terraces in a modern concrete house, tucked away off the road. Breakfast available on request. Good value and friendly. April–Oct. ③.

E Cinque Arcate, 4km east at the Cinque Arcate crossroads (☎04 95 62 02 54). Run-of-the-mill mid-range hotel that's handy if you're travelling by bus (it's next to the bus stop), but otherwise inconveniently far from the village. May–Sept. ③.

Filosorma, on the beach road in the centre of the lower village (☎04 95 62 03 45). Galéria's poshest hotel has comfortable sea-facing rooms, all with showers and toilets en-suite. ④.

Gîte d'Étape, 2km out of the village on the Mare e Monti trail (☎04 95 62 00 46). A well-equipped gîte with 30 dorm beds and hot showers. Self-catering facilities are available, or you can opt for half board (②). ①.

L'Incantu, route de Calca (☎04 95 62 03 66). An unobtrusive complex of spacious studios and chalets with mezzanine floors, kitchenettes and sea-view terraces. Excellent value, particularly during the week. A good option for divers and watersports enthusiasts. ③.

La Martinella, behind the beach, near the *Loup de Mer* (☎04 95 62 00 44). Five immaculate rooms, some for up four persons, opening onto a small garden with tables and views of the bay. Good off-season discounts. ③.

Stella Marina, opposite the *Loup de Mer* (☎04 94 62 00 03). A dozen large, light rooms in a block behind a restaurant. The top-floor rooms have the best views. ③.

Vallée du Fango

The road into the **Vallée du Fango** follows the Fango River for 15km as far as the base of the Paglia Orba mountain. A forest of pines, chestnuts, beeches and eucalyptus carpets the valley slopes, providing excellent picnic spots and walking possibilities. A couple of villages scattered over the slopes of the valley do little to disperse the desolate feel of the place, and few people venture up the mountain unless it's for trout fishing or hunting, for which the area is renowned.

About 1km from the Cinque Arcate bridge, the D81 along the river becomes the D351 for 13km as far as Barghiana. At this wild junction there are two **hotels**, the *Fango* (☎04 95 62 01 92; ③) and *A Farera* (☎04 95 62 01 87; ③), the only places to stay in the valley, also useful if Galéria is overcrowded. Of the pair, the former is the larger and more welcoming, with a bar and restaurant. The shark's fin of Paglia Orba, visible for most of the onward drive, can be seen to especially good effect 6km along the road from the junction at **Tuarelli**, where a short walk down a track to the left of the road leads to a bridge over the Fango.

Keep heading along the main road and you'll soon come to the turning for the village of **MANSO**, which spreads out over the mountainside. A terrace at the entrance to the village affords a glorious view over the valley: a low screen of olive trees strung across the base of Paglia Orba and Capo Tafonato looming up to the southeast. After Manso the D351 road deteriorates as it comes to an end amidst the chestnut trees at the hamlet of **Barghiana**. A 2km walk up to the **Pont de la Rocce**, a bridge over a tributary of the Fango River, leads off to the right, from which point there's a breathtaking panorama of Capo Rosso and Capo Tafonato, belonging to the Cinto massif (see chapter 6).

Réserve Naturel de Scandola

The 700-square-kilometre **Réserve Naturel de Scandola** (Scandula) takes its name from the wooden tiles (*scandule*) that cover many of the island's mountain houses, but the area's roof-like rock formations are only part of its amazing geological repertoire. The stacked slabs, towering pinnacles and gnarled claw-like outcrops were formed by volcanic eruptions 250 million years ago, and subsequent erosion has fashioned shadowy caves, grottoes and gashes in the rock. Scandola's colours are as remarkable as its shapes, the hues varying from the charcoal grey of granite to the incandescent reds and rusty purples of porphyry, striking a vivid contrast with the deep greens of the maquis and the cobalt-blue sea.

The headland and its surrounding water were declared a nature reserve in 1975, so **wildlife** is as varied here as anywhere in Corsica. Dolphins and seals thrive in the area, which also supports more than 450 types of seaweed and other subaquatic plants – including a rare type of photosynthesizing grass that grows at a depth of 35m due to the exceptional clarity of the water here – as well as some remarkable fish, such as the grouper, a species more commonly found in the Caribbean. Colonies of giant gulls and cormorants inhabit the cliffs, and you might see the odd **peregrine falcon** preying on the **blue rock thrushes** that nest on the bare rock ledges. Ospreys, extremely rare in the Mediterranean, are also found here, their huge nests of twigs crowning the pinnacles; there used to be only seven pairs, but careful conservation has increased the number to 24. Rare plants native to Corsica grow freely, such as the sea daffodil (*Pancratium maritimus*) and the *Senecio cineraria*, with its distinctive furry silver leaves.

Unfortunately for flora-spotters, however, the entire reserve is off limits to hikers, and can be viewed only from the sea, which for tourists means taking one of the daily **boat trips** from Calvi and Porto. These leave from Calvi at 9.15am and 2pm, and from Porto at 9.30am and 2.30pm (April–Oct), the first two stopping for two hours at Girolata (see below) and returning in the late afternoon. The later boat from Porto only stops for 45 minutes. It's a fascinating journey, well worth the 250F, but it's a good idea to take a picnic, as the restaurants at Girolata are extremely pricy.

Starting the round trip from Calvi, the first port of call is the **Baie d'Elbu**, last refuge in Corsica of Europe's largest bat. Two kilometres south of here lies the **Punta Palazzu**, so called because of the soaring rocky towers that spring from the sea like a giant palace. Over the course of the last thousand years or so the seaweed here has formed a thick white band around the base of the cliffs just above the surface of the water – a rare phenomenon that provides invaluable information about the changing sea level.

Beyond this point the boat weaves through the narrow straits by Île de Gargalo, an islet created from volcanic lava where the most westerly point on Corsica is marked by a lighthouse. Excursion boats from Calvi and Porto stop for two hours (the later boat from Porto stops for 45min at Girolata before turning round.

Girolata

Connected by a mere mule track to the rest of the island, and dwarfed by the plunging maquis-shrouded slopes, the tiny fishing haven of **GIROLATA** has a dreamlike quality that's highlighted by the vivid red of the surrounding rocks. For hundreds of years its few inhabitants lived a reclusive life, surviving on fishing and hardly communicating with the rest of the island. In 1530 the notorious corsair Dragut was taken prisoner at Girolata by the Genoese general Andrea Doria, who captured nine galleys. Dragut paid the men and returned eleven years later to get his revenge by razing Girolata to the ground. A short stretch of stony beach and a few houses are overlooked by a stately **watchtower**, built later in the seventeenth century in the form of a small castle by the Genoese, and set high on the hills above the beach.

Nowadays, the hamlet has just fifteen year-round inhabitants, who make most of their money from a couple of expensive restaurants and bars that cash in on the daily boat trips. Though obliged to travel across the bay by boat to Porto to do their shopping, they nevertheless enjoy the luxury of hand-delivered mail: each day, a **postman** hikes here and back from the nearest roadhead at the Col de la Croix, distinguished from amateur ramblers by his thick white beard, Lacoste sweatband and zealous pace.

There are no hotels in Girolata, but you can stay at either of two **gîtes** that cater for the steady flow of hikers through here in the summer. Located on the beach, *La Cabane du Berger* (☎04 95 20 15 55; ① dorm bed, ② cabin or half board) offers a choice of accommodation in a dorm, a small cabin in the garden behind (these accommodate two people), or half board in their quirky woodcarved bar; you can also camp here. The other gîte is *Le Cormorant*, amongst the houses at the north end of the cove (☎04 95 20 15 15), which has eighteen dorm spaces and a small restaurant overlooking the boat jetty.

The Golfe de Porto

The coast of the **Golfe de Porto** is one of Corsica's classic landscapes, famed for the corroded beauty of its crimson granite cliffs. Tucked into a niche in the furthest indent of this gulf, the resort of **Porto** presents a scene that is emblematic of the island's finest qualities: on the flank of the village an imposing tower overlooks a stark crescent of shingle beach, while in the background a band of eucalyptus shimmers against thunderous granite crags. North of Porto, a cliff road zigzags up to the **Col de la Croix** (Bocca à Croce), offering breathtaking glimpses of the gulf round every corner, as well as access to a string of secluded coves. Highlight of the southern gulf are the **Calanche**, 12km of dizzying pinnacles and ravines, ideally explored from a boat or on foot. A couple of fantastically located hotels overlooking the Calanche make the village of **Piana** a tempting alternative to Porto as a base, and two outstanding **beaches** – Anse de Ficajola and Plage d'Arone – lie close at hand.

A **bus** serves the coastal route from Calvi to Porto (April–Oct 1 daily), and the bus from Ajaccio to Porto takes in the Calanche, but for visiting the above beaches you really need your own transport.

Porto

The overwhelming proximity of the mountains, combined with the pervasive eucalyptus and spicy scent of the maquis, give **PORTO** a uniquely intense, loaded atmosphere that makes it one of the most interesting places to stay on the west coast. Except for a watchtower built here by the Genoese in the second half of the sixteenth century, the site was only built upon with the onset of tourism in the 1950s. The location, hemmed in by steep mountain slopes, precludes

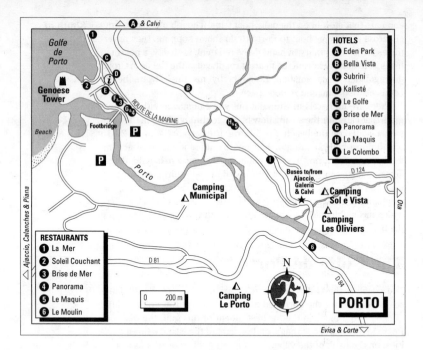

overdevelopment, as hotels can spread only a little way up the road and along the short quay. At the same time Porto is so small that it can become claustrophobic in July and August, when overcrowding – thanks to predominantly German tourists – is no joke. Off season, the place becomes eerily deserted, so you'd do well to choose your time carefully – the best months are May, June and September.

An avenue bordered by eucalyptus, **route de la Marine** links the two parts of the resort. A strip of shops and hotels 1km from the sea makes up the actual village of Porto, but the main focus of activity is the small **marina**, located at the avenue's end. In the nineteenth century Porto was used for exporting Laricio pines from the inland forests, and the route de la Marine was built to accommodate the great carts that used to haul the timber down from the mountains. Clustered around the great red rock that supports the tower, a nucleus of hotels and restaurants vie for the best view of the tower, while the rest of the buildings are crammed into what little space remains.

It's about a fifteen-minute walk from the marina up to the recently restored **Genoese Tower**, a square, chimney-shaped structure that was cracked by an explosion in the seventeenth century, when the tower was used as an arsenal. An awe-inspiring view of the crashing sea and maquis-shrouded mountains make it worth the short climb.

The **beach** consists of a pebbly cove south of the shoulder of the massive rock supporting the tower. To reach it from the marina, follow the little road that skirts the rock, cross the wooden bridge over the River Porto on your left, then walk through the car park under the trees. Although it's rather exposed and the sea is very deep, the great crags overshadowing the shore give the place a vivid edge, and there's some great snorkelling to be had from the rocks to the south of the cove.

Arrival and information

Autocars SAIB's **minibus** from Calvi (April 15–Oct 10 Mon–Sat, Aug daily; ☎04 95 22 41 99) stops a little way north of the village, but leaves for the return journey from the marina. Coaches to and from Ajaccio, also operated by Autocars SAIB, run all year round (Aug to mid-Sept Mon–Sat 2 daily, Sun 1 daily; rest of year Mon–Sat only), stopping at the marina and the roadside further up the avenue opposite *Timy* supermarket; note that the afternoon departure to Ajaccio leaves two hours earlier (ie at noon) on Saturdays. Tickets can be bought on the bus. During July and August, an additional service runs to Corte with M. Mordiconi (☎04 95 48 00 04), costing a stiff 100F one way.

The well-organized **tourist office** is down in the square near the marina (June–Sept Mon–Sat 9am–noon & 2.30–6pm; ☎04 95 26 10 55), and is useful primarily for finding accommodation; they also hand out brochures detailing walks and hikes in the area, and sell topo-maps of the mountain area inland. If you're planning to attempt a long-distance hike, it's worth dropping into the information office of the Parc Naturel Régional close by (same opening hours), which also sells maps and displays the latest weather forecasts. **Changing money** in Porto can be a problem, largely due to the absence of a year-round bank or even a cash dispenser. During July and August, a temporary branch of the Crédit Agricole opens on route de la Marine, but they charge a stiff commission. The only alternative is the small bureau de change nearby (daily June–Sept 9am–noon & 2–5.30pm), whose rates are even worse; the best ploy is to bring plenty of cash with you.

Tickets for the **boat excursions** to Scandola and the Calanche (depart 9.30am & 2.30pm) are available in advance direct from the operator at their office in the marina. For information on **diving** in the Porto area, contact the École de Plongée Sous-Marine "Genération Blue" next to the footbridge in the marina (☎04 95 26 24 28), which runs courses for beginners and will take out more experienced divers with their own equipment for 180F; you can also fill your gas bottles here. Mountain **bikes** and scooters – ideal for exploring the winding coast road and nearby gorges – are available for rent at the café opposite *Timy* supermarket, though they charge well over the odds (90F per day for a mountain bike; 320F for an 80cc step-through).

The Golfe de Porto

Accommodation

Competition between **hotels** is more cutthroat in Porto than any other resort on the island. During slack periods towards the end of the season, most places engage in a full-on price war, pasting up cheaper tariffs than their neighbours to entice the straggling tourists – all of which is great for punters. In late July and August, however, the normal sky-high rates prevail. At this time, queues for the three main **campsites** often trail along the main road, forcing many visitors further north along the gulf, where a string of quieter villages and beaches – notably Bussaglia and Partinellu – harbour a handful of smaller hotels and campsites. All the places listed below are marked on our map of Porto; the rates quoted apply to peak season.

For details of accommodation around Porto, see "The northern gulf" (p.143), Ota, (p.149) and Evisa (p.150).

Hotels

Bella Vista, above the village on the Calvi road, just past *Le Maquis* (☎04 95 26 11 08, fax 04 95 26 15 18). Pleasant, well-furnished rooms in an old pink-granite building with outstanding views of the mountains and sea. Also fully equipped studios, and a good restaurant. Obligatory half board in Aug. April to mid-Oct. ③.

Brise de Mer, on left of route de la Marine as you approach tower from the village, opposite the telephone booths (☎04 95 26 10 28, fax 04 95 26 13 02). A large old-fashioned place with very friendly service and a congenial terrace restaurant. The rear-side rooms have the best views. April to mid-Oct. ③.

Colombo, at the top of the village opposite the turning for Ota (☎04 95 26 10 14). A sixteen-room hotel overlooking the valley. Generous off-season discounts, and a good fall-back if *Le Maquis*, next door, is full. May–Sept. ②.

Eden Park, 4km north of Porto on the Calvi road (☎04 95 26 10 60). Porto's most luxurious hotel is set in its own grounds above Busaglia beach, with a palm-lined pool, piano bar and swish restaurant. April–Oct. ④.

Le Golfe, at the base of the rock in the marina (☎04 95 26 13 33). Small and cosy; every room has a balcony with a sea view. The small restaurant on the ground floor serves good breakfasts, omelettes, steaks and snacks. May–Oct. ③.

Kallisté, in the marina (☎04 95 26 10 30). Despite its ugly exterior, this three-star is the most comfortable hotel in the village centre, with spacious rooms and a relaxing bar. April–Oct. ④.

Le Maquis, at the top of the village just beyond the Ota turning (☎04 95 26 12 19). By far the best low-budget deal in the area: simple rooms, frayed around the edges, but comfortable enough, and at rock-bottom rates. Some en-suite shower-toilets 100F. Advance booking recommended. ①–②.

Panorama, route de la Marine (☎04 95 26 11 05). The most pleasant option in this row of hotels backing the marina, offering competitive rates and sea views from most rooms; their terrace restaurant is a great venue for breakfast. April–Oct. ③.

Subrini, opposite the tower (☎04 95 26 14 94). A very comfortable three-star slap in the centre of things, but with peaceful, air-conditioned rooms. Ideally placed for the sunsets behind Scandola. May–Oct. ④.

Campsites

Camping Municipal, behind the beach (☎04 95 26 17 76). The one to avoid unless you're counting every franc: stony ground and grubby washrooms.

Camping Sole e Vista, at the main road junction near the supermarkets (☎04 95 26 15 71). A superb location on shady terraces ascending a steep hillside with a small café at the top. Great views of Capo d'Orto cliffs opposite, and immaculate toilet blocks.

Funtana al'Oro, 2km up the Evisa road (☎04 95 26 15 48). Too far from the village if you're travelling without your own vehicle, but a shady, well-managed site close to some quiet bathing spots in the river.

Le Porto, on the right as you approach Porto from Piana (☎04 95 26 13 67). Further out of the village than the other sites, but smaller, and with plenty of shade.

Eating and drinking

The overall standard of **restaurants** in Porto is pitiably poor, with overpriced food and indifferent service the norm, particularly during high season. There are, however, a handful of exceptions, notably *La Mer*, which serves some of the most succulent (and expensive) seafood in Corsica. If you're here during the summer and fancy eating somewhere less hectic than the busy pizzerias in the marina, head for *Chez Félix*, 4km up the road at Ota.

Brise de Mer, see hotel, above. Hearty local specialities such as roast lamb in maquis herbs. Inexpensive.

Le Maquis, see hotel, above. Honest, affordable home cooking in a warm bar or on a tiny terrace that hangs over the valley. Friendly service.

La Mer, opposite the tower. *The* place to splash out on fine seafood cuisine. Far from cheap, but their fish is fresh from the gulf and imaginatively prepared, and the location ideal. Set menus from 120F.

Le Moulin, just beyond the village at the junction of the Calvi and Evisa roads. Excellent French food and some tasty regional dishes such as *sanglier en daube*, a rich wild boar stew. Moderate.

Panorama, see hotel, above. Recommended for its fine views and authentic Corsican specialities such as pigeon in eau de vie, and lasagne with wild mushrooms (in season). Set menus 80–100F.

Soleil Couchant, at the foot of the tower. Don't be put off by the green umbrellas, fake foliage and disco lights; this place serves excellent pizzas and there's often a queue. Expensive.

The northern gulf

The D81 north of Porto, a 30km sequence of hairpin bends around the base of **Monte Manganello**, provides breathtaking views across the gulf to the glowing Calanche plus the opportunity to swim or dive at a sprinkling of tiny coves along the way. Autocars SAIB's Calvi bus travels this route daily, but hitching is fairly reliable in season, with droves of visitors driving from Porto to the two viewpoints at **Bocca â Croce** (272m) and **Bocca Palmarella** (374m). You could also cycle up to these passes, or ride by scooter; mountain- and motor-bikes are available for rent from the café opposite *Timy* supermarket in Porto.

About 5km into the route, an abrupt left turn leads to **Plage de Bussaglia** (Bussaghia), the longest strand on this side of the gulf and the first you can get to by car. A sheltered swath of grey pebbles hemmed in by scrubby headlands, it's flanked by a pair of seasonal pizzerias – the one of the left as you face the sea is among the best places in the region for seafood and pasta, popular with locals and visitors alike. You can also **stay** here, at the pleasant and reasonably priced *Hôtel L'Aiglon* (☎04 95 26 10 65, fax 04 95 26 14 77; May–Sept; ③), a large building of local stone with a relaxing terrace, restaurant and comfortable rooms that overlook the valley, or at the more upmarket *Stella Marina* (☎04 95 26 11 18, fax 04 95 26 12 74; May–Sept; ④), further down the road towards the beach, which boasts a small pool. For **campers**, there's the self-contained but rather exposed *Camping Bussaglia* (☎04 95 26 15 72), complete with supermarket and pricy snack bar.

Beyond the turning for Bussaglia beach, the corniche road crosses a dry stream bed and snakes up the folds of the scrub-covered hillside to sleepy **PARTINELLO**, set high above the shore under a carpet of green woodland and maquis. A quiet and friendly place to **stay** here is *Aria Marina* (☎04 95 27 30 33; ②), below the café-bar in the village centre, where half a dozen immaculate, inexpensive rooms (with showers and shared toilets) overlook the vegetable garden to the sea. There are also a couple of interconnecting family suites on the lower floor that are great value if you're travelling in a group of four or more. On the south side of the village, *Le Clos des Ribes* (☎04 95 27 30 36; 4000–5000F per week) is a posher option whose luxurious studios have kitchenettes and verandahs; these are normally rented on a weekly basis, but you may be able to fix a rate for a night or two out of season – ask at the newspaper and postcard shop on the west side of the main road.

A left turn along the D324 from Partinello takes you down a broad valley to the popular **Plage de Caspio**, a steeply shelving mix of pebble and sand backed by a bar. The sun disappears behind the cliff in the afternoon during the summer, so arrive early if you want to catch some rays.

A more enticing cove along this stretch is shingly **Plage de Gratelle**, just north of Caspio, accessible via a narrow signposted road at a point where the road widens about 10km on from Partinello. The deep translucent sea and superb views of the Calanche and Capo d'Orto make this one of the most attractive beaches in the area, though it's far from a well-kept secret and gets crowded in summer with campers from the site behind it.

A short distance beyond the Gratelle turning, the **Bocca â Croce**, or Col de la Croix, has a strategically placed drinks hut from which to relish the view westwards towards Scandola and southwards to the chaos of the Calanche. It also marks the start of the footpath to Girolata (1hr 15min), via Cala di Tuara (see box below). **Col de Parmarella**, a further 10km north, gives more glorious vistas across the Scandola headland and distant hills, and is a popular target for cyclists.

The southern gulf

South of Porto, the sinuous D81 winds gently through the Piana pine forest before entering the spectacularly eroded terrain of the

---

A Round Hike from Bocca â Croce

Bocca â Croce is a key landmark on the Mare e Monti trail from Calenzana to Cargèse (see p.122), a section of which makes a superb six-hour round hike that you can attempt at any time of year. Incorporating a couple of lengthy climbs, it's a strenuous walk, but the scenery is wonderful all the way, with ever-changing panoramic views of the gulf and its mountainous hinterland. Water is in short supply along the route, so carry plenty with you; we also recommend you take along the IGN **topo-map** of the area, or the Parc Naturel Régional de Corse's topo-guide *Corse – Entre Mer et Montagne*, both available at shops and the tourist office in Porto.

From the car park at the pass, head down the signposted path to Girolata, which after around forty minutes ends at a grubby, flotsam-covered cove known as **Cala di Tuara** (30min). Two marked routes continue on from here: a gentle sea-level track around the Punta di Tuara headland, or a more strenuous trail that winds through dense maquis to a pass from where you can spy Girolata far below. Take the latter route, which starts at a gap in the bushes a little way up the Tuara stream bed (it's marked with faded orange or white splashes). Once at the ridge (1hr), follow the right fork further up the hill and keep heading northeast until you reach the **D81** (2hr 15min), where you should turn right. After 300m, a track on the left strikes east up the ridge to **Punta di u Muntitoghju** (640m; 3hr), bending gradually southwards as it skirts the west face of Punta di u Tartavellu (825m) en route to the Bocca Ascenso pass. A short ascent from here, with the crags of Punta Salisei to your left, is followed by a drop down to the **Salisei spring** (4hr), where you can refill your bottles for the steady descent southwest along the Salisei ridge to **Capu di Curzu** (852m; 4hr 50min). The path continues to give ground as it approaches a final pass, marked with an orientation table. Either head due south from here down a series of steep switchbacks to rejoin the main road at the village of **Curzu** (5hr 50min), where there's a gîte d'étape (see p.122), or else continue along the right fork from the pass and follow the north face of the ridge past Capu di Linu (622m) and back down to Bocca â Croce, which you should reach after around six hours.

From mid-April until mid-October, it is possible to pick up Autocars SAIB's **bus** back to Porto at 5.15pm from Bocca â Croce, or from Curzo at 5.30pm (Aug daily, Sept–July Mon–Sat only). Check the times before you set off, as they tend to change slightly from year to year.

Calanche. The village of **Piana** itself, 12km along the route, has this area's main concentration of cafés, restaurants and hotels, and lies within easy reach of several rewarding day hikes, among them the ascent of **Capo d'Orto**, the mountain whose sheer northern crags tower above Porto, draped in vegetation. On the seaward side of Piana, the panoramic **route de Ficajola** connects with the D824, a refreshingly smooth road leading to **Plage d'Arone**, the finest beach in the vicinity. En route, you pass the start of the footpath leading to **Capo Rosso**. Crowned by a Genoese watchtower, this distinctive sugar-loaf lump of pink granite marks the southernmost extremity of the Golfe de Porto, of which its summit affords a sweeping view.

The Porto–Ajaccio **bus** stops at Piana twice daily (July to mid-Sept daily; rest of year Mon–Sat only) – otherwise there's no public transport.

The Calanche

The UNESCO-protected site of the **Calanche** takes its name from *calanca*, the Corsican word for "creek" or "inlet" (in French, *calanque*), but the outstanding characteristics of the Calanche are the vivid orange and pink rock masses and pinnacles crumbling into the dark-blue sea. Liable to unusual patterns of erosion, these tormented rock formations and porphyry needles, some of which reach 300m above the sea, were described by Maupassant as a "nightmarish menagerie petrified by the will of an extravagant god", and have long been traditionally associated with different animals and figures, of which the most famous is the **Tête de Chien** at the north end of the stretch of cliffs. Other figures and creatures conjured up include a Moor's head, a monocled bishop, a bear and a tortoise. An old local legend holds that these fantasic forms were the work of the Devil, who created them in a fit of rage after a shepherdess refused his amorous advances. Unable to punish her pure soul, he conjured the shapes of his enemies from the fiery rocks, among them the giant representations of the shepherdess and her fiancé that tower above the corniche road to this day.

The Calanche has long been the west coast's top tourist site, and the road that winds through its granite archways en route to Piana gets clogged solid with cars, coaches and camper vans during July and August. One way to avoid the jams is to view the cliffs on a **boat excursion** from Porto; these leave daily in summer, cost 120F and last about an hour. Alternatively, head for the *Roches Bleues* café, 8km along the road from Porto, from where a network of marked trails fans through the cliffs, crags and pine trees.

Piana

For some reason, **PIANA**, in a prime location overlooking the Calanche, does not suffer the deluge of tourists that other such picturesque places endure. Retaining a sleepy village feel, it comprises a cluster of pink houses around an eighteenth-century church and

Calanche Walks

Several routes, varying from easy to strenuous, can be followed in the environs of the *Roches Bleues* café (see opposite), marked at regular intervals
with splashes of coloured paint. A monochrome **topo-map** of the area is
featured in the local council's free *Piana Randonnées* leaflet, available at
local tourist offices, and the staff at the café are helpful sources of advice
on the state of the trails.

The most popular short walk in the Calanche is the round hike to the
Château Fort (1hr 15min), a large square chunk of granite resembling a
ruined fort from which an impressive view extends along the coast to Capo
Rosso. Waymarked with blue spots, the trail starts 700m north of the café
at a car park on the right of the Porto road.

The **corniche** walk (about 50min), also marked in blue, starts on a well-
worn track, east off the road directly in front of the *Roches Bleues* before
the bridge. The track, signposted "Corniche", climbs in a loop around to
the main road, coming out a few kilometres down from where you started.

For a more demanding three-hour ramble, another path, beyond the corniche track and signposted "Châtaigneraie", follows a pleasant shady trail
through the **chestnut forest**, indicated by blue-painted marks all the way.

A shorter walk (1hr 30min) begins by the **Oratoire de la Vierge**, a little
chapel 500m south of the *Roches Bleues*, west off the road where two lay-
bys provide parking. A mule track (*chemin des muletiers*) marked by
blue paint leads off to the north of the road. Beginning with a steep ascent
between two massive rocks, the track then follows the coast for an hour,
affording fabulous views over the gulf, before regaining the road.

---

square, with just a few hotels and restaurants. It is well situated for
forays into the Calanche and up the coast, and provides superb views
over the Calanche and across to Porto.

If you want to **stay** here, head straight for *Hôtel les Roches Rouges*,
at the entrance to the village on the Porto side (☎04 95 27 81 81;④);
built in the 1930s, this wonderfully dated building lay empty for nearly twenty years, but was recently been reopened with most of its original fittings and furniture intact. The rooms are huge (make sure you
get one facing the water) and there's a gorgeous restaurant terrace
that juts out over the cliffs, affording a magnificent view of the
Calanche and the sea. Their tariffs are exceptionally low, too, considering the hotel's situation and character; even if you can't afford to
stay here, drop in for coffee and a game of chess on the terrace. A
cheaper alternative is *Hôtel Continental*, on the right as you leave
Piana (☎04 95 27 82 02; ②–③); it's an old house with high wooden
ceilings and a leafy garden. The *Mare e Monti*, between the two (☎04
95 27 82 14; April–Oct; ③), also offers fine views from its sea-facing
side, though the "mountain view" rooms actually overlook the road.

Around Piana

If you've only got time for a very short trip from Piana, just head 2km
south of the village along the D81 to the **Col de Lava**, a famed view-

ing platform for the gulf. Rather more rewarding, though, is the **route de Ficajola** (D624), a short steep road that loops down to the shore from the central junction in Piana. Stunning views of the gulf make it a lovely drive in itself, and ten minutes' walk away from the road's end, accessible via a stone stairway, there's the bonus of the **Anse de Ficajola**, a small cove of red rocks and limpid sea.

Best of all, though, is the drive along the **D824**, which leaves the route de Ficajola a short way outside Piana. About 6km along the road, there's the option of a walk along the marked trail to the **Tour de Turghiu**, a Genoese watchtower occupying the extremity of **Capu Rossu**, the finger of red rocky land that marks the southern boundary of the Golfe de Porto. The headland is a dramatic sight from afar, its sharp point dwarfed by a great tooth-like spur, and the view at the end is even more remarkable, extending south to Cargèse and north as far as the Golfe de Girolata. Indicated from the road by a blue and yellow Parc Naturel Régional panel, the walk to the tower and back takes about three hours and is hard going on the final stretch. Along the way, you pass ruins of old cottages, terraces and animal enclosures dating from an era when the area was intensively farmed. The tower itself has recently been renovated and contains a small fireplace, which means you can bivouac in it and thus be up here for sunset, when the views of the red rocks tumbling down the coast in both directions are sublime.

Continue along the D824 for another 6km and you'll reach another exceptional beach, **Plage d'Arone**. where there's a congenial and clean campsite (☎04 95 20 64 54; June–Sept) and a couple of pricy pizzerias. The beach can get crowded in summer, but tracks lead through the rocks on either side of it to secluded coves. Snorkellers and anglers should head right where the surfaced road leading down to the sea forks, then follow the dirt track that plunges into the maquis at a sharp left-hand bend; ten minutes' walk further down this path brings you to a rocky promontory where the water is crys-

---

A Walk to Capo d'Orto

The walk from Piana east to **Capo d'Orto** (10km) should take between five and six hours, providing you're in good shape and have the right footwear for the rocky terrain. The track begins 2km north of Piana. Follow the D81 halfway, then take the little road on the right just before the bridge. After another 1km this stops at a fork where you can leave the car. Take the right-hand track of the fork and continue alongside the river. After 3km the track gives way to a path marked with flashes of orange paint which ascends east through a pine wood. The orange paint ends at the mountain pass of **Foce d'Orto**, a huge gap between giant mounds of rock, two hours into the walk. For Capo d'Orto head north along the left path which soon peters out and the way to the summit becomes marked by stone cairns. A corridor of rock overgrown with scrub leads up to a plateau, from which point it's an easy scramble to the top and a truly glorious view.

tal clear and the sea bed shelves steeply down, giving glimpses of many kinds of fish and underwater plants.

Inland from Porto

The coast around Porto may be spectacular, but it's positively tame in comparison with the jaw-dropping scenery immediately **inland**. Slicing into the craggy spine of the island, the Spelunca valley snakes from sea level to the **Col de Verghio**. draped in impenetrable maquis and thick pine forests. Its great feature, however, is the breathtaking **Spelunca gorge**, whose colossal granite cliffs can be approached either by the D84 or along the smaller D124, via the attractive village of **Ota**, the administrative centre for the area and the best base for hiking in the valley. From here you can walk up through the gorge along an ancient mule track, pausing at the elegant Genoese bridges and crystalline bathing pools, to **Evisa**, a mountain resort situated in the lap of the mountains. Evisa is also well placed for a visit to the fragrant **Forêt d'Aitone**, which borders the route to the windswept Col de Verghio, the highest point in Corsica traversable by road.

For those without transport, the Ajaccio–Porto **bus** passes through Ota (Aug to mid-Sept 2 daily; rest of year Mon–Sat only). During July and August there's also a daily service to Corte that calls at Evisa before scaling the pass into the Niolu; timetables these are available from tourist offices.

The Spelunca gorge

Spanning the 2km between the villages of Ota and Evisa, the **Spelunca gorge** is a formidable sight, its bare orange granite walls, 1000m deep in places, plunging into the foaming green torrent created by the confluence of the rivers Porto, Tavulella, Onca, Campi and Aitone. The sunlight, ricocheting across the rock walls, creates a sinister effect that's heightened by the dark, jagged needles of the encircling peaks. Not surprsingly, local legend has it that the gorge was hewn by the Devil in a terrible rage.

The most dramatic part of the gorge is best viewed from the road, which hugs the edge for much of its length, but you can explore some beautiful side-valleys and river banks by striking out on foot along the old path between Ota and Evisa (see box overleaf).

Ota

Isolated on a verdant ledge 5km east of Porto, **OTA** is dominated by **Capo d'Ota**, a colossal dome of a mountain whose overhanging summit looks like it's about to topple onto the village. Generations of kids here have grown up believing that the only reason it doesn't is because the rock is held in place by monks tugging on long chains. As a ploy to get them to eat their greens, the children are also told the ecclesiastical strongmen are sustained in their task by spinach *bastelles*, or pasties, delivered to them each week by an old lady on a donkey.

If you're in the area to hike, this village makes a much better base than Porto. An overnight stage on the Mare e Monti trail, it boasts two excellent **gîtes d'étape**: *Chez Félix* (☎04 95 26 12 42), where you can bed down in clean and cosy dorms for 50F per night, and *Chez Marie* (*Le Bar des Chasseurs*), just down the road (☎04 95 26 11 37), which is equally well maintained. Given the choice, however, the former has the edge thanks to its wonderful **restaurant**, whose terrace affords a sublime view of Capo d'Orto on the opposite side of the valley. The food is great, too – ranging from local specialities such as lamb stew and grilled veal or wild boar, to more adventurous couscous dishes – and their deliciously cool draught beer is more than welcome if you've just hiked up from the river.

Evisa

The bright-orange roofs of **EVISA** emerge against a lush background of chestnut forests about 10km from Ota, on the eastern edge of the gorge. Situated 830m above sea level, the village caters well for hikers and makes a pleasant stop for a taste of mountain life – the sky is blue, the air crisp and clear, and the food particularly good.

Buses to Evisa leave Ajaccio twice daily on Monday to Saturday during the summer, via Sagone and Vico, with a reduced service during the winter. Timetables can be found at most tourist offices in the area, or by telephoning Autocars R. Ceccaldi (☎04 95 21 01 24).

The best place to **stay** is the rambling *La Châtaigneraie*, on the west edge of the village on the Porto road (☎04 95 26 24 27, fax 04 95 26 23 11; year round; ③). Set amid chestnut trees, this traditional schist and granite building has a dozen cosy rooms with pine furniture and en-suite bathrooms, and they do good-value half-board deals. *Hôtel du Centre*, opposite the statue in the centre (☎04 95 26 20 92; July–Sept; ③), is a pleasant fall-back, with small rooms but an excellent Corsican speciality restaurant on its ground floor; the 100F menu features wild boar stewed in red wine. Moving upmarket, *Hôtel l'Aitone*, at the north exit to the village (☎04 95 26 20 04, fax 04 95 26 24 18; year round; ③), is a large country hotel with comfortable rooms, a swimming pool, and a relaxing bar-restaurant that enjoys a reputation both for gastronomic prowess and its fine views; the atmosphere here is best around early evening when you can watch the sun set behind the gorge from their terrace. Otherwise, there's the more modest *U Pozzu*, opposite (☎04 95 26 11 45; ②), run by the same family, which has a handful of light and airy rooms that are the cheapest in the village. For an inexpensive meal, *U Mulinu*, downstairs, is the best option, serving pizzas freshly baked in their wood oven from around 45F.

Walks from Evisa

An enjoyable short walk from Evisa runs down to the local **chestnut wood** (*châtaigneraie*) beneath the village. About 250m west of the village square, a stone gateway leads into the wood, from where you soon emerge into a field of bracken. The view here embraces the Golfe de Porto, the Spelunca gorge and Ota. This is a good walk to do at sunset, when the colours can be amazingly vivid.

The three-hour walk from **Evisa to Ota**, which drops down to the Spelunca gorge via dense deciduous and evergreen woodland, is an immensely popular hike, in spite of the fact that for most of the way the views of the gorge are obscured by trees. Cobbled centuries ago by the Genoese and now clearly marked with orange splashes of paint, the route is basically easy-going, though from Ota you may prefer to hitch back to Evisa rather than climb back up the valley. Less-experienced walkers may also prefer to skip the steep descent from Ota to the first of the two Genoese bridges, in favour of the more rambling, scenic stretch along the Spelunca valley floor (see the end of this account).

To pick up the trail, follow the road west of the village as far as the **cemetery**, where a path marked "Ota–Evisa" descends into the gorge, through maquis interspersed with pines and evergreen oak. Continue through the mossy trees, past precipitous walls of bald grey rock, and follow the steepening path as it plunges into the valley. About one-third of the way down, you pass an eternal spring on the left, where you can fill your bottle; from here, the trail descends through an endless series of sharp switchbacks, emerging after around an hour and a half at the picturesque Genoese **Pont de Zaglia**, a row of alders leaning across the confluence of the Aitone and Tavulella. This is a good place for a swim, and a side-track heads northeast up the Spelunca from the bridge, giving access to less-frequented bathing spots. Hugging the left bank of the stream, the path cuts through the rocks below the most spectacular cliffs in the gorge to the confluence of the Onca and Spelunca, reached after around two hours. You can either cross the road bridge here and head up the Onca valley to a chain of beautiful deep-green pools that are perfect for swimming, or else turn left onto the road, follow it for five minutes, and then skirt the village football pitch on your right to pick up the onward trail to Ota. This keeps to the left bank of the river until it reaches another beautiful Genoese bridge, the **Ponte Vecchiu**, from where the path gradually ascends the north flank of the valley to the village. This last section of the walk, between Ota and the Pont de Zaglia, is the most scenic, and makes a very pleasant, undemanding two- to three-hour round hike from Ota.

Forêt d'Aitone

Thousands of soaring Laricio pines, some of them as high as 50m, make the **Forêt d'Aitone** the most beautiful forest in Corsica. Incorporating the mountainous Fôret de Lindinosa, it reaches 1391m at its highest point – the **Col de Salto** – and extends over ten square kilometres between Evisa and the Col de Verghio. Well-worn tourist paths cross the forest at various points, but human disturbance is not yet great enough to upset the balance of local **wildlife**, even if the Aitone foxes have become quite tame owing to visitors feeding them. Wild boar and stoats thrive here, while high up in the remoter parts of Lindinosa, mouflon are sometimes seen. Birds sighted in the forest include eagles, sparrowhawks and goshawks, and if you're lucky you may spot a Corsican nuthatch, a unique species distinguished by a black crown and a white stripe over the eye. The most exotic creature to haunt these parts is a rare, large and savage cat known as a **ghjattu volpe** – literally "fox-cat". A few years ago, a haul of illegal game from Corsica was uncovered by French customs, amongst which one of these cats was discovered. However, sightings of the creature in the wild are extremely rare.

You can park 7km along the road from Evisa by the **Maison Forestière d'Aitone**, the forest headquarters and information centre (daily June–Sept 9am–noon & 2–6pm), and a starting point for walks in the area. In this part of the forest grow the oldest Laricio pines in Corsica, some of them clocking up five hundred years. Fine-grained, strong and very resistant to weathering, the Laricio was highly valued by the Genoese for ships' masts and furniture, and it was they who first built a road down the valley to the coast, later upgraded by the French using convict labour. Throughout the nineteenth century, forests all over Corsica were regularly decimated, as the island has the very best specimens of this species, which only grows in forests higher than 1000m. When the British artist and poet Edward Lear came here in the 1860s, he noted with regret "the ravages of [the] hatchets: here and there on the hillside are pale patches of cleared ground, with piles of cut and barked pines . . . everywhere giant trees lie prostrate."

One of the most popular short walks goes to the **Belvedère**, a great projecting rock 5km north of Evisa. To reach it, follow the signposted track leading into the forest, from beside a wide lay-by on the left-hand side of the road. The magnificent **view** across the valley takes in the rivers Aitone and Porto, which rush between high walls of copper-tinted rocks down to the Spelunca gorge.

Another well-trekked route leads to the multiple **Cascades de la Valla Scarpa**, where the crystalline waters of the Aitone crash into a pool hollowed out by the falls. It's just fifteen minutes' walk from the maison forestière, signposted "Piscines/les Cascades", and thus it does become overcrowded in summer – though you don't have to walk much further along the river to find more tranquil spots for a picnic and a swim.

An account of the Asco valley and gorge appears on p.286.

If you want to reach the higher slopes, an hour's walk from the maison forestière will bring you to the **Col de Salto**, and a further three hours' heavy climbing along the same rocky track will bring you to the **Col de Felce**, for a fantastic vista of the Golfe de Porto. For the more ambitious, the **Col de Cuccavera** – above the tree line at 1500m – can be attained by cutting north before the Col de Felce, striking right up the mountainside. Once you're this far up, you can make out hazy distant views of the Gorges d'Asco.

Just 4km beyond the maison forestière, the road, strewn with pine cones and foraged by herds of semi-wild pigs, runs over the **Col de Verghio** (1477m), gateway to the remote district of the Niolo and the limit of the Fôret de Valdo-Niello. You can park up here and strike out on foot along the marked mountain trail leading north towards the Bergeries de Radule, roughly an hour away. Minutes into the walk, the views improve dramatically, with vistas of Punta Licciola and the lower slopes of the red, wedge-shaped **Paglia Orba** opening up to the north. Keep going long enough and you'll eventually hit the GR20, which winds up to the **Refuge Ciuttulu di i Mori**, springboard for the ascent of Paglia Orba and the adjacent giant rock archway, Capo Tafonata. As long as you overnight in the refuge and set off at dawn, the peak is technically straightforward; don't, however, attempt it without adequate clothing, footwear and maps.

Immediately below the Col de Verghio is one of Corsica's few **ski stations**, an incongruously grim concrete edifice that sees few visitors even in winter, as these days there's rarely enough snow to keep it in use. Desperate for some customers, the entrepreneurial owner "re-directed" the GR20 through his establishment some years back with a couple of tins of red and white paint bought from the local store. His bar and extortionately pricy provisions counter thrived briefly until the Parc Naturel Régional got wind of what he'd done and removed the misleading marks. The road is extremely rocky along the last stretch up to the building, where a café is usually open from May until September.

Inland from Porto

For more on the Niolo, see p.290.

The Corsican origin myth relating to this unusual geological formation is described on p.295.

Théodore Poli: Roi des Montagnes

Théodore Poli was twenty years old in 1817, at a time when the French administration was conscripting young men all over the island in an attempt to curb banditry. A brigadier from Poli's village of Guagno, in an act of spite, neglected to inform Poli that he was due for national service, thereby making him a deserter – an offence on which the French were especially harsh. Poli shot the man in revenge and, in true outlaw tradition, took to the maquis, where his confederation of some 150 bandits soon elected him "Roi des Montagnes". A bandit constitution was drawn up, whereby Poli was named Théodore II, after the Théodore I who had briefly ruled Corsica some sixty years earlier. Hiding out in the Aitone forest, Théodore and his gang proceeded to terrorize the neighbourhood, imposing a heavy "tax" on the rich and the clergy, while exempting the poor. Becoming ever more ambitious, these self-styled champions of the downtrodden poor whipped up anti-French feeling wherever they could, raiding the gendarmeries for arms and even gunning down the local executioner of Bastia when he refused to participate in anti-French demonstrations. In 1827 the Roi des Montagnes' rule came to an abrupt end – lured into a forest glade by a beautiful woman, he was shot dead by one of his many enemies.

Travel details

TRAINS

Algajola to: Ajaccio (2 daily; 4hr 15min); Bastia (2 daily; 2hr 45min); Belgodère (2 daily; 35min); Corte (2 daily; 2hr 10min); L'Île Rousse (2 daily; 15min).

Calvi to: Ajaccio (2 daily; 4hr 40min); Algajola (2 daily; 25min); Bastia (2 daily; 3hr 15min); Belgodère (2 daily; 1hr); Corte (2 daily; 2hr 30min); L'Île Rousse (2 daily; 40min); Ponte Leccia (2 daily; 2hr).

L'Île Rousse to: Ajaccio (2 daily; 4hr); Algajola (2 daily; 10min); Bastia (2 daily; 2hr 30min); Belgodère (2 daily; 20min); Corte (2 daily; 1hr 20min).

BUSES

Calvi to: Ajaccio, via Ponte Leccia (1 daily; 3hr); Bastia (1 daily; 3hr); Calenzana (1 daily; 30min); Galéria (2 daily; 1hr 20min); L'Île Rousse (1–2 daily; 40min); Lumio (1–2 daily; 10min); Porto (1 daily; 2hr 45min); St-Florent (1 daily; 3hr).

Evisa to: Ajaccio (1 daily; 1hr 45min).

Galéria to: Calvi (1 daily; 1hr); Porto (1 daily; 2hr 20min).

L'Île Rousse to: Ajaccio, via Ponte Leccia (1 daily; 2hr 30min); Algajola (1–2 daily; 10min); Bastia (1 daily; 2hr 30min); Calvi (1–2 daily; 40min).

Porto to: Ajaccio (2 daily; 2hr 15min); Calvi (1 daily; 3hr 15min); Cargèse (2 daily; 1hr 15min); Galéria (1 daily; 2hr 20min); Ota (2 daily; 20min); Piana (2 daily; 15min).

FERRIES

For ferry details, see pp.102 and 117.

Chapter 3

The Ajaccio region

A jaccio is Corsica's largest town, capital of the *département* of Corse-du-Sud and seat of the island's Assemblée Regionale, yet the image it immediately projects is that of the classic French Mediterranean resort, with its palm trees, street cafés and yacht-filled marina. Modern blocks are stacked up behind the town, but they do little to diminish the visual impact of its warm yellow-toned buildings and sturdy citadel, set in a magnificent bay and framed by a shadowy mountain range. Unlike Bastia, Ajaccio makes most of its money from tourism, a fact partly attributable to its own attractions, partly to its proximity to the west coast's wonderful beaches, and partly to its having been the birthplace of Napoléon Bonaparte. The prime Napoleonic sites – the Maison Bonaparte and the Salon Napoléonien – are not, however, the best of Ajaccio's cultural assets: that distinction goes to the Musée Fesch, which boasts France's most important collection of Italian paintings outside the Louvre.

The **Golfe d'Ajaccio**, an ethereal vista of mist-shrouded mountains by day, is transformed at night into a completely different but equally evocative scene by the lights of the bay's sprawling tourist developments. Flung out at the northern tip of the gulf, beyond the hotels, the islets known as the **Îles Sanguinaires** are perhaps the most popular excursion from the town, rivalled by **Porticcio** on the gulf's southern shore, a trendy outpost for weekending Ajacciens. Of greater appeal to most visitors are the secluded beaches that punctuate this side of the bay towards **Capo di Muro**, ideal targets for a picnic and a swim.

Inland from Ajaccio, the craggy **Gorges du Prunelli** edge the river as far as **Bastelica**, birthplace of Corsican freedom fighter Sampiero Corso but an uninspiring village that owes its popularity to the nearby Val d'Èse ski station. North of Ajaccio lies the **Cinarca**, a region of gently sloping vineyards whose produce you can sample in pleasant villages such as Sari d'Orcino and Casaglione. Adjoining the Cinarca is the vast **Golfe de Sagone**, where long stretches of sand have incited a build-up of hotels at the tired resorts of Tiuccia and

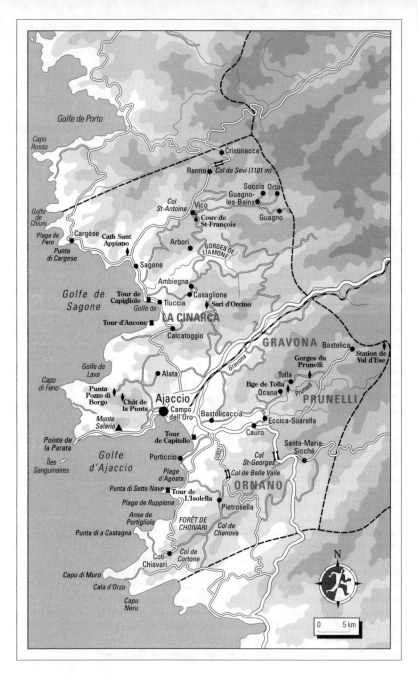

Sagone, both of which are eclipsed by the enchanting village of
Cargèse, sited high on a cliff at the northern extremity of the gulf.
East of here, the sombre town of **Vico** provides a base for excursions
into some of the remoter mountain regions, the lovely **Gorges du
Liamone** and the rocky region around **Orto** being two of the least-
visited areas in the interior of the island.

Apart from the train line to Bastia and a few long-distance bus connections, **public transport** in this region is confined to a few shuttle
services past the holiday complexes of the Golfe d'Ajaccio.

Ajaccio

Edward Lear claimed that on a wet day it would be hard to find so
dull a place as **AJACCIO** (Aiacciu), a harsh judgement with an
element of justice. The town has none of Bastia's sense of purpose
and can seem to lack a definitive identity of its own, as if French
domination has sapped its energy. On the other hand, it's a
relaxed and good-looking place, with an exceptionally mild climate (the average temperature for the year is 17°C), a wealth of
cafés, restaurants and chic shops, and a more welcoming attitude
to tourists than you are likely to encounter anywhere else in
Corsica.

Napoléon gave Ajaccio international fame, but though the self-des-
ignated Cité Impériale is littered with statues and street names relating to the Bonaparte family, you'll find the Napoleonic cult has a less
dedicated following in his home town than you might imagine. The
emperor is still considered by many Ajacciens as a self-serving
Frenchman rather than as a Corsican, and from time to time their
disapproval is expressed in a dramatic gesture – such as painting his
statue yellow, as happened a few years ago. Napoléon's impact on
the townscape of his birthplace wasn't enormous, either. Spacious
squares and boulevards were laid out during Ajaccio's brief spell as
island capital, but Napoléon's efforts did little to alter the intrinsic
provinciality of the place, and Ajaccio remains memorable for the
things that have long made it attractive – its battered old town, the
pervasive scents of fresh coffee and grilled seafood, and the encom-
passing view of its glorious bay.

A brief history of Ajaccio

Although it's an attractive idea that Ajax once stopped here, the name of Ajaccio in fact derives from the Roman *Adjaccium* (place of rest), a winter stop-off point for shepherds descending from the mountains to stock up on goods and sell their produce. This first settlement, to the north of the present town in the area called Castelvecchio, was destroyed by the Saracens in the tenth century, and modern Ajaccio grew up around the citadel that was founded in 1492 by the **Bank of St George**, a Genoese military organization that handled the administration of Corsica. Built to intimidate the local nobility, who had been launching regular assaults on the oppressive Genoese, the citadel was packed with Ligurian immigrants and remained off limits to Corsican settlers for half a century. In 1553, the Corsican patriot Sampiero Corso took control of the citadel, having sided with the French, but within six years the former rulers had returned, inaugurating a period of expansion fuelled in part by an influx of people fleeing Moorish raids on the surrounding countryside. The town's population rose from 1200 to 5000 between 1584 and 1666, a period that saw the reinforcement of the citadel, the construction of a new cathedral and the improvement of the **port**, which by 1627 was doing better trade than Bastia, at that time a far more important military and political centre. Nonetheless, the infertility of the immediate hinterland kept many Ajacciens in extreme poverty and made the town reliant on imports of Genoese olive oil and wheat, while trading restrictions imposed on the town's merchants fostered resentment among the rising bourgeoisie.

Yet, when Pascal Paoli launched his first campaign for an independent republic in 1739, the Ajacciens stayed faithful to their Genoese masters. In 1796, however, the **French** finally prevailed, and the ramparts were demolished on the orders of Napoléon. In its new role as capital of Corsica, Ajaccio expanded more rapidly than ever before and maintained its economic momentum right through the nineteenth century, largely due to the success of the wine trade. Since World War II – when Ajaccio, a centre for resistance fighters, was the first Corsican (and thus French) town to be liberated – the tourist industry has become the most important income-provider, yet Ajaccio continues to suffer from the malaise that afflicts the rest of the island, with many young people emigrating to France as soon as they leave school. It is the determination to reverse this trend that lies behind the success in elections to the Assemblée Regionale of **Corsica Nazione**, a union of politicians committed to the development of Corsica's economy and to the planning of future independence from France.

Traditionally confined to the south of the island, **nationalist violence** has also been on the increase here over the past couple of decades. In January 1980, the *Hôtel Fesch* was the scene of a tense standoff in which RPR militants from Bastelica held hostage three French Secret Service agents discovered on active service in their area. The siege ended peacefully, with the arrest and imprisonment of the Corsican activists involved, but since then the number of bombings and shootings has spiralled, mainly because of the intensifying feud between rival factions in the nationalist movement. That said, the violence rarely, if ever, affects tourists. The only outward signs of the unrest you're likely to come across are the heavily armed CRS police who routinely patrol the port and streets around the gendarmerie and Assemblée Régionale, and the façade of the Palais de Justice, which remains riddled with bullet holes after being sprayed with gunfire in August 1996.

Arrival and information

Served by regular direct flights from France, northern Europe, and North and West Africa, Ajaccio's **airport**, Campo dell'Oro, is 6km south of town. All of the island's main car rental companies have offices lined up outside the terminal building (see "Listings", p.170), and metered taxis queue up here at flight times. For budget travellers, three buses per hour provide a shuttle service into the centre, stopping on cours Napoléon, the main street – buy your ticket on the bus (25F), and stamp it in the machine behind the driver's cab. Long-distance buses pull in at the **bus station**, or terminal routière, next to the port de Commerce, a five-minute walk from the centre. Ferries from the mainland also dock in this spanking new complex, where you'll find Ajaccio's least expensive **left-luggage** facility (10F per article), a **bureau de change**, and arguably the cleanest toilets in town. The SNCF **train station**, however, lies almost a kilometre north along bd Sampiero, a continuation of the quai l'Herminier.

There are two free **car parks** flanking quai l'Herminier, close to the **tourist office** on the ground floor of the Hôtel de Ville (May–Oct Mon–Sat 8.30am–8.30pm, Sun 8.30am–1pm; Nov–April Mon–Fri 8.30am–6pm, Sat 8.30am–1pm; ☎04 95 51 53 03), which is useful primarily for checking travel departure times. Anyone planning a long-distance hike should head for the office of the national parks association, the **Parc Naturel Régional de Corse**, 2 rue Sergeant-Casalonga, around the corner from the Préfecture on cours Napoléon (Mon–Thurs 9am–noon & 2–6pm, Fri 9am–noon & 2–5pm; ☎04 95 51 79 10), where you can buy topo-guides, maps, guidebooks and leaflets detailing regional trail networks, and check the latest weather reports for the mountains. They are also a good source of advice on how to combine different stages of their long-distance footpaths, and will help you sort out gîte d'étape accommodation and transport to the trailheads.

Accommodation

Ajaccio suffers from a dearth of inexpensive **accommodation**, but there are a fair number of moderate to upmarket places scattered

Ajaccio

*Bastelicaccia's
and Porticcio's
hotels and
campsites are
reviewed on
pp.177 & 190.*

around town, chiefly along cours Napoléon and the coast road lead-ing to the Îles Sanguinaires. Whatever your budget, it's a good idea to book ahead by telephone from June through September, and bear in mind the numerous out-of-town hotels within thirty or forty min-utes' drive of the centre, at Bastellicaccia and Porticcio. All those places listed below are open year-round unless specified otherwise.

Only one **campsite** lies within striking distance of the centre. Located 3km northwest, *Camping Mimosa* (☎04 95 20 99 85; May–Oct) is a shady and well-organized site with clean toilet blocks, friendly manage-ment and fair rates, but rock-hard ground. It's a long trudge if you're loaded with luggage, but you can catch bus #4 from cours Napoléon to the **Brasilia** stop, and walk north from there to the roundabout at the bottom of the hill. After crossing the intersection, head up the lane on its far side and turn left at the signpost, passing a tennis club soon after on your right. The site lies another 1.5km uphill from here.

Hotels

Bella Vista, 20 bd Lantivy (☎04 95 21 07 97, fax 04 95 21 81 88). Large, rather imposing place on the seafront offering views of the gulf from its front-side rooms. ③.

Bonaparte, 1 rue Étienne-Conti (☎04 95 21 44 19). Rooms are small and a little overpriced but immaculately clean, with views of the covered market; ask for one on the upper storey. Handy for the restaurants in the same lane. Closed Nov–March. ③.

Colomba, 8 av de Paris (☎04 95 21 12 66). Cheapest place in Ajaccio: an old-style pension with eleven rooms, most of which share toilets on the corridor. Very basic, but central. Reception's on the third floor (no lift). ②.

Le Dauphin, 11 bd Sampiero (☎04 95 21 12 94, fax 04 95 21 88 69). Clean, impersonal place opposite the port de commerce. Bar downstairs is straight out of a French *policier*, complete with jukebox, pinball machine and old men sipping *pastis* under a cloud of Gauloise smoke. ③.

Fesch, 7 rue Cardinal-Fesch (☎04 95 21 50 52, fax 04 95 21 83 36). Among the oldest-established hotels in Ajaccio, and famous thanks to the 1980 siege (see p.158). The sheepskin furnishings and medieval-style decor were designed by Corsicada, a group of local artisans, but the effect is rather som-bre. All rooms have air-con and TVs; balconies cost extra. ④.

Du Golfe, 5 bd du Roi-Jerôme (☎04 95 21 47 64, fax 04 95 21 71 05). Popular with tour parties, this large, slick hotel has modern balconies over-looking the bay, and TVs in every room.⑤.

Idéal, 97bis cours Napoléon (☎04 95 22 17 51, fax 04 95 10 14 24). Moderate-sized rooms in a recently renovated two-star, 10min walk north of the centre. No views, but quiet and very good value. ③.

Kallysté, 51 cours Napoléon (☎04 95 21 34 45, fax 04 95 21 79 00). Third-floor hotel slap in the centre, with an international atmosphere. Sound proofed rooms for up to four people, plus studios with kitchenettes (self-catering 35F extra) and TVs. Proprietor speaks English. ③.

Marengo, 12 bd Mme-Mère (☎04 95 21 43 66, fax 04 95 21 51 26). 10min walk west of centre, up a quiet side-street off bd Mme-Mère. Pleasant, small hotel away from the city bustle, with rooms overlooking a flowery courtyard. Open April to mid-Nov. ④.

Du Palais, 5 av Beverini-Vico (☎04 95 23 36 42). Dingy looking exterior, but the rooms are clean and spacious, and all have bathrooms; those to the rear of the building are quieter. ③.

San Carlu, 8 bd Danielle-Casanova (☎04 95 21 13 84). Sited opposite the citadel and close to the beach, this recently renovated hotel is the poshest option in the old town. Well-appointed rooms, own parking facilities, and a special room for disabled guests in the easy-access basement. ④.

The town

The core of the old town holds the most interest in Ajaccio: a cluster of ancient streets spreading north and south of **place Foch**, which opens out to the seafront by the port and the marina Tino Rossi.

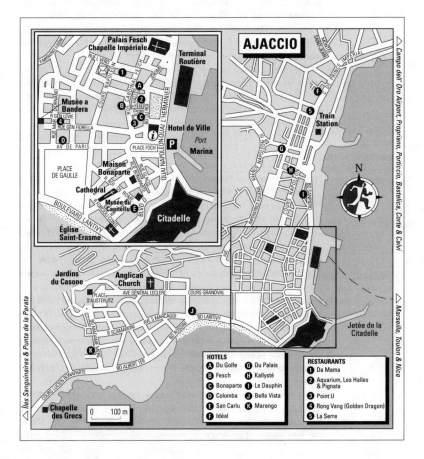

Nearby **place de Gaulle** forms the town centre and is the source of the main thoroughfare, **cours Napoléon**, which extends parallel to the sea almost 2km to the northeast. Lined with chic boutiques, stores and brassy cafés, this is Ajaccio at its posiest – an endless procession of designer clothes, clipped poodles and huge motorbikes. West of place de Gaulle is the town beach where Ajaccio's beau monde top up their tans, overlooked from the north by the honey-coloured citadel.

Around place de Gaulle and the new town

Place de Gaulle – otherwise known as place du Diamant, after the Diamanti family who once owned much of the property in Ajaccio – is the most useful point of orientation, even if it's not much to look at, being just a windy concrete platform surrounded by a shopping complex. The only noteworthy thing on the square is the huge **bronze statue** of Napoléon at the southern end: nicknamed *L'Encrier* (The Inkstand), this pompous lump was commissioned by Napoléon III in 1865, and shows Napoléon clad in Roman garb on horseback, surrounded by his four brothers.

The only museum in this part of town, **A Bandera**, is a short way north of the square, in rue Général-Levie, behind the *préfecture* (May–Sept Mon–Sat 10am–noon & 3–7pm; Oct–April Mon–Fri 9am–noon & 2–6pm; 20F). Scruffy and underfunded, this small military museum houses few objects of note, and is only likely to be of interest if your French is up to the lengthy written explanations that accompany the pictorial exhibits. A English guide may be borrowed from the desk when you buy your ticket, but this translates only a fraction of the material set out on the walls.

The first room is devoted to prehistoric times, with a model of a Bronze Age settlement or *castellu* alongside bronze daggers and pottery fragments; the more interesting second room deals with the Moorish raids, displaying beautiful ivory-handled stilettos and several pictures of flamboyantly dressed corsairs. Among them is the notorious Dragut, a Moorish pirate who allied himself with the French during the campaign of 1553 when Sampiero Corso recaptured Corsica from the Genoese. The Wars of Independence are covered in the third room, featuring statutes drafted by Pascal Paoli and Sir Gilbert Elliot during the Anglo-Corsican alliance of 1794–96. The last room has a section on World War II and the Corsican resistance, though the highlights are the press cuttings and photos presenting the island's **bandits** as genial, popular, local heroes and showing notorious figures such as Spada hobnobbing with aristocratic ladies in forest glades.

Devotees of Napoléon should take a stroll a kilometre up cours Grandval, the wide street rising west of place de Gaulle and ending in a square, the **Jardins du Casone**, where gaudily spectacular son et lumière shows take place in summer. On the way you'll pass the

Assemblée Nationale, an enormous yellow Art Deco building front-ed by a jungle of palms and a couple of armoured police vans. An impressive **monument** to Napoléon dominates the square – a replica of the statue at Napoléon's burial place, Les Invalides in Paris, stand-ing atop a huge pedestal inscribed with the names of his battles. Behind the monument lies a graffiti-bedaubed **cave** where Napoléon is supposed to have frolicked as a child.

Place Foch

Once the site of the town's medieval gate, **place Foch** lies at the heart of old Ajaccio. A delightfully shady square sloping down to the sea and lined with cafés and restaurants, it gets its local name – place des Palmiers – from the row of mature palms bordering the central strip. Dominating the top end, a fountain of four marble lions pro-vides a mount for the inevitable statue of Napoléon, this one by Ajaccien sculptor Maglioli. A humbler effigy occupies a niche high on a wall south of the fountain, above a souvenir shop – a figurine of Ajaccio's patron saint, **La Madonnuccia**, her base bearing the text *Poserunt me custodem* ("They have made me their guardian"). The image dates from 1656, a year in which Ajaccio's local council, fear-ful of infection from plague-struck Genoa, placed the town under the guardianship of the Madonna in a ceremony that took place on this spot. Ajaccio was saved on this occasion and again in 1745, when *La Madonnuccia* was paraded around the ramparts to dispel the Anglo-Sardinian fleet that was bombarding the city – whereupon the enemy beat a miraculous speedy retreat. If you're here on March 18 you can witness Ajaccio's big event, the **Fête de la Miséricorde**, in which the statue is conveyed through the old town as a prelude to a big party and firework display.

Taking up the northern end of place Foch, the **Hôtel de Ville**, with its prison-like wooden doors, was built in 1826. The first-floor **Salon Napoléonien** (May–Oct daily 9am–noon & 2–5pm, Nov–April Mon–Sat 9am–noon & 2–5pm; 5F) consists of two rooms that are really only for dedicated Napoléon fans. A replica of the ex-emper-or's **death mask** takes pride of place in a chamber bedecked with vel-vet, crystal chandeliers and a solemn array of Bonaparte family por-traits and busts. Next door, the smaller medal room has a batch of minor relics – a fragment from Napoléon's coffin, some earth from his garden, and part of his dressing case – plus a model of the ship that brought him back from St-Helena, and a picture of the house where he died.

South of place Foch

The **south side of place Foch**, the former dividing line between the poor district around the port and the bourgeoisie's territory, gives access to **rue Bonaparte**, the main route through the latter quarter. Built on the promontory rising to the citadel, the secluded streets in this part of town – with their dusty buildings, bistros and bar fronts lit by flashes of sea or sky at the end of the alleys – retain more of a sense of the old Ajaccio than anywhere else. Of the families who lived here in the eighteenth century, one of the most eminent was the **Pozzo di Borgo** clan, whose house still stands at 17 rue Bonaparte, its façade adorned by trompe l'œil frescoes. Carlo Andrea Pozzo di Borgo was a distant cousin and childhood friend of Napoléon, but was later to become one of his bitterest enemies. A supporter of Paoli, he was elected to the Corsican legislature and became president of the Council of State under the short-lived Anglo-Corsican rule of 1794–96. Described as "a man of talent, an intriguer", Pozzo was not content with this domestic position and in 1803 he became the ambassador to Russia, later befriending Wellington, with whom he fought at Waterloo. He went on to become a favourite at the English court, where Queen Victoria referred to him affectionately as "Old Pozzo".

Maison Bonaparte

Napoléon was born in the colossal **Maison Bonaparte**, on place Letizia, just off the west side of rue Bonaparte (May–Sept Mon

---

Napoléon and Corsica

"M. de Choisel once said that if Corsica could be pushed under the sea with a trident it should be done. He was quite right. It is nothing but an excrescence." This sentiment, expressed by Napoléon to one of the generals who had followed him into exile on St-Helena, encapsulates his bitterness about his birthplace. Corsica's opinion of its most famous citizen can be equally uncomplimentary.

The year of **Napoléon's birth**, 1769, was a crucial one in the history of Corsica, for this was the year the French took over the island from the Genoese. They made a thorough job of it, crushing Paoli's troops at Ponte Nuovo and driving the Corsican leader into exile. Napoléon's father, **Carlo**, a close associate of Paoli, fled the scene of the battle with his pregnant wife in order to escape the victorious French army. But Carlo's subsequent behaviour was quite different from that of his former leader – he came to terms with the French, becoming a representative of the newly styled Corsican nobility in the National Assembly, and using his contacts with the French governor to get a free education for his children.

At the age of nine Napoléon was awarded a scholarship to the Brienne military academy, an institution specially founded to teach the sons of the French nobility the responsibilities of their status. The French were anxious to impress their values on the potential leaders of a now dependent territory, and with Napoléon they certainly appear to have succeeded. Give or take a rebellious gesture or two, this son of a Corsican Italian-speaking household used his time well, leaving Brienne to enter the exclusive École Militaire in Paris. At the age of sixteen he was commissioned into the artillery. When he was twenty the Revolution broke out in Paris and the scene was set for a remarkable career.

9am–2pm, Tues–Sat 9–11.45am & 2–6pm, Sun 9am–noon; Oct–April Mon 2–6pm, Tues–Sat 10am–noon & 2–5pm, Sun 10am–noon; 20F). The Bonaparte family first appeared in the chronicles of Ajaccio in the fifteenth century, when they lived in a house that was demolished in 1555 by the French attack on the citadel. This later residence, acquired piecemeal over the years, passed to Napoléon's father Carlo in the 1760s and here he lived, with his wife Letizia and their family, until his death. Soon after, in May 1793, Letizia and her children were driven from the house by Paoli's partisans, who stripped the place down to the floorboards. Requisitioned by the English in 1794, Maison Bonaparte became an arsenal and a lodging house for English officers, amongst whom was Hudson Lowe, later Napoléon's jailer on St-Helena. Though Letizia later paid for its restoration with an indemnity given to those Corsicans who had suffered at the hands of the English, her heart wasn't in the job – she left for the second and last time in 1799, the year Napoléon stayed here on his return from Egypt. Owned by the state since 1923, the house now bears few traces of the Bonaparte family's existence, and barely warrants the 20F admission charge unless you have a penchant for Napoleonic memorabilia.

Always an ambitious opportunist, he obtained leave from his regiment, **returned to Ajaccio**, joined the local Jacobin club and – with his eye on a colonelship in the Corsican militia – enthusiastically promoted the interests of the Revolution. However, things did not quite work out as he had planned, for Pascal Paoli had also returned to Corsica.

Carlo Bonaparte had died some years before, and Napoléon – though not the eldest son – was effectively the head of a family that had formerly given Paoli strong support. Having spent the last twenty years in London, Paoli was pro-English and had developed a profound distaste of revolutionary excesses (it was his determination to keep the guillotine out of Corsica that, as much as anything else, led him into the later failed experiment of union with Britain). Napoléon's French allegiance and his Jacobin views antagonized the older man, and his military conduct didn't enhance his standing at all. Elected second-in-command of the volunteer militia, Napoléon was involved in an unsuccessful attempt to wrest control of the citadel from Royalist sympathizers. He thus took much of the blame when, in reprisal for the killing of one of the militiamen, several people were gunned down in Ajaccio, an incident which engendered eight days of civil war. In June 1793 Napoléon and his family were chased back to the mainland by the Paolists.

Napoléon promptly renounced any special allegiance he had ever felt for Corsica. He Gallicized the spelling of his name, preferring Napoléon to his baptismal Napoleone. And although he was later to speak with nostalgia about the scents of the Corsican countryside, and to regret he did not build a grand house there, he returned only once more to the island (after being forced to dock here during his return voyage from Egypt) and put Ajaccio fourth on the list of places where he would like to be buried.

The visit begins on the second floor, but before you go up look out for the wooden sedan chair in the hallway – Letizia was carried back from church on it when the prenatal Napoléon started giving her contractions, and it's one of the very few original pieces of furniture left in the house.

Upstairs, an endless display of portraits, miniatures, weapons, letters and documents gives the impression of having been formed by gathering together anything that was remotely connected with the family and unwanted by anyone else. Amongst the highlights of the first room are a few maps of Corsica dating from the eighteenth century, some deadly "vendetta" daggers and two handsome pairs of pistols belonging to Napoléon's father. The next-door Alcove Room was, according to tradition, occupied by Napoléon in 1799 when he stayed here for the last time, while in the third room you can see the sofa upon which the future emperor first saw the light of day on August 15, 1769. Adjoining the heavily restored long gallery is a tiny room known as the Trapdoor Room, whence Letizia and her children made their getaway from the marauding Paolists.

The Cathedral and St-Érasme

Napoléon was baptized in 1771 in the **Cathedral**, around the corner from Maison Bonaparte in rue Forcioli Conti. Generally known as *A Madonnuccia*, it was built in 1582 on a much smaller scale than originally intended due to lack of funds – an apology for its diminutive size is inscribed in a plaque inside, on the wall to the left as you enter. The interior is interesting chiefly for a few Napoléonic connections: to the right of the door stands the font where he was dipped at the age of 23 months; and his sister, Elisa Baciochi, donated the great marble altar in 1811. Before leaving, take a look in the chapel to the left of the altar, which houses a gloomy Delacroix painting of the Virgin holding aloft the Sacred Heart.

Further down the same road stands **St-Érasme**, a Jesuit chapel built in 1617, then dedicated to the town's fishermen in 1815. Should you find it open, you can see inside some model ships, a statue of St Erasmus and a pair of wooden Christs.

Musée Capitellu and the Citadelle

A left turn at the eastern end of rue Forcioli-Conti brings you onto bd Danielle-Casanova. Here, opposite the citadel, an elaborately carved capital marks the entrance to **Musée Capitellu** (May–Oct Mon–Wed 10am–noon & 2–6pm; 20F), a tiny museum mainly given over to offering a picture of domestic life in nineteenth-century Ajaccio. The house belonged to a wealthy Ajaccien family, the Baciochi, who were related to Napoléon through his sister's marriage, though he doesn't figure at all here.

Watercolour landscapes of Corsica line the walls of the first room, which also contains a marble *Madonnuccia* whose head was cut off

with a sabre during the French Revolution. Busts of Sampiero Corso, **Ajaccio**
a common adornment of smart nineteenth-century households, are
dotted about the second room, with some elegant copies of figures of
Venus from Herculaneum. The glass display cases hold the most fascinating exhibits, however, which include a rare edition of the first
history of Corsica, written by Agostino Giustiniani, a bishop of the
Nebbio who drowned in 1536, and the 1796 *Code Corse*, a list of
laws set out by Louis XV for the newly occupied Corsica. The last
room contains a bronze bust of a chubby-cheeked Pascal Paoli, and
a striking painting titled *Sunrise over Bavella*, attributed to
Turner's nephew.

Opposite the museum, the restored **Citadelle**, a hexagonal
fortress and tower stuck out on a wide promontory into the sea, is
occupied by the military and usually closed to the public. Founded in
the 1490s, the fort wasn't completed until the occupation of Ajaccio
by Sampiero Corso and the powerful Marshal Thermes in 1553–58.
The building overlooks the town beach, **Plage St-François**, a short
curve of yellow sand facing the expansive mountain-ringed bay.
Several flights of steps lead down to the beach from bd Danielle-
Casanova.

To get a better view of the town, follow the waterfront back to the
marina and walk to the end of the **Jetée de la Citadelle**, which juts
into the sea under the shadow of the fortress.

North of place Foch

Immediately **north of place Foch** behind the Hôtel de Ville, **square
César-Campinchi** is the venue for the island's largest fresh produce
market, held here on weekday and Saturday mornings throughout
the year, and an essential part of Ajaccien life. Alongside the usual
array of cut flowers, vegetables and fruit laid out under colourful
stripy awnings are stalls selling artisanal delicacies such as barbary
fig jam, honey *aux fleurs du maquis*, wild boar sauces and ewe's
cheese from the Niolo, as well as muscat wines and myrtle liqueurs.
The goods on sale are not cheap, but the quality is consistently high,
and the cafés lining the west side of the square are among the liveliest breakfast spots in town – ideal for crowd-watching after you've
finished browsing.

Behind the market, the principal road leading north is **rue Cardinal-
Fesch**, a delightful meandering street lined with boutiques, cafés and
restaurants. Halfway along the street, set back from the road behind
iron gates, stands the **Palais Fesch**, home of Ajaccio's best gallery, the
Musée Fesch (June 15–Sept 15 daily except Tues 10am–5.30pm, Oct
16–June 14 Tues–Sat 9.30am–noon & 2.30–6pm; no flash photography; 25F). Cardinal Joseph Fesch, whose image in bronze presides
over the courtyard, was Napoléon's step-uncle and Bishop of Lyons, a
lucrative position from which he invested in large numbers of paintings, many of them looted by the French armies in Holland, Italy and

Germany. A highly cultured man with an eye for a bargain, he bequeathed a thousand paintings to Ajaccio on the condition that an academy of arts was created in the town. His wishes were contested by Napoléon's brother Joseph, who turned a quick profit by dispersing much of the collection on the art market. Luckily for Ajaccio, however, Renaissance art was less highly regarded in those days than in later years, so many of the more valuable works remained here.

The collection is housed on four storeys; if you're pushed for time, skip the basement – which harbours an uninspring assortment of Napoleonic memorabilia – and head via the temporary exhibition room on the ground floor to **Niveau** (Level) **3** upstairs. where the cream of the sixteenth- and seventeenth-century Italian works are displayed. The paintings are ordered chronologically, starting in the gallery immediately to the right of the stairhead and progressing in an anticlockwise direction. In this first room hangs one of Fesch's greatest treasures, Sandro Botticcelli's exquisite *Virgin and Child*, painted when the artist was just 25 years old. Dating from a later period, Titian's smouldering *Man with a Glove*, at the end of the corridor, is shown opposite Veronese's *Leda and the Swan*, an uncompromisingly erotic work for its time. **Niveau 4** is given over primarily to seventeenth- and eighteenth-century paintings, where the absence of the Dutch masters sold off by Napoléon's brother is most keenly felt. Highlights here include Poussin's *Midas à la Source du Pactole*, in the first gallery on the right after the stairs, and a vibrant array of still lifes, notably Giuseppe Recco's *Ray on a Cauldron with Fish in a Basket*, noted for its subtle mix of silver-tinged hues. The largest gallery on this floor, **La Grande Galérie**, houses a collection of outsize canvases, of which Gregorio de Ferrari's *La Ste Famille* is the most famous.

You'll need a separate ticket for the **Chapelle Impériale** (same hours; 10F), which stands across the courtyard from the museum. With its gloomy monochrome interior the chapel itself is unremarkable; the interest lies in the crypt, which holds various members of the Bonaparte family. It was the cardinal's dying wish that all the Bonaparte family be brought together under one roof, so the chapel was built in 1857, and the bodies subsequently brought in – as recently as 1951 Charles Bonaparte was reburied here, alongside Letizia, Cardinal Fesch and half a dozen other Bonapartes.

Lucien Bonaparte laid the first stone of the adjacent **Bibliothèque Municipale**, which contains a huge collection of rare antique books. You're not allowed to handle any, but are welcome to browse and read periodicals and magazines on the long, polished table stretching down the middle of the chamber.

Eating, drinking and nightlife

Restaurants in Ajaccio vary from basic bistros to trendy pizzerias and pricy fish restaurants, the majority of which are found in the old town and off rue Cardinal-Fesch. Most places compensate for unadventurous menus by an appealing location, with tables set outside in the thick of city life. **Bars** and **cafés** jostle for pavement space all over town but especially along cours Napoléon, which is generally lined with young people checking out the promenaders, and on place de Gaulle, where old-fashioned cafés and *salons de thé* offer a more sedate scene. If you fancy sipping a drink with a view of the bay, you can go to one of the flashy cocktail bars that line the seafront beyond the citadel on bd Lantivy, but you do pay a lot more for the privilege.

What **nightlife** there is in Ajaccio consists chiefly of eating and drinking, though there are two cinemas, a busy municipal **casino** on bd Lantivy, and a few trashy **discos** to cater for the tourists and the more adventurous Ajacciens. *A l'Aghjia*, 13 chemin de Biancarello, north of cours Napoléon, occasionally hosts Corsican shows and plays.

Cafés and bars

La Belle Époque, rue Cardinal-Fesch, opposite the *Hôtel Fesch*. Large, shady terrace café that's a good venue for a croissant-and-coffee breakfast or afternoon ice cream.

Café Flore, 33 rue Cardinal-Fesch. Ersatz turn-of-the-century Parisian place, opposite the Musée Fesch, with Toulouse Lautrec posters and an old brass still setting the tone. Renowned for its copious lunchtime salads.

A Cantina, 18 bd du Roi-Jerôme. Unpretentious place opposite the port, serving simple Corsican snacks such as charcuterie, sandwiches and salads, as well as steaks and pasta.

L'Empéreur, 12 place de Gaulle. Elegant Art Nouveau salon de thé looking onto the square.

Le Menestrel, 5 rue Cardinal-Fesch. Dubbed "le rendez-vous des artistes" because local musicians play here most evenings after 7pm; traditional mandolin and guitar tunes, with the odd popular singalong number.

Safari, 18 bd Lantivy. Enormous cocktail bar with a lively terrace backing onto the promenade; a young evening hang-out.

Restaurants

L'Aquarium, rue des Halles. One of the best places in town for seafood – everything comes straight from the fish market across the square. Set menus 70–120F.

Les Halles, rue des Halles. Open since 1920, and the favourite lunch venue for market-stall holders and local office workers. They do a great value 70F menu with wild boar, fresh fish of the day and a choice of omelettes.

Da Mamma, passage Guinghetta. Tucked away down a narrow passageway connecting cours Napoléon and rue Cardinal-Fesch. Authentic but affordable Corsican cuisine, such as *cannelloni al brocciu*, roast kid and seafood, on good-value set menus starting at 60F. Slick service and a lively atmosphere.

A Pignata, 15 bd du Roi-Jerôme. The classiest of a clutch of small restaurants around rue des Halles and the market. House specialities include *marcassin* (baby wild boar) and unusual fresh pasta dishes. Set menus from 70F.

Point U, 30 rue Cardinal-Fesch. Among the town's top three restaurants. Strictly traditional Corsican cooking (artisanal charcuterie, rabbit cooked in myrtle wine, veal with olives, etc), served in cosy surroundings. Pricy, but not prohibitive.

Rong Vang (Golden Dragon), opposite the Bandera Museum on rue Maréchal-d'Ornano. One of Corsica's few Chinese restaurants, serving French-influenced Cantonese cuisine (frogs legs *à la pékinoise* or with lemon curry); no set menus, but à la carte dishes are a reasonable 40–50F. Closed Sun.

La Serre, 91 cours Napoléon. Inexpensive, filling main meals – including moussaka, roast lamb, quiche, and imaginative salads – from a self-service counter in an Art Deco-style cafeteria, close to the train station. Recommended if you're on a tight budget.

Discos and clubs

Casino, 5 bd Lantivy. Flashy Europop disco. Expensive.

A Cassetta, 4 av Sebastiani. Corsican nightclub with traditional singing as well as modern music.

Pennies, 13 rue Bonaparte. Popular nightclub hidden in the old town. Good music.

Ricantu, route du Ricanto. Ajaccio's only gay club is well out of town, near the airport, and hosts regular revues and cabarets.

Listings

Airlines Air France/Air Inter, 1 bd du Roi-Jerôme, next to the *Hôtel du Golfe* (☎04 95 29 45 45); Corse Air (☎04 95 21 55 55); TAT /British Airways (☎04 95 71 00 22).

Airport enquiries ☎04 95 21 07 07.

Banks and exchange Most of the main banks have branches on place de Gaulle or cours Napoléon, while the BNP is near the market place, on bd du Roi-Jerôme; the Société Générale, just up from the Parc Naturel Régional office on rue Sergeant-Casalonga, changes Thomas Cook French-franc travellers' cheques without commission.

Bookshops Maison de la Presse, 2 place Foch (☎04 95 25 81 18), stocks Ajaccio's best selection of books on Corsica, as well as a good range of international newspapers, including the *Guardian*, *Independent*, *New York Times*, and *Washington Post*. François Desjobert, on the opposite side of the square (☎04 95 23 30 17), is better for books in French, and sells audio cassettes by Corsican musicians.

Bus information ☎04 95 21 28 01.

Car rental Aloha, at the airport (☎04 95 23 57 19); Avis-Ollandini, 1 route d'Alata (☎04 95 23 92 50) and at the airport (☎04 95 21 28 01); Citer, bd Lantivy (☎04 95 21 40 65) and at the airport (☎04 95 20 52 32); Europcar, 16 cours Grandval (☎04 95 21 05 49) and at the airport (☎04 95 23 18 73); Hertz-Locasud, 8 cours Grandval (☎04 95 21 70 94) and at the airport (☎04 95 22 14 84).

Cinemas *Empire*, 18 cours Napoléon, is a 1930s-style mainstream cinema; *Laetitia*, 48 cours Napoléon, opposite the post office, screens art-house films.

Diving Popular diving sites around Ajaccio include Les Dentis, a shallow shelf 200m offshore near the citadel; La Castagne, dramatic rock formations rich with underwater life on the southern extremity of the bay; and Les Îles Sanguinaires, 12km west of town (see p.175). Winds and currents can be a problem in all three; for advice, transport and training, contact any of the following reputable diving clubs: Société Nautique d'Ajaccio, Fossé de la Citadelle (☎04 95 21 07 79); Homopalmus, 3 route d'Alata (☎04 95 22 68 12); Club les Calanques, route des Sanguinaires (☎04 95 52 09 37); or Aquasub Center, Hôtel Stella di Mare (☎04 95 52 01 07).

Hospital Centre Hospitalier, 27 av Impératrice-Eugénie (☎04 95 29 90 90).

Laundry Bottom of rue Maréchal-Ornano, off cours Grandval.

Left luggage In the terminal maritime; 10F per article per working day (8.30am–7pm), or part thereof.

Motorbike rental Cheapest of the three companies in Ajaccio is Locacorse, at 10 rue Bévérini (☎04 95 20 71 20), close to the train station, which rents mainly 80cc scooters; for trials bikes, try Corse Évasion, Monté St-Jean (☎04 95 20 52 05); also worth checking out is BMS Locations, in the Port Tino Rossi (☎04 95 21 33 75).

Pharmacies Several large pharmacies on place Foch and cours Napoléon.

Police rue Général Fiorella (☎04 95 29 95 29); emergencies ☎17.

Post office 8 cours Napoléon.

Sports facilities The Complexe Municipal Pascal Rossi, on av Pascal-Rossini (☎04 95 21 08 30), is Ajaccio's largest public sports centre, with a pool, gym, weights room and running track. The municipal tennis courts are out of town on route des Sanguinaires (☎04 95 52 00 25).

Taxis The main taxi rank is on the north side of place de Gaulle (☎04 95 21 00 87).

Telephones There are booths (*cabines téléphoniques*) all over the centre; phone cards are available in the post office, and at tobacconists and photography shops along cours Napoléon.

Train enquiries Gare SNCF (☎04 95 23 11 03).

Travel agents Corse Publitours, 6 rue Cardinal-Fesch, just off place Foch (☎04 95 21 68 80, fax 04 95 21 70 63); Nouvelles Frontières, 14 place Foch (☎04 95 20 13 69); Havas Kallistour Voyages, 11 place de Gaulle (☎04 95 21 17 36, fax 04 95 21 39 47); Ollandini, 3 place de Gaulle (☎04 95 21 10 40, fax 04 95 51 05 54).

Moving on from Ajaccio

Ajaccio's ferry port is the second busiest on the island after Bastia, and its terminal routière on the quai l'Herminier forms the nexus of the long-distance bus network, so most independent travellers come here at some point to pick up onward transport.

By plane

Campo dell'Oro airport, 6km south of Ajaccio, is served by daily scheduled flights to cities on the French mainland, including Marseille, Nice and Paris on Air France/Air Inter, as well as weekly charter flights to northern Europe between April and October; Gatwick is the main destination for British charter operators, but there are also weekly departures to Stansted and Manchester. You can also fly direct from here twice daily in summer to Figari and Calvi with Kyrnair, or once each week to Bastia. Details of airline companies and travel agents in Ajaccio appear in "Listings", on p.170. The cheapest way to get to the airport from town is on the shuttle bus that runs three times per hour from place de Gaulle and cours Napoléon; taxis cost around 100F.

By ferry

Most of the car and passenger ferries sailing out of Ajaccio go to Marseille, with less frequent departures to Toulon and Nice. SCNM operate one to two crossings daily from July until mid-September, five to seven each week from then until the end of October and during late June, and three weekly for the rest of the year. The crossing takes seven hours by day and eleven hours on the night service, or four-and-a-half hours on the superfast NGV 1, which only sails in June and October. Tickets cost 260–310F per person, depending on the destination and time of year, and are available up to two hours before departure time from SNCM's counter inside the arrivals hall of the terminal maritime (☎04 95 29 66 63), or in advance at their office directly opposite on the quai l'Herminier (Mon–Fri 8–11am & 2–6pm, Sat 8–11.45am; ☎04 95 29 66 99). You can also book through any of the travel agents named in "Listings" on p.171.

By train

The four-hour trip from Ajaccio across the mountains to Bastia ranks among the island's most memorable journeys, taking in the wild valleys and pine forests of the interior around Corte, and a string of sleepy village stations. At Ponte Leccia the line forks, with a branch veering northwest along the coast to Île Rousse and Calvi; taking five hours with a change at the junction, this route is longer, but equally scenic, and with the added attraction of seascapes along the way. Four trains leave Ajaccio daily in summer for Bastia, and between two and four in winter depending on the day; Calvi is served by two departures all year round, although the timetables changes between September and June. You can check the timings at the tourist office, or by telephoning the station direct (☎04 95 23 11 03).

By bus

Ajaccio is well connected by bus to other towns on the island, though finding out which one you need can be difficult, as the routes are all run by different companies. The tourist office on place Foch keeps a set of up-to-date timetables, but the best source of information is the spanking new terminal routière on quai l'Herminier, where all the operators have individual counters. Their destinations and departure times are displayed on boards, and you can pay for tickets in advance up to a couple of hours before the bus leaves; they'll also look after your luggage for free. A full list of destinations reachable by bus from Ajaccio appears in "Travel details" on p.194.

Around Ajaccio

The maquis-carpeted ridge of hills north of Ajaccio, known as **Les Crêtes**, holds a few interesting possibilities for a half-day excursion, as long as you have your own transport. Chief of these is the **Punta di Pozzo di Borgo**, which provides an excellent view of Ajaccio and its bay and is reached by a road that takes you close to **Les Millelli**, the country residence owned, but seldom visited, by the Bonapartes. Walkers can take the gentle stroll west of town to **Monte Salario** to see the **Fontaine de Salario**, or chance the more strenuous ascent up the pink granite masses of the **Rochers des Gozzi**, a landmark in the Gravona valley northeast of town.

Les Millelli and Punta di Pozzo di Borgo

Situated 5km northwest of Ajaccio, off the D61, **Les Millelli** (daily except Tues 9am–noon & 2–6pm; 5F) came into the Bonaparte family in 1797, but was used rarely. In 1793, before it came into the family, Letizia was forced to hide out here on her way to the Tour du Capitello in her flight from the Paolists, and Napoléon stayed here with Murat in 1799 on his return from Egypt – but that's about the extent of its relevance. Nonetheless the house is a firmly established stage on the Napoleonic trail. It's a stolid, plain, eighteenth-century building whose real attraction is the surrounding terraced olive grove that overlooks the gulf – a pleasant picnic spot. Inside there's just a small and dreary ethnographical museum.

If, instead of taking the turn to Les Millelli, you go 6km further along the D61 you'll come to the Col de Pruno, where a left turn along a narrow twisting road will bring you after another 6km to the **Punta di Pozzo di Borgo** and its ruined **chateau**. Built by the Pozzo di Borgo family in 1886, the chateau was constructed with materials provided by the demolition of the Tuileries in 1871 and is the exact reproduction of one of the pavilions of that palace – an inscription on the wall states that it was built to preserve a precious souvenir of the home country. In the nineteenth century the Pozzo di Borgo family still owned everything round here, but virtually nothing remained of their native village, which was razed by pirates in 1594; a tower on the track up to the Punta is the sole remnant. From the terrace of the chateau you get fine **views** of the gulfs of Sagone and Ajaccio, and of Monte d'Oro and Renoso to the east.

La Fontaine de Salario

It's a 5km walk or drive from Ajaccio, or a ride on the #7 bus from place de Gaulle, to the **Fontaine de Salario** (or Funta Salamandra), a spring on a 300m hill at the base of Monte Salario. Named after the salamanders that once crawled all over this part of the country, the spring offers another magnificent view of the Golfe d'Ajaccio. From here a trail leads up to **Monte Salario**, a half-hour walk, and from the summit a rocky trail known as the Chemin de la Serra leads directly back down to town.

The Rochers des Gozzi

A solid pink-tinted clump of bare rock rising from the dense maquis and cultivated fields and vineyards northeast of Ajaccio, the **Rochers des Gozzi** provide the Ajaccio area's finest panorama of the mountains and the sea. The 10km hike should take between two and three hours from the village of **Appietto**, 20km from Ajaccio. From Ajaccio take the **bus** to Listincone (16km), which drops you off in the village, just by the signposted turn-off for Appietto, another 4km up a narrow road. Drivers can take the car as far as Appietto.

The track to the summit begins by Appietto's cemetery, leading initially to the church standing on the facing ridge, and continuing as a goat track to the top of the ridge. Following the crest of the ridge, the track cuts through the maquis. After about 4km from the church you'll come to a fence that you can cross by means of a large boulder. Some 300m further, climb the crumbling stone wall that runs down the ridge, then continue to the right of this wall for a few metres before you reach a rocky platform, which affords tantalizing vistas and a place to catch your breath. Heading along the right-hand branch of the path, which skirts the hillside from the platform, you'll come to a faint trail that crosses the ridge over some difficult ground – follow it for 1km to another fork. Either branch will do, and you'll soon reach a trickle of a stream by a precipice facing a derelict stone building. You need to take care from now on as you walk along the wall and scramble down into the easily visible gap across the neck of the Rochers. After a stiff climb of 485m, with deep ravines dropping on either side, you'll reach the top.

The Golfe d'Ajaccio

West of Ajaccio the **route des Sanguinaires** (as the D111 is known) hugs the coast for 12km, passing a succession of tourist developments and sandy beaches before coming to an end at the northern tip of the gulf, the **Punta della Parata**. This headland faces the cluster of crumbling granite islets called the Îles **Sanguinaires**, a miniature archipelago ideally seen from the sea. If you're not lucky enough to have your own boat, you can opt for an **excursion** from Ajaccio marina, though you'll have to contend with a banal running commentary; the trip costs about 100F and lasts two hours, stopping for an hour at the largest island, **Mezzo Mare**. Although the **beaches** along this stretch don't rate as highly as the more secluded strands of the southern gulf, they are more accessible to those without a vehicle. Regular buses from place de Gaulle follow the route: buses #1 and #2 go as far as Ajaccio's cemetery, whereas #5 will take you all the way to Punta della Parata, stopping at **Barbicaja**, **Scudo** and **Terre Sacré**.

The liveliest spot along the southern arm of the Golfe d'Ajaccio – known as **La Rive Sud** – is **Porticcio**, the largest and most established resort along this stretch. Once a hang-out for the rich and famous, the place nowadays has lost its elitist appeal and gets swamped by watersports enthusiasts and weekenders from Ajaccio as soon as summer sets in. Quieter spots are found south of Porticcio, where the coast is less developed and the scent of the maquis takes over, the shrubland clearing at intervals to reveal superb sandy beaches such as **Plage de Verghia** and **Portigliolo**. Genoese watchtowers again feature on every headland, the most prominent being the **Tour de la Castagna** and the enormous construction on **Capo di Muro**, the southernmost point of the gulf. An alternative to the coast road is the inland route from Pisciatella, crossing a series of lovely mountain passes surrounded by maquis and dense woodland, through the belvedere village of **Coti-Chiavari** and then down to Capo di Muro.

Route des Sanguinaires

The first landmark along the coast north of Ajaccio, the **Chapelle des Grecs**, lies 3km along the route. Built in 1632 by Artilio Pozzo di Borgo, it was allocated for the use of the Greeks in 1733, who settled in Ajaccio after being driven out of their small colony at Paomia by Corsican rebels (see p.186) and forced to take refuge here.

The **beaches** start about 1km beyond the cemetery with **Barbicaja**, a usually crowded sandy stretch providing adequate swimming. **Marinella**, another 2km on, is the next beach and the most popular, backed by bars and restaurants. About 4km further, **Terre Sacré** gets its name from the metre-high stone urn, containing the ashes of soldiers killed in World War I, that stands on the beach; this stretch is quieter and boasts an excellent restaurant, the *Auberge du Terre Sacré*. **Cala Lunga** is the last strand, stretching as far as **Punta della Parata**, the narrow, rocky headland that was once connected to the Îles Sanguinaires. Tremendous views of the gulf reward the ten-minute clamber up to the **Tour de la Parata**, a tall Genoese construction built in the sixteenth century to ward off Moorish pirates.

Îles Sanguinaires

Composed of four humps of red granite, the **Îles Sanguinaires** might be named after Sagone or after *Sagonarri* (black blood), from the colour they turn at sunset. A protected site, the islands harbour large colonies of gulls, and it's forbidden to pick flowers or take eggs from the land.

Walk to Capo di Feno from Punta Della Parata

A good way to see the westernmost point of the Golfe de Sagone is to do the walk north of Parata along the coast as far as **Capo di Feno**, a route that also has the attraction of giving access to some fine beaches. The distance of 15km should take about four hours; it's an easy walk but there is quite thick maquis to plough through, so you'll need strong shoes and covered legs.

Start by the restaurant facing the tower, from where a broad path leads into the maquis, skirting round a deep cove with a rifle range to your right. Follow the track uphill, passing through a fence before you reach a wider path where you should go left. Cross a low ridge, passing another rocky inlet below: a track on the left goes down to the sea, the broader path continuing to Capo di Feno, which emerges ahead after a few metres. Proceed along the coast for about 2km, when you'll start to descend through thick maquis, emerging onto a track above the white sandy cove at **Capigliolo**. Beyond the next cove a clear path leads to the **Anse de Minaccia**, a nudist beach. Pass the bar, and after 1km you'll see a fence blocking the way: go under it, following the path through more scrub onto another track. After another 1km you'll come to a glade shaded by pines and mimosa. Pass a house and fork left, continuing as far as a T-junction and a fence. Go through the gate or climb over, and continue straight until you join the main trail to Capo di Feno. Follow the descent into a secluded cove before picking up the trail again at the end of the beach, where a view of Capo di Feno emerges, with a Genoese watchtower crowning the promontory.

The largest islet, **Mezzo Mare** (or Grande Sanguinaire), is topped by a lighthouse, where Alphonse Daudet was inspired to write one of his *Lettres de Mon Moulin*, in which he waxed lyrical about the islet's "reddish and fierce aspect". Tufts of gorse, a ruined tower and crashing surf give the place a dramatic air, which is perhaps why Joseph Bonaparte wanted to be buried here, though his wish wasn't realized.

The southern gulf

Following the main road along the N193 south of Ajaccio for 8km will bring you to the junction with the D55, which follows the Rive Sud as far as Port de Chiavari, some 40km from town. A minor road continues to Punta de la Castagna. Buses along the coast depart hourly from Ajaccio's terminal routière for Plage de Ricanto, near the airport, with hourly buses in summer going as far as Plage de Ruppione.

To reach the inland route along the **southern gulf**, you need to follow the N196 from Ajaccio to the airport in the direction of Porticcio, until you reach Pisciatella, where you switch to the D302. There are no buses along this route.

La Rive Sud

Four kilometres before Porticcio, the massive **Tour du Capitello** appears at the end of a short track leading off to the right of the road across the bridge. The tower's cracks were the result of a famous siege in 1793, when Napoléon and fifty men from the French fleet were stranded waiting for backup in preparation for an attack on Ajaccio. With only one cannon to protect them from the army of Corsican patriots, they were holed up for three days. This was also the scene of Napoléon's reunion in 1793 with his mother and Cardinal Fesch, who sought refuge here after being chased out of town by Paolists before their flight to Toulon.

PORTICCIO village, 18km south of Ajaccio, basically comprises a loop of modern hotels and shops dominated by a huge shopping complex – however, the **beach** is fabulous, a wide sandy stretch commanding a great view of the gulf. Come summer, the place is overwhelmed by Ajacciens in a constant stream of cars, but on the other hand there's the compensation of the lively nightlife, as the cinemas and discos get cranked up for the holidaymakers.

A small **tourist office** in the shopping complex (Mon–Sat May–Aug 9am–8pm, Sun 9am–1pm & 4–8pm; ☎04 95 25 01 01) can be helpful for finding somewhere to stay. Much of the **accommodation** is

The Golfe d'Ajaccio

More background to these events appears on p.164.

The Mare e Monti Sud Trail

The recently inaugurated **Mare e Monti Sud** hiking trail runs from Porticcio to Propriano, divided into five relatively easy stages of between 3hr 45min and 6hr, and waymarked with orange splashes of paint. The scenery along the route, which winds southwest along the ridge dividing the Golfe d'Ajaccio from the Golfe de Valinco, is nowhere near as dramatic as on the original Mare e Monti trail (see p.122), but the gentle, maquis-covered hills and rocky coastline make it an enjoyable hike that will particularly appeal to less experienced walkers. It also takes you within striking distance of the windswept beaches at Capo di Muro (covered on p.180), the prehistoric site at Filitosa, and the picturesque resort of Porto Pollo (see pp.197–203). The only real drawback is that, unlike most of the long-distance footpaths in Corsica, this one does not have gîtes d'étape at each stage, which means you have to shell out on hotels or campsites for at least three of the four or five nights.

Once again, the Parc Naturel Régional de Corse's **topo-guide** is an indispensable companion, giving contour maps and detailed descriptions of each stage; copies are available at most good bookshops on the island, and at the Parc Naturel Régional's office in Ajaccio (see p.159). You should also check the general introduction to hiking on p.25 of "Basics".

Mare e Monti Sud accommodation

The trail's only two gîtes d'étape are at Bisinao (☎04 95 24 21 66) and Burgo (☎04 95 76 15 05). Both are heavily booked during the summer, when you should reserve at least a couple of days in advance to ensure a bed. For reviews of hotels and campsites in Porticcio, Côti-Chiavari, Porto Pollo, Olmeto, and Propriano, check the relevant accounts on pp.178, 180, 203, 201 and 205.

---

aimed at rich, sporty types and is very expensive during July and August, but tariffs are reasonable at *Hôtel de Porticcio*, at the crossroads in the centre of the village (☎04 95 25 05 77; ④); breakfast is included in the price, rooms are light and airy, and the hotel has its own tennis courts. Otherwise you can try *Isolella*, 500m to the south of the village (☎04 95 25 41 36; ③), a smaller place with balconied rooms. If you fancy splashing out, go to *Le Maquis*, 2km south of Porticcio (☎04 95 25 05 55; ⑥), set in a secluded cove and done up like a Palladian villa. For **campers**, there's the three-star *Camping Prunelli* (☎04 95 25 19 23; year round), which has a pool, supermarket and small restaurant, and *Camping Benista* (☎04 95 25 19 30; May–Oct), both 4km north of the village near the junction with the N196, on the Ajaccio road (D55). Apart from their high prices, the main drawback with these places is that they are 2km from the nearest beach.

Pizzeria l'Ostaria, south of the centre on the main street, is the cheapest **eating** place around and boasts a terrace with a view. Another popular joint is the very Corsican *Crêperie Marie*, on the road to Ajaccio, which does inexpensive and tasty crêpes of every description.

A Walk in the Forêt de Chiavari

From the Plage de Verghia it's a gentle climb into the **Forêt de Chiavari**, a dense mass of eucalyptus, maquis, oak and cork trees shrouding the slopes above the beach. The more or less circular 16km walk described below should take about three hours.

Just before the D55 veers inland, a wide forest track signposted "Forêt Domaniale de Chiavari" strikes up through the trees. Pass the picnic tables and ignore the first track to the right, taking instead the right track at a junction 500m ahead. After 2km you'll pass a graveyard; 200m beyond here, continue straight at the junction where the path broadens into an avenue of eucalyptus trees. You will hit the D55 after another 1km; at this point you re-enter the forest along the track above the road, heading back in the direction you came, then pass through a fence, snatching views of Ajaccio and the gulf through the trees. After another 3km, a break in vegetation affords views over the Port de Chiavari, with the Punta di Sette Nave to the north. Great rocks piercing the maquis-shrouded hills characterize the surrounding landscape. Head towards the open valley, crossing the stream twice before you reach the ruins of a penitentiary hidden amongst the trees. Once used to house convicts serving sentences of hard labour (many of them buried in the overgrown graveyard), it's now a shell of ghostly passageways and dark cellars.

Behind the building, take the left fork downwards, past a drinking fountain, then left at the next fork. The track narrows in its descent to the coast but provides expansive views over the bay. After 6km, cross a stone wall and you'll soon reach an intersection; carry on straight, skirting round the wood of gnarled eucalyptus. Ignore the right fork and carry on until a junction, where you must bear left down the track through vines and lavender-carpeted ground. You'll hit the D55 by Ruppione beach, 5km north of where you began.

Beaches south of Porticcio

South of Porticcio the D55 narrows in its progress along the coast, a high bank of maquis screening expensive villas and private beaches from the passing cars. Some 5km along you'll come to **Plage d'Agosta**, a popular, wide, sandy beach sheltered in the south by the Punta di Sette Nave, a narrow, rocky headland crowned by the Tour de l'Isolella. A couple of **hotels** here are worth checking out: *Motel Agosta Plage* (☎04 95 25 40 26; April 15–Oct 15; ④) offers moderately priced self-catering chalets overlooking the beach, while the unpretentious *Kallisté* (☎04 95 25 54 19; May–Sept; ③–⑥), 1km from the beach, has a range of variously priced en-suite rooms, some with baths.

By far the finest beach along this stretch, and a less frenetic spot than Plage d'Agosta, is **Plage de Ruppione**, a half-moon-shaped cove 8km south of Porticcio – perfect for sheltered swimming and snorkelling. Campers can stay here at the well-sited *Camping le Sud* (☎04 95 25 40 51; May–Oct), one of the less expensive campsites along this coast.

From here onwards the coast becomes gloriously rural, with folds of woodland backing onto tapering rocky headlands and golden coves. At PORT DE CHIAVARI, some 5km south of Ruppione, the beautiful **Plage de Verghia** has a makeshift bar and a **campsite**, *La Vallée*, set back from the main road close to the beach (☎04 95 25 44 66; May–Oct). At this point the D55 narrows and turns sharply inland towards Côti-Chiavari. The road ahead deteriorates on the approach to the **Anse de Portigliolo**, a delightful, almost circular sandy cove. Beyond here the road climbs and crumbles as it gets nearer to the **Tour de la Castagna**, a great Genoese tower on the promontory jutting into the gulf. Camping wild is possible beyond the Punta di a Castagna.

The inland route

Some 10km from Pisciatella, where the D302 peels south off the main Ajaccio–Bonifacio road (N196), the **Col de Belle Valle** (522m) opens out with views of Ajaccio and the Sanguinaires laid out to the west. The right fork here will take you more directly to the Chiavari forest, but to get the most out of the landscape, take the left fork, in the direction of Bisinao. This latter road twists through a dark rocky gorge, giving a great view of the Punta di Sette Nave, before reaching the **Col d'Aja Bastiano** (638m). At this point the D55 cuts south up the ridge at a gentle gradient amidst heavy scrubland of broom, mimosa, gorse and wild thyme, a mixture known as the *maquis dense*. Some 4km ahead, the **Col de Chenova** (629m) offers more expansive views, then the continuation of the D55 brings you into the eucalyptus-lined route shouldering the **Forêt de Chiavari**.

The **Col de Cortone** (523m) lies towards the southern edge of the forest, and from here it's a short way to CÔTI-CHIAVARI, a pretty orange-stone village overlooking the Golfe d'Ajaccio. You can **stay** here at the *Hôtel Belvedère*, a family-run place recently relocated to a wonderful site 1km below (south of) the village (☎04 95 27 10 32; ③, optional half board ⑤); it does excellent home-cooking, served on a terrace overlooking the sea, and has a loyal following – so make sure you book ahead if you want to stay. Several people rent out apartments and rooms in the village; the *Belvedère* can point you in the right direction.

North of the village, a road favoured by practising rally drivers hairpins down to Port de Chiavari, while the D55 continues deeper into the headland. About 4km along the D55, a narrow track leading off to the right will take you almost as far as **Capo di Muro**, where a watchtower marks the southern limit of the Golfe d'Ajaccio. There's a magnificent **beach** here called **Cala d'Orzu**, accessible along a rough but motorable dirt track. In summer you should try the shack **restaurant** here, *Chez Francis*, to which people drive from as far as Ajaccio to enjoy its fresh, no-nonsense seafood from the gulf.

The Cinarca

Contained within mountains approaching 1000m high to the north and south, the **Cinarca** forms the hinterland to the Golfe de Sagone north of Ajaccio. Once the seat of the powerful Cinarchesi, a family of corrupt self-titled nobles who ruled the country in the thirteenth century, the region is today renowned for its *appellation contrôlée* wine, produced near the banks of the River Liscia, in a cluster of sleepy villages along the **Route des Vins**. A tour of the Cinarca can easily be made in about two hours, passing through **Calcatoggio** en route to the chief village of the region, **Sari d'Orcino**, an appealing little place set deep in the verdant countryside. From here you continue through the villages of **Casaglione** and **Ambiegna** before returning to the coast road.

The villages

Two kilometres from the main D81, just over 20km north of Ajaccio, **CALCATOGGIO**'s bleached houses rise from a jungle of vineyards and orchards, creating a scene that's typical of the Cinarca. The terraced hillside location gives a pleasant view of the azure Golfe de la Liscia, and there are more marvellous views if you continue for about 1km beyond the village and then turn right along the D101, descending to the sinuous corniche of the lush Liscia valley.

Passing through Sant'Andrea d'Orcino and Canelle, two villages nestled close together amidst vines and fig trees, the road threads its way up to **SARI D'ORCINO**, a village composed of two hamlets stacked up the slopes of Punta San Damiano. In the second, Acqua in Giu, the parish church's terrace gives a panorama of the whole of the Cinarca, its green carpet of fruit trees sliced by the river, which you

Giudice della Cinarca

The medieval **Cinarchesi**, a loose association of feudal lords, many of them distantly related, controlled wide tracts of the wilder southern half of Corsica, maintaining an especially tight grip on the Cinarca region. The most famous of these chieftains was Sinucello della Rocca, better known as **Giudice della Cinarca**, described by fifteenth-century historian Giovanni della Grossa as "one of the most extraordinary men who has ever existed on the island".

Born in Olmeto in 1219, Giudice began his career allied to the Genoese, but he refused to give up his feudal rights and become a vassal to the republic. Constantly battling against the rival Cinarchesi from his base in the castle of Istria, he managed to gain effective control of the whole of the south of the island, and at one point was able to summon all the region's lords and chieftains to form a national assembly before the Genoese eventually had him chased out of Corsica. Thereupon Giudice took up the Pisan cause, distinguishing himself at the battle of Meloria in 1284, the naval engagement that was Pisa's downfall. After that he returned to the mountain fastnesses of Corsica to resume his war on Genoa and his neighbouring warlords.

It was during this period that Giudice (meaning "judge" or "governor") set himself up as a figure of public authority, arbitrating vendettas, forcing the rich to pay high taxes, and punishing wrongdoers and enemies with extreme brutality – blinding his adversaries was a favoured tactic. He consolidated his position by allowing a greater degree of freedom to the burgeoning peasant bourgeoisie than was accorded by other Cinarchesi tyrants, and married off his six daughters to local counts to ensure the continuation of his power. In 1289 and 1290 the Genoese launched two massive and unsuccessful attempts to overthrow Giudice, who by this time was nearly blinded by venereal disease, yet he was only captured when betrayed by one of his many illegitimate sons. Thrown into a common prison on the French mainland, he died of fever in 1307.

Dorothy Carrington, in her book *Granite Island*, recalls a popular folk tale concerning Giudice. According to the story, the mighty warlord, who started life miserably poor and hunchbacked, fell in love with a wealthy and beautiful widow named Sibilia, whom he asked to marry him. On receiving her refusal, Giudice threatened to abduct her, whereupon the lady asked him to her castle at Istria. But the invitation was a trap, and on arriving there the young suitor was imprisoned. To rub salt in the wound, it is said that Sibilia had him thrown into an iron cage in her dungeon and "paraded herself in front of him, in all her loveliness, stark naked". However, Giudice bribed the guards to set him free and soon exacted a cruel revenge. Capturing the castle, he took Sibilia in the same cage to a nearby mountain col and prostituted her to passers-by until she perished of hunger and humiliation. The story is mostly myth, but retains a few bones of historical truth: Giudice (neither poor nor hunchbacked) did indeed court a beautiful widow, Sibilia de Franchi, who had him thrown into prison for a reason that has been lost over time. When the insulted nobleman eventually escaped from her clutches, he restored his honour by committing Sibilia to a place that was, in the words of a chronicler, "less than honest".

can see flowing into the Golfe de la Liscia. Just beyond the village, you can stop and **taste wine** at the *Clos d'Alzeto*, owned by Pascal Albertini (☎04 95 52 24 67).

North of Sari d'Orcino, the D1 skirts a high rocky wall for 3km as far as **AMBIEGNA**, an elegant village bordering the Liamone valley and a soaring pine wood. Head south from here along the D25 for 3km to **CASAGLIONE**, an ancient cluster of silvery stone buildings grouped around a church that houses a painting of the Crucifixion dated 1505. From here it's a gentle meander back down to the coast.

The Golfe de Sagone

Long curves of sandy beach characterize Corsica's largest gulf, the **Golfe de Sagone**, which stretches 40km from Capo di Feno up to the Punta di Cargèse. The gulf lacks the wild allure of much of the west coast, with new holiday villages, bungalows and campsites springing into existence every year, but the resorts make acceptable bases for a few days if you have your own transport. Tucked into the **Golfe de la Liscia** at the easternmost indent of the gulf, the resort of **Tiuccia** is the most sheltered spot, with a fine golden **beach** close by. North of here, **Sagone** thrives as a centre for scuba diving and watersports, but it can't match the appeal of **Cargèse**, a lovely and increasingly chic clifftop village at the northern tip of the bay.

Tiuccia and Sagone

Once the D81 hits the coast, the first concentration of hotels and campsites can be found at **TIUCCIA**, some 25km north of Ajaccio at the northern end of the Golfe de la Liscia, a half-moon bay set within the Golfe de Sagone. Consisting chiefly of a line of modern buildings bordering the main road, Tiuccia has a trio of minor historic sights – two seventeenth-century Genoese watchtowers and the ruined **Castello di Capraja**, seat of Giudice della Cinarca – but its strong point is **Plage de la Liscia**, a broad golden strand 500m to the south.

Tourist information is handled by *Hôtel Cinarca*, on the main street (☎04 95 52 21 39; ④), whose rooms afford a good view of the bay. You'll find the least expensive beds at *Le Bon Accueil*, in the middle of the resort (☎/fax 04 95 52 21 01; ③), a comfortable inn with ten rooms and an excellent, moderately priced restaurant specializing in Corsican food. Other options include the nearby *Beau Rivage* (☎04 95 52 21 09; ③), and the more upmarket *Hôtel Nerval*, 3km south of Tiuccia at Liscia (☎04 95 52 25 35; April–Oct; ④), a luxurious modern complex near the beach, with tennis courts and a patio pool.

Buses from Ajaccio stop next to the **campsite** by the main road just outside the village, but if you have your own vehicle, a better place is the three-star *Les Couchants*, 3km out of Tiuccia on the D25 to Casaglione (☎04 95 52 26 60; May–Oct), which occupies an attractive site in fields overlooking the valley to the sea. Alternatively, head 3km south along the Ajaccio road to *La Liscia* (☎04 95 52 25 35; April–Oct), another large and well-equipped site with a disco, shop and snack bar.

The next significant place along this stretch is **SAGONE**, formerly a bishopric and important fishing port until marauding Saracens destroyed the town in the sixteenth century. The only evidence of Sagone's past glory is the cathedral of **Sant'Appiano**, a crumbling ruin dating from the twelfth century sited a kilometre north of the village. The village itself is a string of tired-looking hotels and restaurants, slightly redeemed by **Plage du Liamone**, a long sandy beach to the north of the resort. Despite its minimal charm, Sagone gets pretty crowded in high season, principally on account of the watersports facilities offered along the beach.

Accommodation is strung out along the main road thruugh the centre of the village. *Hôtel Cyrnos*, next door to *Immeubles les Mimosa* in the centre (☎04 95 28 00 01; ④), is functional but nothing special – it is, however, the base for the Centre Subaquatique (same phone number), whose staff can guide you to the excellent **diving** sites around the Pointe Leccia, a headland with a sheer underwater drop of 80m. Alternative hotels, just beyond the village, are *La Marine*, an attractive stone building on the left of the road to Ajaccio (☎04 95 28 00 03, fax 04 95 28 03 98; closed Jan; ③), whose terrace jutting into the sea gives it the edge on other hotels in the vicinity; and the *Motel Funtanella*, 4km along the road to Cargèse (☎04 95 28 03 36; ④), which is shady and secluded but doesn't have a restaurant. The best **campsite** in the area, *Camping Sagone*, lies 3km inland on the road to Vico (☎04 95 28 04 15, fax 04 95 28 08 28; May–Oct), and offers riding, tennis and underwater fishing. The only commendable **restaurant** in the area is the *Kallisté*, an inexpensive pizzeria on the beach that serves a good range of seafood dishes, including anemone soup (*soupe d'oursin*).

Worth considering if you're staying in Sagone is a **boat trip** to Girolata and the Scandola reserve. Departing from the *Aneura* restaurant at 8.30am, the trips cost 180F (half-price for kids) and last all day; the boats are narrow enough to penetrate several of the most impressive breaches in the red cliffs and sea caves around Porto, and return via the Calanche at around 5pm. Tickets should be reserved the day before (☎04 95 28 04 13).

Cargèse

Sitting high above a deep blue bay on a cliff scattered with olive trees, **CARGÈSE** (Carghjese) oozes a lazy charm that attracts hundreds of well-heeled summer residents to its pretty white houses and hotels, giving the place an air of an exclusive holiday resort. The full-

The Scandola nature reserve and Girolata, an isolated fishing village, are located along one of the most dramatic stretches of the coast in Corsica, see pp.137–139.

*Cargèse marks
the end of the
popular Mare
e Monti long-
distance foot-
path, which
starts in
Calenzana, see
p.122.*

time locals, many of them descendants of Greek refugees from the
Peloponnese in the seventeenth century (see box on p.186), seem to
accept this inundation and the proximity of a Club Med complex with
generous nonchalance, but the best time to visit is September, when
Cargèse empties and you can enjoy its distinctive qualities in peace.

Two **churches** stand on separate hummocks at opposite sides of
the valley head, one Catholic and one Orthodox, a reminder of the
old antagonism between the two cultures. The **Greek church**, the
more interesting of the two, is a large granite neo-Gothic edifice built
in 1852 to replace a church that had become too small for the congregation. Inside, the outstanding feature is the **iconostasis**, a gift
from a monastery in Rome, decorated with **icons** painted by monks
from Mount Athos and brought over from Greece with the original
settlers in the late seventeenth century – the graceful *Virgin and
Child* is thought to date from as far back as the twelfth century.
Flanking the iconostasis are a number of thirteenth-century paintings on canvas, including one of a winged St John the Baptist, his
severed head at his feet. The icons are currently being restored by a
team of European fresco painters who are also working on new frescoes for the walls, giving the church a rather too vibrant look.

Built for the minority Corsican families in 1828, the **Catholic
church** is one of the latest examples of Baroque in Corsica and has a
trompe l'œil ceiling that can't really compete with the view from the
church's terrace.

You can swim off the rocks beneath the hotel *Bel'Mare* (see
opposite), if you climb down the cliff through the gate just past the
hotel. There's also another quieter sand and gravel beach 2km south;
head towards Ajaccio and turn off along the track where you see the
Hertz sign, leading to a small marina. However, by far the best beach
in the area, **Plage de Pero**, is 2km north of Cargèse – walk up to the
junction with the Piana road and take the left fork down to the sea.
Overlooked by a Genoese tower, this white stretch of sand has a couple of bars and sailboard stalls, but it's large enough to absorb the
crowds that descend here in summer. **Plage du Chiuni**, a further 2km
along the same road, is much busier thanks to its full-on watersports
scene and the high profile of the Club Med resort that backs the beach.
A more secluded spot lies a kilometre south of the village at **Plage du
Monachi**; this small, sandy cove is reached by climbing down the
track at the side of the road past the little chapel on the cliff side.

Practicalities

There's an unusually helpful **tourist office** on rue Docteur-Dragacci
(daily July–Sept 9am–noon & 4–7pm, Oct–May 3–5pm; ☎04 95 26
41 31), which can provide you with a map of the area and will help
you find accommodation; it also sells tickets for the **boat trips** up to
the Calanche (see p.146), leaving at 9am daily in summer and costing about 150F for the day.

Buses running between Ajaccio and Porto pull in for a ten-minute pit stop at the *Bar des Amis*, in the village centre. Two services operate all year round from Monday to Saturday in either direction, with an additional departure on Sundays during the summer. Timetables can be consulted at any tourist office, or telephone Autocars SAIB in Porto (☎04 95 26 13 70); note that services on Saturdays leave one hour earlier than during the week.

All the best **hotels** are located within a few minutes' walk of the centre, with the budget places at the top end of the village. Pick of the bunch, though, is the characterful *Bel'Mare*, 400m south of the centre on the Ajaccio road (☎04 95 26 40 13 or 04 95 26 48 24; ③), which occupies a great location overlooking the bay. The rooms in both the main building and annexe below are en-suite and spacious, and have sweeping views from their balconies; the restaurant here is also pleasant, with a breezy terrace and a varied, good-value set menu that changes daily. If it's full, ignore the overpriced *Spelunca*, an ugly modern building directly opposite the *Bel'Mare*, and head to the top of the village where the *Continental*, on the right as you leave Cargèse along the main Piana road (☎04 95 26 42 24; ③), has four modest rooms (with shared toilets) above a small restaurant. Moving upmarket, the *St Jean*, overlooking the nearby crossroads (☎04 95 26 46 68, fax 04 95 26 43 93; ④), offers more luxurious rooms, some of them with mezzanine floors and self-catering facilities; ask for one on the front side with a sea view. The other commendable option hereabouts is the *Cyrnos*, on the main street (☎04 95 26 40 03, fax 04 95 26 41 25; ③), which is plain but immaculately clean, central, and just about the cheapest place to stay in Cargèse. For a room slap on the beach, however, you'll have to drop down the road leading north off the crossroads at the top of the village to the *Thalassa* (☎04 95 26 40 08; ④), 1.5km from the centre. Among the oldest-established places in the area, this is Cargèse's most attractive hotel, an intimate place swathed in bougainvillea, right behind the sands, and with friendly owners; it's also extremely popular in season, when advance booking is essential. The only **campsite** within easy reach of Cargèse is *Camping Toraccia*, 4km north along the main road (☎04 95 26 42 39; May–Oct). Well shaded under olive groves, the site's best pitches are at the top of the hill, looking inland towards Capo d'Orto; they also have simple wood cabins that can be rented on a daily basis out of season, or for 2500F per week from late June through August.

There are a fair number of **restaurants** scattered about the village, as well as the standard pizzerias. *A Volta*, next to the Catholic church, serves interesting fare (including game and stuffed pasta) on a spectacular terrace jutting out over the sea. The bizarre *Restaurant/Bar Le Select*, in rue Dragacci, is worth a visit for its fairy lights and accordion music; the menu features mainly inexpensive French bistro food, plus pizzas until they run out of dough in the early evening. Down in the marina, *Chez Antoine*, is a renowned seafood joint that does a legendary bouillabaisse – don't be fooled by its rustic fishing-shack appearance: catering mainly for well-heeled yachties from the moorings opposite, it's a lot more expensive than the previous places, but well worth the extra. For a **drink**, go no further than the main square, where you can watch all the action from

The Greeks of Cargèse

Some 730 Greek settlers from Mani, in the southern Peloponnese, originally landed on Corsica in 1676, fleeing the Muslim attacks and persecution that followed the conquest of Crete seven years earlier. They came as part of a Genoese plan to weaken Corsican resistance by colonizing the island with different nationalities; the deal involved the payment of a large sum of money in return for guaranteed protection from any hostile Corsicans who might object to their presence. The Greeks were allowed to maintain their own customs, including their Orthodox religion (though they had to recognize the supremacy of the pope), but were forced to Italianize their surnames: thus Papadakis and Dragakis became Papadacci and Dragacci, two prominent names in the village to this day.

The first settlement was 4km northeast of Cargèse at a place they called **Paomia**. Within a year they had built five hamlets, proving so successful as farmers that they began to incur the wrath of the locals, who resented Genoa's patronage. Peace came to an abrupt end in 1715, when Paomia was ransacked by Corsican patriots enraged by the Greeks' refusal to take up arms against their Genoese benefactors. After much bloodshed, the Greeks were forced to take refuge in Ajaccio, where they remained for forty years until the arrival of the French brought temporary peace to the island.

Their deliverance came in the form of a Count **Marbeuf**, an ambitious French nobleman who in 1773 attempted to integrate the communities by forming a united regiment of Greeks and Corsicans, and offered the Greeks Cargèse as compensation for the loss of Paomia. Unfortunately, the building of 120 family houses and a castle for Marbeuf again provoked the locals, who in the same year descended from the hills to burn the castle and drive the Greeks into hiding in the towers of Plage de Pero. In 1793 the Greeks were attacked once more; their village was burned to the ground and they had to flee to Ajaccio. Four years later, only two-thirds chose to return. Gradually the Corsicans came to join them in their reconstructed village, marking the beginning of an uneasy coexistence which, largely through intermarriage, eventually led to integration. In the nineteenth century the Corsicans built their own church, after which the Greeks built one opposite and adopted some Catholic rites as a gesture towards integration.

There are still three hundred Greek families in Cargèse, well assimilated into the Corsican way of life but still observing the Greek liturgy and conducting weddings in the traditional Greek style, with the bride and groom crowned with vine leaves and olive branches. Also distinctively Greek are the festival of St Spiridion on December 12, when fireworks light up the village, and the Easter Monday blessing of the village, when all the women dress in black, the lights in the village are extinguished and the villagers form a candlelit procession to the church.

Bar des Amis, which has a pool table, or *Bar Chantilly*, which commands the best vantage point.

The least expensive places to change money are the **banks** along the main street, just up from the *Bar des Amis*, two of which have cash machines.

Vico and around

Vico, a dismal outpost in one of the remoter parts of Corsica, crouches in the mountains 15km northeast of Sagone. Although there's not much to recommend the place itself, its single hotel is an ideal base for drives into the surrounding granite peaks. Close by you can visit the **Couvent St-François** on the way to the beautifully wild **Gorges du Liamone**, which extend to the south of the village. To the north, the **Col de Sevi** provides fine views across the mountains, or you can strike eastwards and visit the thermal springs at **Guagno-les-Bains**. Intrepid drivers can venture further up this way to the dramatically situated hamlets of **Soccia** and **Orto**, perched on a ledge in front of the crags of Monte Sant'Eliseo.

The only public transport in this region is the twice daily **bus** from Ajaccio to Evisa (see p.194) via Vico and the Col de Sevi.

Vico and the Gorges du Liamone

Dominated by the dome of La Sposata, **VICO** lies at a crossroads amidst a high wooded valley, remaining invisible until the final approach. Its tough ambience is heightened by the tall dark houses and cold mountain air, but it does have the only **hotel** hereabouts, *U Paradisu*, on the outskirts of town along the road to Arbori (☎04 95 26 61 62, fax 04 95 26 67 01; ④, obligatory half board July–Aug ⑤). Its rooms are quite plain, but it does good Corsican mountain food and has a pool. An alternative place to **eat** is the excellent *Auberge du Col*, at the junction of the D70 and D23 on the Evisa road (☎04 95 26 61 58). Don't be put off by its unpromising exterior: the restaurant serves variously priced, good-value set menus, including one with delicious *loup de mer* in cream sauce, and there's a choice of pungent local cheeses.

You can travel to Vico by direct **bus** from Ajaccio, via Sagone; the service operates twice daily on Mondays to Saturdays during the summer (depart Ajaccio 7.45am & 3.30pm; 1hr 15min), with a reduced timetable in the winter. For more information, contact Autocars R. Ceccaldi (☎04 95 21 01 24).

For two hundred years Vico was the residence of the bishops of Sagone after their settlement was destroyed by the Saracens in the tenth century. It went on to become the seat of the da Leca clan, a Cinarchesi family who ruled the district in the fifteenth century. One day in 1456, 23 members of this rebel family were put to death by the Genoese governor Spinola, who had their throats cut out on the slopes east of town, where they were left to die a lonely death. Gian'

Paolo da Leca escaped this massacre and in 1481 founded the only surviving remnant of Vico's past: the **Couvent St-François**, a great white building encircled by vivid green woods and gardens, 1km along the road to Arbori. These days it's the headquarters of an old-style Roman Catholic missionary movement that culls converts from the poorer corners of the world. Worth a look here is the seventeenth-century church (daily 2–6pm), whose chief treasures are the carved **chestnut furniture** in the sacristy and the fifteenth-century wooden figure of Christ above the altar, thought to be the oldest in Corsica.

South of the convent the D1 follows the River Liamone for 7km through the **Gorges du Liamone**, a gloriously remote landscape of sweeping valleys shrouded in chestnut trees, framed by shadowy ridges covered in patches of deep maquis. Wild pigs roam the route as far as **ARBORI**, an exquisite village of russet buildings strung out on a ledge jutting into the valley. Unless you want to continue down to the Cinarca, this is a good point to turn back.

Col de Sevi

Aside from the obvious draw of the mountain views, a drive up to the **Col de Sevi** gives you an unadulterated taste of the rural Corsican way of life. By regaining the D70 north of Vico, you'll start the ascent along a high maquis-clad ridge. A detour 5km along will bring you to the apple-growing village of **RENNO**, spectacularly set amidst swaths of orchards and chestnut trees – be sure to taste the marvellous pippins that are sold in summer along the roadside. At first sight solely populated by pigs and chickens, the village hosts the annual **St-Roch fair** (August 16–18), a traditional country jamboree which involves selling livestock, honey- and chestnut-related products, as well as the usual pastis-imbibing.

Back on the D70 it's not far up to the **Col de Sevi** (1110m), the pass that links the Liamone basin with the Porto valley. From up here there's a tremendous **vista**, but for an even better view of the Golfe de Porto you can walk up to a spot called **L'Incinosa**, an easy-going two-hour stroll there and back – just follow the path to the right of the road for 4km along the ridge until you reach the top.

After the Col de Sevi, the road continues to rise for 1km before descending into the valley on the approach to Evisa.

Guagno-les-Bains, Soccia and Orto

A tedious winding route east of Vico passes goat enclosures and muddy green countryside before coming to **GUAGNO-LES-BAINS**, 12km along the D23. A couple of hot springs were first exploited here in the eighteenth century, when illustrious personages such as Pascal Paoli made the trip by mule to take a thermal bath. The spa was renovated quite recently and is open from May to October. Well-heeled visitors stay in the village's one hotel, the *Hôtel des Thermes* (☎04

Hike to Lac de Creno

Surrounded by thick Laricio pine forest on the lower western slopes of the
Rotondo massif, the **Lac de Creno** makes an ideal picnic spot if you're driving around the Vico area – easily accessible, well shaded and in the lap of
the high mountains. The hike there and back takes around two hours; to
pick up the trail, follow the recently tarmacked road up the valley from
Soccio. After the second switchback you come to a car park with a large
cross and information panel, from where the path strikes uphill across the
northeast flank of Sant'Eliseo. En route you pass a couple of tumbledown
bergeries and the little **Lac d'Arate**, and cross the trail leading to the lake
from the village of **Orto**, on the far side of the Eliseo ridge. This latter route
is harder and double the distance, but the scenery is more varied and the
chestnut forest covering the lower part of the trail one of the healthiest and
least spoilt on the island (for more on Corsica's chestnut forests, see p.274).

95 28 30 68, fax 04 95 28 34 02; ④), the only three-star in central
Corsica, boasting a pool, tennis court and gourmet restaurant.

Just beyond Guagno-les-Bains, a left turn up the unsignposted
D123 to Poggiolo, followed by another left turn, will bring you to **SOC-
CIA**, where the *U Paese* (☎04 95 28 31 92 or 04 95 28 33 13; ③) provides comfortable **accommodation** for hikers attempting the **Lac de
Creno** (see box above). Its restaurant is popular, so if you want to take
advantage of their good-value half-board deals, book at least two days
in advance. Perched on a high mountain shelf across the valley, **ORTO**
is also only accessible from Poggiolo, from where a pitted track
squirms up to the village. The attraction here is the forbidding proximity of **Monte Sant'Eliseo**, a peak crowned with a tiny chapel that is
the object of a popular pilgrimage in August. Only masochists would
take the road from Guagno-les-Bains to Guagno, 9km to the east.

The Gorges du Prunelli

A drive up through the **Gorges du Prunelli** provides an easy but
immensely varied excursion inland from Ajaccio, as the landscapes
change dramatically from gardens and orchards to the bare jagged
granite of the gorges themselves. Two roads climb the opposite
flanks of the valley for 20km before converging on the run-up to
Bastelica, a mountain village equipped with restaurants and hotels
and providing access to the **Val d'Èse** ski station. The road on the
north side of the valley, the D3, passes through the villages of
Bastelicaccia and **Ocana** on its way to the dam at **Tolla**, where the
route becomes increasingly hair-raising. To view the gorges from the
other side, you can descend from Bastelica along the D27 via the **Col
de Crichetto** and the attractive village of **Cauro**. The first route
affords the best views, while the second is more easily negotiable by
car; no public transport reaches these parts.

Bastelicaccia to Tolla

Fully cultivated since the nineteenth century in order to feed the growing population of Ajaccio, the plain around **BASTELICACCIA** has an air of cornucopian opulence, with its overflowing orchards of orange and lemon trees mingled with flower gardens and deep maquis. This is among the most pleasant places to stay within a short radius of Ajaccio, and one of the best local hotels is *L'Orangeraie* (☎04 95 20 00 09; ④–⑤), situated 1km beyond the village amidst an orchard and a beautifully kept garden of palms and indigenous Mediterranean plants. In addition to rooms, you can rent studios here by the night or the week; advance booking is essential. Another good place is *Le Vieux Chêne*, 2km up the D303 in the hamlet of **BOTTACINA** (☎04 95 20 00 13; ④), a modern place where all rooms have terraces in a garden overlooking the Golfe d'Ajaccio.

Beyond Bastelicaccia the road threads through the maquis alongside the River Prunelli, past hordes of roaming wild pigs. Some 10km along you'll come to **OCANA**, a tiny village set in a small valley beneath a belt of fig trees, olive trees and cactus. Here they make *brocciu*, a milky cheese you'll find on sale in the market in Ajaccio – hence the abundant herds of ewes.

Beyond Ocana the scenery undergoes a dramatic change, as high rock walls and pointed granite teeth begin to emerge from the greenery. After 2km you'll see **TOLLA**, a pretty village strung out on a ridge overlooking an immense reservoir of the **Lac de Tolla**. Trees abound: a bank of apple, walnut and chestnut orchards overhangs the valley in the approach to Tolla. Before you reach the village you can stop at the **Col de Mercuju** (716m) dominated by two great pyramids of rock rising from the circular hollow of the gorges. At the col, a Corsican **restaurant**, *Chez Baptiste*, is set back from the road and overlooks the gorges. Opposite the restaurant a path leads down to a platform above the dam, affording an impressive view across the lake, and various gentle forest paths thread through the woodland lining the banks.

Tolla itself is a lively place in summer, popular with Ajacciens who, returning to visit the family home, flock to the open-air pizzeria at the entrance to the village on the left. The only place to stay is a well-placed **campsite** down by the lake, *A Selva* (☎04 95 27 00 28; May–Oct), which also offers tasty Corsican cooking.

Once past Tolla the landscape continues to be wild – rocky walls strewn with high maquis border the road, overlooked by the ragged crest of Punta di Forca d'Olmu to the south. After the roads converge it's only a short ascent of 4km up to Bastelica.

Bastelica

Set at 800m on the lower slopes of Monte Renoso, **BASTELICA** is a stark and unusually unprepossessing spot with a few rows of cold granite houses and an ugly modern church. It attracts a fair number of visitors, however, partly because it's close to the **Val d'Èse** ski station, and partly because it is the birthplace of Sampiero Corso (see box overleaf), whose statue, dating from the 1890s, stands in the village centre. To visit the spot where Sampiero was born, walk up the road east of the church towards the adjoining hamlet of Dominicacci; take a left a turn at the *U Renosu* restaurant, and then the first right up the lane running behind this building, which brings you to a T-junction; head right here and follow the backstreet for 20m or so; the house is on your right. The original building was burned down by the Genoese in 1554, but the façade of its replacement (1855) is adorned with an inscription that extols "the most Corsican of Corsicans, a famous hero amongst the innumerable heroes that love of the country, superb mother of male virtues, has nursed in these mountains and torrents".

Bastelica has remained a hotbed of nationalism. In 1980, it witnessed one of the more dramatic encounters between Corsican activists and the state when, on January 6, a group of RPR militants discovered three undercover Secret Service agents operating in the village. The men were captured and taken at gunpoint to Ajaccio's *Hôtel Fesch*, where they were held to draw attention to the French government's covert activities on the island. Paris, however, refused to negotiate with the Bastelica nationalists, whom they dubbed "racketeers and hostage takers", and ordered the storming of the hotel. On January 12, armed police liberated the three agents and seized the militants, who were subsequently tried and imprisoned on the mainland. Coming only a few years after the siege at Aléria (see p.266), the event enraged the FLNC and plunged the island into a period of spiralling violence during the early 1980s.

For more background on Corsican nationalism, see Contexts.

Accommodation and eating

Bastelica has a few **hotels** open in summer. The most central is *Le Sampiero*, a large modern building opposite the church (☎04 95 28 71 99, fax 04 95 28 74 11; ③), which, though lacking the character of its competitors, enjoys uninterrupted views of the mountains from

---

Hike to Canal de la Volta

A pleasant and relatively easy walk (2hr 30min) begins on the edge of Bastelica, taking in a representative cross-section of the area's diverse landscapes via the route of an old irrigation channel. Passing waterfalls, streams and lush woodland, the waymarked trail is gentle enough for kids, and the views of the mountains through the trees are great. The path starts at the east side of the village near *Chez Paul* (see overleaf), between a blocked-off spring and a concrete lane. Striking up through the chestnut forest, it arrives after around 30min or less keeps to the canal, reaching the Ortala falls an hour later. Return by the same path.

The Gorges du Prunelli

Sampiero Corso

"The most Corsican of Corsicans", **Sampiero Corso** was born into a peasant family in 1498 and first took up arms in 1517, when he entered the service of the Medici as a mercenary – a career followed by many of his poorer compatriots. Gaining himself a reputation for audacious ambition – he is said to have put forward a plan to assassinate Charles V in 1536 – he arrived in France in the company of Catherine de' Medici, and went on to distinguish himself in several campaigns, becoming renowned as the most valiant captain in the French army. At Perpignan in 1543 he saved the life of the future Henry II, husband of Catherine de' Medici, thereby ensuring his promotion in 1547 to colonel of the Corsican infantry. He returned to Corsica a proud and popular figure, and promptly married a young noblewoman named Vannina d'Ornano. The match was not approved by her brothers, who saw their inheritance about to slip from their fingers – and their enmity was to have dire consequences.

Around this time the Genoese, suspicious of Sampiero's prestige, decided to lock him up for a spell, accusing him of having plotted an uprising against the republic. Their action engendered a hatred of Genoa that Sampiero was to hold for the rest of his days. It was the French declaration of war against Genoa in 1553, and their attempt to "liberate" Corsica from the despotic republic, which established Sampiero's legendary status. Setting out with Marshal Thermes and an expeditionary force of seven thousand mercenaries, amongst them a Turkish contingent led by the notorious Dragut, he managed a rapid takeover of Bastia, Ajaccio and Corte. Bonifacio and Calvi weren't such an easy proposition, however, being populated primarily by Ligurian settlers and thus more firmly entrenched as Genoese strongholds. Long and relentless sieges ensued, with Turkish ships ruthlessly bombarding the towns in a prelude to massacre and pillage.

The subsequent Genoese alliance with the Spanish resulted in Sampiero's return to the continent in 1557, and two years later the treaty of Cateau-Cambresis gave Corsica back to Genoa. Sampiero passionately wanted independence for the island, but could not command the backing of France after strangling his wife, in Aix-en-Provence, after he found out she had betrayed him to the Genoese and sold most of his possessions. Escaping with some of her fortune, he returned to Corsica in 1564 to organize another revolt. He rapidly took over much of the island's interior but failed to take the ports, and enthusiasm for his cause soon diminished, a process doubtless hastened by the 2000-ducat price the Genoese put on his head. In 1567 Sampiero was decapitated in an ambush near Bastelica, a murder engineered by the Ornano brothers, who had never forgotten their grudge. His head was impaled on the town gate of Ajaccio, a warning to would-be rebels that ensured his martyr's status.

most of its rooms, and has a friendly bar on the ground floor. More comfortable is *U Castagnetu*, past Sampiero's birthplace 1km north of the church (☎04 95 28 70 71, fax 04 95 28 74 02; ④), which has fifteen well-appointed rooms set amid chestnut trees, and stunning views over the valley from its sunny terrace. *Chez Paul*, 200m further along the same road (☎04 95 28 71 59; ③), is more modest but less pricy, and rents out apartments for longer stays; it also has an excellent little **restaurant** where you can enjoy traditional home-cooking for around 100F per head. Bastelica is famous for its fine cheeses and charcuterie, and a good place to sample these is *Chez François Urbani*, next door to *Chez Paul*, which stocks a range of traditional local hams, sausages and ewes' cheese; the prices are high, but so is the quality.

Bastelica to Cauro

On the way back down the main D27, there's the option of turning off the road 4km south of Bastelica to follow a parallel road which gives a stunning view of the gorges. If you're in a sturdy vehicle, you can enjoy even better views by taking the rough mountain track that branches off just before this junction at the **Col de Menta** (762m); this runs parallel to the D27, merging with it at the **Col de Crichetto**. The D27 is bordered by the **Forêt de Pineta**, whose carpet of Laricio pines, chestnut and beech trees makes it good place for a picnic. From the maison forestière, 3km along the same road, it's a ten-minute marked walk to the **Pont de Zipitoli**, a single arc of Genoese stone spanning the River Èse.

After regaining the D27 at the **Col de Marcuggio** (670m), you descend through an increasingly pastoral terrain of verdant vineyards interspersed by fields and folds of woodland. About 6km along from the col, just before the hamlet of Radicale, a bridge on a sharp left bend marks the start of a fifteen-minute trail to the **Cascade de Sant'Alberto**, a high waterfall hidden amidst the forest. CAURO, a pleasant but unremarkable village at the junction of the D27 and N169, has a good **hotel** – *Sampiero*, in the centre opposite the post office (☎04 95 28 44 84; ③). Buses from Ajaccio to Bonifacio pass through here daily before crossing the **Col St-Georges**, 7km further south, where there's an excellent little roadside **restaurant**: in a small dining room behind a bar, the *Auberge du Col* serves traditional and tasty Corsican dishes such as cannelloni made with chestnut flour, and wild rabbit stew.

From Cauro, it's an easy 13km detour south to **SANTA MARIA SICCHÉ**, set amid dense swaths of coastal maquis just off the main road. The village would be a pretty but otherwise undistinguished place were it not for the fact that Sampiero Corso's wife, Vannina d'Ornano, was born here. The old stone house Sampiero built for her in 1554, the **Palazzo Sampiero**, still stands; follow the lane leading left around the village church for about 500m and you'll see it on your left, marked with a plaque. Its derelict state was caused by a fire in the forge that formerly occupied the ground floor. Vannina's family home, by contrast, has remained in fine condition, though it's harder to locate and unmarked: take the main road leading downhill past the church towards the highway for 300m – the house, a fifteenth-century tower, stands on the right, at the top of a black tarmac lane.

Travel details

TRAINS

Ajaccio to: Bastia (4 daily; 4hr); Bocognano (4 daily; 1hr); Calvi (2 daily; 5hr 15min); Corte (4 daily; 2hr 15min); L'Île Rousse (2 daily; 4hr 45min); Ponte-Leccia (4 daily; 3hr 25min); Venaco (4 daily; 1hr 15min); Vizzavona (4 daily; 1hr).

BUSES

Ajaccio to: Aullene (1 daily; 1hr 25min); Bastia (2 daily; 3hr); Bavella (1 daily; 2hr 5min); Bonifacio (2 daily; 3hr 30min); Cargèse (2 daily; 1hr 10min); Corte (2 daily; 2hr); Evisa (2 daily; 2hr); Levie (2 daily; 2hr 45min); Olmeto (4–6 daily; 1hr 35min); Porticcio (6 daily; 15min); Porto (2 daily; 2hr 10min); Porto-Vecchio (2–5 daily; 3hr 10min–3hr 45min); Propriano (2–6 daily; 1hr 50min); Quenza (1 daily; 1hr 45min); Sagone (4 daily; 40min); Sartène (2–6 daily; 2hr 15min); Ste-Lucie-de-Tallano (1 daily; 1hr 30min); Santa Maria Sicché (2 daily; 45min); Tiuccia (2 daily; 25min); Vico (2 daily; 1hr 15min); Vizzavona (2 daily; 1hr); Zonza (1 daily; 2hr).

Cargèse to: Ajaccio (2 daily; 1hr); Ota (2 daily; 1hr 30min); Piana (2 daily; 30min) Porto (2 daily; 1hr); Sagone (2 daily; 15min); Tiuccia (2 daily; 25min).

Porticcio to: Ajaccio (6 daily; 15min).

Sagone to: Ajaccio (4 daily; 50min); Cargèse (2 daily; 30min); Piana (2 daily; 1hr); Porto (2 daily; 1hr 30min); Tiuccia (2 daily; 10min).

FERRIES

For ferry details, see p.172.

Chapter 4

The south

For the sheer variety of its landscapes, **the south** of Corsica is the most stunning part of the island, its coast of white sands and translucent turquoise sea hemming scrubland deserts, huge granite peaks, mountainous forests of Laricio pine, limestone plateaus, and slopes covered by orchards and vineyards. It's also the most militant and Mafia-ridden region; many of the seemingly tranquil mountain villages are riven by age-old family rivalries and political divisions that have been exacerbated in recent times by an upsurge in organized crime and nationalist violence. Visitors, however, are very seldom affected by this seemier side of island life, which to outsiders is discernible only in the odd bombed-out holiday villa or government building, and by the ubiquitous graffiti sprayed over roadside signs and posts. More likely to linger in your memory are the ghostly rock formations and mysterious ancient monuments lurking in the maquis of the southwest. Of these, **Filitosa**, accorded World Heritage status by UNESCO, is the most important, strewn with clusters of skilfully carved standing stones and prehistoric fortifications.

A good base from which to visit Filitosa is **Porto Pollo**, a delightful seaside village at the northern end of the vast **Golfe de Valinco**. Alternatively, there's **Propriano**, a livelier modern port in the centre of the bay, offering the widest choice of hotels, shops and restaurants in the area. From here you can also explore the southern section of the Golfe de Valinco, with the secluded sandy beach at **Campomoro**, or roam into the island's richest wine-producing country, taking in **Fozzano**, famed for its blood feuds and stalwart granite tower houses. A bit deeper inland, the region of **Alta Rocca** has an abundance of historic villages and prehistoric sites – the architecture of **Santa Lucia di Tallano** pays testimony to the wealth of the area's former overlords, the della Rocca family, while a visit to the Bronze Age ruins of the **Pianu di Levie** is an essential complement to the Filitosa trip. In the heart of Alta Rocca, the village of **Zonza** stands on the threshold of the south's major natural attraction, the sublime granite "needles" of **Bavella**.

Moving southwest, **Sartène** is in many ways the quintessential Corsican town, its history saturated with stories of vendetta and its

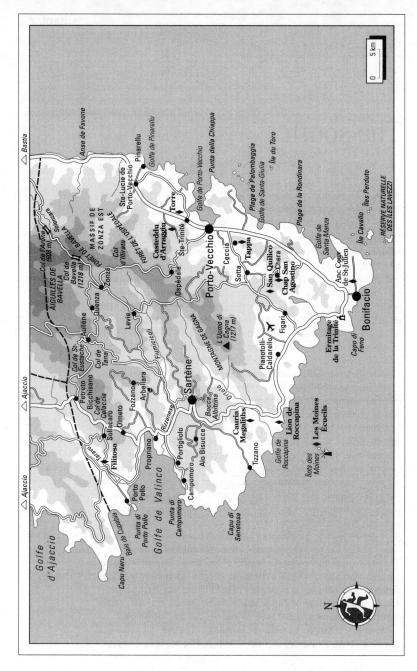

Accommodation Prices

Throughout this guide, hotel accommodation is graded on a scale from ①
to ⑥. These numbers show the cost per night of the cheapest double room
in high season, though remember that many of the cheap places will have
more expensive rooms with en-suite facilities. In such cases we list two
price codes indicating the range of room rates.

① under 100F	③ 200–300F	⑤ 400–500F
② 100–200F	④ 300–400F	⑥ over 500F

stark, fortified buildings redolent of the harshness of life in the not-
so-distant past. South of Sartène, a wild landscape of thick maquis
and parched rock makes an appropriate background for the **megaliths of Cauria** and **Alignement de Palaggiu**, Corsica's largest
arrays of prehistoric standing stones.

Marking the southern extremity of Corsica, **Bonifacio** is one of the
most dramatically sited towns in the whole Mediterranean, its old quarter sitting atop vertiginous white cliffs and almost severed from the
mainland by a deep natural harbour. It's a popular holiday centre for
the island's wealthier tourists, as is **Porto-Vecchio**, a former Genoese
citadel that's close to the island's most beautiful, and popular, beaches and to the majestic forest scenery of the **Massif de l'Ospédale**.

The area is reasonably served by **public transport**, with buses running four times a day from Ajaccio to Bonifacio via Propriano and
Sartène, and up to four times daily from Bonifacio to Porto-Vecchio.
Daily buses also pass through the mountains from the west coast as far
as Zonza, but for Bavella and for all the prehistoric sites you will need
your own vehicle. The *micheline*, Corsica's idiosyncratic train, doesn't
reach as far south as this, though there are plans for a line in the future.

The Filitosa region

Set deep in the countryside of the fertile Vallée du Taravo, **Filitosa** is
one of the most important prehistoric sites in the western
Mediterranean, a wonderful array of statue-menhirs and prehistoric
structures enfolded by meadows and deep-green hills. Situated some
40km south of Ajaccio and 17km north of Propriano, the site lies
within easy reach of **Sollacaro** and **Olmeto**, two attractive inland villages, and of the tiny village resort of **Porto Pollo**, the only coastal
base on the north side of the Golfe de Valinco.

Filitosa

Eight thousand years of history are encapsulated by the extraordinary
Station Préhistorique de Filitosa (daily March–Oct 8am–7.30pm,
out of season by arrangement only; ☎04 95 74 00 91; 22F). Little is
known about the peoples who inhabited this spot, a fact that adds an

element of mystery to Filitosa's statue-menhirs, which glare amid intensely green meadows, patches of wild orchid and gnarled olive trees – a scene little changed since their creation. The site remained undiscovered until Charles-Antoine Cesari came upon the ruins on his farmland in the late 1940s. He and Roger Grosjean, who was to become head of the centre for archeological research in Sartène, set about a full-scale excavation, discovering some menhirs lying face down in the maquis, others broken at waist level inside what is now known as the central monument (you can read an evocative first-hand account of the discovery in Dorothy Carrington's *Granite Island*, see p.330). When the digging was completed the menhirs were set into lines, and the site was opened to the public in 1954.

There's no public **transport** to this site, but the Propriano–Porto Pollo bus will take you as far as the D157/D57 junction, just before the Taravo bridge, from where you can hitch the remaining 6–7km; hitching is fairly reliable during the summer, when nearly all the traffic on these back roads is heading to or from the site.

A brief history of Filitosa

Filitosa was occupied from 6000 BC when it was settled by **Neolithic** farming people who lived here in rock shelters. Flakes of obsidian, used to make arrowheads and only available from the Aeolian Islands and Sardinia, have been unearthed, indicating that the first Filitosans must have engaged in trade, but little else is known about them, other than the fact they were colonized sometime between 3500 and 3000 BC by **megalithic** peoples from the East. Believed to have been missionary navigators, these early invaders came in search of converts to their faith, as well as land and metals, and were the creators of the first menhirs, the earliest of which were possibly phallic symbols worshipped by an ancient fertility cult. Later statues display stylized human features, making them quite distinct from nearly all other European menhirs of the megalithic period – such as those at Stonehenge and Avebury – which would seem to have been abstract expressions of devotion to a godhead rather than tributes to humankind. Most archeologists believe that the representational menhirs were memorials to dead chieftains and warriors. Grosjean, however, maintained that they were portraits of enemy **Torréens**, who – most people agree – arrived in the Golfe de Porto-Vecchio from the eastern Mediterranean around 1700 BC. To back up his theory, Grosjean cites Aristotle, who claimed the ancient Iberians used to raise stones around the tombs of slain enemies; moreover, very few knives or daggers like the ones depicted have ever been found in megalithic sites on the island, nor at the time of the invasions did the farmers of Filitosa have the technology to make them.

As they settled, the Torréens built conical structures known as **torri** (towers) all over the south of Corsica. Again, no one is absolutely certain of their function; it's generally agreed that the smaller of these beehive-like towers are likely to have been used as

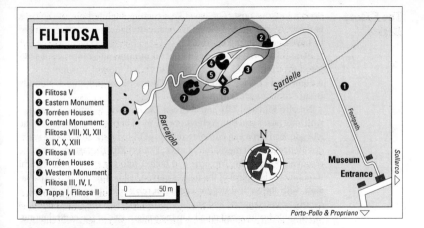

FILITOSA

1. Filitosa V
2. Eastern Monument
3. Torréen Houses
4. Central Monument:
   Filitosa VIII, XI, XII
   & IX, X, XIII
5. Filitosa VI
6. Torréen Houses
7. Western Monument
   Filitosa III, IV, I,
8. Tappa I, Filitosa II

0   50 m

N

Sardelle

Barcajolo

Footpath

Sollarco ▷

Museum
Entrance

Porto-Pollo & Propriano ▽

places of worship to some divinity, though traces of ashes and bones in the vicinity also suggest these could have been where the Torréens burned or buried their dead. The larger *torri*, too small for human habitation, are thought to have served as stores for weapons or food, or perhaps as refuges or lookout towers.

When the Torréens conquered Filitosa around 1300 BC, they destroyed most of the menhirs, incorporating the broken stones into the area of dry-stone walling surrounding the site's two *torri*. Around the towers, the remains of which are the central and western monuments, they constructed a village of Cyclopean stone shacks – a complex known as a **casteddu**. As such *casteddi* became more numerous, their inhabitants were forced into attacking neighbouring settlements in order to protect their land and livestock. Grosjean believed that competition between the *casteddi* forced Torréen expeditions to migrate to northern Sardinia, which would explain the existence on that island of **nuraghi**, larger and more technically advanced versions of *torri*. A rival theory, however, suggests that the Torréens were in fact indigenous Corsicans who simply acquired their technical expertise from the Sardinian *nuraghi* builders.

The site

Vehicles can be left in the small **car park** in the hamlet of Filitosa, where you pay the entrance fee; from here it's a five-minute walk to the site, which includes a small **museum** (best seen after the site) and a workshop producing reproduction prehistoric ceramics.

Filitosa V looms up on the right shortly after the entrance. The largest statue-menhir on the island, it's an imposing sight, with clearly defined facial features and a sword and dagger outlined on the body. Beyond a sharp left turn lies the oppidum or central monument, its entrance marked by the **eastern platform**, thought to have been a lookout post. The cavelike structure sculpted out of the rock is the only evidence of Neolithic occupation and is generally agreed to have been a burial mound.

Straight ahead, the Torréen **central monument** comprises a scattered group of menhirs on a circular walled mound, surmounted by a dome and entered by a corridor of stone slabs and lintels. Nobody is sure of its exact function.

Nearby **Filitosa XIII** and **Filitosa IX**, implacable lumps of granite with long noses and round chins, are the most impressive menhirs on the site – indeed Grosjean considered Filitosa IX to be the finest of all western Mediterranean megalithic statues. Filitosa XIII, the last menhir to be discovered here (the Torréens had built it into the base of the central monument), is typical of the figures carved just before the Torréen invasion, with its vertical dagger carved in relief – **Filitosa VII** also has a clearly sculpted sword and shield. **Filitosa VI**, from the same period, is remarkable for its facial detail. On the eastern side of the central monument stand some vestigial Torréen houses, where fragments of **ceramics** dating from 5500 BC were discovered; they represent the most ancient finds on the site, and some of them are displayed in the museum.

The **western monument**, a two-roomed structure built underneath another walled mound, is thought to have been some form of Torréen religious building. A steep flight of rough steps leads to the foot of this mound, where a tiny footbridge leads into the meadow, on the other side of which five statue-menhirs are arranged in a wide semicircle beneath a thousand-year-old olive tree. A bank separates them from a jumble of contorted, nobbly grey rocks – the **quarry** from which the megalithic sculptors hewed the stone for the menhirs. A granite block, marked ready for cutting, has been propped up on stakes to make a seat from which you can survey the site.

The **museum** is a shoddy affair, with poorly labelled exhibits and very little contextual information (the owners have even put the light on a timer switch so that you're plunged into darkness every two or three minutes), but the artefacts themselves are fascinating. The major item here is the formidable **Scalsa Murta**, a huge menhir dating from around 1400 BC and discovered at Olmeto. Like other statue-menhirs of this period, this one has two indents in the back of its head, which are thought to indicate that these figures would have been adorned with headdresses like the horn that's been attached to Scalsa Murta. Other notable exhibits are **Filitosa XII**, which has a hand and a foot carved into the stone, and **Trappa II**, a strikingly archaic face. Explanatory notes and photographs around the walls sketch the progression of the excavations.

Filitosa to Olmeto

East of Filitosa, the D57 threads through hilly hedged-in pastures for about 8km before the village of **SOLLACARO** (Suddacaru) rises into view. A compact, reddish-toned collection of houses, the village boasts the distinction of having been the setting for the first meeting of James Boswell and Pascal Paoli on October 21, 1765 (see box overleaf) – a plaque opposite the post office commemorates the occasion.

Heading south along the coast road from Ajaccio, your first glimpse of the stunning Golfe de Valinco comes just below **Col de Celaccia** (583m), where a series of steep turns brings you down to **OLMETO**, situated 4km below the pass. With its grandstand view over Propriano, Olmeto was once a favourite spot with amateur sketchers such as Edward Lear, and it remains a captivating place, close to the coast but far enough from Propriano to retain a village atmosphere, compromised only by holiday traffic clogging up the main road through the centre in summer. Once off the main road, however, you're instantly hemmed in by lofty, mellow buildings and sleepy back alleys.

Contrary to appearances, life in Olmeto has not always been peaceful. The village was actually established on this high, easily defensible site to provide protection from the constant pirate raids that menaced the gulf from the fifteenth to seventeenth centuries; in 1617, for example, some fifty villagers were abducted and taken as slaves to North Africa. The village is also renowned for its bloody **vendettas**, some of which carried on well into the present century; in *Granite Island* (see p.330), Dorothy Carrington recalls meeting an old man who could name twenty people murdered here in his lifetime. Most famous of all the Corsican vendettas was the one instigated by **Colomba Carabelli**, the heroine of Merimée's novel *Colomba*, who died here in 1861, aged 96, in the forbidding mansion facing the mairie. Her reputation still attracts a few admirers, but what brings most tourists to Olmeto today are the incredible views from the village's two streets, which are linked by steep stairways, with the foundations of the houses vanishing into a valley whose olive groves once sustained the local economy.

Just before you enter the village, you'll notice the ruined **Castello della Rocca** crowning an isolated peak. This inaccessible castle was inhabited in the fourteenth century by Arrigho della Rocca, the fiery great-grandson of Giudice della Cinarca. Exiled to Spain in 1362, Arrigho enlisted the support of the King of Aragon and returned to Corsica ten years later, intent on taking over the whole island. He virtually succeeded, with only Calvi and Bonifacio holding out against him, and as Count of Corsica ruled the island for four years until his death at Vizzavona in 1401, poisoned by one of his own vassals.

Olmeto's small **information office** (July & Aug daily 9am–noon & 2–6pm, Sept–June 9am–noon; ☎04 95 74 65 87) can help you find **accommodation** in the area, but much the most popular hotel hereabouts is hard to miss. Overlooking the church square, the old stone *U Santa Maria – Chez Mimi* (☎04 95 74 65 59, fax 04 95 74 60 33; obligatory half board in Aug; ③) has smart, comfortable rooms above an excellent little **restaurant** whose set menus of classy Corsican cuisine range from 120F to 160F. For less expensive food,

The Filitosa Region

A feature on piracy in Corsica appears on p.89.

For more background on Colomba and the Corsican vendetta, see p.212.

A short biography of Giudice appears on p.181.

The Fïlitosa
Region

Boswell in Corsica

Dr Johnson's biographer courted men of genius as assiduously as he pursued women, and one of his early conquests was the Corsican patriot **Pascal Paoli**. In 1765, at the age of 25, **James Boswell** contrived to make the acquaintance of the great French philosopher Rousseau in Switzerland. The Corsicans, struggling to formalize their independence, had asked the author of the *Social Contract* to give them a new set of laws. In certain circles Corsica had something of the appeal that Greece was to offer Byron's generation sixty years later, and Boswell promptly suggested that Rousseau make him his ambassador to the Corsicans. He duly received a letter of introduction, which he was able to present to Paoli the following year.

The meeting was a far more nerve-racking experience for Boswell than his encounter with the philosopher. "I had stood in the presence of many a prince but I never had such a trial as in the presence of Paoli," he wrote. "For ten minutes we walked backwards and forwards through the room hardly saying a word, while he looked at me with a steadfast, keen and penetrating eye, as if he searched my very soul." A student of physiognomy, Paoli also feared an attempt on his life, so the close scrutiny was scarcely surprising, and it didn't hinder the development of a friendship that was to hold throughout Paoli's later exile in London.

The success of Boswell's book about his visit, *An Account of Corsica – the Journal of a Tour to that Island and Memoirs of Pascal Paoli*, helped launch his social and literary career in London, and commemorated a passion that endured throughout his life. In 1769, the year of the book's publication, he attended the first annual celebration of Shakespeare's birthday in Stratford-on-Avon, an event organized by the actor David Garrick. Boswell appeared at the celebrations dressed in the Corsican national costume and wearing in his hat a card that read "Corsica Boswell".

try *Le Colomba*, a locals' bar on the main street, cours Balisoni, where you can eat well for under 100F.

Porto Pollo

From Fïlitosa it's a short drive down to the narrow iron bridge across the River Taravo, then on to the seafront village of **PORTO POLLO**, 18km northwest of Propriano; it's also accessible by peeling west off the N196 just below Olmeto, and winding along the north coast of the Golfe de Valinco on the D157. Despite its long popularity with holidaymakers, this place is still an attractive spot in summer, mainly due to the sublime view of the Golfe de Valinco and the long stretch of golden sand that fronts the village. Constantly ravaged by pirate raids in former times (whence its Corsican name, *Porti Poddu*, meaning "troubled port"), the harbour today provides peaceful and sheltered moorings for yachts, and a few fishermen still venture out to supply the local restaurants with fresh langoustine from the gulf.

From June till September, **minibuses** provide the only public transport in the area, shuttling between Propriano and Porto Pollo (Mon–Sat; ☎04 95 74 05 58 or 04 95 74 01 88). They stop at various points along the road that runs behind the beach, dominated by a string of mid-range **hotels**. Of these, *Kallisté*, right in the centre of the village (☎04 95 74 03 38, fax 04 95 74 06 26; ④), is the best place to stay. An immaculately renovated period building, it boasts the distinction of being owned by a descendant of Pascal Paoli; its restaurant also serves the best fresh seafood on this side of the gulf, though it's quite pricy, with set menus starting at 120F. Otherwise, try the equally central *Les Eucalyptus* (☎04 95 74 01 52, fax 04 95 74 06 56; mid-May to Sept; ④); best value are its three budget rooms, which are basic and don't have views, but are clean and affordable even in high season. **Campers** have *Camping Alfonsi*, at the entrance to the village (☎04 95 74 01 80; June to mid-Oct), which has a good pizzeria.

You can rent surfing and windsurfing equipment at the Centre Nautique de Porto Pollo, at the entrance to the village, though the best **windsurfing beach** is the beautiful half-moon **Baie de Cupabia**, northwest of Porto Pollo – take the D155 in the direction of Serra di Ferro, then turn left along the D155a about 4km from Porto Pollo. In the other direction there's **Plage de Taravo**, a fabulous, wide, sandy stretch just 1500m east of the village, but with no facilities other than a makeshift bar. **Diving** enthusiasts should note that that the water at this end of the gulf is some of the clearest on the island. For tips on where to dive, contact the Taravo diving club through the *bar-tabac des Oliviers* in Porto Pollo (☎04 95 74 01 67).

Propriano and around

Tucked into the narrowest part of the Golfe de Valinco, the small port of **Propriano** has most of the area's hotels and campsites, and is handy for some good beaches as well as for the menhirs at Filitosa and the historic town of Sartène. The attractions of the minimally developed southern Golfe de Valinco culminate in **Campomoro**, an enchanting fishing village set behind a glorious long beach, while **Fozzano**, a pretty village renowned for a particularly virulent vendetta, provides an easy inland excursion, taking in some pastoral landscapes along the way.

Public transport serving Propriano consists of a twice-daily bus from Ajaccio to Bonifacio and Porto-Vecchio. For Campomoro and Fozzano, however, you'll need your own transport.

Propriano

Bracketed by the promontory of Scogliu Lungu, the fine natural harbour of **PROPRIANO** (Prupria) was exploited by the ancient Greeks, Carthaginians and Romans, but became a prime target for pirate raids and by the eighteenth century had been largely destroyed. The

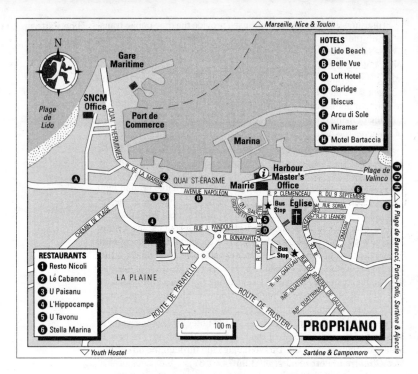

port, developed at the beginning of this century, now handles **ferries** to the French mainland and Sardinia, but still has an unfinished appearance. This is due in part to terrorist bombs: the post office, a symbol of the French administration and especially targeted for its isolated position here, has had to be rebuilt three times over the last ten years after nationalist attacks.

The amount of building work going on here also bears witness to the pace of change in Propriano, which has, in a little over fifteen years, metamorphosed from a sleepy fishing village into a busy tourist resort capable of accommodating 23,000 visitors. Chief among the architects of this rapid transformation is the mayor, **Émile Mocchi**, who has led the local council for more than a decade. A second-generation Italian immigrant whose father made a fortune selling army surplus supplies after World War II, Mocchi owes his longevity to friends and family in high places, including a nephew who's one of the leaders of the nationalist group, A Cuncolta. He's also a close associate of southern Corsica's most powerful godfather, Jean-Jérôme ("Jean-Jé") Colonna, veteran of the infamous "French Connection" and the number-one tobacco smuggler on the island.

The strength of this coalition has somewhat held in check power struggles between the area's political and Mafia organizations, though

Ferries

Ferries depart from the Port de Commerce for Marseille and Toulon from the last week of March to the end of September. There's also an all-year service to Porto Torres in Sardinia.

SNCM, quai l'Herminier (☎04 95 76 04 36). To Marseille (March–May 1 weekly, June to mid-July 1 weekly, mid-July to Aug 5 weekly, Sept 4 weekly); Toulon (March–May 1 monthly, June to mid-July 1 weekly, mid-July to Aug 5 weekly, Sept 4 weekly). Prices start at around 300F per passenger, plus another 450F for a car. Daytime crossings take 9hr 30min, overnight 12hr.

Compagnie Méridionale de Navigation, quai l'Herminier (☎04 95 76 04 36). To Sardinia: twice weekly. The 4hr crossing costs 150F per passenger, 260F for a car.

reports of mob and nationalist shootings in Propriano still crop up from time to time in the local press. The occasional eruption of violence, however, doesn't seem to deter the tourists, who come for the beaches, the sailing and watersports facilities, and the comparatively flourishing nightlife. Even if you're just passing through, this resort provides useful amenities (supermarkets and cashpoint machines, for example) at the midway point between Ajaccio and Bonifacio.

For the nearest beach, head west of the ferry quay and around the headland with the lighthouse to **Plage de Lido**, a steep crescent of yellow sand surveyed by lifeguards during the summer. Just north of the town, **Plage de Baracci**, a long, sheltered stretch of sand spanning the narrowest part of the gulf, is less than ideal: locals avoid it because of the strong undertow and unsightly heaps of rubbish littering the wasteland behind. Around 3km further north, the D157 branches off to the left and continues along the coast, which is built up with hotels and package-tour holiday blocks until **Olmeto Plage**, 10km west, where there's an abundance of campsites (see p.206). From June until September, you can travel all the way along this stretch by **minibus** from Propriano.

Practicalities

Ferries dock in the Port de Commerce, west of the town centre and ten minutes' walk from where the **buses** pull in at the top of rue Général-de-Gaulle, the town's main street, which runs at right angles to the water. The **tourist office** down in the marina (July & Aug daily 8am–8pm, June & Sept Mon–Sat 9am–noon & 3–7pm, Oct–May Mon–Fri 9am–noon & 2–6pm; ☎04 95 76 01 49) issues a glossy brochure with a plan of the town and lists of hotels, gîtes and restaurants in the area. They also have up-to-date timetables for transport services all over the island.

Propriano has a disproportionate number of tourist beds for its size (7000 of them in hotels, 4000 in camping places, and 12,000 more in holiday villas), and finding **accommodation** is rarely a problem, even during peak season. There are several good mid-range hotels in the centre of town, but if you have a car and the means, you could try the more alluring places along the coast or on the quieter route de Baracci, 3km northeast. Cafés, bars and restaurants are concentrated along av Napoléon, with the best of the bars being those closest to the marina. The **theatre**, in the sports complex 1km along the road to Sartène (visit the tourist office for details), hosts concerts, plays and films in the summer.

Hotels

Arcu di Sole, route de Baracci (☎04 95 76 05 10, fax 04 95 76 13 36). A large pink building with green shutters, just off the main Ajaccio road, 3km west of town (turn inland by the gas station). No views, but there's a pool and gourmet restaurant, and they do excellent off-season discounts. Half board obligatory in July & Aug. April–Oct. ④.

Belle Vue, av Napoléon (☎04 95 76 01 86, fax 04 95 76 27 77). The cheapest central hotel, halfway down av Napoléon and overlooking the marina; all rooms have balconies with a view of the gulf and are cheerfully decorated; downstairs there's a lively crêperie frequented by locals. ③–④.

Claridge, rue Bonaparte (☎04 95 76 05 54, fax 04 95 76 27 77). A modern building in the middle of town, with comfortable rooms but grim views. March–Oct. ⑤.

Ibiscus, route de la Grande-Corniche (☎04 95 76 01 56). A modern pink concrete block on the outskirts, whose front rooms have large balconies and good views over the gulf. Restaurant and parking. ⑤.

Lido Beach, av Napoléon (☎04 95 76 17 74, fax 04 95 76 06 54). Not to be confused with the *Lido*, at the far west end of the beach and currently being renovated. A large four-storey block overlooking the Port de Commerce, whose rooms are spacious and comfortable but a little bland and overpriced. ⑥.

Loft Hotel, 3 rue Camille-Pietri (☎04 95 76 17 48). Former wine and flour warehouse imaginatively converted into gleaming hi-tech hotel, with bright, clean rooms overlooking a parking lot. Good value. Closed Feb. ④.

Miramar, route de la Grande-Corniche (a continuation of route de Baracci), 3km towards Ajaccio (☎04 95 76 06 13, fax 04 95 76 13 14). This four-star is the place to go if you want to splash out – a splendid luxury hotel with a huge swimming pool and sauna. May–Sept. ⑥.

Motel Bartaccia, 1km east of the centre off the Ajaccio road (☎04 95 76 01 99, fax 04 95 76 24 92). Inexpensive studios with fully equipped kitchenettes, tucked away in leafy gardens behind the *Miramar Hotel*. Usually rented out by the week during July & Aug, but out of season they go for around 250F a night. ③.

Hostels and campsites

Auberge de Jeunesse (LAFJ), Résidence des Lauriers, route de Paratelle (☎04 95 76 29 81, fax 04 95 76 29 83), lies a stiff fifteen-minute walk from the bus stop: head uphill from the roundabout outside the post office and you'll see it at the top of the rise. Beds in their small, immaculately clean dormitories cost 85F per night, including breakfast; the only catch is that the place gets overrun in summer by parties of boisterous teenagers.

Centre Équestre Baracci, on the route de Baracci, 3km northeast of town (☎04 95 76 19 48). The excellent gîte d'étape here is an even cheaper option than the youth hostel, and one that's better situated if you're hiking around the long-distance trails in the area. Beds in their four-person dorms cost 50F, or 75F for a rooms with a shower, and they serve quality evening meals to order for 80F; bring your own sleeping bags.

Chez Angelini, further up the Baracci valley at Burgo, 7km northeast of Propriano (☎04 95 76 15 05). Run by the friendly and knowledgeable M. Angelini, this is one of the largest hikers' hostels in Corsica, with room for thirty people, though its proximity to the trailhead means advance booking is recommended during peak season.

Camping Colomba, 3km north along the route de Baracci (☎04 95 76 06 42). Take the right-hand turning off the main road by the Elf gas station to reach this medium-sized, peaceful three-star with good facilities and plenty of shade – the best of the sites within walking distance of town.

Camping Lecci e Murta, on the Campomoro road (☎04 95 77 11 20). A good site near the beach, with a tennis court, pizzeria and store.

Chez Antoine, in Marina d'Olmeto (☎04 95 76 06 06). Situated on the north side of the gulf, 5km from Propriano, this campsite is basic but slap next to one of the least-frequented beaches in the area.

Propriano and around

A description of the Mare a Mare Sud trail, which starts in Propriano, features on p.208; for an account of the Mare e Monti Sud hike, which starts in Porticcio and ends here, see p.177.

Restaurants

Le Cabanon, rue des Pêcheurs. Gourmet fish restaurant, with terrace, at the west end of the marina towards the port. Their special 70F lunch menu is excellent value, but the pricier options include more imaginative dishes such as ray's wing served with haricot beans and lemon sauce.

L'Hippocampe, rue Pandolphi. Tucked away behind the port, this is the best place for classy seafood at affordable prices, and their 95F set menu offers unbeatable value for Propriano. Dine inside, where nautical bits and bobs provide the decor, or outside on a flowery terrace.

U Paisanu, av Napoléon. Ersatz rustic peasant place serving copious Corsican dishes, including mountain charcuterie, pigeon pâté, roast piglet and delicious vegetables *farcies à la Sarté* – a local speciality. Count on 150F per head, including wine.

Resto Nicoli, at the far end of rue Napoléon. An Italian-style café near the port that's just about the cheapest place to eat; excellent 65F omelettes served with Parmesan and gnocchi, and they do their own tiramisu (also available to take away).

Stella Marina, 21 rue du 9-Septembre, near *Hôtel Ibiscus*. Laid-back seafood restaurant with a shady terrace overlooking the gulf. Reasonable prices, and the garrulous owner serenades his customers with guitar and songs.

U Tavonu, rue Capitaine-Pietri. Bright and cosy tourist restaurant slap in the centre of town, whose inexpensive menu features Corsican dishes as well as pizzas *au feu de bois*.

Bars and nightlife

Shanghai, rue Général-de-Gaulle. Rub shoulders with the local gangsters at this bar, whose owner sports a gold chain and spats.

The Mare a Mare Sud Trail

Crossing the rocky spine of the island between the Golfe de Porto-Vecchio and the Golfe de Valinco, the **Mare a Mare Sud trail** takes in the full cross-section of Corsican landscapes, from the deep-blue inlets of the coast to the pale-grey needle peaks of the Alta Rocca region, dusted for half the year in snow. Divided into five stages of between four and six hours, this hike can be attempted at any time of year, even high summer, thanks to the amount of tree cover along the route. Moreover, you rarely stray out of sight of a village, and every night halt has a good gîte d'étape, so it isn't necessary to carry more than a day's worth of food. The path is marked at regular intervals with signposts and splashes of orange paint, but you shouldn't rely solely on these; without the Parc Naturel Régional de Corse's essential **topo-guide** (see *Basics*), which contains the relevant sections of the IGN contour maps, you'll find yourself getting lost in dense maquis or wandering down dead-end game tracks, as the waymarks have faded along some stretches, and the path has become overgrown in others (notably between Loreto di Tallano and Burgo).

This is one of the most popular long-distance footpaths on the island, so if you want to avoid your fellow hikers, walk it from west to east, beginning at Propriano. The trailhead is actually another 7km up the Baracci valley at **Burgo**; no buses run up this road, but if you're carrying a rucksack you shouldn't find it too hard to hitch a lift. Alternatively, walk along the road and spend the night in the gîte d'étape here (see below), which will allow you to get an early start the following day.

From Burgo, the trail drops down to the river through dense forest, before climbing up the other side of the valley to **Fozzano** (see p.214), where there's a small store. Climbing southwest out of the village, it then veers north around the flank of Pointe de Zibo and begins the long haul up to the Punta d'Arja Vecchia pass, from where you get superb views of the interior mountains. A sharp descent via the ruined *bergeries* of Altanaria brings you out at some old quarry workings just outside the hamlet of Erbajolu. Turn left here and head up the road until you see a signpost pointing down to the Rizzanese River. Ascending steeply through lush old-growth forest, the final stretch up to **Santa Lucia di Tallano** (see p.216) is hard going, but you can break the walk at the Romanesque chapel of St-Jean-Baptiste, an account of which appears on p.217.

Le Midnight, on the steps in rue Bonaparte. Situated behind the *Shanghai*, and under the same ownership, this is Propriano's hottest night spot, with a cabaret every night.

Listings

Car rental Avis, 22 rue Général-de-Gaulle (☎04 95 76 00 76); Budget, rue Jean-Pandolfi (☎04 95 76 00 02); Citer, Location Valinco, 25 av Napoléon (☎04 95 76 11 84); Europcar, 2 rue Général-de-Gaulle (☎04 95 76 00 02).

Diving Valinco Plongé (☎04 95 76 21 03) and U Levante (☎04 95 76 23 83), both in the marina.

The second stage of this walk covers some of the most beautiful forest in the Mediterranean, between Santa Lucia and **Serra di Scopamène**. At the latter village is a superbly sited gîte d'étape, whose terrace looks south down the serene Rizzanese Valley. Stage three takes you up onto the Coscionu plateau – known by locals as *U Pianu* (The Plateau) – dominated by the summit of l'Alcudina (2136m) and by the needles of Bavella emerging to the east. Crisscrossed by numerous streams, this high, rocky basin formerly provided pasture for nomadic herders, and you'll come across several ruined *bergeries* punctuating the route to the picturesque mountain village of **Quenza**, one of the main settlements in the Alta Rocca. At this point, the trail swings south and follows a fairly level course to **Levie**, skirting the edge of the extraordinary Castellu di Capula archeological site (see p.219).

The penultimate day of the hike takes you south of Levie, through deep vallies carpeted with pine forests, to the lonely hamlet of **Carbini** (see p.219), and thence east towards the Col de Mela, reached via the hardest climb on the trail. From here, it's a gentle ascent through more old maritime pine forest around the Punta di a Vacca Morte (1314m) to the Foce Alta pass (1171m), which offers an awesome view of the Golfe de Porto-Vecchio, with the shadowy ridges of Sardinia clearly visible on the southern horizon. You can break this stage at **Cartalavonu**, an old stone herders' hamlet where there's a gîte d'étape, or continue on the **Ospédale**. Rather than complete the walk with a long zigzagging descent through the Ospédale forest, many hikers call it a day here and jump on the evening Ollandini bus to **Porto-Vecchio**, which passes through at 6.40pm.

Mare a Mare Sud gîtes d'étape

Excellent **gîtes d'étape** mark all five stages of this walk. Dorm beds cost around 60F per night if you're cooking for yourself, and 170F for half board. From June to September it's essential to book ahead, especially if you require an evening meal.

Burgo (☎04 95 76 15 05).

Santa Lucia di Tallano (☎04 95 78 80 13).

Serra di Scapomène (☎04 95 78 64 90).

Quenza (☎04 95 78 65 19).

Levie (☎04 95 78 46 41).

Cartalavonu (☎04 95 70 00 39).

Doctors Dr Peninon, 11 av Napoléon (☎04 95 76 01 98), Dr Quilichini, 3 av Napoléon (☎04 95 76 00 96).

Horse riding The Centre Équestre de Baracci, 2km northeast on the route de Baracci (5min walk from the Elf station; ☎04 95 76 08 02), offers rides for 100F per hour on beautiful horses. They also do longer trips from 500F per day, accompanied by an expert guide, across relatively unfrequented parts of the interior.

Hospital The nearest hospital with a casualty department is in Sartène.

Laundry Two self-service laundries (*laveries automatiques*): one just down from the tourist office on rue Général-de-Gaulle, the other opposite the Port de Commerce on av Napoléon.

Mountain- and motorbike rental Mountain bikes (*vtt*) and 50cc or 80cc scooters for rent through TCC Sarl, 25 rue Général-de-Gaulle (☎04 95 76 15 32), and Location Valinco, 25 av Napoléon (☎04 95 76 11 84); the latter also has a couple of 125cc trials bikes.

Taxis ☎04 95 76 11 03.

Travel agent Ollandini Valinco Voyages, 22 rue Général-de-Gaulle (☎04 95 76 00 76), for plane tickets and buses to Ajaccio.

The southern Golfe de Valinco

Separating from the Sartène road at the Rena Bianca bridge, 2km south of Propriano, the D121 winds down the coast, shouldering some gentle cliffs and deep-green maquis which sets off the intensely blue sea. Some 7km along the route you'll come to **Portigliolo**, an exceptionally white and quiet curve of sand with a shady **campsite**, *Lecci e Murta* (see p.207). Five kilometres beyond, at the hamlet of **BELVÉDÈRE**, at the top of the cliff before you descend to Campomoro, there are two more campsites on the crest of the hill, *La Vallée* (☎04 95 74 21 20) and *Les Roseaux* (☎04 95 74 20 52), which are less crowded than the site by the beach.

A cluster of sturdy old buildings and a tiny chapel make up **CAMPOMORO**, a fishing village, 17km southwest of Propriano, enjoying tranquil isolation amongst eucalyptus trees at the foot of a maquis-covered hill. The main attraction here is the beach nearly 2km of gently curving golden sand and pellucid sea, overlooked by an immense Genoese watchtower. In late July and August it's swamped by Italian families from the nearby campsites, but for the rest of the year Campomoro remains a sleepy place, with barely enough permanent residents to support a year-round post office. The village basically consists of one road, which turns left when it arrives at the beach and then runs in a curve around the bay, coming to a dead end below the promontory, which you can scale in ten or fifteen minutes to reach the **tower** (summer 9am–7pm; free), a stunning lookout point.

Background on Corsica's distinctive Genoese towers appears on p.89.

The rocks on the far side of the tower mark the beginning of a superb coastal walk, described in the box opposite.

You may have trouble finding a place to stay in July and August, as Campomoro possesses only two **hotels** and a couple of campsites. *Le Ressac*, about 100m behind the chapel (☎04 95 74 22 25; June–Sept; ③), is a friendly family concern where the rooms afford excellent views across the bay or over the olive trees behind; half board (315F per head) is obligatory in peak season. *Le Campomoro*, overlooking the beach about 500m from the post office towards the tower (☎04 95 74 20 89; ④), is more expensive and less welcoming, but the rooms are adequate if rather sparsely furnished. A possible alternative is Mme Carbini, who rents out **rooms** overlooking the beach, but you will need to reserve these in advance (☎04 95 74 20 69). *Bar des Amis*, opposite the beach near the chapel, will also rent out rooms, but don't expect luxury. The

Les Bandits d'Honneur

The most romantic of all Corsican folk heroes is the bush bandit, or **bandit d'honneur**. Coined during the nineteenth century, the term was used to distinguish between common highway robbers and men who had taken to the maquis after committing a vendetta killing. Protected by impenetrable scrub and granite, these fugitives could survive for years in caves, ruins or makeshift shelters accessible only by a labyrinthine network of game trails.

The true *bandit d'honneur* never stole or murdered anyone except his sworn adversaries, and could rely on the support of local villagers in times of need. Wandering the maquis in a broad-brimmed hat, a gun slung over his shoulder and a dog at his heels, he was felt to epitomize the *âme corse*, or "Corsican soul" – the spirit of rugged defiance, pride and separateness with which islanders had traditionally regarded their colonial rulers. As such, the *bandits* were respected, and even revered: travellers, artists and famous authors would seek them out in their camps, wealthy women fell in love with them, and a spate of nineteenth-century novels romanticized their footloose lifestyles, steeped in the spirit of Jean-Jacques Rousseau's "noble savage". During a visit to the Lauretti brothers in their Fiumorbo hideout, for example, Flaubert wrote the following: "Great and valiant heart that beats alone in freedom in the woods . . . purer and nobler, no doubt, than most people in France" (quoted by Dorothy Carrington in *Granite Island*; see "Books", p.330).

While some *bandits* lived up to this ascetic ideal, many more took to drink, robbery, rape and murder, safe in the knowledge that they were beyond the reach of the *gendarmes*. In time, a new breed of outlaw emerged; one who adopted the wild life as a means to personal gratification rather than to escape the stringent ancestral code of vendetta. Playing on their reputation for ruthlessness, the new *bandits* – dubbed *bandits percepteurs*, or "tax-collecting bandits" – began to racket businesses and wealthy landowners. Far from being Corsican Robin Hoods, however, they sometimes amassed fortunes and large factions of followers, as well as widespread notoriety, and are these days regarded as the precursors of the modern Mafia.

Around the turn of the century, the atrocities committed by *bandits* such as the Bellacoscia brothers (an account of whose career appears on p.313) spurred the police to mount a sweeping crackdown. Hideouts were raided, outlaws rounded up and imprisoned and their protection rackets rumbled. Today, there are no longer any bona fide *bandits d'honneur* remaining in the Corsican maquis, but their racketeering tactics, heroic self-image and hold over the local population have become distinguishing traits of the FLNC paramilitaries, who regularly invite journalists to their hideaways in the dead of night to be photographed wearing black jumpsuits and balaclavas, brandishing automatic weapons.

A biography of one of the first, and most notorious, Corsican *bandits*, Théodore Poli ("Le Roi des Montagnes") appears on p.153, while the story of Muzarettu, among the only traditional *bandits d'honneur* to have lived in the postwar period, is featured in our account of Sartène on p.229.

Alta Rocca and Bavella

A region of evocative prehistoric sites, delightful villages and stark mountain peaks, **Alta Rocca** also contains some of the most fertile parts of Corsica – **Vallée du Rizzanese**, in the south of the region, is cultivated with orchards and the most prolific vineyards on the island. In the upper part of the Rizzanese valley the highlight is **Santa Lucia di Tallano**, an outstandingly attractive village, while high in the valley of the Fiumiccicoli tributary lies **Levie**, where you can see a Bronze Age settlement and medieval castle. Many of the Alta Rocca villages have hotels, with the majority concentrated at **Zonza**, thanks to its proximity to the magnificent **Bavella**, whose granite needles and dense forests form one of the most celebrated Corsican landscapes.

If you're approaching Alta Rocca from Propriano, you can either follow the D19/119/69 from the village up to **Aullène**, or head south from Propriano along the N196, then turn onto the D69, which switches to the west bank of the Rizzanese River, leaving the D268 to continue to Santa Lucia. The approach from the other side of Corsica, via the Ospédale route, is covered on p.253. A twice-daily **bus** runs from Ajaccio through Bicchisano, Santa Lucia di Tallano and Levie on its way to Zonza and Bavella, but there's no bus to Aullène.

Propriano to Carbini

The first diversion along the N196/D69 route from Propriano – the **Spin a Cavallu** bridge – comes 3km after the junction with the N196, and is reached by a track from the parking space down to the river. This elegant Pisan stone arch, beautifully set off by a background of rippling vineyards and olive trees, has survived intact since the thirteenth century, and provides room for two horses to pass – its name means "horseback bridge".

Santa Lucia di Tallano

Perched high above the Vallée du Rizzanese, the exquisite village of SANTA LUCIA DI TALLANO has been wealthy since Rinuccio della Rocca made it his stronghold. An eminent patron of the arts as well as a fearsome warlord, Rinuccio donated many works of art to the parish church in between his desperate attempts to oust the Genoese in the first decade of the sixteenth century. Graceful balconied houses remain as a legacy of the illustrious families who once resided here, while the prosperity of many present-day residents is attested by the Mercedes lined up in the square. Some of the money comes from gangsterism, but there are two more legitimate sources of income: locally produced **Fiumiccicoli** wine, and an extremely rare rock called *diorite orbiculaire* – a greyish-blue stone with concentric rings of black and white, like a leopard pelt – which is quarried close by.

A wide street sweeps through the village in a loop, widening out in the centre to form **place des Monuments aux Morts**, whose terrace gives a glorious view of vineyards and verdant hills that is interrupted by the prominent red roof of **Chapelle St-Jean-Baptiste**, a few kilometres to the south. Reached via a twenty-minute walk along the waymarked Mare a Mare Sud trail (follow the signposts for Fozzano), the floor of the monument, now used as a cattle shed, incorporates the local **diorite**, though it's hard to pick any out under the layer of straw and cow dung. Portable pieces of this strange stone can be bought for about 50F from Mme Françoise Renucci, just down the road from the *Hotel Léandri* (look for the sign "pierre corse" outside her house), whose family own the only workable diorite mine in the area. It was closed fifteen or so years ago, but before sealing the shaft, Mme Renucci extracted four final tonnes of rock that she now keeps in a cellar, chipping chunks off from time to time to sell to tourists.

The anonymous **Église Paroissiale** has precursors going back to Roman times, but was rebuilt many times until its seventeenth-century Baroque incarnation that you see today. Inside there's a marble font in the form of a hand, dating from the 1490s and bearing the della Rocca arms, but the real treasure is the finely worked marble bas-relief of the *Virgin and Child*, commissioned by Rinuccio della Rocca in 1498 – it's attached to a column on the left inside the church entrance. The church's late fifteenth-century *Crucifixion*, attributed to the Catalan painter known as the Master of Castel Sardo, is now locked away in the mairie next door, where you can ask to see it.

Behind the church stands the **Maison Forte**, a huge, impenetrable, grey granite house built to shelter the population in times of danger. For a view of the village you could walk north for five minutes to the **Couvent St-François**, founded by Rinuccio in 1492 and set squarely on a plateau overlooking the valley. Another good **walk** takes you along the route of the Mare a Mare Sud footpath, which cuts between switchbacks in the road from the village centre to the hamlet of Altagène; from here, a motorable track hugs the shoulder of the hillside, bending northeast as it enters a dense and beautiful evergreen oak forest sliced by babbling streams. You can follow this easy trail through the woods for miles, but most people turn back as it begins the steep climb up to the **Col de Tarava** (reached after 2hr 30min; allow 4hr for the return trip to the pass, and take plenty of water with you).

Santa Lucia has just two places to **stay**: the attractively converted gîte d'étape, on the north edge of the village (☎04 95 78 80 13 or 04 95 78 80 54); and the *Léandri*, on the main street south of place des Monuments-aux-Morts (☎04 95 78 80 82; ③). The latter is a creakingly inviting establishment trapped in a delightful time warp, with portraits of the Léandri family on the walls and old furniture in its three simple rooms; nothing at the front of the building suggests it's a hotel, except a handful of tatty green café tables. For a **meal**, try the *Pizzeria Santa Lucia*, next to the monument, which turns out run-of-the-mill pizzas, salads and local cheeses, and whose terrace is the best place to watch the *pétanque* players next to the fountain. The streetside tables outside the village **bar**, the *Ortini*, provide another good vantage point from which to follow the comings and goings in the square, plus they serve fresh croissants and pains au chocolat for breakfast.

Levie

In the eighteenth century **LEVIE** (Livia) was the capital of Alta Rocca, its Genoese families prospering from the fertile countryside and presiding over a village more populous than Sartène. Today the village is rather dull, its main attraction being the proximity of the **Pianu di Levie** (see below), whose prehistoric sites provide much of the substance of the **musée départementale** (July–Sept daily 9.30–6.30pm; Oct–June Mon–Fri 10am–noon & 2–4.30pm; 10F), underneath the mairie off the main street. The star exhibit is the so-called *Dame de Bonifacio*, a human skeleton discovered near Bonifacio and dated around 6570 BC, making this the oldest to be found in Corsica. The remains are those of a woman in her mid thirties whose legs were badly crippled by old fractures; to have lived to such an age she must have been cared for by her community. The other noteworthy artefact on display here is a beautiful ivory statue of Christ by a pupil of Donatello, given to Levie in the 1580s by Pope Sixtus V.

In the summer, a small **tourist office** operates in the centre of the village on rue Sorba (July & Aug Mon–Fri 9am–noon & 3–6pm). There's only one place to **stay** hereabouts: the small B&B-style guesthouse run by Annie de Peretti, above *Le Gourmet* restaurant at the entrance to the village (☎04 95 78 41 61; ③). As well as the simple rooms, they have more expensive studios with kitchenettes to let. A good and moderately priced place for a hearty **meal** is *La Pergola*, opposite the museum, which serves plain home-cooking and will make charcuterie sandwiches on request. Lovers of quality regional cuisine, however, should note that one of the island's finest **gourmet restaurants**, *A Pignata* (☎04 95 78 41 90), lies close to Levie. Among the best-kept secrets of Corsican gastronomy, it's hidden deep in serene countryside near **Cucuruzzu**, 5km west. To find it, head 3km out of the village on the Santa Lucia road, turning right at the signpost for the Pianu de Levie archeological site. Roughly 1.5km further on the left you'll see a narrow, unsignposted lane marked by a couple of large rubbish bins; a short way up the lane lies the gateway to the auberge. They serve a single set menu, reasonably priced at 160F (plus wine), and the food is refreshingly unpretentious, with everything straight from the garden and prepared on the premises.

The Pianu di Levie

The most interesting prehistoric site on Corsica after Filitosa, the **Pianu di Levie** (daily June to mid-Sept 9am–8pm; 20F) is reached by taking the signposted road off the D268, 3km west of Levie. A further 2km will bring you to a field where you can park and buy your ticket – you get a ninety-minute cassette-guided tour of the site for no extra charge.

A fifteen-minute walk through a Tolkienesque tract of gnarled old oak trees brings you to the **Casteddu di Cucuruzzu**, the remains of a Torréen habitation dating from 1400 BC. Emerging from the forest and integrated into the chaos of eroded, moss-covered granite boulders, this is the best example of a *casteddu* in Corsica. The complex, dominated by a circular *torre* and surrounded by a thick high wall, was inhabited by Bronze Age artisans and farmers, who lived in the chambers surrounding the *torre* and in dry-stone shacks close by. The *casteddu* is entered by a steep and narrow stairway. Storerooms are ranged on the right, opposite a series of chambers with openings above to let the light in and the smoke out. Straight ahead, the *torre* has retained its vaulted roof of wide granite slabs, below which stones jutting out sideways from the walls suggest the existence of another floor. Stone tools, bronze belt links and domestic utensils, found in the course of excavations here, all point to the tower's having a functional rather than religious purpose. From the top you get a magnificent panoramic view of the region, from the needles of Bavella to the gulf of Propriano.

*For more on
the Torreans
and their enig-
matic towers,
see p.198.*

Another twenty minutes through the woods brings you to **Capula**, a site occupied from the Bronze Age until 1259, when its so-called **castle**, an impressive circular monument, was partly destroyed. Just below the entrance stands a headless menhir, and other pieces of Bronze and Iron Age stonework are incorporated into the monument, mixed with hundreds of small granite bricks from the medieval period. About 200m beyond the castle stands **Chapelle San Lorenzu**, a tiny thirteenth-century Romanesque building extensively restored this century.

Carbini

South of Levie, the D59 runs 8km through a twisting valley to **CARBINI**, whose isolated bell tower heads a straight road lined with lime trees and low cottages. Adjacent to the tower, which is all that remains of the Église St-Quilico, stands **San Giovanni**, built in the first half of the twelfth century and decorated with elegant early Romanesque arcading. In 1354, in the aftermath of the Black Death, this stately building saw the birth of a sect called the **Giovannali**, a bizarre Franciscan offshoot whose religious meetings were rumoured to end with orgies – their doctrine of the equal division of property extended to the sharing of wives as well as all worldly goods. Despite persecution the Giovannali spread throughout the east of Corsica until, in 1362, Urban V dispatched an expedition that resulted in the massacre of a hundred people here. The village then had to be repopulated by families from Sartène.

Carbini does not have anywhere to stay or eat, nor even a café; the only facility for visitors is a small tap dispensing springwater – a welcome sight for hikers ambling through on the Mare a Mare Sud trail.

An account of the Mare a Mare Sud long-distance footpath is featured on p.208.

Aullène and around

Aullène, lying at a crossroads of four main inland routes, is most easily approached from Propriano by following the D69 across the Rizzanese or by taking the D19 directly out of Propriano, a route that becomes the D69, then meanders north through the verdant **Vallée du Coscione**. From Aullène you loop back to Propriano via the **Col de St-Eustache** and **Petreto-Bicchisano**, or alternatively head east for the mountains to **Quenza**, in the direction of Zonza.

Aullène

Lush vegetation characterizes the region around the dispersed village of **AULLÈNE** (Auddé), whose inhabitants relied for centuries on the surrounding chestnut woods for survival. Set midway between the east and west coasts, the village makes a pleasant place to stop, its long-established *de la Poste* **hotel**, rue Principal (☎04 95 78 61 21; May–Oct; ②–③), incorporating a cosy restaurant renowned for its charcuterie and pork dishes. If you're just passing through, pause at the seventeenth-century **church**, whose pulpit displays wooden carvings portraying pirate raids and is supported by twisting sea monsters emerging from a Moor's head.

Aullène to Petreto-Bicchisano

Striking **west from Aullène** along the D420, a looping road rises through a spectacular rocky landscape, with enormous boulders dominating the road as far as the **Col de la Tana** (975m), situated some 7km along. Beyond this pass a high narrow road hugs the mountainside above a belt of pinewood, overshadowed by the pink granite bulk of the Punta di Taccaluccjia. At the **Col de St-Eustache** (995m), a further 3km, the view extends north over the mountains to the Vallée du Taravo, its mass of greenery swamping the slopes.

A further 10km will bring you to **PETRETO-BICCHISANO**, an imposing sixteenth-century village made up of two hamlets. The church at Petreto is worth a look for its wooden statues representing St Francis of Assisi, St Claire and the Immaculate Conception.

Aullène to Quenza

Southeast of Aullène, the D420 passes through two particularly pretty villages clinging to the lush, steep sides of the Rizzanese valley. The first, **SERRA-DI-SCAPOMENA**, is a night halt on the Mare a

Mare Sud trail (see p.208) and has an excellent gîte d'étape (☎04 95 78 64 90 or 04 95 78 60 13), whose terrace affords a glorious view across the pale-blue Bavella, Zonza and Ospédale massifs. You can also **camp** here at the *Camping de l'Alta Rocca* (☎04 95 78 62 01; June 15–Sept 15), a rambling two-star site tucked away above the village under a chestnut wood; a stone's throw from the footpath to the Coscione plateau, it makes a great base for day walks in the area, details of which are available from the *gardien* of the gîte.

The next village along the main road, **SORBOLLANO** marks the start of a spectacular, but rarely travelled, backroute down the hidden Rau di Codi valley, a tributary of the Rizzanese. Twisting around a sharp spur, it veers north through dense woodland to cross the stream at Ponte de la Nova, where it switches south again. A short way beyond the bridge, at the hamlet of **Campu**, a Parc Naturel Régional signpost on the left of the road, marked "Santa Lucia", points the way to an idyllic bathing place and picnic spot at the confluence of two boulder-choked streams, a gentle ten-minute walk.

From here, either continue south to Santa Lucia di Tallano, or return to Sorbollano and pick up the D420, which eventually winds to sleepy **QUENZA**. Set on a granite eminence smothered in pines and chestnut groves, with Bavella as a spiky backdrop, Quenza has a spectacular location and a fine Romanesque church, **Santa Maria**, which stands at the entrance to the village. Dating from 1000, it's built on a single nave plan with an oven-shaped apse, and retains some traces of its original frescoes. The church next door has a wooden pulpit supported by a couple of dragons and a Moorish head, as well as a curious fifteenth-century multicoloured wooden panel of the Virgin and Child, in a chapel to the left of the altar.

Lying within easy reach of Bavella and the Coscione plateau, Quenza is also a prime destination for **outdoor pursuits** enthusiasts. Corsica's most renowned mountaineer, the distinctively bearded Jean-Paul Quilicci, lives here. Dubbed "l'Homme de Bavella" because of his unrivalled knowledge of the local peaks, he leads **guided walks** into mountains during the summer (for more details, call ☎04 95 78 64 33).

Quenza's **hotel**, the *Sole e Monti*, is just past the centre along the road to Zonza (☎04 95 78 61 56, fax 04 95 78 63 88; ⑤). It's a large, recently converted granite building, with good food served in the small triangular garden out the front; non-residents can eat here for around 150F. Hikers passing through on the Mare a Mare Sud, however, tend to hole up in the more modest gîte d'étape, *I Muntagnoli Corsi* (☎04 95 78 65 19), which has an adjacent **campsite**. Located 1km north of the village at the end of an appallingly rutted dirt track, the site/gîte enjoys stunning views and has a congenial common room with easy chairs and a guitar.

Five kilometres northwest of Quenza in the hamlet of **JALICU**, Pierrot Milanini's stables (☎04 95 78 63 21 or 04 95 78 61 09) offer

---

An Alta Rocca Round Walk: Quenza–Zonza–Quenza

A circular walk from **Quenza to Zonza** via the St-Antoine river bridge is a relatively easy, but hugely rewarding, hike (about 4hr 15min) offering glimpses of the mountains and opportunities for swimming in the crystal-clear rivers along the way. Don't attempt this route without a map, as the area is riddled with other trails confusingly marked with the same-coloured orange paint. Failing an IGN map of the region or a copy of the Parc Naturel Régional's topo-guide, try to get hold of the *Balades en Corse: Alta Rocca* leaflet from any tourist office, which has a black-and-white contour map of the area with the route marked on it.

The path begins about 600m from Quenza's eastern exit, signposted to the right. Dropping gently down through deciduous woodland, it crosses the **Rizzanese river** and steadily climbs the opposite side of the valley to meet the D420. Follow this into **Zonza** (1hr 45min); the onward trail is indicated 400m south of the village with a post marked "Quenza", on the right-hand side of the main road to Levie (D268). After crossing fairly level, open farmland, it enters the trees and zigzags sharply down, crossing onto the left (south) bank of the **de Rian stream**, which it follows through the woods for around forty minutes to rejoin the **St-Antoine river** (3hr). Once on the other side, you climb steeply through more beautiful oak and chestnut forest until the path runs alongside the tall fences of a **deer enclosure**. Deer were hunted out in Corsica by 1970, but have been re-introduced on the island from this twenty-hectare farm, which releases five or six fawns into the woods each year. After following a motorable dirt track for 1km, bear left at the signpost for Quenza, reached after a gradual, hour-long ascent through broken plantations and grassy fields.

---

the chance to explore the stark surrounding countryside on horseback. A day's **pony trekking** will set you back a stiff 550F, but the horses are are lovingly looked after, and the landscape superb. The Milaninis also run an independent gîte: a combination of budget dormitory accommodation and classy half-board cooking for the excellent all-in price of 175F per head – ideal if you want to explore the area on foot.

Zonza and the route de Bavella

One of the main tourist centres of Alta Rocca, **Zonza** lies at a junction of roads to Levie, Ospédale, Quenza and Bavella. The road north from here is perhaps the most dramatic in all Corsica: crossing the bleak **Col de Bavella**, it plunges through the forests of Zonza, Bavella and Tova, with sublime views of the **Aiguilles de Bavella**, before descending steeply to the coast from **Col de Larone**, alongside the sparkling River Solenzara. No public transport serves the route, but in summer there's enough tourist traffic to make hitching feasible.

Zonza

Set against the snow-dusted needles of the Bavella massif, **ZONZA** looks like something off the top of a chocolate box, and its prominence on postcard racks and brochure covers ensures that this picturesque granite village is transformed during summer with the influx of tourists – hikers, climbers and horse riders, as well as a steady stream of motorists and backpackers. Its most illustrious visitors were probably Muhammed V, Sultan of Morocco, and his son, who turned up here with three limousines in October 1952 after the family had been deposed in a coup d'état. The French ministry of the interior had requisitioned the village's now-defunct *Mouflon d'Or* hotel to accommodate the royals during their two-year exile. But the winter snow and rain got the better of them, and after only five months the sultan demanded the government find him a place on the coast. Another hotel was subsequently requisitioned: the palatial *Napoléon Bonaparte* in L'Île Rousse.

A cluster of **hotels**, all with more than decent **restaurants**, cater for today's less affluent crowds. Pick of the bunch has to be the long-established *L'Aiglon*, in the village centre on the main road (☎04 95 78 67 79, fax 04 95 78 63 62; April–Dec; ③), which has comfortable, tastefully furnished rooms and a wonderful restaurant on the ground floor where you can sample classy local cuisine such as *fettuccini al brocciu* and smoked salmon, or melt-in-the-mouth kid stew, rounded off with cakes baked from chestnut flour. A slap-up à la carte meal here should set you back a little over 150F per head, plus wine, and they have a couple of less expensive fixed menus and dishes of the day to choose from. Roughly in the same price range is *Le Tourisme*, north of the village, set back on the west side of the Quenza road (☎04 95 78 67 72; ③–④). Their more costly rooms have fine views over the valley, but the smaller, less expensive options are comfortable enough, if a little dark; and the restaurant is renowned throughout this area. Otherwise there's the pleasantly old-fashioned *L'Incudine*, at the entrance to the village if you're coming from Ospédale (☎04 95 78 67 71; ③); affiliated to the Logis de France chain, it offers good value for money, with cosy en-suite rooms and a busy restaurant serving mountain charcuterie, cheeses and local game in season. Finally, beer lovers should check out the *Alta Rocca* **café**, just below the war memorial junction, which dishes up over fifty kinds of draught lager.

Zonza's only **campsite** is set in a pleasant pine wood 4km out of the village on the D368, the main Ospédale/Porto-Vecchio road (☎04 95 78 62 74). If you're on foot, it's worth noting that a courtesy minibus is laid on during July and August to ferry visitors out of the site, connecting with the **buses** that stop in the village. Three scheduled services pass through during the summer. Autocars Ricci's coaches (☎04 95 51 08 19 or 04 95 76 25 59) run twice each evening from Ajaccio's terminal routière via Propriano, Santa Lucia di Tallano and Levie, arriving here at 6.15pm or 7.15pm and returning early the next morning. From Porto-Vecchio there's Balesi Evasion's daily minibus (☎04 95 70 15 55 or 04 95 21 05

17), which leaves at 7am, and pulls in here an hour later en route to Ajaccio via Quenza and Aullène. Coming in the other direction, this service departs Ajaccio at 4pm, arriving in the village at around 6.15pm.

The Parc Naturel Régional **information office**, where you can pick up maps, topo-guides and leaflets for the Alta Rocca walk described above, is situated 500m north of the village (May–Sept daily 9am–noon & 3–5pm; ☎04 95 78 66 58).

Zonza to Solenzara: the route de Bavella

North of Zonza, the D268 penetrates the Forêt de Zonza, a dense expanse of pine and chestnut trees, as it rises steadily to the **Col de Bavella** (1218m). A towering statue of Notre-Dame-des-Neiges marks the pass itself, which has a bleak and blasted look, the pines flattened by the wind, their jagged branches sharply black against the green-hued granite peaks. An amazing panorama of peaks and forests surrounds the col: to the northwest the serrated granite ridge of the Cirque de Gio Agostino is dwarfed by the pink pinnacles of the **Aiguilles de Bavella**; behind soars Monte Incudine; and the east is dominated by the ruddy shades of Punta Tafonata and the distant sea.

The hamlet of **BAVELLA**, a cluster of neatly painted tin- and stone-roofed huts and chalets just beyond the col, was built in the early nineteenth century for the inhabitants of the eastern plain to take refuge from the suffocating summer heat of the lowlands. It's a lonely spot, especially in winter, and a sign erected in the car park voices the residents' complaints of neglect by the local *commune* council, who have failed to provide refuse collection and common sanitation for the village. Nevertheless, this is an ideal place to base yourself for **hikes** in the area (see box opposite). The *Auberge du Col* (☎04 95 57 43 87; April–Oct; ①) offers clean and comfortable dormitory accommodation, with the option of good-value half board in their restaurant, where you can tuck into groaning plates of local charcuterie and cheese on a sunny terrace.

From the auberge, it's a steep descent through what's left of the **Forêt de Bavella**, which suffered a devastating fire in 1960 but still features some huge Laricio pines. The winding road offers numerous breathtaking glimpses of the Aiguilles de Bavella, whose granite pinnacles are roamed by the rare mouflon. About 10km from the pass you'll come to the **Col de Larone** (608m), which offers stunning vistas of the mountains and the **Forêt de Tova** in the north. Vast cliffs and rock falls tower on all sides as the road winds through a landscape reminiscent of the American Wild West, with dizzying drops to a river full of smooth white rocks and turquoise pools. Towards the bottom of the gorge, you can pull over in several places for a dip.

Walks from the Auberge du Col

A waymarked variant of the GR20 trail gives you an eighty-minute walk around the Col de Bavella. Begin by following the GR20, leading to the right of the *Auberge du Col* and clearly marked with red and white paint; after 1500m leave the GR20 and ascend the path indicated by red paint flashes that runs alongside the river and after 3km leads to a stream. Continue up the left bank for a short stretch until you reach a grassy platform scattered with twisted pines. From here there's a view of the Aiguilles de Bavella and both the east and west coast of Corsica. Descend by the right-hand path along the larger slope down to the chapel, from which a path leads back down to the auberge.

A very enjoyable two-hour walk from the auberge goes to the Trou de la Bombe, a circular opening that pierces the Paliri crest of peaks. From the auberge follow the GR20 for 800m, then take the first path to the right, signposted "Trou de la Bombe". The track rises through a wood as far as a ridge where a path follows the line of the crest, the *trou* emerging to the right of the Calanca Murata mountain. Those with a head for heights should climb right into the hole for the dizzying view down the sheer 500m cliff on the other side.

Sartène

A "town peopled by demons" is how German chronicler Gregorovius described SARTÈNE (Sartè) in the nineteenth century, and the town hasn't shaken off its hostile image. Located near the coast and therefore vulnerable to foreign invaders, it was persistently attacked by pirates in the Middle Ages, and from the twelfth to the sixteenth centuries became the seat of the ferocious Sgio (from *signori*), feudal lords who preferred to implement justice without interference from the island's rulers and thus turned Sartène into an asylum for refugees from the law of the state. A bloody vendetta in the nineteenth century sealed the town's reputation and left a legacy of tall, grim fortress houses. An insular outlook continues to this day, and outsiders can be put off by the implacable ambience of the place, and by the heavy presence of wealthy-looking godfather types. On the other hand it's a smarter, better-groomed town than most in Corsica, with a perfectly preserved medieval heart that's blissfully free of ferroconcrete. One of the main reasons for this is the communist mayor, who has passed laws banning unsightly buildings, neon signs, and even overhead cables. Another is the money brought in from the Sartène wine – the best on the island.

Despite its turbulent history, the town doesn't offer many diversions once you've explored the enclosed vieille ville and paid a visit to the Musée de la Préhistoire Corse. The only time of year Sartène teems with tourists is at Easter for U Catenacciu, its highly charged Good Friday procession (see p.230).

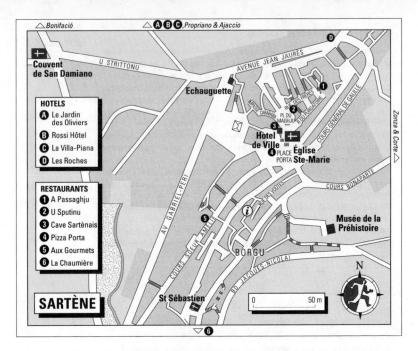

A brief history of Sartène

Sartène was formed when, in the tenth century, the inhabitants of this region's agglomeration of hamlets were forced to congregate in one place by Saracen raids. In the twelfth century the **della Rocca** family held sway over the area with the consent of its Pisan governors, but when the Genoese took over in the thirteenth century, Sartène became a centre of discontent. The laws giving Genoa a monopoly on Corsica's trade were anathema to the local nobility, the **Sgio**, who continued to resist the Genoese until the final stand of Rinuccio della Rocca, defeated after a long struggle in 1502.

It was not until early in the sixteenth century that Sartène became a Genoese administrative centre, and even then their tenure was deeply troubled. In 1565 Sampiero Corso's army destroyed the town after a 35-day siege, then the Genoese took it back, only to lose it again in 1583 to **Hassan Pasha**, the mad king of Algiers, who ransacked the town and abducted four hundred of its inhabitants, a third of the population. Thereafter Sartène remained faithful to Genoa, so much so that Paoli had a struggle to win Sartène to his cause in the fight for a Corsican republic.

The nineteenth century saw the re-emergence of the Sgio: recognized as members of the nobility by the French monarchy, these powerful aristocrats prospered under privileges granted by

Napoléon III; and, whereas other parts of Corsica suffered depopulation and decline, the Sgio oversaw the development of a wine industry that still underpins the local economy. Today, as the *sous-préfecture* of southern Corsica – France's second-largest *commune* – Sartène is the most important town in the region after Ajaccio.

Arrival, information and accommodation

If you're arriving in Sartène by **bus** you'll be dropped either at the top of av Gabriel-Péri or at the end of cours Général-de-Gaulle, just off the main square. On the opposite side of place Porta, a short way down rue Capitaine-Benedetti, is a tiny **tourist office** (summer Mon–Fri 9am–noon & 2.30–6pm; ☎04 95 77 15 40), which can help you find accommodation in the area if the hotels listed below are full – only likely during Catenacciu. The nearest **campsite** to Sartène is the three-star *Camping Olva (Les Eucalyptus)*, 5km out of town towards Castagna on the D69 (☎04 95 77 11 58, fax 04 95 77 05 68; May–Oct). Travellers without their own vehicle can telephone for a courtesy *navette* from the bus stop. Drivers are advised to park in rue Général-de-Gaulle or outside the *Super U* supermarket at the bottom of cours Sœur-Amélie, and walk up into town.

Accommodation

Le Jardin des Oliviers (Chez Jean Rossi), 1km west of town on the Propriano road (☎04 95 77 02 72). Moderately priced maisonettes set amid a beautiful garden full of citrus fruits, figs and cacti, with a tiny pool. June–Sept. ③.

Les Roches, av Jean-Jaurès (☎04 95 77 07 61, fax 04 95 11 19 93). A large, family-run hotel on the edge of the old town, most of whose well-appointed en-suite rooms command panoramic views of the Vallée du Rizzanese. The only place actually in the centre, which means it can get a little noisy. Restaurant. ④.

Rossi Hotel (Fior di Riba), 800m west of town on the Propriano road (☎04 95 77 01 80). Run by the same family as *Le Jardin des Oliviers*, but with more modern and marginally posher rooms, or tastefully furnished studios for longer stays. April–Sept. ③.

La Villa-Piana, 1km west of town on the Propriano road (☎04 95 77 07 04). Pretty rooms, most of them with views of the old town; also tennis court and pool. Good value at this price. May–Oct. ④.

The town

Place Porta – its official name, place de la Libération, has never caught on – forms Sartène's nucleus. Once the arena for bloody quarrels, it's now a well-kept square opening onto a wide terrace overlooking the rippling green valley of the Rizzanese. Somnolent by day, place Porta comes alive for the early evening *passeggiata*, when it fills with snappily dressed townsfolk, and hunters in their green camouflage gear.

Flanking the south side of place Porta is **Église Ste-Marie**, built in the 1760s but completely restored to a smooth granitic appearance.

Sartène

The chief interest here is historical – it was in this church that the warring families of nineteenth-century Sartène were forced to make their peace, though the truce often lasted only until they got outside again. Inside the church you can see the weighty wooden cross and chain used in the Catenacciu procession (see p.230), but otherwise the only notable feature is the Baroque altar, a present from the town's Franciscan monastery, no longer in existence.

Formerly the palace for the Genoese governor, the nearby **Hôtel de Ville** serves as an archway into the Santa Anna district of the *vieille ville*; the building is not open to the public and its archives have been closed since the 1880s, due to the endemic corruption of local politics, it's said.

The vieille ville

A flight of steps to the left of the Hôtel de Ville leads past the Maison de la Culture and cinema to the post office, behind which stands to the ruined **échauguette**, a small lookout tower which is all that remains of the town's twelfth-century ramparts. This apart, the best of the **vieille ville** is to be found behind in the **Santa Anna** district, a labyrinth of constricted passageways and ancient fortress-like houses reached via the archway directly beneath the Hôtel de Ville, which rarely harbours any signs of life. Featuring few windows and often linked to their neighbours by balconies, these houses are entered by first-floor doors, a necessary measure against unwelcome intruders; dilapidated staircases have replaced the ladders that used to provide the only access. The main "road" across Santa Anna is rue des Frères-Bartoli,

---

Vendetta in the Vieille Ville

In the villages of nineteenth-century Corsica it was common for blood feuds to start over something as trivial as the theft of a cockerel (see box on p.212), but Sartène's vendetta had its roots in a political dispute between the rich **Roccaserra** family of Santa Anna – supporters of the Bourbons – and the anti-monarchist Ortoli family of the poorer Borgo district. In 1830, on the occasion of the overthrow of the Bourbons in France, a group of Ortolis and their cohorts marched through Santa Anna to provoke the mayor, a royalist Roccaserra. In the ensuing fight Sebastien Pietri, a leading light in the Roccaserra clan, was killed and five of his comrades were wounded, which provoked an invasion of the town by a thousand Roccaserra allies from the mountains. The scene was witnessed by French chronicler A.C. Pasquin Valéry, who wrote, "The French are powerless against the nature, manners and passions of the Corsicans." After a series of violent confrontations in the maquis, where many members of both factions were killed, a mediator was brought in, a peace treaty drawn up and in 1834, at a Mass in Église Ste-Marie, the survivors of the vendetta were forced to swear to live in peace. Even then, street corners were guarded and windows bricked up, the feud only relaxing on the election of Napoléon III in 1848, when the children of the families were allowed to dance together at the celebrations.

---

to the left of which are the strangest of all the vaulted passageways, where outcrops of rock block the paths between the ancient buildings. Just to the west of the Hôtel de Ville, signposted off the tiny **place Maggiore**, you'll find the **impasse Carababa**, a remarkable architectural puzzle of a passageway cut through the awkwardly stacked houses. A few steps away, at the western edge of the town, **place Angelo-Maria-Chiappe** offers a magnificent view of the Golfe du Valinco.

Musée de la Préhistoire Corse

Set in a shady garden a short distance east of place Porta, the **Musée de la Préhistoire Corse** (Mon–Fri 9am–noon & 2–4pm; 25F) is Corsica's centre for archeological research and is packed with findings from digs throughout the island, dating mostly from 6000 to 500 BC. Beyond the entrance hall, where a chart traces the history of human habitation in Corsica, the first room contains Neolithic exhibits, mainly pottery fragments, and covers the early development of agriculture, fishing and hunting. More sophisticated items are found in the second room, where finely carved arrowheads and tools of polished obsidian are presented alongside more accomplished fragments of decorated ceramics, gold jewellery and statuettes, as well as a pile of human bones deformed by fire, discovered near Bonifacio.

Next door, in the fourth room, a model of Cucuruzzu gives a good idea of what a Bronze Age settlement looked like, while specimens of functional Torréen pottery contrast with the more elaborate examples in the previous section. Two **statue-menhirs**, one of them coloured red as it would have been during the megalithic era, stand opposite cases containing colourful **bracelets** from the Iron Age, a period also represented by weaponry and decorated pottery. Painted ceramics from the thirteenth to the sixteenth centuries complete the museum.

An account of the Cucuruzzu ruins, the most important archeological site in Corsica after Filitosa, appears on p.219.

Couvent de San Damiano

A ten-minute walk along the road to Bonifacio will take you to the **Couvent de San Damiano**, the building in which the Catenacciu penitent spends the night before the procession, when he has to be guarded from curious outsiders by police. One of the last of the old-style bandits, a formidable character called **Muzarettu**, died here in the 1940s at the age of ninety, having been given refuge by the monks. Cast out from his village for killing a nephew who had slapped his face, Muzarettu took to the maquis, then proceeded to terrorize the neighbourhood from his cave hideout near Propriano, where he hosted wild parties for the fishermen who brought him food and drink. A few more murders along the way kept him outlawed for many years, but as an old man he developed cancer and came to this convent to die; repenting his sins right at the very end, he was visited by the chief of police on his deathbed. The convent is now home to a brotherhood of Belgian monks and is out of bounds to the public, but there's a fine view of the valley from the outside.

For a background feature on Corsican bandits, see p.215.

Sartène

U Catenacciu

Sartène's Good Friday ceremony of U **Catenacciu**, generally considered to be the most ancient ritual in Corsica, is a frighteningly authentic imitation of Christ's walk to Golgotha, despite a touch of exploitation in recent years. The nocturnal procession through candlelit streets is headed by the **Grand Pénitent** or Pénitent Rouge: dressed in a scarlet hooded robe which covers his face, he carries a heavy wooden cross and is chained on the ankle – *u catenacciu* means "chained one". In former times the penitent was usually a bandit whose identity was officially known only to the priest. Nowadays the Grand Pénitent is still anonymous and there's a waiting list of twelve years to take part, which means that some of the penitents are very old men. If the Grand Pénitent is too frail to shoulder the cross alone, he's helped out by the **Pénitent Blanc**, who follows behind, representing Simon of Cyrena. Behind him comes a troop of **Pénitents Noirs** bearing the statue of Christ on a bier. Accompanied by the continuous unearthly chanting of an ancient Corsican prayer, *Perdonu miu Diu*, the penitents pass slowly from Église Ste-Marie through the streets of the *vieille ville*, ending up three hours later in place Porta, where they receive benediction at midnight.

In the past it was a dangerous event, as the penitents were often known murderers at whom onlookers would fling stones – though this was one time of year when a truce was observed between sworn enemies, so nobody got killed. It's still a rough affair, with a lot of pushing and shoving to get the best view among the throng of tourists, and shots are often fired into the air at the end of the ceremony, by which time excitement is running high.

Eating and drinking

Hotels may be thin on the ground in Sartène, but there is no shortage of restaurants, most of them cosy, traditional places in old stone buildings. A handful of inexpensive snack bars and pizzerias also line the main square, and are ideal for a light lunch or ice cream.

La Cave Sartènais, place de la Libération. Directly beneath the Hôtel de Ville, and the most congenial place in town to taste and buy quality local wines.

La Chaumière, rue Capitaine-Benedetti. A cosy ersatz rustic restaurant specializing in local cuisine such as *tripettes sartènais*, river trout and wild pork. One of the few places open all year.

Aux Gourmets, cours Sœur-Amélie. Small, unpretentious bistro just south of the main square, serving inexpensive omelettes and a good-value 70F set menu that includes wild-boar steaks and chips. Ask for a seat on the tiny terrace to the rear, which juts over the valley.

A Passaghju, at the end of rue des Frères-Bartoli, in the *vieille ville*. Slap in the centre of the old town, and a good place for *grillades*: charcoal-grilled beef and lamb steaks, served with salads and chips. Moderate.

Pizza Porta, place Porta. *Paninis* (toasted sandwiches), fresh salads, crêpes and pizzas at reasonable prices.

U Sputinu, 13 rue des Frères-Bartoli, in the *vieille ville*. Mostly salads and fresh pasta, with a fair choice of Corsican dishes such as stuffed courgettes, and local wines. Moderate.

Around Sartène

You get captivating views of Sartène and the Golfe de Valinco by driving along the D50 southeast of Sartène, which descends into the Ortolo valley before reaching the tiny hamlet of **MOLA**. This nest of reddish houses lurks in the shadow of the **Uomo di Cagna**, a gigantic globular rock perched on top of the mountain, which dominates the landscape of the Sartènais district south of Sartène.

West of Sartène, the prehistoric monument of **Alo Bisucce** is reached by a lovely road that leads eventually to Campomoro (see p.210). To get there, take the N196 south as far as the Col de l'Albitrina, branching right towards Tizzano and then soon after veering along a sudden, unsignposted right turning which worms around the hillside in the direction of Grossa. After about 4km the unsignposted site emerges as a mound on the left-hand side of the road. Neolithic settlers occupied this rocky peak around 1700 BC, before the arrival of the Torréens, building a double wall of Cyclopean boulders surmounted by a structure measuring 8m across and centring on a hearth. East of here lies a rough platform, probably used for surveying the surrounding countryside for possible attackers.

Southwest Corsica: the megalithic sites

Sparsely populated today, the rolling hills and deep maquis of the southwestern corner of Corsica, known as the **Sartènais**, harboured a healthy population until the Saracen pirate raids of the fifteenth and seventeenth centuries, when the majority of its inhabitants were abducted and carried off as slaves to North Africa. Since then, this windswept, forbidding area, studded with outcrops of weirdly eroded granite, has been all but deserted, though it remains rich in myth and folklore. Many of the old stories relate to the numerous standing stones and prehistoric sites scattered across the countryside, and these, along with a handful of remote beaches, remain the chief incentive to pull off the main road as it cuts inland between Sartène and Bonifacio.

For more background on the North African pirates who plagued the Corsican coast, see p.89.

Standing in ghostly isolation 10km southwest from Sartène, the **megaliths of Cauria** comprise the **Dolmen de Fontanaccia**, the best-preserved dolmen on Corsica, and the nearby alignments of **Stantari** and **Renaggiu**, an impressive congregation of statue-menhirs. More than 250 menhirs can be seen northwest of Cauria at **Palaggiu**, another rewardingly remote site. The coast hereabouts is equally wild, with deep clefts and coves providing some excellent spots for diving and secluded swimming. Closest to the ancient sites is the miniature port of **Tizzano**, while further east there's the exquisite white cove of **Roccapina** and then the village of **Pianottoli-Caldarello**, set on the deserted plain inland from the narrow **Baie de Figari**.

The only public transport in this region is the four-daily **bus** from Ajaccio to Bonifacio, which keeps to the main N196.

The megaliths of Cauria

To reach the **Cauria** megalithic site you need to turn off the N196 about 2km southwest of Sartène, at the **Col de l'Albitrina** (291m), taking the D48 towards Tizzano. Four kilometres along this road a left turning brings you onto a winding road through vineyards, until eventually the **Dolmen de Fontanaccia** comes into view on the horizon, isolated in a clearing amidst a sea of maquis. A blue sign at the parking space indicates the track to the dolmen, a fifteen-minute walk away.

Known to the locals as the *Stazzona del Diavolu* (Devil's Forge), a name that does justice to its enigmatic power, the Dolmen de Fontanaccia is in fact a burial chamber from the second phase of the megalithic era, around 2000 BC. This period was marked by a change in burial customs – whereas bodies had previously been buried in stone coffins in the ground, they were now placed above, in a mound of earth enclosed in a stone chamber. What you see today is the great stone table, comprising six huge granite blocks nearly 2m high topped by a stone slab, which remained after the earth rotted away.

The 22 "standing men" of the **Alignement de Stantari**, 200m to the east of the dolmen, date from the same period. All are featureless except the two distinctly phallic stones, which both have roughly sculpted eyes and noses, with diagonal swords on their backs and sockets in their heads where horns would probably have been attached.

Across a couple of fields to the south you'll find the **Alignement de Renaggiu**, a gathering of forty menhirs standing in rows amid a small shadowy copse, set against the enormous granite outcrop of Punta di Cauria. Some of the menhirs have fallen, but all face north to south, a fact that seems to rule out any connection with a sun-related cult.

Palaggiu and Tizzano

For the **Alignement de Palaggiu**, the largest concentration of menhirs in Corsica, you regain the D48 and continue southwards until you reach the Domaine la Mosconi vineyard, 3km south of the Cauria turning. From here a dirt track marked "Propriété privée" leads 1.5km inland to the stones, lost in the maquis, with vineyards spread over the hills in the half-distance. Stretching in straight lines across the countryside like a battleground of soldiers, the 258 menhirs include three statue-menhirs with carved weapons and facial features – they are amidst the first line you come to. Dating from around 1800 BC, the statues give few clues as to their function, but it's a reasonable supposition that proximity to the sea was important – Grosjean's theory is that the statues were some sort of magical deterrent to invaders.

TIZZANO (Tizza), at the end of the road about 3km south of Palaggiu, is a secluded little marina tucked into a sheltered inlet. The village consists of a couple of ancient buildings and a chic terraced café set on the rocks overlooking the yacht moorings. Just south of the village, a glorious **beach** of white sand draws increasing numbers of tourists every year, among them surfers undeterred by the strong undertow that wells up here when the waves are high. A string of even more enticing little coves lies a short scramble over the rocks northwest of Tizzano.

Self-reliant hikers in search of coastal wilderness may consider pressing on up the coast to the **Capo di Senetosa**, a remote headland crowned with a bleached white Genoese tower. The path peters out in dense maquis at several points, forcing you back to the rocks lining the shore, but the scenery is superb, and once beyond the tower the tangled wild-boar trails merge to form a more easily discernible path that you can follow all the way to Campomoro – a hike described in more detail on p.211. If you do decide to give it a try, start early in the day, take a sunhat, and carry plenty of food, water and a tent and/or sleeping bag in case you have to camp out.

The road to Bonifacio

South of Sartène, the N196 undulates through a strange landscape of gentle barren hills and vivid blue sea, dominated by the Uomo di Cagna. Once the road hits the coast, about 25km along, the huge roseate rock of the **Lion de Roccapina**, a lump of fawn-coloured granite bizarrely weathered into the shape of a lion's head, comes into view. Sheltered by crumbling granite cliffs, the **Golfe de Roccapina** below it is a dazzling turquoise-blue bay accessible to vehicles via a rocky and rutted dirt track (look out for the turning at Asinaja, signposted "Camping Roccapina"). Shallow bathing, soft white sand and crystal-clear water make this a strong contender for the best beach in Corsica, though it's far from a secret. During the summer, large numbers of tourists from the campsite descend on the cove, designated a protected site – hence the fence safeguarding the dunes. To reach the old Genoese watchtower, head up the stony path that leads right off the main approach to the beach, and bear left when you reach a fork five minutes later (the right fork of this path will take you to the Lion de Roccapina). From the ridge, the views south across the cove, and north over a stunning deserted bay, are superb; you can also follow the path downhill from the watchtower to the headland dividing the two bays, giving access to a wild and rocky shore that is great for diving, snorkelling and fishing.

Southwest Corsica: the megalithic sites

The account of Corsica's most famous prehistoric site, Filitosa, on p.197, includes more background information on the Torrean invasions.

Roccapina and the Queen-Emperor's Jewels

The Golfe de Roccapina witnessed one of the most notorious **shipwrecks** of the nineteenth century when, on the night of April 17, 1887, the luxury P&O steam liner *Tasmania* ran aground onto the treacherous Des Moines rocks a short way out to sea. En route to Southampton from Bombay, she was carrying in her holds a trunk whose contents were worth an estimated eight times the value of the entire ship – precious gems sent by the Rajahs of India to Queen Victoria on her jubilee. Once they learned of the cargo, rescuers began to search for the trunk, but it was eventually picked up by crew members of a salvage vessel, the *Stella*, three weeks later. Local legend has it, however, that some of the jewels found their way into the possession of the *bandit* **Barrittonu**, who used to hide out in the hollows around the Lion de Roccapina. No one has ever proven this rumour to be true, though it is known that a purse of Indian diamonds sent as part of the gift to Queen-Emperor was never recovered; its whereabouts are still subject of speculation in the bars of Sartène.

Pianottoli-Caldarello

Back on the main road the first sign of civilization for miles comes at **PIANOTTOLI-CALDARELLO**, the largest settlement between Sartène and Bonifacio. Two hamlets make up the village, and their names tell you everything about the locale: Pianottoli, the northern half straddling the main road, is derived from the word for "plain", and Caldarello, 1.5km south, means "extreme heat". There's nothing much to see in either, but a handful of unfrequented coves lie within easy reach, and if you're catching a plane from nearby Figari airport, the *Kevano Plage* **campsite**, 3km southeast on the Baie de Figari (☎04 95 71 81 00; April to mid-Oct), is a convenient place to spend your last night on the island.

Figari

Cut through by the main Porto-Vecchio–Ajaccio road, the village of **FIGARI** sees a disproportionate amount of through-traffic thanks to its proximity to south Corsica's largest **airport** (☎04 95 71 00 22), spread over the floor of the valley below. Most charter and scheduled flights to northern Europe leave at civilized times of day, and visitors generally drive here on the day of their departure, depositing hire cars at the row of rental company offices outside the main terminal before checking in. If, however, you're travelling without the luxury of your own vehicle, and catching a morning flight from Figari, you'll have to get here by **bus** the night before. Two services per day pass through in both directions, from Ajaccio and Porto-Vecchio. Make sure you're dropped off in Figari village proper, not at the previous junction on the N196 (confusingly signposted "Aeroport"), from where the D22 branches inland to approach the airport from the far northeastern side, leaving you a very long walk along a disconcertingly quiet country road. From Figari, you can arrange a taxi at the one bar in the vil-

Mazzeri

Of all the occult phenomena recorded in Corsica – from vampire witches
(*stregoni* and *strèga*), evil-eye (*occhiu*) healing, *orii* (see p.256),
Christian sects and pagan cults – the strangest has to be the existence of
mazzeri, dubbed by Dorothy Carrington in her recent book on the subject
as "dream hunters". Also known as *colpadori* (from the Latin *culpi*, "to
strike"), *mazzeri* (from the Corsican *ammazza*, "to kill") are those who
possess the power to foresee death. They do this by slipping into the
maquis in the dead of night and waiting silently, usually next to a stream,
to kill the first living creature that passes. On retrieving the body, the
mazzeri will recognize in its face, or hear in its death cries, the identity of
a person they know well, usually someone from their own family or village,
who will shortly die. If the *mazzeri* has only managed to wound the animal, the person concerned will suffer a grave illness, for the quarry temporarily harbours the spirit of the doomed individual.

Bizarrely, these nocturnal hunting expeditions rarely take place in the
literal sense, for the *mazzeri's* realm is that of dreams. Nevertheless,
records exist of *mazzeri* who are known to leave their house at night in a
state of trance and return covered in scratches from the maquis – whence
another of their Corsican names: *sunnambuli*, or "sleepwalkers". Despite
the ambiguity surrounding the nature of the *mazzeri's* hunting activities,
the outcome is invariably unequivocal. Once the death of an individual has
been foretold, it always occurs, usually within a week or two, certainly
before a year has passed.

Although the *mazzeri* may have predicted the event and performed a
symbolic or dream killing of the deceased's spirit, he or she is not held
directly responsible, nor regarded as a murderer. In some villages they are
actually held in high esteem for the protective role they play in a former
pagan festival marked on the last night of July. At this time it is said that
mazzeri from different villages form teams (*milizia*) to wage phantom
battles (*mandrache*) against each other on lofty mountain passes dividing
districts. Using an armoury of traditional weapons – knives, axes, lances,
human bones and asphodel plants (known in Corsica as *fiori di morti*,
"flowers of death") – they fight the opposition until one side is forced to
retreat. Once again, although the killing occurs in the dream world the outcome is real enough, and any *mazzeri* slain in a battle on July 31 is des-
tined to die within twelve months. Moreover, the village whose side loses
the ghost battle will sustain more unexpected deaths during the year. For
this reason, villagers all over the island still light fires outside churches
and place knives above doorways on the last night of July, to ward off evil
sprits.

All this may sound like mere folk myth, but *mazzeri* still exist in many
areas (notably the far south around Sartène and Figari), albeit in far smaller numbers than a century ago. Recent interest by local ethnologists has
unearthed a wealth of lore surrounding the phenomenon, and several eru-
dite books and papers have been published – well worth hunting out if
you're interested in the esoteric side of island life. Of these, Dorothy
Carrington's *The Dream Hunters of Corsica* (see "Books", p.330) is the
most detailed, but if your French is up to it ask in any good bookshop for
the special edition of *L'Origine* magazine devoted to Corsican *mazzeri*
and related subjects.

lage, or hitch the remaining 5km. Note, too, that during the summer *navettes* run out here from opposite the marina in Porto-Vecchio to meet flights; more details of this service appear on p.252.

There's no accommodation in the village, but the *Ferme-Auberge Pozzo di Mastri*, 1km northeast of Figari on the D859, serves wonderfully simple gourmet **food** in authentic surroundings. Virtually everything on the menus comes from either the farm or the maquis, including the olive oil, wine and meat (locally shot *sanglier* is often available). Count on spending around 170F for a four-course meal with all the trimmings.

Bonifacio

BONIFACIO (Bonifaziu) enjoys a superbly isolated situation at Corsica's southernmost point, a narrow peninsula of dazzling white limestone creating a town site unlike any other on the island. The **haute ville**, a maze of tortuous streets, rises seamlessly out of sheer cliffs that have been hollowed at their base by the buffeting waves, while on the landward side the deep cleft between the peninsula and the mainland forms a perfect natural harbour. A haven for boats for centuries, this harbour is nowadays a marina that attracts yachts from all around the Med, with a plethora of hotels and restaurants to cater for the thousands of summer visitors.

Separated from the rest of the island by an expanse of maquis, Bonifacio has maintained a certain temperamental detachment from Corsica, and is distinctly more Italian than French in atmosphere. It has its own dialect based on Ligurian Italian, a legacy from the days when it was practically an independent Genoese town. The old town retains Renaissance features found only here, and with Sardinia just a stone's throw away, much of the property in the area is owned by upper-echelon Italians.

Such a place has its drawbacks: exorbitant prices, crowds in August, and a commercial cynicism that's atypical of Corsica as a whole. However, it's perhaps the island's best-looking maritime town, with a livelier than average nightlife.

A brief history of Bonifacio

It could be that Bonifacio's first documented appearance is as the town of the cannibalistic Laestrygonians in the **Odyssey**; Homer's description of an "excellent harbour, closed in on all sides by an unbroken ring of precipitous cliffs, with two bold headlands facing each other at the mouth so as to leave only a narrow channel in between" fits the port well. The unploughed land which Odysseus comes across inland of the harbour could be a reference to the plain beyond the Bonifacio promontory, and it's also possible that the Neolithic tribes that once lived in this area were the barbaric attackers of Odysseus's crew.

In Roman times there was a village on this site, but the town really came into being in 828AD when **Count Bonifacio of Tuscany** built a castle on the peninsula. Like other towns on the Corsican coast, this one suffered continuous pirate raids, but its key position in the Mediterranean made various powers covet the port. Subject of dispute between Pisa and **Genoa** in 1187, the town eventually fell to the Genoese, who then proceeded to massacre the local population and replace them with Ligurian families, to whom they offered exemption from tax and customs duty in Genoese ports. Two hundred and fifty families duly settled here, and soon the town developed into a mini-republic with its own constitution and laws, governed by elected magistrates called *Anziani*.

In 1420 **Alfonso V** of Aragon set his sights on Corsica, and for five months his fleet blockaded the port, hoping to starve the Bonifaciens into submission. Every citizen joined in the defence of the citadel, with clergymen, women and children flinging wooden beams, rocks and blinding chalk dust down on the attackers – they even tried to demoralize the enemy by pelting them with cheese, an action masterminded by one **Marguerita Bobbia**, whose ingenuity is commemorated by a street named after her in the old town. Eventually Genoese warships sailed into the port just as the townspeople were about to surrender, but it was a last show of bravado from the starving Bonifaciens that broke the resolve of the Aragonese. Donning the uniforms of their dead soldiers, the women processed around the citadel to create the illusion of a large army, causing their attackers to lose heart and decamp.

Another celebrated siege occurred in 1554, when the town was recovering from an outbreak of plague that had claimed two-thirds of the population. **Henri II** of France arrived with the Turkish fleet, led by the fearsome corsair Dragut. The town held on through eighteen days and nights of cannon fire, and then a member of the eminent Cattacciolo family was despatched to Genoa to raise help. He was seized on his return by the Turks, who forced him to carry a forged letter refusing them the assistance of the republic, a ploy that brought about Bonifacio's surrender. The invaders pillaged the town, which was then rescued by Sampiero Corso. There followed a brief period of French rule, which came to an end when the Treaty of Cateau-Cambresis returned Corsica to Genoa in 1559.

Thereafter the Genoese port enjoyed relative prosperity until the late eighteenth century, when the French gained control of the island. No longer permitted their special autonomy, the merchants moved away and the town suffered a commercial decline that was really only reversed with the advent of tourism. Fishing, however, still brings in some income for a few Bonifaciens.

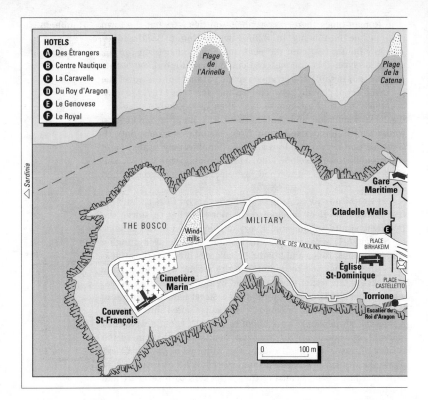

HOTELS
- Ⓐ Des Étrangers
- Ⓑ Centre Nautique
- Ⓒ La Caravelle
- Ⓓ Du Roy d'Aragon
- Ⓔ Le Genovese
- Ⓕ Le Royal

Arrival, information and accommodation

Arriving by plane, you'll land at **Figari** airport, 17km north of Bonifacio. There's no bus service from here so have to take a taxi into town – around 220F. If you're coming by **bus** you'll be dropped at the car park by the **marina**, close to most of the hotels. Drivers can either park here or head straight up av Général-de-Gaulle to the *haute ville*. This is where you'll find the **tourist office**, in rue des Deux-Moulins (July–Sept daily 9am–8pm; Oct–June Mon–Fri 8.30am–12.30pm & 1.30–5.15pm), opposite the *Genovese* hotel. The most they will give you is a map of the town and a list of hotels.

Finding **accommodation** can be a chore, as Bonifacio's few hotels are quickly booked up in peak season, so if you want to stay centrally ring in advance. Be prepared, too, for higher than average tariffs, though out of season it's usually possible to pick up a room for around 220F. Most of the **campsites** are located on the road to Porto-Vecchio.

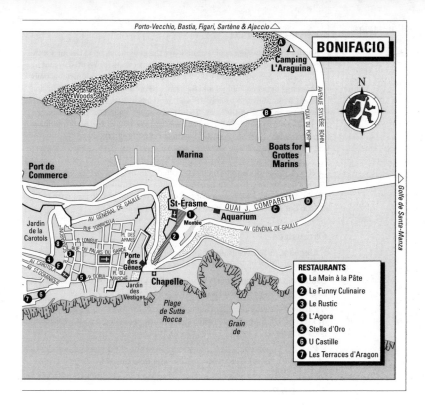

BONIFACIO

Camping
L'Araguina

Woods

Marina

Boats for
Grottes
Marins

Port de
Commerce

AVENUE SYLVÈRE BOHN

QUAI DU PORT

Golfe de Santa-Manza

Jardin
de la
Carotols

AV GÉNÉRAL DE GAULLE

RUE TORREICELLA

R. LONGUE

RUE DU PALAIS DU GARDE

AV CAROTOLA

AV ST-DOMINIQUE

PL DES
ARMES

Porte
des
Gênes

PL DU
MARCHÉ

R. DORIA

Jardin
des
Vestiges

Chapelle

St-Érasme

Montée

Aquarium

QUAI J. COMPARETTI

AV GÉNÉRAL-DE-GAULLE

Plage
de Sutta
Rocca

Grain
de

RESTAURANTS
1 La Main à la Pâte
2 Le Funny Culinaire
3 Le Rustic
4 L'Agora
5 Stella d'Oro
6 U Castille
7 Les Terraces d'Aragon

Hotels

La Caravelle, 37 quai Comparetti (☎/fax 04 95 73 00 03). Stylish olde-worlde place whose excellent restaurant occupies a prime location on the marina. ⑤.

Centre Nautique, the marina (☎04 95 73 02 11, fax 04 95 73 17 47). Chic but relaxed hotel on the waterfront. All rooms are tastefully furnished and consist of two storeys connected with a spiral staircase. The best upmarket option. ⑥.

Des Étrangers, 4 av Sylvère-Bohn (☎04 95 73 01 09, fax 04 95 73 16 97). On the road to Ajaccio just past the port, this is the cheapest place in the south, gathering an interesting mix of travellers who compensate for the dull decor. April–Oct. ④.

Le Genovese, la Citadelle (☎04 95 73 12 34, fax 04 95 73 09 03). The only luxury hotel in the *haute ville*, hence the sky-high rates. No pool, but the views over the marina from some of the (priciest) rooms are great. ⑤.

Du Roy d'Aragon, 13 quai Comparetti (☎04 95 73 03 99, fax 04 95 73 07 94). A stylish, recently renovated three-star overlooking the marina, with better-than-average off-season discounts. ⑥.

Ferries to Sardinia

Ferries for Santa Teresa di Gallura leave the gare maritime at the far southern end of the marina. The Mobyline company (☎04 95 73 00 29) and its competitor Saremar (☎04 95 73 00 96) operate ten to fourteen daily crossings between July 19 and September 1, reduced to between four and seven from March 3 to July 18 and September 2 to September 29, with none for the rest of the year. The 1hr crossing costs 70F per passenger, (130F return) plus 210F per car. You can get tickets for both operators from Agence Gazano, Port de Bonifacio (☎04 95 73 02 47).

Le Royal, place Bonaparte/rue Fred-Scamaroni (☎04 95 73 00 51, fax 04 95 73 04 68). Above a modern bar-restaurant at the entrance to the *haute ville*. Bright, clean place with views of the citadel and the sea. Prices soar in high season but are reasonable at other times of the year. ⑥.

Campsites

L'Araguina, av Sylvère-Bohn, opposite the Total service station near *Hotel des Étrangers* (☎04 95 73 02 96). Closest place to town, so it gets overcrowded.

Campo di Liccia, opposite *U Farniente* (☎04 95 73 03 09). Well shaded and large, so you're guaranteed a place.

U Farniente, Pertamina, 3km along the road to Porto-Vecchio (☎04 95 73 05 47). Very flash four-star site with all mod cons, including a pool – essential to book in summer.

U Pian del Fosse, route de Santa-Manza, 7km out of Bonifacio along the D58 (☎04 95 73 16 34). Very basic, but cheaper than the rest.

The town

Apart from the cafés, hotels and restaurants of **quai Comparetti**, the only attraction in the lower town is the marina's **Aquarium** (daily 10am–8pm; 25F), where the blue lobsters are the star attractions. At the far end lies the port, from which ferries depart for Sardinia and, in between, a cluster of restaurants and shops lies at the foot of **Montée Rastello**, the steps up to the *haute ville*.

The haute ville

Many of the houses in the **haute ville** are bordered by enormous battlements which, like the houses themselves, have been rebuilt many times – the most significant modifications were made by the French during their brief period of occupation following the 1554 siege, after they had reduced the town walls to rubble. Remnants of cannonshot-peppered buildings still scatter the *haute ville*, especially around the **Bosco** area at the tip of the promontory, where the barbed wire fences round the military facility and the rubbish flying about in the wind all add to the war-torn appearance. The *haute ville* has been sparsely populated since the Genoese merchants moved out in the eighteenth century, and the precariousness of many of its buildings is no enticement to settle – on the southeast side the hous-es have no surrounding wall to protect them, and in 1966 one house fell into the sea, killing two people. Since then various plans have been put forward to reinforce the cliff, but the state of the buildings is still a great problem.

From the top of the Montée Rastello steps, dubbed locally as the *grimpette* (literally "little climb"), you can cross av Général-de-Gaulle to **Montée St-Roch**, which gives a stunning view of the white limestone cliffs and the huge lump of fallen rock face called the **Grain de Sable**. At the **Chapelle St-Roch**, built on the spot where the last plague victim died in 1528, more steps lead down to the tiny beach of Sutta Rocca, which is great for snorkelling.

At the top of the Montée St-Roch steps stands the drawbridge of the great **Porte des Gênes**, once the only entrance to the *haute ville*. Through the gate and to the right, on place d'Armes, you can see the **Bastion de l'Étendard** (July & Aug daily 10am–9pm, April–June & Sept Mon–Sat 11am–5.30pm; 10F), sole remnant of the fortifica-tions destroyed during the siege of 1554. Inside is a small museum whose only noteworthy exhibit, aside from some decidedly unlifelike mock-ups of historical scenes using dummies, is a facsimile of the *Dame de Bonifacio*, a remarkably intact prehistoric skeleton of a woman found in a cave shelter near the town. You can also climb over the battlements to the tiny **Jardin des Véstiges**, which affords the *haute ville*'s best views of the cliffs to the east.

The original Dame de Bonifacio is housed in Levie's musée départementale; *see p.218.*

Back in the square, a few paces from the bastion lies **rue des Deux-Empereurs**, where at no. 4 you'll see the flamboyant marble escutcheon of the Cattacciolo family, one of many such adornments on the houses of this quarter. In 1541 the emperor Charles V, having been caught in Bonifacio by a storm, stayed in this house as a guest of Filippo Cattacciolo; after the departure of his illustrious visitor, Cattacciolo shot the horse he had loaned to him, on the grounds that nobody else was worthy to ride the poor beast after it had supported the ruler of half the known world. Opposite stands the house in which Napoléon resided for three months in 1793.

Cutting down to rue Palais-du-Garde brings you to **Église Ste-Marie-Majeure**, originally Romanesque but restored in the eigh-teenth century, though the richly sculpted belfry dates from the four-teenth century. The façade is hidden by a **loggia** where the Genoese municipal officers used to dispense justice in the days of the repub-lic. If you look up you can see buttresses connecting the houses in the adjoining streets to the roof of the church – these were vital not just as support but also for draining rainwater into a huge cistern underneath the porch, which provided the town with water in times of siege and during the dry summers. This church's treasure, a relic of the **True Cross** said to have been brought to Bonifacio by St Helena, the mother of Constantine, was saved from a shipwreck in the Straits of Bonifacio; for centuries after, the citizens would take the relic to the edge of the cliff and pray for calm seas whenever storms raged. The relic is kept in the sacristy, along with an ivory cask containing relics of St Boniface, and you'll only be able to get a glimpse if you can find someone to open the room for you. In the main body of the church the highlight is the marble **tabernacle** to the left of the door; decorated with bas-relief carvings of Christ support-ed by eight glum-faced cherubs, it's thought to have been created by a north Italian sculptor in 1565. The holy water stoup below it is a third-century **sarcophagus**, the sole Roman item in town.

Rue du Palais-de-Garde, which runs alongside the church, is one of the most handsome streets in Bonifacio, with its closed arcades and double-arched windows separated by curiously stunted columns. The oldest houses along here did not originally have doors; the inhabitants used to climb up a ladder which they would pull up behind them to prevent a surprise attack, while the ground floor was used as a stable and grain store.

South of here, rue Doria leads towards the Bosco (see below); at the end of this road a left down rue des Pachas will bring you to the **Torrione**, a 35-metre-high lookout post built in 1195 on the site of Count Bonifacio's castle. Descending the cliff from here, the **Escalier du Roi d'Aragon**'s 187 steps (daily June–Sept 11am–5.30pm; 10F) were said to have been built in one night by the Aragonese in an attempt to gain the town in 1420, but in fact they had already been in existence for some time and were used by the people to fetch water from a well.

The Bosco

To the west of the tower lies the **Bosco**, a quarter named after the wood that used to stand here in the tenth century. In those days a community of hermits dwelt here, but nowadays the limestone plateau is open and desolate. The only sign of life comes from the military training camp where young Corsicans sweat out their national service. The entrance to the Bosco is marked by **Église St-Dominique**, a rare example of Corsican Gothic architecture – it was built in 1270, most probably by the Templars, and later handed over to the Dominicans.

Beyond the church, rue des Moulins leads onto the ruins of three mills dating from 1283, two of them decrepit, the third restored. Behind them stands a memorial to the 750 people who died when a troop ship named *Sémillante* ran aground here in 1855, on its way to the Crimea, one of the many disasters wreaked by the straits.

The tip of the plateau is occupied by the **Cimetière Marin**, its white crosses standing out sharply against the deep blue of the sea. Open until sundown, the cemetery is a fascinating place to explore, with its flamboyant mausoleums displaying a jumble of architectural ornamentations: stuccoed façades, Gothic arches, classical columns, even flashing lights. Next to the cemetery stands the **Couvent St-François**, allegedly founded after St Francis sought shelter in a nearby cave – the story goes that the convent was the town's apology to the holy man, over whom a local maid had nearly poured a bucket of slops. Immediately to the south, the **Esplanade St-François** commands breathtaking views across the bay to Sardinia.

Eating, drinking and nightlife

Eating possibilities in Bonifacio might seem unlimited, but it's best to avoid the chintzy restaurants in the marina, few of which merit their exorbitant prices – the places in the *haute ville* are less pretentious. The **bars** and **cafés** on quai Comparetti are the social focus for much of the day and in the evening, but the main nightspot is the *Amnésia* club, 10km north on the Porto-Vecchio road, which has an open-air stage, three bars and an over-the-top terrace with fountains. It's one of the island's main venues for live rock and dance music, and entrance costs 50–120F depending on who's on. You can get there in a free *navette* from the marina (☎04 95 72 12 22).

Restaurants

L'Agora, 2 av de Carotola. Excellent 50F pizzas, steaks, fresh fish and the local speciality, *merrizzane* (here billed as *aubergines à la bonifacienne*), served at a wonderful location overlooking the marina. Moderate.

Boulangerie-Pâtisserie Faby, 4 rue St-Jean-Baptiste, *haute ville*. Tiny local bakery serving Bonifacien treats such as *pain des morts* (sweet buns with walnuts and raisins) and *fugazzi* (brioches flavoured with eau de vie, orange, lemon and aniseed), in addition to the usual range of spinach and *brocciu bastelles*.

U Castille, rue Simon-Varsi, *haute ville*. Two cosy, cavernous retaurants off place Fondaco-Montepagano: one is a classy stone-walled pizzeria; the other specializes in pricy Italian-style dishes based mainly on lamb, veal and fresh seafood – try their wonderful *terrine de sanglier*, fresh pasta à la carbonara, or tomato and mozzarella salads steeped in fresh basil.

Le Funny Culinaire, Montée Restello. Copious salads, crêpes and freshly squeezed fruit juices at reasonable prices. A good spot to break the haul up the steps to the *haute ville*.

La Main à la Pâtes, 1 place Bonaparte, at the bottom of the Montée Rastello. Three dozen different kinds of fresh pasta, including some imaginative concoctions such as pasta with cocoa, mint or seaweed. Not cheap, but you get what you pay for here, which makes a change in Bonifacio.

De la Poste, 6 rue Fred-Scamaroni. A very popular pizza joint serving some of the best-value food in the *haute ville*: oven-baked lasagne, spaghetti *al brocciu*, stuffed mussels and delicious pizzas.

Le Rustic, 16 rue Fred-Scamaroni. The town's most self-consciously Corsican restaurant, offering good-value set menus at 75F and 85F (for seafood). A great place to eat during the winter, when they keep a wood fire burning.

Stella d'Oro (Chez Jules), 23 rue Doria, near Église St-Jean-Baptiste. Pricy à la carte place with stone walls and wood beams, whose classy Corsican dishes include the definitive *merrizzane* (stuffed aubergine) – *the* local speciality.

Les Terraces d'Aragon, at the top of the Escalier du Roi-d'Aragon. A predictable mid-range terrace restaurant (set menus from 70F) whose main attraction is its stunning sea views. Opening early, this makes a great breakfast venue.

Bars

L'Émeraude, 5 quai Comparetti. Shady, relaxing bar close to the aquarium. Draught beer and ice creams.

Laetitia, 12 quai Comparetti. Good place for breakfast, overlooking the marina.

Langoustier, quai Comparetti. Popular among young Bonifaciens, with midnight karaoke sessions.

Listings

Airport Figari, 17km north of town, off the D859 road (☎04 95 71 00 22).

Banks and exchange Societé Générale, 2 rue St-Érasme, at the foot of the steps to the *haute ville*. Avoid the bureaux de change dotted around town – they charge extortionate commission rates.

Bookshops A couple on the quai Comparetti, of which the Librairie-Papeterie Simoni is the largest, selling a range of imported newspapers, pulp fiction and guidebooks.

Car rental Avis, quai Banda-del-Ferro (☎04 95 73 01 28); Hertz, quai Banda-del-Ferro (☎04 95 73 06 41); Citer, quai Noel-Beretti (☎04 95 73 13 16). All of the above also have branches at Figari airport.

Hospital 1 route de Santa-Manza, at the entrance to town (☎04 95 73 95 75). For an ambulance, ☎04 95 73 06 95 or 04 95 73 06 94.

Laundry *Laverie automatique*, northeast side of the port.

Mountain- and motorbike rental Tam Tam, route de Santa-Manza (☎04 95 73 11 59); Corse Moto Services, quai Nova, on the north side of the port (☎04 95 73 15 16).

Pharmacy 17 quai Comparetti.

Police route de Santa-Manza (☎04 95 73 00 17).

Post office on place Carrega in the *haute ville* (Mon–Fri 9am–noon & 2–5pm, Sat 9am–noon), opposite the tourist office.

Taxis ☎04 95 73 19 08.

Travel agent Voyages Gazano, quai Banda-del-Ferro, near the gare maritime (☎04 95 73 02 47).

Around Bonifacio

Some beautiful beaches lie northeast of Bonifacio, along a stretch of coast that has become the preserve of the Côte d'Azur's jet set. Unlike in some areas of the island, where the FLNC routinely bomb holiday villas, here the paramilitaries have spared the swish second homes of the big stars, tycoons and industrial magnets that move in for the summer, allegedly because the publicity generated by such

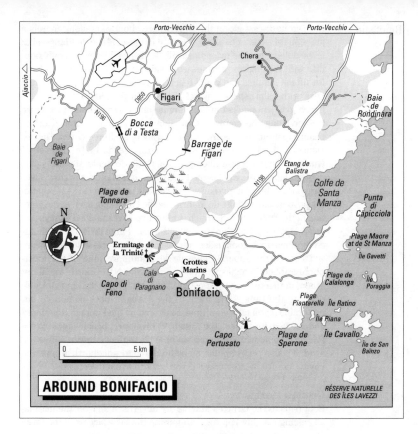

AROUND BONIFACIO

attacks would be detrimental to their cause. A string of luxurious houses fringe the silvery **Golfe de Santa Manza**, but further north up the coast, **Plage de la Rondinara**, an exquisite, almost circular cove midway between Bonifacio and Porto-Vecchio, is more of a day-trip destination, with few permanent constructions. Other enjoyable excursions include the **Grottes Marins**, a beautiful set of sea caves west of the town, the **Ermitage de la Trinité**, which affords impressive views of Bonifacio from the west, **Capo Pertusato**, which marks the southernmost point of Corsica, and the nature reserve of the **Îles Lavezzi**.

Beaches

The nearest accessible beach, **Plage de la Catena**, is small and picturesque but gets a lot of flotsam – it's a kilometre to the west on the opposite side of the marina, accessible via a track that begins just before *Camping L'Araguina* (see p.240). For the best local beaches head northeast along the D58, where about 3km along there's a junction for a trio of beaches. The first of these, **Plage de Pianterella**, is the dullest, backed by an unsavoury-smelling swamp and only popular with watersports enthusiasts. Walk south around the headland for fifteen minutes and you'll reach **Plage de Sperone**, a pearl-white cove with calm, shallow water that's ideal for kids. However, this beach gets jam-packed in the summer and you may want to venture further along the coast to **Cala Lunga**, where you stand a better chance of escaping the crowds at a string of sheltered coves. Further along the D58, a second right-hand turn leads to the hamlet of **Gurgazu**, on the southern edge of the **Golfe de Santa Manza**.

Stretching to the right is the **Plage de Santa Manza**, a narrow silver strip backed by a rough road where you can park your car. A less enticing proposition is **Plage de Maora**, reached by taking a left at the junction of the D60 and D58, which is more exposed and filled with yachts and and jet skis. The third beach of the gulf, **Plage de Balistra**, situated by a marshy lagoon, is less pleasant and not accessible from here.

To reach the superb **Plage de la Rondinara**, one of the most-photographed beaches in Corsica, take the N198 north for about 10km, until a turning signposted "Camping Rondinara" appears suddenly to the right – the track to the sea is in poor condition, but motorable if you take your time. Sheltered by the Punta di Rondinara and backed by dunes, the small, shell-shaped beach looks like a Pacific lagoon, with turquoise water and a perfect curve of soft white sand; it's also very popular, so be prepared to walk north around the bay to less-frequented coves if you want to avoid the crowds.

Grottes Marins

Boat trips to the **Grottes Marins** are advertised all over the marina, all costing roughly 75F for a 45-minute trip. The largest of the three sea caves, the **Grotte du Sdragonatu**, is worth the money on its own – it's a magnificent grotto where the water takes on an extraordinary luminosity and the rocks glitter indigo and gold. Most excursions take in the Bonifacio cliffs, giving an awe-inspiring view of the town, but you can also take a separate three-hour trip out to the Îles Lavezzi (see opposite).

Ermitage de la Trinité

The **Ermitage de la Trinité**, 7km west of Bonifacio, off the N196, stands on a site that has been inhabited since prehistoric times and was a hermitage right at the beginning of the Christianization of the island. Heavily restored in the thirteenth century, the whitewashed convent sits beside a terrace of olive trees, a backdrop of gigantic boulders lending it a bizarre quality. There's a fine view of Bonifacio from here, and an even better one if you follow the track to the left before you reach the building, which arrives at the **Mont de la Trinité** after about 25 minutes' gentle climbing.

Capo Pertusato

The deeply scored limestone cliffs southeast of Bonifacio culminate in the wide headland of **Capo Pertusato** (Pierced Cape), a steepish climb of about 45 minutes, preferably attempted in the cooler evening air. Leaving town along the D58, almost immediately bear right along the D260, a narrow road hugging the cliff side as far as the **Phare du Pertusato**, the lighthouse at the edge of the point. (Driving is very dangerous, as there's no room for passing and no barriers at the side of the road.) At the end of the walk you'll be rewarded with an incredible seascape embracing Sardinia, the crested islands of Lavezzi and Cavallo, and Bonifacio itself, just discernible to the west.

Îles Lavezzi

The **Îles Lavezzi**, part of the archipelago to the east of the straits of Bonifacio, can be seen on a boat trip from the marina (2 daily in summer; 3hr; 100F). Having passed the Grain de Sable, the Phare du Pertusato and the heavily guarded private island of Cavallo, the boat moors at the main island of **Lavezzi**, beside a graveyard containing the victims of the *Sémillante* shipwreck of 1855, when 750 crew members and soldiers bound for the Crimean war were drowned. Their bodies were washed ashore over the following fortnight, but so disfigured were they that only one could be identified. A stone pyramid on the western tip of the isle commemorates the tragedy. Classified as a nature reserve since 1982, the island is home to several rare species of **wild flower**, such as the yellow-horned poppy, the white sea daffodil and the stonecrop, distinguished by its fleshy red leaves beneath heads of small blue flowers. The boat stops here for an hour, and there's a small beach where you can swim.

Further north, **Cavallo** and its adjoining islet, **San Bainzo**, are the sites of Roman quarries. Huge monolithic columns lie at the water's edge, cut from horizontal trenches in the rock nearby and discarded, seemingly in haste. The stone quarried here was not used in Corsica, but transported to the mainland to fuel the decadent building boom at the end of the Roman empire. Most touching of the remains here is an image of Hercules Saxanus, the patron saint of hard labour, carved by slaves on the face of a large boulder.

The Porto-Vecchio region

Corsica's highest concentration of tourists is found in the area around **Porto-Vecchio**, a small town that seems entirely populated by Italians in summer. Spectacular beaches lie to the south of town, with **Palombaggia** the most popular and **Golfe de Santa Giulia** coming a close second; while to the north, the deep inlet of the **Golfe de Porto-Vecchio** boasts some luscious pine-backed strands. Continuing north, the bays of **San Ciprianu** and **Pinarellu** form a

prelude to the **Côte des Nacres**, a chain of sandy beaches stretching towards the eastern plain.

Most people make at least one trip to one of the many **prehistoric sites** dotted around Porto-Vecchio – north to the Bronze Age settlements of **Torre** and the **Casteddu d'Araggiu**, or south to the monuments at **Ceccia** and **Tappa**. To get right away from the sultry coast, you could head inland up to the cool, scented **Forêt de l'Ospédale**, one of the highlights of southern Corsica.

Porto-Vecchio is connected by regular **buses** to Bastia, via the east coast highway. You can also get here on direct services from Ajaccio, either via the mountain route through Ospédale, Zonza and Bavella, or on the Route Nationale that loops south through Propriano and Figari. In addition, *navettes* run throughout the busy summer months from the town to the most popular beaches in the area, including Santa Giulia and Palombaggia.

Porto-Vecchio

Set on a hill above a deep and beautiful gulf, surrounded by gigantic outcrops of pink granite, **PORTO-VECCHIO** was rated by James Boswell as one of "the most distinguished harbours in Europe". Nowadays its success as a tourist attraction is due more to its proximity to some fine beaches than to its own character. Once rife with malaria, the town still has a rather insalubrious atmosphere, with its approaches ruined by a confusing network of roads, its outskirts marred by tasteless modern architecture, and a cramped centre jammed solid with traffic during the summer. Nonetheless, if you treat it purely as a base for some serious beach-work, Porto-Vecchio is worth a couple of days of anyone's time.

It was founded in 1539 as a second Genoese stronghold on the east coast, Bastia being well established in the north. The location was perfect: close to the unexploited and fertile plain, the site benefited from secure high land and a sheltered gulf. Unfortunately, however, the Genoese hadn't counted on the mosquito problem, and within months malaria had wiped out the first Ligurian settlers. Sampiero Corso occupied the port for a brief period in 1564, having failed to take Ajaccio, but Genoa got it back a few months later, and things began to take off soon after, mainly thanks to the cork industry, which thrived until this century. Today a third of Corsica's wine is exported from here, but most revenue comes from the rich tourists who flock to the town each year, spending a fortune in Porto-Vecchio's flashy clothes shops.

Around the centre of town there's not much to see, apart from the well-preserved **fortress** and the small grid of ancient streets backing onto the main **place de la République**. East of the square you can't miss the **Porte Génoise**, which frames a delightful expanse of sea and through which you'll find the quickest route down to the modern **marina**, lined with cafés and hotels.

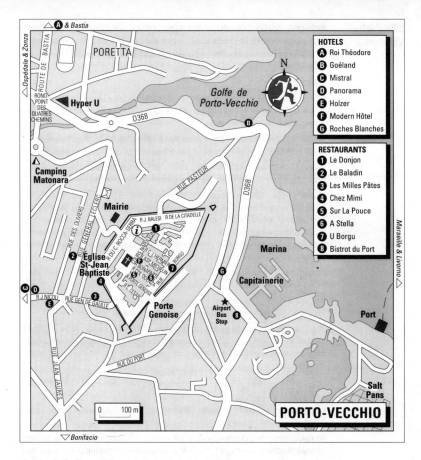

Arrival, information and accommodation

Buses from Bastia, Bonifacio, Propriano, Bavella and Ajaccio stop outside their companies' offices on rue Jean-Jaurès, a stone's throw southwest of the walled centre. From here it's a ten-minute walk north-east to place de l'Hôtel-de-Ville, site of the modern and efficient **tourist office**, just west of place de la République (July & Aug Mon–Sat 9am–9pm, Sun 10am–noon & 5–7pm; June & Sept Mon–Sat 9am–1pm & 3–6pm), which hands out brochures featuring colour maps of the town and is a good place to check transport timetables. Two hundred metres from the tourist office, the **Maison d'Information du Parc Régional**, at the bottom of rue Col-Quenza (daily mid-June to mid-Sept 9am–12.30pm & 4.30–7.30pm; ☎04 95 70 50 78), is a good source of advice on hiking and the long-distance footpaths in the area.

Finding somewhere to stay is only a problem during peak season, when prices soar even higher than elsewhere in Corsica. **Hotels** are

grouped mostly around the old town, with a handful of more expensive places down in the marina, while **campsites** line the route north
of the centre towards Pinarellu beach and Bastia.

Hotels

Goéland, port de Plaisance (☎04 95 70 14 15). Pleasant and good value, in
an excellent location overlooking the marina; large rooms, convivial atmosphere. Tariff includes breakfast. ④.

Holzer, 12 rue Jean-Jaurès/rue Jean-Nicoli (☎04 95 70 05 93). Labyrinthine
place with airless, boxed-in rooms, but immaculately clean and very central. ③.

Mistral, rue Jean-Nicoli (☎04 95 70 08 53). Smart, comfortable, mid-range
hotel slightly removed from the noisy centre of town. ④–⑤.

Modern'hotel, 10 cours Napoléon (☎04 95 70 06 36). One of the island's few
bona fide budget hotels, slap in the centre overlooking the square. Most rooms
have shared toilets on the corridor, but there are some en-suite options; particularly recommended are nos19–21 on the roof, which have gulf views.
Tariffs are low even in high season and it's always popular with backpackers,
so book ahead. ③.

Panorama, 12 rue Jean-Nicoli (☎04 95 70 07 96). Simple, family-run place
with parking spaces, just above the old town. Inexpensive for the area. ③–④.

Roches Blanches, quai Syracuse, route du Port-de-Plaisance (☎04 95 70 06
96). Well-placed hotel with rooms overlooking the sea. May–Oct. ③–④.

Roi Théodore, route de Bastia, 500m north of Porto-Vecchio (☎04 95 70 14
94, fax 04 95 70 41 34). The best upmarket option: a splendid, tranquil hide-
away boasting a gourmet restaurant, swimming pool, tennis courts and extensive grounds. ⑥.

Campsites

Les Amis de la Nature, Araggio (☎04 95 70 21 57). Basic site set in a pine
wood, 4km north of town.

Arutoli, route de l'Ospédale (☎04 95 70 12 73). Large, well-equipped site
located 2km northwest along the D368. Enormous swimming pool makes this
a good option.

Îlots d'Or, Trinité de Porto-Vecchio, 5km north of town along the Bastia road
(☎04 95 70 01 30). Very upmarket site with swimming pool and many more
facilities.

La Matonara, carrefour des Quatre-Chemins (☎04 95 70 37 05). A large site
shaded by cork trees, with clean *sanitaires* blocks and washing machines. By
far the best choice if you don't have your own vehicle, as it's within walking
distance of the centre (see map, p.249).

Mulinacciu, Lecci de Porto-Vecchio (☎04 95 71 47 48). Popular, shady place
by the river, 5km north of Porto-Vecchio along the N198.

Eating, drinking and nightlife
On the whole, Porto-Vecchio's **eating places** are substandard tourist
traps, but there are a couple of decent addresses where you can get quality fresh fish and seafood at affordable prices, and pizzerias and pasta

places are found all over the centre. Cafés line place de la République and cours Napoléon, which runs along the east side of the square – *Au Bon Coin*, facing the church, is the nicest and least expensive.

Apart from when the Italians swamp the town in August, **nightlife** is fairly low-key, revolving around the cafés in the square and a handful of unwelcoming gambling joints. Among the few places that stand out is *Objectif Lune*, on rue Jérôme-Léandri, which sports lively Tintin decor and hosts regular rock and jazz music sessions during the tourist season. Also worth checking is the rustic *Le Taverne du Roi*, near the Porte Genoise, where you can hear more traditional music – a mixture of Corsican choral and folk tunes, and French standards, accompanied by guitar and piano. Admission to both these places is free, but you're expected to shell out on at least a couple of exorbitantly priced drinks for the privilege.

Restaurants and snack bars

Le Baladin, rue Général-Leclerc. Expensive French joint serving excellent fresh fish and other gourmet delights, in dimly lit, luxurious surroundings. Evenings only; closed mid-Nov to Jan.

Bistrot du Port, port de Plaisance. Sailors' hang-out serving omelettes and steaks as well as good Corsican food. Moderate.

U Borgu, rue Borgo, parallel to cours Napoléon in the old town. Upscale pizzeria in the old town. Their à la carte dishes are overpriced, but the pizzas are affordable and the views over the gulf sublime.

Chez Mimi, 5 rue Général-Abbatucci. Run-of-the-mill streetside restaurant from the outside, but their 70F Corsican menu is one of the best deals in town, offering a choice of three or four dishes such as squid or the local speciality, stuffed aubergine. The portions are generous, too, and house wine is only 50F a bottle.

Le Donjon, rue S-Casalonga. Tucked away in a backstreet in the old town, this cosy, established bistro offers good-value 65F menus and plenty of tasty Corsican specialities.

Les Milles Pâtes, 4 rue Général-de-Gaulle. Popular with locals for its wide variety of fresh pasta at average prices. They also serve mouthwatering ravioli with crab, salmon and langoustine in basil sauce.

A Stella, rue de Col-Quenza. Tiny Spanish joint down a narrow alley in the old town, serving paella for a reasonable 65F, or paella "royale" with lobster and crab for 95F, in addition to a range of inexpensive tapas.

Sur la Pouce, rue de la Porte-Genoise. Various *paninis* and other light snacks to take away for around 20F, many using quality local cheeses (try their delicious *panini* "Corse", with real goat's cheese filling). A real find if you're on a tight budget.

Listings

Ambulance ☎04 95 70 00 05.

Banks All the big banks have branches in the town centre and will change travellers' cheques, but only the Société Générale has a cash dispenser, on the Quatre-Chemins crossroads near the *Super U* supermarket.

Car rental Budget, port de plaisance (☎04 95 70 25 70); Citer, route de
Bonifacio (☎04 95 70 16 96); Europcar, route de Bastia, Poretta (☎04 95 70
14 50); Hertz, Fillipi Auto, 1 quai Pascal-Paoli (☎04 95 70 28 04).

Diving La Palanuée CIP, Les Marines (☎04 95 70 16 53); Club Plongée
Kallisté, Plage de Palombaggia.

Motorbike rental Garage Legrand, 3km south on the route de Bonifacio (☎04
95 70 15 84); Corse Moto Service, Yamaha Garage, route de Bastia, beyond
the *Géant* supermarket (☎04 95 70 45 51); Suzuki Garage, route du Port-de-
Plaisance (☎04 95 70 36 05).

Taxis ☎04 95 70 08 49.

Moving on from Porto-Vecchio

Porto-Vecchio's proximity to Figari airport means this is the first
port of call for many independent travellers. Thankfully, it's well
served by **public transport**, so you shouldn't have to spend more
time here than you need to catch a bus somewere else.

By plane

Figari airport, 28km southwest, is served by weekly charter **flights**
to various destinations in northern Europe, including London
Gatwick, and by domestic departures to several cities on the French
mainland. If money is no object, you can catch a plane from here to
Calvi, and during the summer there are special helicopter flights for
tourists around the gulf, costing 220–730F per person; for more
details, contact the Société Figari Aviation-Transports, on route du
Port (☎04 95 72 07 12). **Getting to Figari** without your own vehicle is straightforward during the summer, when a bus leaves from
opposite the *Capitainerie* (harbourmaster's) in the marina to connect with flights; tickets cost 50F single. At other times of year, you'll
have to take a taxi or catch the Ajaccio bus there. Reviews of accommodation in Figari are listed on p.236.

By ferry

Car and passenger **ferry** services from Porto-Vecchio to Marseille
and Livorno operate from July to September, with none during the
rest of the year.

Corsica Marittima, Port de Commerce (☎04 95 31 46 29). To Livorno (July
& Aug 1–2 weekly; 3 in first week of Sept). The 8hr crossing costs 200F per
passenger, 650F per car.

SNCM, Port de Commerce (☎04 95 70 06 03, fax 04 95 70 33 59). To
Marseille (mid-June to Sept 3 weekly). The overnight crossing on the *Monte
d'Oro* (14hr 30min) costs 310F per passenger, 640F per car.

By bus

Buses to **Ajaccio** via **Figari**, **Sartène** and **Propriano** are operated by
Eurocorse Voyages (☎04 95 70 13 83), leaving two to three times
daily from in front of the offices on rue Jean-Jaurès (see map,

p.249). From June through September you can also travel to the capital via a longer and more convoluted mountain route that takes you through **Ospédale, Zonza, Quenza** and **Aullène**; this service is run by Balesi Évasion (July & Aug Mon–Sat, June & Sept Mon & Thurs; ☎04 95 17 15 55), and leaves from outside Île de Beauté Voyages, on the junction of rues Jean-Jaurès and Général-Leclerc at 7am. For **Bonifacio**, there are two buses each day with Autocorse Voyages, taking 30min. Rapides Bleus (☎04 95 70 10 36) also run coaches up the east coast to **Bastia** (3hr).

Tickets for all these services can be bought on the bus. Note that in the winter timetables are scaled down slightly; departure times may be checked at any of the travel agents in town or at the tourist office.

Finally, if you're spending any time in the area and need transport to the beaches south of Porto-Vecchio, it's worth knowing that during July and August buses run out to **Santa Giulia** and **Palombaggia**, leaving two to four times daily from the *Matonara* campsite; you can also pick up the bus down from the *Capitainerie* in the marina, or flag it down at various points along the N198.

Massif de l'Ospédale

Broadly covering the hinterland of the Golfe de Porto-Vecchio, limited in the northwest by the Massif de Bavella and in the southwest by the Montagne de Cagna, the **Massif de l'Ospédale** is a forested upland characterized by enormous granite boulders emerging from the deep greenery. Attractions up here include an impressive artificial **lake**, which makes an ideal picnic spot, and a magnificent beech forest, the **Forêt de l'Ospedale**. Although much of the woodland was devastated by fire recently, enough remains on the higher slopes to make this a rewarding area for short hikes, with spellbinding views across the gulf.

Leaving Porto-Vecchio by the D368 northwest of town, a twisty drive of 19km up the slopes will soon get you to **OSPÉDALE**, a village that has long been used as a summer resort by the inhabitants of Porto-Vecchio. Plumb in the middle of the forest, within a backdrop of massive clumps of granite, it provides fine views through the trees across L'Alta Rocca and over the Golfe de Porto-Vecchio to Sardinia in the other direction. A great place to make the most of the views is the **restaurant** in the centre of the village, *Chez Paul – Le Vieux Lavoir*. It's a pricy place serving fussy French-influenced Corsican food, but you can opt for a coffee on the sunny terrace, from where the rippling hills and coast of Sardinia are clearly visible to the south. A less expensive place to eat lies just above the village, hidden among the giant pines and granite boulders of the massif. *Le Refuge* is popular with tourists and locals alike for its fragrant home-made charcuterie and wild-boar pâté, and a full four- or five-course meal costs around 150F.

In the intense heat of summer, most people pass through Ospédale and head straight for the **lake**, which emerges a couple of kilometres up the road. A shimmering blue expanse backed by lines of spindly black trees, the lake is surrounded by marked forest trails in every direction. A particularly enjoyable walk goes to the **Piscia di Gallo** (Piss of the Cockerel) waterfall, a two-hour walk that provides plenty of opportunities to stop and bathe. The route begins about 1km past the dam on the right-hand side of the road, beyond the large parking area. From here the trail meanders through the pines and the maquis and crosses two streams before veering to the right. When you reach an opening in the pines, follow the stream for about 1km, keeping it on your right, and listen out for the sound of the waterfall about to come into view. Some 50m high, it's an impressive sight, plummeting between giant rocks into a swirling green pool.

North of the lake lies the **Forêt de Barocaggio-Marghèse**, a magnificent pine forest dominated by the pyramidal **Punta di u Diamante** (1227m); just past here the road crosses the **Col d'Illirata** (991m), 25km from Porto-Vecchio and 15km south of Zonza (see p.222).

The coast around Porto-Vecchio

Much of the coast of the **Golfe de Porto-Vecchio** and its environs is characterized by ugly development, bombed-out building sites and hectares of dismal swampland, yet some of the clearest, bluest sea and whitest beaches on Corsica are also found around here. The most frequented of these can be reached by **bus** from town in the summer (see p.252); at other times of year you'll need your own transport.

Heading **south of Porto-Vecchio** along the main N198, take the turning signposted "Palombaggia" about 1km along and you'll find yourself on a narrow road leading to the hamlet of Picovaggia. Here you can veer left for the headland marking the southern limit of the Golfe de Porto-Vecchio, the **Punta di a Chiappa**, or keep going 3km south to **Plage de Palombaggia**, a golden semicircle of sand edged by short twisted umbrella pines that are punctuated by fantastically shaped red rocks. This might be the most beautiful beach in Corsica were it not for the crowds, which pour onto the beach in such numbers that a wattle fence has had to be erected to protect the dunes. A few kilometres further along the same road takes you to the **Golfe de Santa Giulia**, a sweeping sandy bay backed by a lagoon. Despite the presence of several holiday villages and facilities for windsurfing and other watersports, crowds are less of a problem here, and the shallow bay is an extraordinary turquoise colour.

North of Porto-Vecchio, the first beach lies some 4km along the D468, a small bay within the Golfe de Porto-Vecchio called **Baie de Stagnolu**, one of the cleaner strands in these parts. Avoid the next one, **Plage de Cala Rossa**, as this is bordered by ugly swampland and blackened by fires from bomb-struck villas – head instead for **Baie**

de San Ciprianu, a half-moon bay of white sand with an unobtrusive development, reached by turning left at the Elf garage. About 7km by road from here lies the best beach in this area – **Golfe de Pinarellu** – featuring a long sweep of soft white sand, a Genoese watchtower and smaller crowds.

Beyond here, north of the village of Ste-Lucie-de-Porto-Vecchio, the **Côte des Nacres** covers the distance from Favone to Solenzara. The beaches at the **Anse de Favone** and **Canella** are pretty average by Corsican standards, but they gain immensely from the backdrop of towering crags behind.

The prehistoric sites

Torréen settlements are concentrated south of a line running from Ajaccio to Solenzara, with the majority located around Porto-Vecchio. The most fully preserved example is **Torre** itself, situated not far to the north of Porto-Vecchio. Nearby **Casteddu d'Araggiu**, another Bronze Age settlement set higher on the mountain slopes above the gulf, is also worth a visit, and to complete the prehistoric tour you should go south of Porto-Vecchio to visit the sites of **Ceccia** and **Tappa**, also impressive legacies of the Torréen civilization. Finally, a worthwhile side-trip from the main Porto-Vecchio–Figari road takes you south to the tiny hamlet of Chera, where two enigmatic natural rock formations, known as **orii**, have become the objects of much local folklore.

Torre and the Casteddu d'Araggiu

Just follow the N198 north of Porto-Vecchio for 8km to reach **Torre**, which stands on its own a little way from the main road on the right-hand side. Built against a massive granite rock and covered in broad stone slabs, the semicircular construction, an impressive if small-scale Torréen edifice, crowns a granite hillock above a tiny farming hamlet, and is thought to have been used as a crematorium.

More background on the Torréans appears on ☎ 198.

The **Casteddu d'Araggiu** lies on the other side of the main road, about 4km up the D759; from the site's car park it's a twenty-minute stiff climb through maquis and scrubby woodland, much of it burned out in the recent fire, along a well-defined path. Built in 2000 BC and inhabited by a community that lived by farming and hunting, the *casteddu* consists of a complex of chambers built into a massive circular wall of pink granite, splashed with vivid green patches of lichen. The site is entered via a ten-metre-long corridor covered in stone slabs. Immediately to the left you'll see a small triangular enclosure, in the centre of which would have been a clay fireplace, a forerunner of the *zidda* (hearth) found in traditional Corsican households. Continuing in a clockwise direction you come to the *torre* itself, comprising a central chamber of which only the foundations remain. Past the tower, the next chamber – measuring 10m across – also has the remains of a fireplace, and a little further on it's

possible to make out a well built into the thick walls, beyond which
stands another small hut with fireplace.

Ceccia and Tappa

The **Ceccia** site lies about 5km southwest of Porto-Vecchio along the
D859, a twenty-minute walk from the village of the same name. Set
on a conspicuous spur, this isolated tower was raised around 1350
BC, possibly for scanning the surrounding countryside for invaders,
or for cult purposes. Unlike other Torréen sites, no traces of
dwellings remain here.

About 1km west of Ceccia along the D853 you'll find the **Tappa**
casteddu signposted to the south of the road, opposite an abandoned farm building. Set on a granite mound about ten minutes' walk
away, the site lies on private property and is approached on foot,
passing through the gate and following the direction indicated.

The surrounding wall is considered to be more recent than the rest
of the *casteddu*, which was developed in the half-millennium prior to
1000 BC. A large *torre* at the southern end of the site consists of several small rooms around a central chamber. A ramp leads up to the
main structure, entered by a narrow corridor, inside which another
ramp winds up to a second level. The excavation of various clay pots,
pounding implements and grindstones here has led archeologists to
propose that this building was used for milling as well as storage.

The Orii of Sotta and Chera

Amidst the chaos of rocks by the side of the roads in southern
Corsica, you occasionally come across large boulders whose overhanging crevices have been bricked in with masonry. Known as **orii**
(*oriu* in the singular), these distinctive rock formations, whose name
is thought to derive from the Latin for "granary", *horreum*, have
been used for centuries to store grain and hay, and to provide shelter for animals. They crop up with surprising frequency in old folk
songs and legends, suggesting they were at one time central to the
life of rural communities; some have even been "Christianized" and
are the focus of religious rituals.

One such *oriu* stands in the far-flung hamlet of **CHERA**, roughly
midway between Porto-Vecchio and Bonifacio (turn south off the
D859 at **Sotta**). The most famous of its kind, it overlooks the village
from the top of a rocky outcrop, crowned by a crucifix. Local people
believe the artificial cave sheltered their pastoralist ancestors when
they fled here centuries ago to escape a vendetta in the mountains,
since when it has been revered as a kind of guardian spirit of the
Culioli clan. The English author Dorothy Carrington – who was
shown the *oriu* by one of the island's most renowned bards, the long-
white-bearded Jean-André Culioli – was told it was haunted by a
phantom goat whose hoof-steps could occasionally be heard trotting
over the rock in the dead of night.

Even spookier is the *oriu* of CANI, 4km north down the valley
from Chera (look for a hand-painted sign on the right, or east, side
of the road). Pull over outside the farmhouses where the road ends
and follow the track as it bends right; once over two stiles, you come
to a breach in a wall, from where a faint trail cuts uphill through the
woods to the *oriu*, perched on a rock platform above the tiny hamlet. An unfeasibly contorted lump of granite with a strange high-
pitched "roof", the structure looks like one of Salvador Dali's night-
mares, and it's not hard to see why local people believe it was once
inhabited by a witch. In fact, the last recorded resident was one
Vinceguerra Pietri, the local landowner, who lived here until a ripe
old age at the end of the nineteenth century.

Travel details

BUSES

Bonifacio to: Ajaccio (4 daily; 3hr 30min); Olmeto (2–4 daily; 1hr 55min);
Porto-Vecchio (1–4 daily; 30min); Propriano (4 daily; 1hr 40min); Roccapina
(2–4 daily; 45min); Sartène (1–4 daily; 1hr 25min).

Levie to: Ajaccio (1–2 daily; 2hr 45min); Bavella (1–2 daily; 30min); Santa
Lucia di Tallano (1–2 daily; 15min); Zonza (1–2 daily; 15min).

Olmeto to: Ajaccio (2–4 daily; 1hr 30min); Bonifacio (2–4 daily; 2hr 15min);
Porto-Vecchio (2–4 daily; 1hr 45min); Propriano (2–4 daily; 15min);
Roccapina (2–4 daily; 45min); Sartène (2–4 daily; 40min).

Porto-Vecchio to: Ajaccio (2–4 daily; 3hr 30min); Bastia (2 daily; 3hr);
Bonifacio (1–4 daily; 30min); Olmeto (2 daily; 2hr 20min); Propriano (2–4
daily; 2hr 10min); Roccapina (2–4 daily; 1hr); Sartène (2–4 daily; 1hr 55min).

Propriano to: Ajaccio (2–4 daily; 1hr 50min); Bonifacio (2–4 daily; 1hr
40min); Olmeto (2–4 daily; 15min); Porto-Vecchio (2–4 daily; 2hr 10min);
Roccapina (2–4 daily; 40min); Sartène (2–4 daily; 20min).

Roccapina to: Ajaccio (2–4 daily; 2hr 30min); Bonifacio (2–4 daily; 45min);
Olmeto (2–4 daily; 45min); Porto-Vecchio (2–4 daily; 1hr); Propriano (2–4
daily; 40min); Sartène (2–4 daily; 30min).

Santa Lucia di Tallano to: Ajaccio (1–2 daily; 2hr 20min); Bavella (1–2 daily;
45min); Levie (1–2 daily; 15min); Zonza (1–2 daily; 30min).

Sartène to: Ajaccio (2–4 daily; 2hr 10min); Bonifacio (1–4 daily; 1hr 25min);
Olmeto (2–4 daily; 40min); Porto-Vecchio (2–4 daily; 1hr 55min); Propriano
(2–4 daily; 20min); Roccapina (2–4 daily; 30min).

Zonza to: Ajaccio (1–2 daily; 2hr 45min); Bavella (1–2 daily; 15min); Levie
(1–2 daily; 15min); Santa Lucia di Tallano (1–2 daily; 30min).

FERRIES

For ferry services, see pp.205 & 240.

Chapter 5

Eastern Corsica

Comprising a hundred and fifty square kilometres of vine-striped plains backed by rippling hills, the landscape of Corsica's east coast is restrained in comparison with the rest of the island. If you do visit the region, it'll probably be to take advantage of the smooth, straight N198, the island's main north–south artery, from which windier side-roads penetrate the more varied and rugged interior. That said, the *littoral oriental* does have its attractions, not least of which are several vast sandy beaches, where scattered resorts and a string of large self-contained campsites offer plenty of inexpensive accommodation. **Solenzara**, for example, is one of the area's more alluring small seaside towns, at the head of the spectacular road leading to the Col de Bavella. North of here, beyond the rather tired resort of **Ghisonaccia**, you move into the eastern plain, an enormous malaria-ridden swamp until the Americans sprayed it with DDT after World War II. Now supporting of clementine orchards and vineyards, this patchwork of fields is punctuated by shimmering lagoons, of which the **Étang d'Urbino** and **Étang de Diane** are the largest, supplying plentiful oysters and seafood for the local restaurants. Set on a rise between these lagoons is the Roman capital of **Aléria**, which boasts an excellent museum, a beach close by, and a few hotels straddling the main road.

Inland, you could drive up to the terraced villages of the **Fiumorbo** region for a grand view of the plain and the Tuscan islands offshore, or venture into the craggy gorges and precarious villages of the **Vallée du Tavignano** and the **Bozio**, either as a diversion on the drive to or from Bastia or as a route into the core of the island. North of here, the verdant **Castagniccia** is a fascinating region to explore, its tunnelled roads twisting past waterfalls and through an enormous forest of chestnut trees that's peppered with the highest concentration of highland villages in Corsica. A bed around here can be found at **Cervione**, the largest village in these parts, or **Piedicroce**, an old village occupying a fantastic location on the slopes of Monte San Petrone. North of the Castagniccia lies the **Casinca**, a more compact

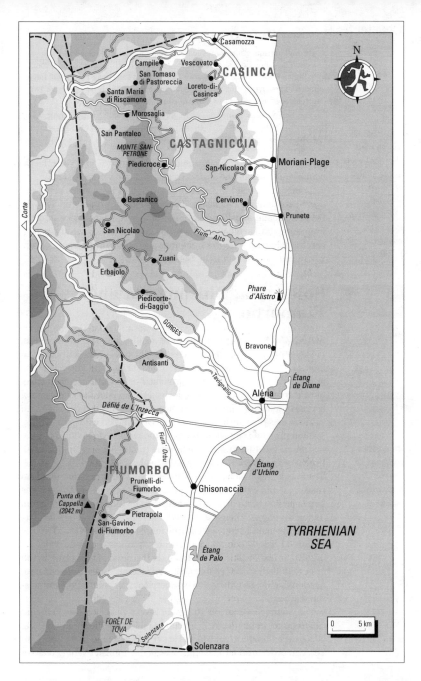

Corsica's most challenging long-distance hiking trail, the GR20, ends at the village of Conça, near the east coast. For a description of the route, see p.120.

region of delightful villages such as **Vescovato** and **Venzolasca**, which could feasibly be seen on a day excursion from Bastia.

Transport around the east isn't too bad: a bus passes along the coast stopping at Solenzara, Ghisonaccia and Aléria on its way between Bastia and Porto-Vecchio, but there's no service into the Fiumorbo and Tavignano valleys. For the Castagniccia you'll need a car, though the *micheline* train does pass through Casamozza, from where you can hitch into the region.

Solenzara, Ghisonaccia and Fiumorbo

SOLENZARA might not be the most scintillating of coastal resorts, but its strip of shops and busy marina give it a pleasantly lived-in look, and it does have a good clean beach. In addition, the village lies at the junction of the **route de Bavella**, one of Corsica's most spectacular mountain roads, whose lower reaches hug the river, giving access to numerous bathing and picnic spots.

An account of the route de Bavella appears on p.224.

There are a few **hotels** here as well: try the *Mare è Festa*, a pink-painted place at the southern end of the village (☎04 95 57 42 91, fax 04 95 57 43 23; ④), which rents cabins backing onto a small beach; or the *Maquis et Mer*, on the main street (☎04 95 57 42 37; ③–⑥) – a huge old-fashioned three-star with a solemn Corsican restaurant and a swish bar (ask for a room in the old wing, which has flagstone floors, an original granite staircase and pale-blue shutters on the windows). The cheapest option is the family-run *Orsoni*, further up the main street, just past the tourist office (☎04 95 57 40 25; ②–③). *La Solenzara*, above the beach north of the village (☎04 95 57 42 18, fax 04 95 57 46 84; ⑤), is the most stylish place in the area, with high stucco ceilings, gilt candelabras and a gorgeous pool overlooking the sea; they also have a restaurant and do good off-season discounts.

The **tourist office**, on the main street opposite the *Prisunic* supermarket in the centre (mid-June to mid-Sept daily 9am–noon & 5–10pm, mid-Sept to mid-June Tues–Fri 9am–noon; ☎04 95 57 43 75), can provide additional addresses in the unlikely event that these

THE GUIDE: CHAPTER 5

hotels are booked up. For those intending to **camp**, there's *Camping de la Côte des Nacres*, set amid eucalyptus trees 500m north of Solenzara next to the river and beach (☎04 95 57 40 09; May–Oct), or the cheaper *Camping Eucalyptus*, 1.5km further up the main road (☎04 95 57 44 73; April–Sept).

Solenzara, Ghisonaccia and Fiumorbo

Ghisonaccia

The one sizable village between Solenzara and Aléria is dusty **GHISONACCIA**, whose pejorative "accia" suffix (meaning "bad") seems just as applicable today as it was when the town was a malarial bog. That said, the place has enjoyed a certain prosperity ever since the late 1950s, when pieds-noirs from Algeria bought much of the hitherto useless agricultural land in the area to plant vineyards. The wine they eventually produced became France's leading brand of cheap *vin de table*, stimulating a boom that lasted until the 1970s, when it was discovered that most of Ghisonaccia's farmers had been mixing sugar and dodgy chemicals into their wine to bump up production. Since then, the vines have been replaced by orchards of clementines, kiwis and other soft fruit, picked by the low-paid Arab agro-workers you'll see hanging around the main crossroads. The village's other main source of revenue, after tourism and farming, are the close-cropped national service lads from the nearby air-force base who fill the bars on weekends.

For more background on this scandal, and its violent repercussions, see box on p.266.

If you have to **stay** in Ghisonaccia, make for the welcoming *De la Poste*, an old-fashioned place just north of the crossroads on the Ghisoni road opposite the war memorial (☎/fax 04 95 56 00 41; ③), whose pink and frilly restaurant has good-value 90F set menus featuring Corsican home-cooking. Otherwise there's the posher and pricier *Franceschini*, on the other side of the crossroads (☎04 95 56 05 32; ④).

The nearest **beach**, Plage de Tignale, lies 4km east; it's clean and large enough, but gets inundated during the summer by thousands of Germans and Italians from the enormous **campsites** behind it. These are all flashy four-star places complete with restaurants, shops, coin-operated fridges and the like. The most homely of the bunch is the *Arinella Bianca*, reached via a signposted turning off the main beach road (☎04 95 56 04 78, fax 04 95 56 12 54; May–Oct). A pleasant and relatively inexpensive place to **eat** in this area is *Les Deux Magots*, at Plage de Tignale, where you can enjoy locally caught seafood such as mussels and *loup de mer* on a breezy beachside terrace.

Making your way north from Ghisonaccia, you could turn off for the **Étang d'Urbino**, one of the half-dozen lagoons that break the monotony of the plain. Accessible via a dirt track, 10km along the main road from Ghisonaccia, this is a delightfully peaceful spot, fringed by reed beds.

The Mare a Mare Centre Trail

The **Mare a Mare Centre** footpath slices diagonally across the middle of Corsica, between Ghisonaccia on the eastern plain and Porticcio at the southern tip of the Golfe d'Ajaccio. Accessible to all from late April to November, it sees relatively few hikers, though the route is as varied and scenic as any on the island, with some particularly memorable stretches along remote ridges overlooking the sea. The trail is also punctuated at each of its seven stages by **gîtes d'étape**, and you can make several worthwhile side-trips to picturesque interior villages along the way.

Marked with orange splashes of paint, the Mare a Mare Centre starts 2.5km south of Ghisonaccia on the N198, near a bridge called Pont de l'Abatescu, which you can reach on any of the buses running between Bastia and Porto-Vecchio. From here the trail cuts across fruit orchards and vineyards, nutured by the River Fium'orbu from which this region takes its name, to begin a gradual ascent of the coastal range, peppered with red-roofed granite villages. Once over the snow-prone Col de Laparo (1525m), you enter the region of Haut Taravo, named after the river that drains into the Golfe de Valinco near Propriano, and thence head west via remote Cozzano and Tasso to Guitera-les-Bains, where the path climbs out of the Taravo valley and over a thickly forested ridge into Frasseto. Exposed ridges characterize the remaining few stages of the trail as it strikes north from Quasquara to scale the rocky Punta d'Urghiavari, before bending southwest to cross the main Ajaccio–Bonifacio road at the Col St-Georges. From here, another sharp ascent takes you onto a high ridge, and the path gives little ground until its junction with the Mare e Monti trail near the isolated village of Bisinao, where it swings northwest towards Porticcio.

Although it's divided into seven **stages** (of between 3hr and 6hr 30min), you can complete the route in six days by combining the first two stages, making a longer than average first day from Ghisonaccia to Catastaghju (7hr). Essential, as ever, is the Parc Naturel Régional's topoguide *Corse: Entre Mer et Montagne*, which indicates the route on a full-colour contour map, with a description of the trail and its chief highlights in French.

Mare a Mare Centre gîtes d'étape

Ghisonaccia see p.261
Serra di Fiumorbu Mme Guidicelli (☎04 95 56 70 14)
Catastaghju Mme Paoli (☎04 95 56 70 14)
Cozzano M. Pantalacci (☎04 95 24 41 59)
Zicavo see p.311
Guitera les Bains M. Lafranchi (☎04 95 24 42 54)
Tasso M. Tasso (☎04 95 24 52 01)
Col St-Georges Mme Renucci (☎04 95 25 70 06)
Porticcio see p.177

Fiumorbo

The little-explored region of **Fiumorbo** (or Fium'orbo), immediately inland from Ghisonaccia, has been renowned for the independent spirit of its inhabitants ever since 1769, when a group of shepherds who had refused to ascribe to French laws were struck down in an ambush along the road to Corte. Thirty years later a coalition of royalist, Paolist and pro-British Corsican exiles organized another anti-French rebellion which spread as far as the Sartenais before it was crushed by the French authorities. This tradition continued into the early nineteenth century, when an insurrection broke out and five thousand troops hired by Louis XVIII's government were unable to suppress the hordes of mountain people who seized control of the region. Eventually the ringleaders were either gunned down or deported to the French mainland by General Morand, who was nevertheless obliged to accede to them an area of coastal land. By the end of the century the Fiumorbo had become notorious bandit country, ruled by outlaws who terrorized the villages, untouched by the police, but today this is one of the quietest, and most untroubled parts of Corsica.

The region is reached by taking the D244 west off the main road 2km south of Ghisonaccia, then turning onto the D145, a route that takes you into the valley of the **River Albatesco**, a tributary of the River Fium'orbu ("troubled waters") and location of the chief villages of the region. Once on the D145, you can either take the amazingly contorted sideroad up to **SERRA-DI-FIUMORBO**, which gives a fantastic view of the coastal plain, or continue to **PIETRAPOLA**, whose **thermal baths** attract suffers from arthritis and rheumatic disorders throughout the year. The village is also thought to have been the site of an encounter between local bandits and a detachment of Roman soldiers en route from Sardinia in 231BC. Ambushed and relieved of their booty, the Romans pursued the Corsican robbers into the hills, only to nearly die of hunger and thirst trying to find a way down again. Eventually they discovered a spring at Pietrapola and survived, consecrating a special "Temple of the Spring" at the gates of Rome on their return. The façade of the village church, Santa Maria, sports a remnant of this era: an incongruous 4m column salvaged from a Jupiter-Saturn temple that once stood in a now-defunct hamlet further up the hill.

Beyond here the road forms a loop round the northern flank of the valley, twisting through San Gavino di Fiumorbo, Isolaccia-di-Fiumorbo and the especially attractive **PRUNELLI-DI-FIUMORBO**, approached from the west along an avenue of oak trees and pines. Clustered like an eagle's nest on top of a hill, with the austere peaks of Monte Renoso looming behind, the village gives a panoramic view of the eastern plain, with the best vantage point outside the church. You can stay up here at *Santa Susini*, a huge villa **hotel** in the centre of the village (☎04 95 56 02 29; ②). There are no restaurants.

The Défilé de l'Inzecca

Northwest of Ghisonaccia, the D344 scythes straight across a broad tract of fruit orchards and vineyards towards a narrow niche in the

*Details of
walks and
accommoda-
tion in Ghisoni
are featured
on p.309.*

wall of coastal mountains. Formed by the fast-flowing Fium'orbu torrent, the **Défilé de l'Inzecca** is a sheer granite trench bounded in the
south by the jagged needles of the Kyrie peaks and in the north and
west by the grey, snow-flecked Monte Renoso massif. The road that
winds through the gorge, leading from the coast to the village of
Ghisoni, provides one of the most spectacular approaches to the
interior, cutting across dramatic pale-green serpentine cliffs speck-
led with stunted trees. Below, colossal boulders choke the river,
which has been dammed to form a reservoir for a small hydroelec-
tricity station.

A good place to break the trip through the *défilé* is the *U Sampolu*
restaurant, 8km west of Ghisoni on the banks of the river (☎04 95
57 60 18; April–Oct Tues–Sat), where you can enjoy copious local
cuisine at reasonable prices. The accent here is on meat, with grilled
local lamb, veal and beef featuring prominently on both their 80F
and 100F set menus. It's also very popular, so book a table in
advance if you plan to lunch here.

Aléria

Built on the estuary at the mouth of the River Tavignano, **ALÉRIA** was
the capital of the Corsican province during the Roman era, remaining
the east coast's principal town and port right up until the eighteenth
century. Little is left of the historic town except the **Roman ruins** and
the Genoese fortress, which stands high against a background of chequered fields and green vineyards. A sizable proportion of the local
population is employed in farming oysters and mussels in the neighbouring **Étang de Diane**, formerly the Roman harbour and now an
excellent place for a swim. (During his exile on Elba, Napoléon kept
in contact with his homeland by ordering boatloads of oysters from
the lagoon.) To the south, a strip of modern buildings straddling the
main road makes up the modern town, but it's the village set on the
hilltop just west of here that holds most interest.

A brief history of Aléria

This area was first settled in 564 BC by a colony of Greek Phocaeans
who had been chased from their land by the Persian invasion. Calling
their new port Alalia, these Greeks initiated the island's trade routes
around the Mediterranean, selling the copper and lead they mined
from the land, and the wheat, olives and grapes they farmed here. In
535 BC they managed to survive a battle with the Carthaginians, but
were left considerably weakened as a colony. Eventually fleeing to
the mainland, the Phocaeans established a new capital at Massiglia
(Marseille), retaining Alalia as a trading link between their colonies
in southern Italy, Greece, Carthage and Spain.

In 259 BC the Romans arrived and conquered what was left of the
port, which was by that time controlled by Carthaginians. It wasn't

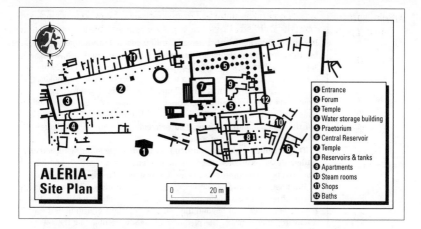

ALÉRIA-
Site Plan

0   20 m

❶ Entrance
❷ Forum
❸ Temple
❹ Water storage building
❺ Praetorium
❻ Central Reservoir
❼ Temple
❽ Reservoirs & tanks
❾ Apartments
❿ Steam rooms
⓫ Shops
⓬ Baths

until around 80 BC, however, that they built up a naval base here, calling the town Aléria and re-establishing its importance in this part of the Mediterranean. As the only town of significant size, Aléria was named administrative capital of the province, before long boasting a population of some thirty thousand. Under the orders of the emperor Augustus a fleet was harboured in the Étang de Diane and public buildings were constructed here, including baths, a forum and a triumphal arch, the remains of which are visible today. Light industries also flourished during this period as Aléria developed into a thriving crafts centre, producing jewellery, ceramics and clothes. Honey and wax were also marketed here, and seafood from the Étang de Diane found a ready trade with the continent.

Aléria's Roman days came to an end in 410 AD, when the city was struck by a fire which destroyed buildings and people alike. Malaria epidemics put paid to many of the survivors and the town was wiped out by Vandals later that century. Aléria was revived by the Genoese in the thirteenth century and was the seat of a bishopric for two hundred years thereafter. A fort was constructed in the sixteenth century, and when Theodor von Neuhof was received here in 1736 this was still one of the principal ports on the east coast.

The Musée Jerôme Carcopino and ancient Aléria

Your best plan is to begin your visit with the **Musée Jerôme Carcopino** (May 16–Sept daily 8am–noon & 2–7pm, Oct–May 15 Mon–Fri 9am–noon & 2–5pm; 10F), which is housed in **Fort Matra**. Pending the completion of building work on the ground floor, the collection – comprising remarkable finds from the Roman and Greek sites – is crammed into three interconnected rooms on the first storey of the fort, where ceramics, metal objects and jewellery form the bulk of the exhibits.

Aléria

The **first room** contains magnificent evidence of ancient Aléria's importance as a trading port. Hellenic and Punic rings and belt links are ranged alongside elaborate oil lamps decorated with Christian symbols, amphorae and some fragments of water pipes. In the first case on the left, a large Attic plate, depicting a faded red-grey elephant against a black background, takes up the middle of one display case, with various glazed dishes using the same painting method ranged beneath. The real highlight of this first room, however, is a second-century marble bust of Jupiter Ammon, which was discovered near the forum.

Moving clockwise, most notable of the exhibits in the **second room** is a shallow-stemmed Attic bowl featuring a masturbating Dionysus, with twisting erotic figures on its rear face. Thought to date from 480 BC, this piece is attributed to master artist Panaitios and ranks among the museum's most treasured exhibits. There are also painted earthenware Etruscan goblets and more fine red and black ceramics, many in perfect condition. among them two remarkable drinking vessels or "rhytons", one representing the head of a mule, the other the head of a dog

Finely worked Etruscan bronzes fill the **third room**, where you can also see jewellery from the fourth to the second century BC and objects discovered in the tombs of ancient Aléria, one of which, uncovered in 1966, revealed a priceless collection of elegantly curved, exquisitely made Greek swords, lances and daggers from the fifth century BC. Iron weapons, armour and hundreds of finely painted cups called "craters", one featuring a picture of Hercules and the Lion and another representing Dionysus, this time overseeing the grape harvest, are housed in the end room, along with a reconstruction of a fourth-century BC tomb.

The Roman site

Outside it's a stone's throw to the **Roman site** (closes 30min before museum), where most of the excavation was done as recently as the 1950s, despite the fact that Merimée noticed signs of the Roman settlement during his survey of the island in 1830. Most of the site still lies beneath ground and is undergoing continuous excavation, but the balneum (bathhouse), the base of Augustus's triumphal arch, the foundations of the forum and traces of shops have been unearthed. The proximity of the sea, the strong scent of wild tarragon and the arresting view of snow-capped mountains and Fort Matra add to the atmosphere.

First discovered was the **arch**, which formed the entrance to the governor's residence – the praetorium – on the western edge of the **forum**. In the adjacent **balneum**, a network of reservoirs and cisterns, the **caldarium** bears traces of the underground pipes that would have heated the room, and a patterned mosaic floor is visible inside the neighbouring chamber. To the north of the site lie the foundation walls of a large house, while at the eastern end of the forum the foundations of the **temple** can be seen, and at its northern edge, over a row of column stumps, are the foundations of the apse of an early Christian church.

Some traces of the Greek settlement, comprising the remains of an acropolis, have been discovered further to the east. It's believed that the main part of the town would have extended from the present site over to this acropolis and down to the Tavignano estuary. The port was located to the east of the main road, where the remnants of a second-century bathhouse have been found.

L'Étang de Diane and Plage de Padulone

A large saltwater lagoon, the **Étang de Diane** lies just north of Aléria. To get there, follow the main road north for 2km until you reach a turning on the right. A narrow dirt track leads down to *Le Chalet* restaurant (see below) and the banks of the lagoon, a glittering stretch of water dotted with fish-farm tanks, whose northeastern edge is marked by a lookout tower. The best places for swimming are the sandy eastern banks, which also make a pleasant picnic spot. **Plage de Padulone**, 3km due east of Aléria, is the most accessible beach in the area, reached via the narrow N200 from the Cateraggio crossroads. A row of modest seafood restaurants and downbeat cafés overlooks the sands, among them the old-style *Le Casabianca*, where groups of locals gather in the evenings to sing, play the accordion and cast fishing lines from the rear terrace.

Practicalities

If you decide to stay, there are a few **hotels** worth checking out: *Les Orangers*, situated 50m north of the Cateraggio crossroads in the centre of the modern part (☎04 95 57 00 31; June–Sept; ②–③), is the best place; the slightly pricier two-star *l'Atrachjata*, a little further north (☎04 95 57 03 93; ③), does good **meals** and provides adequate accommodation; *L'Empereur*, a big chalet-style building a little further up from *Les Orangers* (☎04 95 57 02 33; ③), is clean and comfortable, and a very good deal, with large motel-style rooms opening onto a central garden. One of the most pleasant **campsites** on the east coast lies 3km east of the Cateraggio crossroads: the *Marina d'Aléria* (☎04 95 57 01 42, fax 04 95 57 04 29; Easter–Oct) backs onto the beach and is well equipped. If it's full, try the smaller site at **Bravone Plage**, 12km further north along the main road (☎04 95 38 84 08).

Those with a passion for **oysters** can sample them fresh from the lagoon at *L'Auberge le Chalet*, 500m north of the crossroads, which also serves other excellent seafood dishes. During the summer, you can enjoy the same high-class cuisine at *Le Chalet*'s lagoon cabin, a smart wooden shack on stilts in the Étang de Diane (see above for directions). It's pricy, with most main dishes costing around 100F, but the food, which according to the menu comes "fully furnished", is topnotch and the setting wonderful; ask for a table on the rear terrace.

Vallée du Tavignano

Running northwest from Aléria, the **Vallée du Tavignano** forms an exhilarating approach to Corte, its craggy gorges and dark rocky slopes dotted with red-roofed villages. The N200, which tracks the river all the way to Corte, is the quickest route, but if you're in no hurry you could take the upland road through the savage country of the **Bozio**, on the north flank of the valley. If, however, you've only got time for a quick detour on your way across the eastern plain, you might drive up to the village of **Antisanti**, which over-looks the coast and Corsica's mountainous spine from the south side of the valley.

Antisanti

Located at an altitude of 700m, 20km west of Aléria, the rocky grey outpost of **ANTISANTI** offers views that more than reward anyone making the effort to get to it along the tortuous D43. In the twelfth century the village was an important stop-off point for merchants travelling between Corte and the coast. Resisting Pascal Paoli's revolution, the town was burned down in 1753. Today it consists of only one street, but there's a café from which, on a clear day, you can see all the main peaks of Corsica, the craggy needles of Bavella and Incudine rising to the south, Monte d'Oro to the west, while east-wards the islands of Elba, Capraia and Monte Cristo can be made out way beyond the plain.

The gorge route

Following the River Tavignano, one of the island's principal rivers, the main N200 road from Aléria to Corte (around 48km) provides a direct scenic route into the heart of the island. The road meanders across the plain for about 10km until, past the hamlet of **Buggione**, it begins an ascent into the mountainous country of the interior, narrowing in the approach to a magnificent **gorge** a further 10km onwards. Slicing through the denuded schist walls of the valley, the route affords occasional glimpses of hilltop villages to the south, and after the same distance again you emerge from the gorge at the sparse hamlet of **VOLTA**, where a triple-arched Genoese bridge takes you across the river. Visible on the right bank is a tenth-century Romanesque chapel dedicated to John the Baptist, a tiny edifice built of patterned stones alternating with plain blocks of granite, now used as a shepherds' shelter.

From here on it's an easier road along the southern flank of the river; to the north you can make out the flinty villages of the Bozio, ridged high on the distant valley slopes.

The Bozio

Tucked between the Tavignano gorge and the Castagniccia, the Bozio is a grimly mountainous terrain, its maquis littered with Romanesque churches and sombre villages that were hotbeds of Corsican nationalism in the eighteenth century. There are two routes through this region from Aléria: the D14, which leaves the N200 about 12km from town; or the D16/D116, which begins 5km north of Aléria, crossing the plain before rising to the north side of the Cursiglièse valley.

If you take the former road, the landscape becomes really wild at **PIEDICORTE-DI-GAGGIO**, a protuberance of red roofs above the bleak rock, with a central square that gives you a panorama of the eastern plain plus a hazy view of the giant peaks. The village church boasts an eighteenth-century façade and a huge clock tower, and the base of the building incorporates carved twelfth-century remnants. About 4km beyond lies **ALTIANI**, whose houses are attached to a spur amidst great blocks of granite, and from here it's another 9km of switchback road to **ERBAJOLO**, which offers a fantastic view of the Tavignano valley and of Monte d'Oro and Monte Renoso. From here you can take a walk to the remote Pisan chapel of **San Martino**, a gentle thirty-minute hike along a mule track through the maquis from the church in the centre of the village. A further twenty minutes from San Martino lies the ruined hamlet of **Casella**, another spectacular belvedere.

The alternative route becomes increasingly tortuous once you've joined the D116, winding through the flinty semi-derelict villages of **Tallone** and **Zuani** on its way to the **Col de San Cervone** (899m), where there's a fine view across the Tavignano in one direction and towards the distant sea in the other. Beyond here you could make a loop down to Erbajolo (see above) or continue to **ALANDO**, the birthplace of Sambucuccio d'Alando, a legendary fourteenth-century rebel. Leader of a popular movement against the region's despotic nobility, he is credited with the invention of the "Temps du Commun", an organization which from 1359 to 1362 united villages all over Corsica under one administrative body of elected magistrates.

From Alando you can head north through the stark hills as far as **BUSTANICO**, the village said to be the source of the War of Independence. It began in 1729 when an old man named Lanfranchi, or Cardone, sparked off a local rebellion against the Genoese after a tax collector threatened to carry off all his possessions. Outraged at such injustice, fellow villagers rose up in his defence, triggering riots and raids all over eastern Corsica, culminating in the sack of Bastia in 1730. The village church has a graceful wooden figure of Christ, sculpted by a local craftsman in the eighteenth century.

For more on a
paghjella
singing, see
p.292.

If you head west along the D441 you'll soon come to **SERMANO**, famous for *a paghjella* singing, which is performed once each year during the Jour des Morts festival at the Pisan chapel of **San Nicolao**. The chapel is fifteen minutes' walk from the church in the centre of the village, and is decorated with naive fifteenth-century frescoes of Christ, the Virgin, the Apostles and saints.

The Castagniccia

Famous for the herds of pigs that roam its tortuous backroads, **Castagniccia**, pronounced "Castan*eetch*", takes its name from the dense forests of chestnuts (*castagna*) first cultivated here by the Genoese in the fifteenth century, which later made this the richest and most densely populated part of the island. Today, many of the beautiful grey-green and silver schist hamlets perched on its ribbon-thin ridges lie virtually deserted or derelict, but the region remains a rewarding one to explore, particularly during the autumn, when whole valleys are carpeted in vivid gold and russet, and in wet weather, when wisps of mist and cloud cling to the lush canopy.

Castagniccia covers roughly a hundred square kilometres, extending south of the River Golo as far as the Bozio, and westwards just beyond the shadowy crest of Monte San Petrone (1767m), its highest mountain. Fuelled by a lucrative trade in chestnut flour and fine woodcarving, the region's golden era occurred during the Genoese peace between 1569 and 1729, when the majority of its opulent Baroque churches, convents, chapels and lofty stone houses were built. In the eighteenth century the arms industry thrived here as well, and its products found a ready market during the Corsican Revolution, during which Castagniccia was a bastion of support for Pascal Paoli (see box overleaf), a native of **Morosaglia**. Decline only set in towards the end of the nineteenth century, with the completion of the railways through the interior of the island. Easing the transport of timber to the coast, this hastened the process of **deforestation**, which ultimately undermined the area's traditional agro-pastoral economy, and stimulated an exodus to the coastal towns and French mainland. These days, Castagniccia only comes alive during August, when families return from Marseille to visit their grandparents in their native villages.

Exploring the Castagniccia requires a vehicle and some caution: although there's a larger concentration of roads here than anywhere else on Corsica, routes are extremely winding and narrow, with the added hazard of roaming pigs, cows and goats. Daily **trains** from Bastia stop in Casamozza and Ponte Leccia, but unless you're prepared to walk or hitch this isn't much help for exploring the area. Furthermore, hotels and restaurants are to be found only at La Porta, Piedicroce and Cervione – though you could always stay on the coast at Moriani Plage and see the Castagniccia on a day's tour. You have a choice of routes into the region: from the east coast you can penetrate the forest from either Prunete or Moriani Plage; from the north, strike in from Casamozza; or, from the west, drive the small distance from the west – it's a short drive from Ponte Leccia to Morosaglia.

Moriani Plage and around

One of a string of virtually indistinguishable resorts along the coast north of Aléria, **MORIANI PLAGE** is a bland strip of kitsch souvenir shops and cafés huddled around a crossroads on the N198. For a foray into Castagniccia, however, this is as convenient a base as any, boasting the last decent beach before Bastia, a reasonable choice of accommodation, a large *Champion* supermarket (300m south of the

Pascal Paoli

"He smiled a good deal when I told him that I was much surprised to find
him so amiable, accomplished and polite," wrote Boswell on first meeting
Pascal Paoli in 1765, "for although I knew I was to see a great man I
expected to find a rude character, an Attila king of the Goths, or a
Luitprand king of the Lombards." By this time Paoli was forty years old
and famous throughout Europe, widely admired by the liberal intelli-
gentsia of the time, among them Jean-Jacques Rousseau.

Paoli was born in **Morosaglia** (see p.281) with the cause of Corsican
independence in his blood – his father, Giacinto, a doctor, was a first-gen-
eration rebel, one of the three primates elected in 1731 by the independent
assembly. At the age of fourteen Pascal accompanied his father into exile
in Naples where the boy became a keen student of political enlightenment.
At the time of Gaffori's assassination, Pascal was a 29-year-old sublieu-
tenant in a Neapolitan regiment, but his brother Clemente was in the thick
of the rebellion. Appointed one of four regents after Gaffori's death,
Clemente invited his younger brother to take over the position of **General
of the Nation**, a title he accepted in 1755 and was to hold for the next
fourteen years.

Paoli's intention was to drive out the Genoese by force of arms, but
despite his military background he wasn't an experienced soldier, and was
anyway always short of the necessary supplies. However, he proved to be
adept at the art of government, giving the island a **democratic constitution** which anticipated that of the United States of America, founding the
university at Corte, building a small navy that was strong enough to break
the Genoese blockade, and establishing a mint, a printing press and an
arms factory. Furthermore, the system of justice instituted by Pascal Paoli
was effective enough to bring about a decline in vendetta killings.

Then in 1768 everything collapsed. The French moved in once more,
this time intending to stay after having bought out the Genoese under the
terms of the Treaty of Versailles. Determined to crush the rebels for good,
the French overwhelmed the Corsican troops at **Ponte Nuovo**, where-

crossroads), a cash dispenser (the only one for miles if you're heading inland), a self-service laundry (on the road leading to the beach)
and a small **tourist office** (Mon–Fri 9am–noon & 2–5pm; ☎04 95 38
41 73).

Best of the budget **hotels** here is the small and recently renovated
Le Lido, slap on the seafront (☎04 95 38 50 03; ③), which has ten
en-suite rooms, some with sea views, and painted wood shutters; its
restaurant is also the most attractively situated in the village. The
more modern *L'Abri des Flots*, set back a little further from the
beach (☎04 95 38 40 76; ②), is the least expensive option, whose
plain but clean rooms all have shower-toilets attached. For **campsites**, you've a choice between the flashy four-star *Camping
Merendella*, 700m south of the crossroads (☎04 95 38 53 47;
May–Oct), or the more modest *Camping Calamar*, 6.5km south at
PRUNETTE (☎04 95 38 03 54; May–Oct). The latter is situated

upon Paoli went into exile in London. However, his political life was not over.

In **1789**, at the start of the French Revolution, the people of Corsica were declared to be subject to the same laws as the revolutionary state, and it was in this changed political climate that Paoli returned triumphantly to the island in the following year. Initially he sympathized with the new republicanism, but the Corsican Jacobites – the Bonaparte family amongst them – owed too much to France to have much sympathy with separatist politics. Disagreements came to a head with Paoli's arraignment in June **1793**. His response was dramatic. Setting up an independent government in Corte, he approached the British government for help, who, having been driven out of Toulon by the French, were in search of a naval base in the area; and so there followed one of the more curious episodes of Corsican history.

The British sent **Sir Gilbert Elliot** to evaluate the situation, and agreement was quickly reached. English troops and naval forces moved in and after some fighting – during which the future Admiral Nelson lost the sight in one eye – the French moved out. A new constitution was drawn up that gave Corsica an attachment to the English crown, but with a large degree of autonomy. It's questionable whether Paoli was ever entirely happy with the course of events, but he was in a difficult situation, as the guillotine was waiting for him if France ever regained control. There seems no doubt that he expected to be appointed viceroy of the island, and when Elliot was given the job things began to turn sour. The parliament of 1795 elected Paoli as president, but Elliot objected; soon after, rioting was provoked by a rumour that Paoli's bust had been deliberately smashed at a ball given in the viceroy's honour. When the English began talking again to the republican French the game was over. In 1796 Paoli was persuaded to return to London, shortly before Elliot withdrew as Napoléon's army landed to secure the island for France.

Given a state pension, Paoli **died in London in 1807** at the age of 82, a revered figure. He was initially buried in his place of exile – there's a bust of him in Westminster Abbey – but his body now lies in his birthplace.

right next to the beach amid an old olive grove, and ranks among the most pleasant sites on the island; it's small, with only simple facilities, but is kept immaculately clean (the young *patronne* has even planted beds of aromatic herbs outside the toilet block), and has a sociable little snack bar that stays open late.

A great place to make the most of the stunning views available from the west-facing flanks of the coastal hills lies a short way inland from Moriani Plage along the D34. Signalled by the prominent bell tower of its church, the village of **SAN NICOLAO** emerges after 6km of tight bends and dense chestnut woods. You could pull over here to admire the colourful decor and trompe l'œil in the seventeenth-century parish church, or continue 4km further uphill to the hamlet of **SAN GIOVANNI DI MORIANI**, where the wonderful *Bar-Restaurant Cava* (☎04 95 38 51 14; June–Sept) serves wholesome Castagniccian specialities (including *migliacci*, goat's cheese

The
Castagniccia

A Castagna

The chestnut tree (*la chataîgnier* in French, **a castagna** in Corsican)
grows in most areas of the island that lie between 500m and 800m, but
only in Castagniccia – whose mild, moist climate and schist soils create the
optimum environment – does it form such extensive forests. Planted in the
fifteenth century by the Genoese, these were the linchpin of the local economy for more than four hundred years, providing fuel, carving and building material, pollen for bees and, most importantly of all, a ready source
of food.

The first chestnut pods, or *pelous*, appear on the trees in mid-August,
but the harvest doesn't usually start until two months later, while the
leaves are falling. Removed from their spiky pods, the nuts are shelled and
stored in special double-storey stone sheds called **sèchoirs**, where they dry
over the winter. Traditionally, the largest and most succulent were eaten
whole, while the rest were taken to water mills and ground into flour (*fari-
na*). This formed the mainstay of the peasant diet in many areas of upland
Corsica, where it was mixed with salt and water to make **pulenda**, a kind
of polenta, or, on special occasions, baked into cakes and biscuits. Any
surplus was bartered for olive oil and wine from the coastal villages.

During the late nineteenth century, the "chestnut economy" of regions
such as Castagniccia went into free fall as hectares of forest were felled for
timber and to provide tannin for leather production. Still more trees died
due to neglect as rural populations dwindled, while a virulent fungal disease has also taken its toll over the past decade. These days, *pulenda* and
chestnut-flour cakes, served as gourmet specialities in expensive restaurants and souvenir boutiques, have become more a symbol of the
islanders' traditional identity than eaten as daily staples; emigrants, for
example, are still often sent parcels of flour from their family land by older
relatives. The only apparent beneficiaries of the chestnut's decline are
Corsica's wild pigs, who gorge themselves on the ungathered windfalls.

doughnuts, on the 100F set menu) on a terrace overlooking the
Tyrrenean Sea. All the Tuscan islands are visible from here, and on a
clear day you can even make out the Italian coast.

Cervione

From San Nicolao, it's 5km south to the largest, busiest and most
welcoming village of the Castagniccia, **CERVIONE**, whose houses,
spread in an amphitheatre around the lower slopes of Monte
Castello, tower over a sloping medieval square that's linked to the
surrounding streets by a labyrinth of alleys and archways. Flanking
the south side of the square is one of the first Baroque churches on
Corsica, the **Cathédrale St-Érasme**, founded in 1578 by St
Alexander Sauli, who was ordained bishop of Aléria in 1570 and soon
transferred the bishopric to Cervione to escape the malaria-ridden
swampland of the plain. Little remains of the old cathedral, which
was restored in the nineteenth century, but the impressive black-and-
white marble floor gives the place some appeal. Opposite the church
stands the **bishop's palace**, once the residence of King Theodor (see

The Mare a Mare Nord Trail

Begining at **Moriani Plage** on the east coast, the principal **Mare a Mare Nord trail**, waymarked with orange paint splashes, winds west through the heart of the country's watershed to Cargèse. The route, which passes through the Bozio to Corte, and thence along the dramatic Tavignano valley into the Niolo, consists of ten stages (lasting 3hr 30min–6hr), and is best attempted from late April to November, heading west.

A longer and more strenuous option is to turn off the trail at Sermano, three stages into the hike, where a **variante** (alternative) path peels south to begin an eight-day loop through the Vivario forest and up a series of cols en route to Guagno and the Incinosa massif. It rejoins the principal route at Marignana, where you follow the Mare e Monti trail for the final two days' walk to the west coast.

Accommodation along the main route is provided by a string of comfortable gîtes, but on the less-frequented *variante* you'll have to check into a hotel or refuge at the end of a couple of stages where no hikers' hostels have so far been built. In either case, advance booking is recommended, especially during high summer when beds in the gîtes can be in short supply.

A stage-by-stage rundown of both routes is given in the Parc Naturel Régional de Corse's essential **topo-guide**, *Corse: Entre Mer et Montagne*, which you can buy at most good bookshops and tourist offices.

Mare a Mare Nord Principal accommodation
Pianello (☎04 95 39 62 66 or 04 95 39 61 59)
Sermano M. Mariani (☎04 95 48 67 97)
Castellare di Mercurio M. Guiducekku (☎04 95 61 05 13)
Corte M. Gambini (☎04 95 46 16 85), see also p.298
Calacuccia M. Mordiconi (☎04 95 48 00 04), see also p.294
Albertacce M. Albertini (☎04 95 48 05 60), see also p.294
Casamaccioli Reservation obligatory (☎04 95 48 03 31)
Evisa Mme Ceccaldi (☎04 95 26 21 28), see also p.150

Mare a Mare Nord Variante accommodation
Poggio di Venaco M. Giorgetti (☎04 95 47 02 29)
Casanova Mme Casanova (☎04 95 47 03 73)
San Petru di Venaco M. Hiver (☎04 95 47 07 29)
Vivario see p.307
Pastricciola mairie (☎04 95 28 91 85 or 04 95 20 78 22)
Soccia *Hotel U Paese* (☎04 95 28 31 92)
Guagno Mme Mariani (☎04 95 28 33 47), see also p.188

box on p.277); its ethnographical **museum** (May–Sept Mon–Sat 9am–noon & 2.30–6pm; 5F) exhibits various geological specimens and farm implements.

The village's only **hotel** is the *St-Alexandre*, below the main road at the bottom of the village (☎04 95 38 10 83; ③), whose rooms have great views across the plains from their balconies. It's a stark, unfinished building with few frills, but the management is welcom-

ing, and the pieces of old family furniture and antique memorabilia dotted around the corridors give the place a quirky air. You can **eat** at the lively *U Casone* pizzeria, through an archway off the square, and there's a good **bar** next door to the church.

The elegant Romanesque chapel of **Santa Cristina** is a forty-minute walk from Cervione – take the road down towards Prunette for about 600m, then a signpost shows the way. Marvellous **frescoes** dating from 1473 decorate the twin apses (you'll find the key on a ledge above the door): on the left side Christ is depicted with the Virgin, St Christina and a kneeling monk; on the right, Christ is surrounded by the symbols of the Evangelists; and over the arch between them is a portrayal of the Crucifixion. A more ambitious three-hour walk into the mountains starts from the west of the village: follow the signs to Notre-Dame-de-la-Scobiccia, a tiny Romanesque chapel about 2km up the slope, from where a mule track wends up into the maquis to the **Punta Nevera**, a rocky eminence overlooking much of the Castagniccia.

Cervione to Carcheto

South of Cervione, after about 12km of tormented hairpin bends (many with dizzying drops and no barriers), comes **Valle d'Alesani**, from where it's a short detour up the D217 to the **Couvent d'Alesani** where King Theodor was crowned. Founded in 1236, the Franciscan monastery is mostly a ruin, but its church holds a beautiful fifteenth-century Sienese painting known as the *Virgin and the Cherry*. The site is also associated with the infamous Giovannali sect, who sheltered here after the destruction of their monastery at Carbini.

Back on the main road it's not long before you reach **FELCE**, whose Baroque church is decorated with simple yet arresting frescoes – on the ceiling you'll see the artist, palette in hand, floating among the clouds. Also of interest is the **tabernacle** above the altar, carved by a penitent bandit. Look out, too, for the wonderful local-produce shop run by Christine Bereni, on the outskirts of the village, where you can buy home-grown chestnut-pollen honey, free-range eggs, charcuterie, jams and tasty goats' and ewes' cheese.

Beyond Felce, the road winds slowly up to the **Col d'Arcarotta**, dividing the Alesani valley from the Caldone basin, the heartland of Castagniccia. The aptly named *Auberge des Deux Valleés*, strad-

The Castagniccia

More background on the Giovannalis, who were persecuted, and eventually exterminated, for their licentious religious practices, appears on p.219.

Théodore von Neuhof

Scorned by Corsican historian Chanoine Casanova as an "operetta king", **Théodore von Neuhof** was crowned King of Corsica on April 15, 1736, a unique title he was to hold for just eight months.

Théodore was an ambitious nobleman with a very colourful past. Brought up in the court of France where he was page to the duchess d'Orléans, mother of the Prince Regent, he travelled around England, Holland and Spain, killed his best friend in a duel, and acquired a fortune through some rather dubious financial speculations. Captured by Moors in Tunis in the early 1730s and put into slavery in Algiers, he managed to bribe his way to freedom, and was soon sending word to a group of Corsican exiles in Livorno that he would provide them with aid in return for the crown of their troubled island. Impressed by his royal connections and fancy talk, and desperate for money and arms, the Corsicans agreed. Soon after, Théodore landed at Aléria, decked out in full Turkish regalia with a retinue of French, Italian and Moorish attendants, and was taken in state to the Couvent d'Alesani to be crowned King Théodore I of Corsica. His powers were severely constrained – a council of 24 men was appointed to advise him, and he was answerable to a Corsican parliament – but Théodore had plenty of opportunities for kingly behaviour. Living it up at the bishop's palace in Cervione, he distributed titles among the wealthier Corsicans, made increasingly exaggerated promises of arms for the liberation of his people, and organized a few ineffectual sieges and pointless military manoeuvres against the Genoese.

Mistrust amongst his ministers increased as the emptiness of his promises became obvious, and in November 1736 the king was forced to flee the island via Solenzara, disguised as a priest. Théodore didn't give up entirely on the Corsicans, however – in 1739 he returned with a small fleet but was deterred from landing by the French. Eventually Théodore returned to England, where he died in 1756 having accumulated massive debts. A plaque in London's Soho Square commemorates him: "Fate poured its lessons on his living head, bestowed a kingdom and denied him bread."

dling the pass (☎04 95 35 91 20; ③), takes in the best of the views, with Monte San Petrone dominating the skyline to the northwest. Its convivial wood-lined bar makes a good place for a pit stop, or you can sample typical Castagniccian cuisine (such as *figatelle*, roast pork or trout in cream cheese) in the restaurant. A la carte dishes cost around 60F, plus there's a good-value 80F "menu corse", served indoors or alfresco on the terrace (for a ten percent surcharge); wines cost 60F and upwards.

The first sizable settlement below the pass is **CARCHETO**, set amidst an ocean of chestnut trees and giving a good view of Piedicroce across the valley. Carcheto's dilapidated **Église Ste-Marguerite**, set by a wood on the edge of the hamlet, is an eighteenth-century edifice packed with decaying examples of local work – luridly painted stucco covers the walls, portraying scenes from the Crucifixion, with an alabaster statue of the Virgin and Child providing a restrained counterpoint. If the church is locked, you can pick up the key from the *Refuge* hotel in Piedicroce (see below). Outside the church, a sign for "La Fontaine" directs walkers through the wood to a glistening **waterfall**, which cascades through an opening in the trees – a fine spot for a dip and a picnic: follow the track indicated, heading straight on where the the main (motorable) trail switches sharply to the right (ignore the orange splashes of paint). You'll know you're going the right way when you pass a cemetery, followed by a spring.

Piedicroce and around

A cluster of hamlets belonging to the commune of **Orezza** lies to the north of Carcheto, strung along the lower slopes of Monte San Petrone. During the mid-nineteenth century, this was the most densely populated commune in the whole of France, with 91 inhabitants per square kilometre. Today, however, barely two hundred permanent residents live in **PIEDICROCE**, the area's principal village, whose **hotel**, *Le Refuge* (☎04 95 35 82 65, fax 04 95 35 84 42; Dec to mid-Oct; ③), is the sole place to stay in the valley. Perched on a steep terrace, the building itself is a pink monstrosity, but its restaurant does excellent Corsican food, including Castagniccia specialities such as chestnut fritters with *brocciu* cheese. Piedicroce's **Église St-Pierre-et-Paul**, built in 1691, harbours a handful of mediocre sixteenth- and seventeenth-century paintings, and a restored organ that is reputedly the oldest in Corsica.

STAZZONA, 2km downhill along the D506 from Pedicroce, was the centre of arms manufacture during the War of Independence – its name means "forge" in Corsican. More recently it's made its money from the **Eaux d'Orezza** spring: as the faded old hotel signs indicate, people used to come up here for the curative waters, among them parties of English aristocrats and colonial hoi polloi from French Indochina. The local council used to bottle the water for export, but had to give up the enterprise a few years ago because sales were poor – no surprise to anyone who's tasted the stuff. To reach the spring, continue down the hill for a couple of kilometres and cross the bridge where a sideroad turns right; the gates to the old bottling plant are a short way further on your left as you start to climb. Few foreign visitors venture down here these days, but you might see a gang of local kids here hanging around the little pavilion where the warm fizzy water bubbles to the surface – mudpacks made with it are reputedly effective against adolescent acne.

While you're on this side of the valley, you could follow the D46 past the spring another 4km to **Valle d'Orezza**, where traditional smoking pipes and boxes are carved from olive and chestnut wood. Formerly this hamlet exported crafted wood objects all over Corsica, France and Italy; now only a handful of elderly artisans still live here, selling their work to visitors direct from tiny cottage workshops.

Heading back through Piedicroce, take the D71 north for the **Couvent d'Orezza**, which stands in a green glade in a bewitchingly silent spot. Reduced to a craggy ruin by the Germans in World War II, when it was temporarily used as a Resistance arms dump, the site has

The Monte San Petrone Hike

Visible all over Castagniccia and central Corsica, the craggy summit of **Monte San Petrone** (1767m) is one of the most thrilling viewpoints on the island, and is accessible on a comfortable four-hour round-hike (2hr 30min ascent, 1hr 30min descent) along a clearly marked trail. Each year in August, hundreds of local villagers, including a fair number of old folk, climb to the top for a special Mass, so the route is relatively easy-going. That said, you'll definitely need sturdy footwear and a good pair of lungs, as the path gets steep towards the top.

The trailhead for the hike is at **Campodonico**, about 2km west of Couvent d'Orezza up a sideroad. Park your car in the lay-by at the entrance to the hamlet and head down the lane through the houses, turning right along the mule track that leads up the valley. From here, the trail – marked at regular intervals with splashes of orange or red paint – zigzags up to a scattering of **bergeries** (1hr 30min) where you should briefly quit the path and follow the hillside around to the north to get the best views of the mountains inland. All of Corsica's principal peaks are visible at this point, from the Cinto massif down to Monte Rotondo.

Once you've rejoined the marked trail, it takes around one hour to reach the summit, passing through beautiful birch woods and mossy boulders. The final thirty minutes are tough going, but the 360-degree panorama from the top, marked with a crucifix and a serpentine-stone carving of St Peter, is breathtaking. In clear weather you can see from the coast of Tuscany to Cap Corse, and across the swath of dramatic snow-capped mountains to the east.

Note that if you have the use of two vehicles or are happy to hitch, a good alternative descent leads north from the *bergeries* mentioned earlier along a clearly marked trail to the **Col de Prato**, a short way east of Morosaglia.

profound historic associations. In the eighteenth century the convent was a centre of resistance to the Genoese republic, and several *consulte* (rebel meetings) took place inside it – on April 20, 1731, twenty representatives of the clergy gathered to discuss whether violent rebellion was against the fundamental principles of Christian morality, and it was here that Paoli was voted commander-in-chief of the Corsican National Guard. Paoli also met Napoléon here in 1793 in an unsuccessful attempt to achieve a truce between their respective armies.

Campana to the Col de Prato

Beyond Piedicroce the D71 continues to twist through the forests on the slopes of Monte San Petrone, past various abandoned hamlets. Just 2km from the Couvent d'Orezza the village of **CAMPANA** merits a stop for its Baroque church of **Sant'André**, which houses a fine *Adoration of the Shepherds* attributed to the Spanish seventeenth-century painter Zurbaran. Renowned for its beautiful light (and, bizarrely, for the faintly demonic expression on the face of the boy carrying the eggs), the painting was given to the parish by a wealthy local resident in 1895. The key to the church is kept by an old lady who lives in the last house on the left as you face the village. After Campana head north for 2km, then veer right at the fork for the village of **CROCE**, which has Castagniccia's only **campsite** (☎04 95 39 21 33; May–Oct) – either phone the owner, M. Mattei, or ask at the mairie in the centre of the village.

Thanks largely to the gigantic five-storey bell tower rising from its terracotta and grey schist rooftops, **LA PORTA**, 6km up the hill from here, is the most distinctive village in Castagniccia. Swathed in lush chestnut forest, with the granite crags of Monte San Petrone looming behind, its centrepiece is the spectacular **Église St-Jean-Baptiste**, erected in 1720 and widely regarded as the high-watermark of Baroque architecture in Corsica. The church's grand façade gracefully unites all the principal features of Rococo, although a tasteless paint job recently submerged its former muted colours in gaudy yellow and white. Inside the building are several noteworthy art treasures, including a gory depiction of the beheading of St John the Baptist (to the left as you face the altar) and, opposite this, a sixteenth-century wood sculpture of the Crucifixion.

There is nowhere to stay in La Porta, but you can **eat** well in the *Restaurant de L'Ampigignani (Chez Elizabeth)*, down the road through the centre of the village from the church (☎04 95 39 22 00). This place looks unpromising from the outside, but is a light and airy dining hall with magnificent views down the valley. The food is superb, too, and reasonably priced (count on 130–150F for a full four-course meal) considering the quality; everything comes from the immediate vicinity, and is prepared according to traditional Castagniccian recipes.

Taking the north road out of La Porta will bring you to the **Col de Prato** (985m), the highest point on the roads of Castagniccia. From the col, a walk to the ruined **San Petrucolo** (a church founded as far back as the sixth century) can be done in half an hour. Follow the narrow track south in the direction of Monte San Petrone, then after 100m take the track on the right into the maquis – follow this for a few steps, then strike left, and you'll see the chapel straight in front of you.

Morosaglia and beyond

A 2km descent west from the Col de Prato brings you to **MOROSAGLIA**, where Pascal Paoli's birthplace stands to the east of the village in the hamlet of Stretta, signposted **Maison de Pascal Paoli** (daily 9am–noon & 3–6pm; 5F). A low-budget video primes you for the tour of the house, whose exhibits comprise a small and uninspiring collection of letters, portraits and other memorabilia, including the very first Corsican newspaper, printed in 1794. Paoli's ashes, brought back from England in 1807, are entombed in a chapel on the ground floor.

Paoli was baptized in the Pisan-founded but extensively rebuilt church of **Santa Reparata**, situated up a track opposite the house. His brother Clement, described by Dorothy Carrington as "a matchless marksman who prayed for his enemies' souls as he shot them down", lived out his retirement here, in the large mansion that's now the village school.

A couple of fine Romanesque chapels are to be found beyond Morosaglia. The nearer, **Santa Maria di Valle di Rostino**, stands to the west of the D15, 5km along the road. Passing the village on your right, continue for 500m to reach the ruined chapel, accessible via a rough track. Dating from the tenth century, the apse displays some fine Pisan stonework created by narrow blocks interspersed with green and grey schist, adorned with slender columns and harmonious arcading. Amongst the primitive sculpture along the external roof band, Adam and Eve on either side of the Tree of Life feature most prominently. **San Tomaso di Pastoreccia**, 10km north of Morosaglia at the end of the zigzagging route through Pastoreccia, is a half-ruined building of grey schist, dating from the tenth century, its interior enlivened by a series of sixteenth-century **frescoes**. Some are in very bad condition, but you won't have any difficulty picking out most of the Apostles and saints (a young St John stands out in a gold surround), or deciphering the scenes from the Passion and the Last Judgment.

The Casinca

Bounded by the Golo and Fiumalto rivers, the **Casinca** covers the eastern slopes of Monte Sant'Angelo, an area swathed in olive and chestnut trees and embellished with stately villages. It's less popular with tourists than the Castagniccia, but is easier to get into if you haven't got your own transport, as there's a twice-daily **bus** from Bastia to **Vescovato**, many of whose inhabitants earn their living in

the city. There's no accommodation on offer, but it's a small area, easily coverable in half a day.

The Casinca villages

CASTELLARE-DI-CASINCA, just 1km up the D6 from the main coast road, about 15km north of Moriani Plage, affords a wonderful view of the eastern plain and has a beautiful tenth-century church, **San Pancrazio**, notable for its triple apse. About 1km out of the village, a road off to the left leads to **PENTA-DI-CASINCA**, the second-largest village in the region. Its dark streets, crammed with lofty schist buildings dating principally from the fifteenth century, open out onto a large square which gives a fine view across the plain.

Heading east for a kilometre along the D206 will bring you to a junction where an abrupt left turn leads onto the spectacular road flanking Monte Sant'Angelo. **LORETO-DI-CASINCA**, the next halt, and the area's most appealing village, perches on a spur overlooking all the villages of the Casinca, its long main street affording a panorama right across to Bastia – the terrace to the left of the church is the best place to make the most of it. A waymarked hike through the chestnut forest up **Monte Sant'Angelo** (1218m) starts 500m south of the village along a recently surfaced road, from the neighbouring hamlet of **Silvarecio** – it's about ninety minutes' fairly strenuous climbing to the summit.

Some 500m north of the village you can cut back east by taking a right turn and following the road across a ridge for 2km until you hit the D237 again. A right here will bring you to **VENZOLASCA**, a remote and lofty village whose slender, lance-like church spire is conspicuous from a long way off. Venzolasca is one of the few places in Corsica where you still see men dressed in traditional black corduroy, complete with silver studs and gun belt.

From here it's a short drive down to **VESCOVATO**, set amongst chestnut trees and olive groves. Capital of the Casinca, this was an important place in the thirteenth century when the bishopric of Mariana was transferred here in a move to escape the malaria-ridden plain (*vescovato* means "bishopric" in Corsican). The bishopric remained until 1570 when it was relocated to the more important town of Bastia. The village is livelier than most places hereabouts – its busy central square, shaded by lines of ancient plane trees, even has an outdoor café, a rare find in these parts.

On the south side of the square, a family coat of arms indicates the house of the historian Filippini, whose *Historia di Corsica* (1594) is a principal source of medieval Corsican history. A further wander through the village reveals various plaques commemorating eminent visitors such as Mirabeau, but Vescovato's main sight is the church of **San Martino**, reached by climbing a flight of steps north of the square. Enlarged by the bishops of Mariana in the fifteenth century, the church contains a fine marble tabernacle, carved by a Genoese sculptor in 1441 and portraying two Roman soldiers sleeping against the tomb.

Travel details

BUSES

Buses along the east coast are operated by Rapides Bleus/Corsicatours (☎ 04 95 31 03 79). The following details apply to July and August; during the rest of the year, only one service runs on most routes (daily except Sun).

Aléria to: Bastia (2 daily; 1hr 30min); Ghisonaccia (2 daily; 15min); Porto-Vecchio (2 daily; 1hr 20min); Solenzara (2 daily; 30min).

Ghisonaccia to: Aléria (2 daily; 15min); Bastia (2 daily; 1hr 45min); Porto-Vecchio (2 daily; 1hr); Solenzara (2 daily; 20min).

Moriani Plage to: Bastia (2–3 daily; 45min).

Solenzara to: Aléria (2 daily; 30min); Bastia (2 daily; 2hr 15min); Ghisonaccia (2 daily; 20min); Porto-Vecchio (2 daily; 45min).

Venzolasca to: Bastia (3–4 daily; 50min); Vescovato (3–4 daily; 10min).

Vescovato to: Bastia (3–4 daily; 40min); Venzolasca (3–4 daily; 10min).

Chapter 6

Central Corsica

*For more on
the GR20, see
p.120.*

C entral Corsica is a non-stop parade of stupendous scenery,
and the best way to immerse yourself in it is to get onto the
region's ever-expanding network of marked trails and forest
roads. The ridge of granite mountains forming the spine of the island
is closely followed by the epic GR20, a trail that can be picked up
from various villages and is scattered with refuge huts offering basic
facilities. Other marked trails wind off the watershed to the surrounding summits. Of these, the island's two highest peaks – Monte
Cinto and Monte Rotondo – provide the most popular routes, accessible in settled summer weather to anyone with sufficient stamina
and a strong pair of boots. For less adventurous hikers, there are also
plenty of lower-altitude trails to exquisite glacial lakes and view
points over the valleys, while the region's roads, though often in dis-
repair, penetrate deep into the forests that carpet the mountain
slopes, crossing various lofty passes along the way.

Corte, set in a dip at the centre of the island on the main road
between Ajaccio and Bastia, provides the perfect base to begin
exploring, as it's well placed to reach anywhere covered in this chapter and has the bulk of the region's accommodation – elsewhere it's
rare to find more than one basic hotel per village. Capital of independent Corsica in the eighteenth century, Corte is a fortress village
par excellence, with its walled citadel, set atop a twisted pinnacle of
rock, piercing the landscape of overlapping mountains and forests.
Despite being the second-ranking town of northern Corsica, it's a
peaceful, slow-moving place where old traditions die hard, making it
a fascinating introduction to the mentality of the interior.

In the immediate environs of Corte the chief attractions are the
spectacular **Vallée de la Restonica** and the parallel **Gorges du
Tavignano**, but the most popular valley in central Corsica – on
account of its comparative proximity to Bastia – is the **Vallée d'Asco**,
which offers another superb gorge and rich wildlife. The Asco road
culminates at Haut'Asco, a ski resort on the northern slopes of
Monte Cinto, Corsica's highest peak. Access to the upper reaches of
Cinto is also possible via the adjacent valley of the **Niolo**, a sheep-

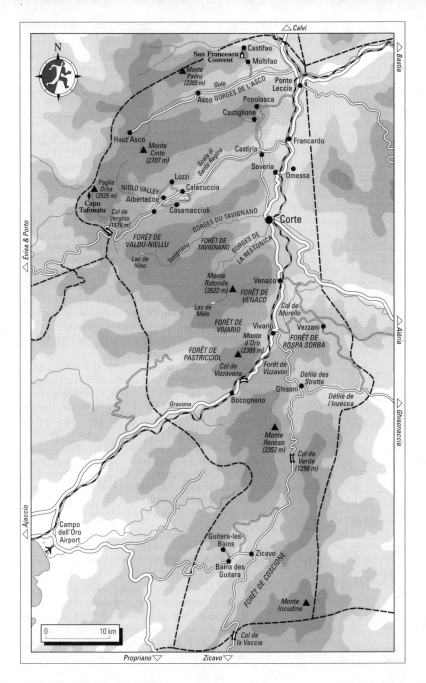

rearing region that was isolated for centuries until the construction
of the road a hundred years ago. Like Corte, the Niolo is an essential
visit for anyone eager to understand *l'âme corse* – "the soul of
Corsica" – so you might want to linger for a night or two in the main
settlement of **Calacuccia**, a centre for walks and drives into the
Forêt de Valdo-Niello, a dizzying forest of Laricio pines.

Such forests cover much of central Corsica, and one of the most
superb drives on the island goes south of Corte from **Vivario** through
the **Forêt de Rospa-Sorba**, the endless trees set against an
omnipresent background of snowy peaks. The nearby village of
Ghisoni is the place to make for if you want to tackle **Monte Renoso**,
while **Vizzavona**, further south along the Bastia–Ajaccio route, is the
springboard for Monte d'Oro, and offers countless walks into the luscious beech forest. Still further south, **Zicavo** is the base for **Monte
Incudine**, the southernmost major peak.

The most memorable way to travel in central Corsica is on the
micheline train, which crosses the mountains from Bastia to
Ajaccio, with a main connection at Ponte Leccia. Four daily services
stop at Ponte Leccia, Corte, Venaco, Vivario and Vizzavona, passing
through a 4km tunnel that is one of the major engineering triumphs
of the mountain railway. If you're pushed for time, however, you'll be
better off travelling this route by **bus** on one of the regular coaches
that run between Bastia and Ajaccio via Corte; the last stop before
the descent to the capital is Bocognano. Public transport away from
this main artery is more sporadic, limited to a seasonal summer service from Porto across the col de Verghio and Niolo valley to Corte.
In July and August and during the skiing season, you can also catch
a bus from Ponte Leccia to Haut'Asco.

The Vallée d'Asco

The **Vallée d'Asco** – the wettest part of Corsica – was once a region
of intensive pastoral farming, whose scattered population lived for
centuries off on small-scale cheese and wool production, supple-
mented by crops such as wheat, tobacco, linen and hemp. During the
Genoese era, the *poix*, or pitch, made by the Aschesi from pine sap,
caused the wholesale destruction of the area's forests, and today

much of the landscape is denuded and bleak. Ringed by a string of 2000m peaks, the valley remains among Corsica's most remote enclaves; only in 1937 was Asco village connected to the road network, which was extended as far as the ski station by the French Foreign Legion in 1968. Today, the Aschesi, like most mountain communities, rely on the seasonal influx of hikers to make ends meet, along with modest sales of cheese and charcuterie, and their famously fragrant **honey**, produced in the ranks of ramshackle hives stacked up the hillsides.

The Vallée
d'Asco

The River Asco starts life as the Stranciacone, which rises at an altitude of 2556m on the lower slopes of **Monte Cinto**, Corsica's highest mountain, then flows through the village of Asco and on through a fantastic **gorge** before reaching the Golo close to Ponte Leccia. In the upper valley, beyond Asco, the scenery is most alpine – up here mouflon roam in carefully protected zones, and bearded vultures and royal eagles are sometimes to be spotted in the magnificent **Forêt de Carozzica**. The road comes to an end 15km west of Asco at the semi-operational ski station at **Haut'Asco**, from where trails lead into the forest and up the flank of Cinto.

*A description
of the two
main routes
up Monte
Cinto features
on p.291.*

There is a summer **bus** service between Ponte Leccia and Haut'Asco, but you'll need your own transport to make a tour of the valley. Starting at Ponte Leccia, it's a good idea to detour up to the delightful villages of **Moltifao** and **Castifao**, before returning to the gorge and the road up to Haut'Asco.

Ponte Leccia, Moltifao and Castifao

Lying 19km north of Corte at the junction of road and rail routes to Bastia, Corte and the Balagne, **PONTE LECCIA** has nothing to recommend it except its supermarkets and service stations, where you might want to refuel before pressing on into the Vallée d'Asco or Castagniccia. A couple of kilometres north, the D47 leaves the N197 to follow the River Asco, initially along a flatland scattered with eucalyptus trees.

*The
Castagniccia
region is
covered on
p.270.*

The best-value place to **stay** hereabouts is the *Cabanella*, just beyond the turning for Moltifao, 7km from the junction with N197 (📞04 95 47 80 29; ③); this modest, unpretentious auberge provides comfortable chambre d'hôte accommodation, with 85F meals of mixed French and Corsican dishes served in a downstairs dining room. Close by, the *Camping A Tizarella* (📞04 95 47 83 92; April–Oct) is a well-equipped two-star site with plenty of shade, a camping-gas bottle depot and pizzeria; it's easy to spot – look for the giant painted wooden flowers at the roadside.

A right along the D247 here will take you up the hillside to **MOLTIFAO**, an amphitheatre of old stone buildings set on a crest separating the valleys of the Tartagine and Asco. Moltifao's church houses a beautiful sixteenth-century **triptych** and some sacristy furniture, including a wooden retable incorporating a fine primitive painting of the Virgin on a gold background.

The Vallée d'Asco

For a great view across to the Tartagine, carry on 3km north to CASTIFAO, a warm-toned settlement that once thrived on its copper mine and marble quarry. At the pass just before the village stands the ruined **Couvent de Caccia**, a former Franciscan convent built in the late-Gothic style. Some of the tombstones in its small cemetery bear the name "Stuart", which historians believe may have been brought to the area by Scottish mercenaries during the wars of Independence. An ideal picnic spot from which to view the spectacular Mori massif, on the opposite side of the valley, is the grassy ledge below the ruin, reached by hopping through a gap in the fence where the road bends sharply towards the pass.

The Gorges de l'Asco and Haut'Asco

Back down the main road, after a further 2km the road penetrates the **Gorges de l'Asco**, following the river's every twitch for 9km, between overhanging rock faces of orange granite that soar to 900m. There isn't much to **ASCO** itself, an austere little place 22km west of Ponte Leccia, famed in the eighteenth century as home of the *paceri* (peacemakers), a tribunal of locally elected magistrates who mediated between families involved in vendettas. Its location, however, couldn't be better: built up the left bank of the river, the village lies at the base of a grandiose crest of mountains, with the crags of Monte Padro immediately to the northwest and the Monte Cinto massif and Capo Bianco to the southwest. You can stay here at the welcoming *Ferme-Auberge d'Ambroise et Nicole Vesperini*, on the way into the village (☎04 95 47 83 53; ②–③), which offers comfortable accommodation in small but cosy rooms, and excellent local cuisine in its **restaurant**, where a four-course meal will set you back around 100F.

A wonderful – if well-known – **swimming spot** can be found on the riverbank below Asco, at the renovated fifteenth-century **Genoese bridge**, a listed historical monument; follow the narrow one-way road west through the village until you reach a potholed lane running sharply downhill. The water on either side of the humpbacked stone bridge is transparent green and fairly deep, but pretty cold even in midsummer. On its far side, an ancient, paved mule track strikes up the **Pinara valley** towards the Col de Serra Piana – formerly the main line of communication with the Niolo valley to the south. Twenty minutes into the walk, you find yourself deep in a wilderness of scrub and towering rock, with only semi-wild goats for company.

Beyond Asco the D147 widens and hugs the **Forêt de Carozzica**, a magnificent forest of maritime and Laricio pines, which extend up the valley walls as far as the 2000m contour. Hugging the river, the road passes clearings and pools ideal for a picnic and a bathe, then becomes increasingly difficult as it ascends to **HAUT'ASCO** (Asco La Neige), a ski station set amidst swaths of lush turf punctuated by stunted pines. Paid for largely by government grants, the unsightly chalet blocks and ski lifts would be more tolerable if they were used regularly, but over the past few years there has been so little snow up here that the station has remained closed. During the summer, however, the place is popular with hikers who come to tackle the ice-flecked crags of the Cinto massif, looming menacingly to the south, and it serves as a major re-provisioning stop for long-distance walkers following the GR20.

Accommodation is provided by the large and impersonal *Le Chalet* (☎04 95 47 81 08, fax 04 95 30 25 59; May–Sept; ①–③), which, in addition to standard chalet-style rooms with balconies, offers budget gîte d'étape rooms. Situated at the head of the valley,

---

Mountain Walks from Haut'Asco

The road up the Asco valley takes you right into the heart of the mountains, and the ski station is a popular springboard for some exceptional high-altitude hiking, most notably the ascent of Monte Cinto. Nearly all of the trails in the area are well frequented and marked every 10m or so with paint splashes, but you should be prepared for sudden and dramatic changes of weather, particularly in August, when electric storms rip across the ridges most afternoons. An IGN **topo-map** of the area is also essential, although you could get by with the Parc Naturel Régional's topo-guide of the GR20, which passes within a stone's throw of the road-head.

A line of broken crags marking the high point of the crest dividing the Niolo and Asco basins, **Monte Cinto** (2706m) is the loftiest, if not the most handsome, mountain in Corsica, and as such attracts greater numbers of hikers than any other peak on the island. Even so, it's a long hard slog to the summit, and you need to be in good shape to complete the climb in a day. The route from Haut'Asco, winding up the massif's wilder north face, is more varied and dramatic than the approach from the south (via the Niolo valley), and is a much better option except in May and early June, when patches of eternal snow clinging to sheltered crevices can be treacherous. A spray-painted rock and regular red spots indicate the way from the ski station car park, from where the trail crosses the Stranciacone torrent, hugging the true right bank before peeling left into the Cirque de Trimbolaccio. Eventually, you arrive at the foot of the gorge leading to the Col de Borba, at the head of the massif, where the trail plunges left into the huge boulder field below the summit. Count on five to six hours for the ascent, and up to four hours for the return trip to the ski station.

Five kilometres south of the station lies the challenge of the **Punta Minuta**, part of the Monte Cinto massif reached via the grandiose Cirque de la Solitude, or you might attempt **Monte Padro**, approached through the Vallée du Stranciacone. Probably the most straightforward option for a day hike, however, is the ascent of the **Muvrella ridge** (Crête de la Muvrella), reached after a two-hour climb up a narrow rock corridor running west from the ski station. From the top, the views are superb, and on a clear day you should be able to pick out the Calvi coast and the needles of the Bonifatu massif. A further thirty minutes will bring you to the little lake on the northwest face of the mountain; allow a good two hours for the descent.

---

the hotel is perfectly placed for high-altitude hikes, lying within easy reach of a number of challenging routes, among them some of the most gruelling stretches of the GR20. If you're **camping**, pull off the road 2km down the valley from Haut'Asco, where the two-star *Monte Cinto* campsite (May–Oct) has fairly level pitches under the pine trees, plus clean toilet blocks and electricity hook-ups for camper vans.

The Niolo

The Niolo – homeland of Corsican freedom, inviolable citadel from which the island's invaders have never been able to expel its mountain folk. This wild trench is unimaginably beautiful. Not a blade of grass, nor a plant; granite . . . nothing but granite.

Guy de Maupassant, *Un Bandit Corse* (1892)

The **Niolo** is the vast basin of the upper reaches of the **Golo**, a river that rises 2000m up in the mountains, is swelled by meltwater from the high peaks of Monte Cinto, Paglia Orba and Capo Tafonato, and expires to the south of Bastia, 80km from its source. The region's name – a corruption of the Corsican *niellu*, meaning "sombre" or "afflicted" – is now more appropriate than ever, for fire has destroyed much of the Niolo's forested land, leaving bleak landscapes of orange granite and shrivelled vegetation. Conifers and chestnut trees scatter the lower slopes of Monte Cinto, but of the great dark forest that once blanketed the whole basin all that remains is the **Forêt de Valdo-Niello**, a majestic swath of Laricio pines in the southwest of the district.

The forest extends east of the frequently snowbound Col de Verghio, the highest mountain pass in Corsica and one of two routes into the Niolo. The other one is the rocky corridor known as the **Scala di Santa Regina**, a vertiginous ravine some 21km long and 300m high, through which a road was built in the late nineteenth century. Until then, people had used hazardous goat and mule tracks (the *scala*) to get into this region, whose isolation and consequent inbreeding perpetuated the singularly tall, blond and blue-eyed appearance of the Neolithic tribes known as the Corsi, from whom the Niolins claim direct descent.

The Niolins have always made their living from the breeding of goats. Shepherds formerly lived a solitary, harsh existence, trekking over the mountains with their herds to the milder coastal plains for winter – mainly to Galéria on the west coast but sometimes as far as Cap Corse – and returning to the high ground with their flocks in summertime. Some of the old, bare stone dwellings still pepper the slopes, but are mostly abandoned these days. In addition, Niolo's craft industry has all but disappeared, though the production of local gastronomic specialities survives: a sharp goats' cheese and some renowned charcuterie, which cures particularly well at this altitude.

Niolo Hikes and Walks

The Parc Naturel Régional recently inaugurated an extensive network of marked footpaths in the Niolo, but by far the most popular mountain hike in the area remains the ascent of **Monte Cinto** (2706m), Corsica's highest mountain, via its southeast face. Although not nearly as dramatic as the approach from the Asco valley (see p.286), this route, boulder-strewn for much of its length, ranks among the island's most frequented trails between mid-June, when the snow melts, and mid-October, when it returns with a vengeance on the high ridges.

To drive as close to the mountain as possible, take the D218 north out of Calacuccia, then turn right along a rough track at the hairpin bend just beyond the hamlet of **Lozzi**, some 6km along. A short way above the village lie two good campsites (reviewed on p.294), from where a motorable dirt track winds via another series of sharp switchbacks to a small car park – the de facto trailhead. Another 35 minutes on foot will bring you to the **refuge de l'Ercu** (1600m), which is open all year but only staffed between July and mid-September. If you're hiking all the way from Lozzi, allow around three hours to reach the refuge. This is where the ascent proper starts, and you should aim to be here shortly after dawn, particularly during the summer, when electric storms and rain frequently force hikers off the mountain by mid-afternoon. The climb to the summit takes between three and four hours, depending on how fit you are, and the views are sublime, taking in both coasts, the Toscan islands and, even on very clear days, the Côte d'Azur and Alps.

For the best views of the Cinto massif itself, however, you have to scale the opposite, southern, side of the Niolo valley. An ancient mule track beginning at the Calacuccia dam cuts up a mountain spur to the **Col de l'Arinella** (1592m), a pass separating the Golo and Tavignano valleys, from which there's a magnificent vista of the surrounding summits. To pick up the trail – a section of the Mare a Mare Nord long-distance footpath – cross the dam and follow the right fork of the road peeling left off the D218. Cutting across the switchbacks, the path (marked with orange splashes of paint) is very steep, especially after the **bergeries de Casartine** (1169m), as it zigzags up to the col. Descend via the same route back to Calacuccia, or continue east to the **refuge de la Sega**, where you can spend the night. From here, the trail follows the Tavignano all the way to Corte, reached in around four hours from the refuge.

The Mare a Mare Nord footpath is detailed on p.275.

A good pair of boots is essential **equipment** for the latter climbs, and you should follow our advice regarding clothing and supplies given on p.25. For the Cinto hike, it's worth investing in a detailed IGN contour **map** of the massif; and if you plan to complete the whole of the Calacuccia–Corte route, the Parc Naturel Régional's topo-guide of the area, available at most tourist offices and bookshops on the island, is invaluable.

If you feel more like a leisurely **low-altitude walk** than a full-on mountain hike, call in at the Calacuccia tourist office for a free copy of the Parc Naturel Régional's excellent *Balades en Corse: Niolu* leaflet (*dépliant*), which outlines five routes (of between 3hr 30min and 7hr) on a monochrome topo-map. Some, like the "Tour des Cinque Frati", involve stiff ascents, but most are leisurely ambles along the valley floor.

The Niolo

Today, though sometimes performed by folk groups, voceri are very seldom heard in their original form.

Corsican Folk Singing

Singing has for many centuries provided a crucial mode of entertainment and expression for the shepherds of poor and remote areas such as the Niolo and, though it is dwindling in its purest form, Corsican song remains an integral part of the island's rich oral tradition.

As recently as the 1960s, remote village streets would still occasionally echo with the wild, searing incantation of the **voceru**, an improvised song by a woman in mourning for a loved one. In the more distant past, when the death of a son or husband often stemmed from a vendetta, the song would register not only the pain of bereavement but also urgency of revenge, aimed at spurring the surviving men to retribution.

Death and separation have also provided inspiration for many shepherds' songs, often sung in the form of the three-part **a paghjella**, a form perhaps dating as far back as the megalithic age. It's performed by three male voices – the first (*a prima*) sets the pace for the chant, the second (*u boldu*) provides the base sound, while the third (*a terza*) sings the mesmerizing melody. Mass used to be sung this way in the more remote churches of the island; today you can hear *a paghjella* at its best at the Santa di u Niolu fair at Casamaccioli.

A third type of singing, known as **chiami e rispondi** (questions and answers), is also an important feature of the Santa di u Niolu. This takes the form of a competition in which two male contestants have to improvise a dialogue in strictly rhyming verse to a repetitive air. They may sing about anything, but it's popular to aim abuse at the assembled company or else proclaim about political issues. The one who first runs out of answers in this battle of wits is the loser.

In the course of this century, the drift of rural populations into the towns and to the French mainland nearly killed off folk singing, but the form enjoyed a dramatic revival during the nationalist upsurge of the 1970s, when young singers such as Jean-Paul Poletti and Petru Guelficci, made a name for themselves performing patriotic songs at political rallies.

Ancient traditions, however, have an extra vitality in the Niolo, and some of the finest *a paghjella* chanting can be heard here (see box below). Improvised singing competitions are still held at Casamaccioli during the three-day **Santa di u Niolu**, a country fair that takes place around September 8.

These days tourism is making itself felt at the far-flung capital of the Niolo, **Calacuccia**, an exposed little place whose basic accommodation makes it a suitable base for exploring the area. Apart from a trip to **Casamaccioli**, you could pay a visit to **Albertacce**, which boasts a small ethnographic museum, to **Corscia**, an impressive stack of hillside hamlets, or to the southeast face of **Monte Cinto**. Southwest of Calacuccia, the glistening **Lac de Nino** makes a rewarding hike from the Forêt de Valdo-Niello, a magnet for walkers and tourists in search of some shade.

Since then, several have formed **folk-rock** groups to spread the national-ist message, mixing modern guitar, keyboard and percussion sounds with traditional harmonies. The most commercially successful of these is the band I Muvrini, who these days play to packed houses in Paris as well as Bastia and Ajaccio, and whose live album, *A Bercy*, topped the island's charts in 1996–1997. Another name to look out for is Les Nouvelles Polyphonies Corses, a five-piece group of young singers who've collabo-rated with musicians from other parts of the world to forge a radically new, ambient reworking of traditional Corsican choral singing. Produced by synth supremo Hector Zazou (of Voix Bulgares fame), their first album was an international "world music" bestseller, while their second offering, *Paradisu*, a collection of sacred music produced by ex-Velvet Underground violinist John Cale, with Patti Smith, looks set to be just as successful.

During the summer months, posters and banners advertise **gigs** by well-known nationalist-oriented bands – such as Chjami Aghalesi and Canta U Populu Corsu – at towns and resorts all over the island, and these are well worth attending. Rooting out pure, traditional *polyphonie* singing, however, can be more difficult. One occasion you're sure to encounter the crême de la crême of Corsican singers is the annual four-day **Rencontres Polyphoniques**, held in Calvi in mid-September. Regular recitals also take place at La Casa Musicale in Pigna, Balagne (see p.126), while during the **Santa di u Niolu** festival, Casamaccioli's village bar bursts at the seams with exponents of most of the island's traditional choral forms. Failing that, splash out on a **cassette** or CD. Recommended titles include *Voce di Corsica: Polyphonies* (Olivi Music/Sony), which features the island's six greatest living male voices recorded in a church in Bonifacio; *A Filetta: Una Terra ci hè* (Olivi Music), with the ethereal singing of Ghjuvan-Claudiu Acquaviva accompanied by traditional instru-ments such as the cittern (*cistre*); and anything by the all-women ensem-ble Donainsulsa (Silex/Auvidis), whose renditions of old *voceri* and laments are sublime.

Calacuccia and the Niolo villages

A clutch of grim grey buildings, **CALACUCCIA** benefits from its unusual location – set high on a wide plain at the heart of the Niolo, in the shadow of the weird jagged ridge of the Cinque Frati moun-tains. West of the village stretches the Lac de Calacuccia, a large reservoir built in 1968 to supply Bastia and the eastern plain. Bathing and sailing on the lake are forbidden, and locals insist the water has caused undesirable climatic changes in the valley – notably an increase in mist and humidity – but its rippled surface, shimmer-ing with reflections of snowy peaks, is an undeniably beautiful sight. The only historic monument here is the white-painted Église de St-Pierre, built on an eminence at the western exit from the village and affording a fine view across the plateau; inside, a seventeenth-centu-ry wooden statue of Christ forms the principal attraction. The main

The Niolo

reason visitors come to the village, however, is to access the network of trails that crisscross the surrounding mountainsides, affording wonderful views of the colossal massifs to the north and south.

Calacuccia practicalities

During the summer, Calacuccia is served by daily **buses** from Corte and Porto via the Col de Verghio. Timetables for this service, operated by Autocars Mordiconi (☎04 95 48 00 04), are available at the village **tourist office**, 200m east of the centre on the Corte road (mid-June to Sept Mon–Fri 8am–noon & 2–7pm, Sat 8am–noon; ☎04 95 48 05 22). This is also a good place for advice on hiking, climbing and kayaking in the area, and they can put you in touch with qualified mountain guides.

For more on the role of song in the Corsican vendetta, see p.292.

If you're after a **room**, the *Hôtel des Touristes*, in the centre of the village (☎04 95 48 00 04; ③), is a welcoming place despite its drab, grey façade, and has a popular restaurant. A posher option is *L'Acqua Viva*, overlooking the lake as you leave the village on the road to Col de Verghio (☎04 95 48 06 90, fax 04 95 48 08 82; ④); its dozen rooms are well appointed, with en-suite bathrooms and balconies, and the views of the mountain and lake are superb. Hikers generally stick to Calacuccia's two **gîtes d'étape**: *Chez José Albertini*, 3.5km west in Albertacce (☎04 95 48 05 60; ③), and *Couvent St-François-di-Niolu*, 2km west, near the museum (☎04 95 48 00 11; ③). Both enjoy scenic, quiet locations, and offer rooms in addition to dormitory beds. The two best **campsites** in the area – *Camping U Monte Cintu* (☎04 95 48 04 45) and *L'Arimone* (04 95 48 00 58) – lie next door to each other at the trailhead of the Monte Cinto hike, in the hamlet of Lozzi, 5km west. The latter also has a handful of inexpensive rooms, and a basic pizzeria. For classier **food**, try the *Auberge du Lac*, 2km west of the village along the road that skirts the lakeside, which enjoys a near-perfect location on the water's edge, and serves authentic Niolo cuisine at reasonable prices; set menus range from 75–130F, with home-made charcuterie and local cheeses featuring prominently.

Around Calacuccia

Occupying the greenest part of the Niolo, **CASAMACCIOLI** lies south of the lake in the middle of a chestnut forest. Its small square, edged by enormous chestnut trees, is the setting for the **Santa di u Niolu** (see box on p.292), Corsica's most important religious festival, when thousands of pilgrims and expatriate natives descend on the village to celebrate the Nativity of the Virgin. The focal point of the event is a statue of the Madonna, **Santa Maria della Stella**, which miraculously transported itself here by mule in the fifteenth century after the convent in which it originally resided was burned down by Turkish pirates. Now venerated for her miracle-working powers, she is carried in procession through the village, but the most visually

Forêt de Valdo-Niello Hikes

Southwest of Calacuccia the D84 follows the river into the **Forêt de Valdo-Niello**, where Laricio pines, some of them 500 years old, grow to a height of 40m. From the **maison forestière de Poppaghia**, 10km from Calacuccia, trails branch off deep into the forest in all directions, providing a choice of wonderful forest walks and hikes to high pasture lands. The area is not covered on the Parc Naturel Régional's *Balades Crose: Niolu* leaflet, so you're advised to shell out on an IGN **topo-map**, available at the tourist office in Calacuccia and Porto.

The most classic route hereabouts winds from the maison forestière to the beautiful **Lac de Nino**, a high-altitude lake reached in a hard three-hour hike from the road. The trail, marked with yellow splashes of paint, follows a mountain stream up to the **bergeries de Colga**, a gathering of stone shacks just above the tree line (1411m), then on – more steeply – up to the **Col de Stazzona** (1762m), between Monte Tozzo (2007m) and Punta Artica (2327m). At the top of the pass there's a weird scattering of black, pointed rocks known as the **Devil's Oxen** – the story goes that the Devil was challenged by St Martin to plough a straight line and, upon failing, his oxen were turned to stone. The Devil hurled his ploughshare in a rage through the distinctively shaped red mountain known as **Capo Tafonato** (Pierced Mountain), visible on the opposite side of the valley. It's only fifteen minutes further to the lake, which from June to September is thronged with flocks of sheep and goats. The surrounding marshy turf declivities, known as *pozzi* (meaning "wells"), are the remnants of lakes gouged by glaciers which subsequently filled up with sediment. To get back to the maison forestière, you can either retrace your steps (allow 5hr for the round-trip), or else follow the GR20 path marked with red and white paint splashes across the slopes of Monte Tozzu until it meets up with the Forêt de Valdo-Niello round-route, which takes you back to the Colga valley, and thence through the pines to the road.

The other recommended hike in the forest is a much easier two-hour round trip to the **Cascades de Radule**, where the River Golo, which has its source high up on Paglia Orba, plunges through a series of waterfalls, forming perfect natural pools. Marked with red and white splashes, the trail (one of the rare easy-going stretches of the GR20), starts at the hairpin bend in the D84 known as *Fer à Cheval* (Horseshoe), 4km below the Col de Verghio. After around thirty minutes you emerge from the pine trees at the **bergeries de Radule**, from where the path descends to the river and falls. The GR20 proper continues north, winding up the stream valley, and is well worth following for another couple of hours as far as the **refuge Ciuttulu di i Mori** (1962m), the usual night halt for mountaineers attempting Paglia Orba.

striking feature of the festival is the famous **Granitola**, when dozens of white-robed and -hooded penitents, drawn from the village's various religious brotherhoods, or *Cunfraterna*, wind and unwind in spirals around a cross (a similar procession takes place in Calvi; see p.107). La Santa has a strongly secular aspect too. Formerly, the event, held at the end of the first week in September, provided the main opportunity of the year for Niolites from remote villages to buy, sell and barter; in exchange for wool, meat, milk, cheese and charcuterie, they would obtain hardware, hats, horse tack, woodcarving from Castagniccia, textiles, shoes and anything else that could not be manufactured in the mountains. Gambling was also central, and remains so to this day, with serious round-the-clock card sessions held in unlicensed home casinos. Afterwards, the participants celebrate, or drown their sorrows, in the village bar – one of the few places in Corsica where you can still hear traditional improvised singing, or *chiami e respondi* (see box on p.292). Outside festival time, however, the only noteworthy sight here is the small **Église de la Nativité**, where you can pay your repects to the crudely repainted and gold-crowned Santa Maria della Stella herself, and enjoy magnificent views of the Cinto massif to the northwest.

Three kilometres west of Calacuccia, **ALBERTACCE**'s row of little cottages makes an interesting contrast with the fortress houses found throughout the rest of the island – people hereabouts thought the mountains were protection enough against uninvited guests. If you knock at the last house on the right coming from Calacuccia, you'll be let into a small folk museum, the **Musée Archéologique Licinoi** (June–Sept Mon–Fri 10am–noon & 2–5pm, Sat 10am–noon; free), where the exhibits include shepherds' implements and clothes, plus some evil-looking knives.

Heading through the village, if you take a left up the D318 around the base of the Monte Cinto massif you'll come to **CALASIMA**, the highest inhabited village in the Niolo, giving a splendid view of the great valley from amid its goat enclosures.

A cluster of high-altitude hamlets 3km northeast of Calacuccia, **Corscia** warrants a visit for its phenomenally steep terraced houses and for the traditional Corsican dwellings – complete with high exterior staircases – in **Costa**, the uppermost hamlet, standing at 900m.

Corte and around

Stacked up the side of a wedge-shaped crag, against a spectacular backdrop of brooding granite mountains, **CORTE** (Corti) encapsulates the essence of *l'âme corse*, or "Corsican soul" – a small town marooned amid an unforgiving landscape, where a spirit of dogged defiance and patriotism is never far from the surface. This has been the home of Corsican nationalism since the first National Constitution was drawn up here in 1731, and was also where **Pascal Paoli**, "U Babbu di u Patria" (Father of the Nation), formed the island's first democratic government later in the eighteenth century. Self-consciously insular and grimly proud, it can seem an inhospitable place at times, although the presence of the island's only **university** lightens the atmosphere noticeably during term-time, when the bars and cafés lining its long main street fill with students. For the outsider, Corte's charm is concentrated in the tranquil **ville**

haute, where the forbidding **Citadelle** presides over a warren of narrow, cobbled streets. Immediately behind it, the Restonica and Tavignano gorges afford easy access to some of the region's most memorable mountain scenery, best enjoyed from the marked trails that wind through them.

A sprinkling of cafés and restaurants in the town provide a spark of life all year round, and the local **cinema** is also a popular meeting place, screening new films and boasting a hi-tech bar. The busiest time of year comes at the end of August, when Corte hosts the **Ghjurnate di U Populu Corsu**, a seven-day celebration of Corsican culture that has become a meeting place for separatists from all over Europe.

A brief history of Corte

Corte's reputation for belligerent independence was born in the ninth century when the occupiers of the strategic post allegedly saw off a group of Saracen raiders. Later on, the Genoese rulers were constantly harried by the local nobles, culminating in 1419 with the takeover by **Vincentello d'Istria**, the king of Aragon's viceroy. After Vincentello's execution in 1434, Genoa ruled relatively undisturbed until the French expedition of 1553, when Corte happily succumbed to Sampiero Corso, though within six years the Genoese were back in charge, and were to stay in control for a long time.

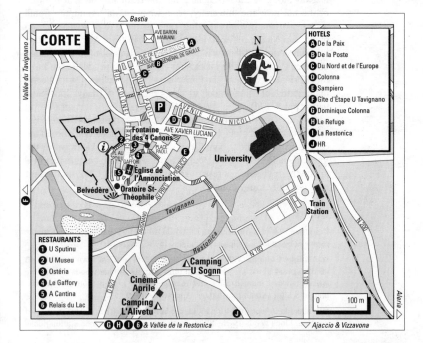

By the early eighteenth century, Corsican nationalism was on the rise in Corte, its success due in part to the town's isolation from the occupied coastal towns. Following a local insurrection in 1731, a National Constitution was drawn up here at the first National Assembly, and in 1752 Gaffori was elected head of state in Corte. After Gaffori's assassination in 1753, Pascal Paoli returned from exile and from 1755 to 1769 made Corte his centre of government. His revolutionary government set up the first Corsican printing press and the **Università di Corsica**, the first university to be established on the island.

However, in 1768, under the terms of the Treaty of Versailles, France bought Corsica from the Genoese, and after the battle of Ponte Nuovu in the following year the period of Corsican independence was at an end. Under the French the town became insignificant, and it's only recently that it has acquired a slightly more exalted status as *sous-préfecture* of Haute-Corse and as the seat of the revived university, whose aims are to re-establish the value of Corsican culture, partly through the compulsory teaching of the indigenous language.

Arrival, information and accommodation

Buses stop in the centre of town on cours Paoli, the main street, and halfway along av Xavier-Luciani, but the **train station** is at the foot of the hill near the university, from where it's a ten-minute uphill walk into town. If you're **driving**, the best place to park is at the top of av Jean-Nicoli, the road leading into town from Ajaccio. Pending the completion of the new museum, Corte's **tourist office** is situated on place Paoli (daily May–Oct 9am–noon & 2–6pm), while the helpful information office of the Parc Naturel Régional lies just inside the main gates of the citadel in the *ville haute* (daily June–Sept 9am–1pm & 4.30–7pm; ☎04 95 46 27 44).

Finding a **accommodation** shouldn't be too difficult – there's not an abundance of hotels, but there are some inexpensive places in the centre of town, and a handful of more upmarket hideaways in the Vallée de la Restonica, 2km out of town. The nearest **campsites** lie a kilometre or so south across the river bridges, with *U Sognu* the best of a generally ropey bunch.

Hotels

Colonna, 1–3 av Xavier-Luciani (☎04 95 46 01 09). Basic but comfortable rooms above a local-oldies-only bar, slap in the centre of town. ②–③.

Dominique Colonna, Vallée de la Restonica, 2km south of town (☎04 95 46 09 58, fax 04 95 61 03 91). A posh three-star set in pine woods next to the stream. Owned, named after and managed by a retired football star who bought it after winning the lottery. April–Oct. ③–④.

HR, allée du 9-Sept (☎04 95 45 11 11, fax 04 95 61 02 85). This converted concrete-block gendarmerie, 200m southwest of the SNCF train station, looks

grim from the outside, but its 125 rooms are comfortable enough and its rates reasonable; bathroom-less options are a good deal. ②–③.

Du Nord et de l'Europe, 22 cours Paoli (☎04 95 46 00 68). Pleasant, clean place right in the centre. The variously priced rooms are basic but huge, and the building has oodles of old-style charm, with a marble-floored entrance hall and high stucco ceilings. ②–③.

De la Paix, 1 av Général-de-Gaulle (☎04 95 46 06 72). Large, smart and central, in an elegant part of town. Closed winter. ③.

De la Poste, 2 place Padoue (☎04 95 46 01 37). The cheapest rooms in the centre, in a huge old building that opens onto a quiet square just off the main drag. ②.

Le Refuge, Vallée de la Restonica, 2.5km southwest of town (☎04 95 46 09 13, fax 04 95 46 22 38). Cosy, unpretentious hotel-restaurant at the roadside, with rooms overlooking the stream (the rearside ones are a touch noisy in spring, but fine in summer), and a sunny terrace. Good half-board deals. Advance booking essential. ③–④.

La Restonica, Vallée de la Restonica (☎04 95 46 20 13, fax 04 95 61 15 79). Sumptuous comfort in a modern, riverside hotel with a pool, 2km southwest of town. Very popular in summer, so book in advance. April–Oct. ④.

Sampiero Corso, 1 av Président-Pierucci (☎04 95 46 09 76, fax 04 95 46 00 08). Sixties-style modern block, with spectacular views from the balcony. April–Sept. ③.

Hostels and campsites

Gîte d'Étape U Tavignanu (Chez M. Gambini), behind the citadel (☎04 95 46 16 85). Run-of-the-mill hikers' hostel with small dorms and a relaxing garden terrace that looks over the valley. Peaceful, secluded, and the cheapest place to stay after the campsites. Follow the signs for the Tavignano trail (marked with orange spots of paint) around the back of the citadel. 80F per bed.

L'Alivetu, faubourg St-Antoine (☎04 95 46 11 09). One of two sites to definitely avoid (the other is the *Batho* behind the citadel): crowded, noisy and with dirty toilet blocks.

U Sognu, route de la Restonica (☎04 95 46 09 07). At the foot of the valley, a 15min walk from the centre. Has a good view of the citadel, plenty of poplar trees for shade, and a small restaurant. Recommended.

U Tavignanu, chemin de Balini, Vallée du Tavignano (☎04 95 46 16 85). The hiker's option: a tiny site next to the gîte d'étape of the same name, only accessible on foot. Follow the road around the back of the citadel, cross over the river bridge and bear right; the site lies another 10min walk up a path.

The town

Corte is a very small town whose centre effectively consists of one long street – **cours Paoli** – with almost all the town's banks, shops and cafés, and far too many cars. This thoroughfare runs alongside the **ville haute**, which is reached by climbing one of the cobbled ramps on the west side of the cours or by taking the steep rue Scoliscia from place Paoli.

At the north end of the *cours* lies **place du Duc-de-Padoue**, an elegant square of nineteenth-century buildings that's strangely out of place in this rough mountain town. Its statue, a grim bronze lump by Bartholdi, designer of the Statue of Liberty, is of Arrighi di Casanova, a general whose service under Napoléon earned him the title of Duke of Padua; his ancestral home can be seen in **place Poilu** in the *ville haute*. Apart from this square, there is only one spot where you might want to hang around: **place Paoli**, at the southern end of the main street in the lower town, a more tourist-friendly zone packed with cafés, restaurants and market stalls, surrounding a cumbersome and self-satisfied statue of Paoli.

The ville haute

Place Gaffori, the centre of the old **ville haute**, is dominated by a statue of General Gian'Pietru Gaffori pointing vigorously towards the church in the midst of the square's restaurant tables. On the base of the statue a bas-relief depicts the siege of the Gaffori house by the Genoese, who attacked in 1750 when Gaffori was out of town and his wife Faustina was left holding the fort. Faced with weakening colleagues, she is said to have brandished a burning torch over a barrel of gunpowder, threatening to blow herself and her soldiers to smithereens if they surrendered, a threat that toughened them up until Gaffori came along with reinforcements. The house stands right behind, and you can clearly make out the bullet marks made by the besiegers.

Opposite the house, the **Église de l'Annonciation**, built in 1450 but restored in the seventeenth century, is where Joseph Bonaparte, Napoléon's brother and future King of Spain, was christened. Inside, there's a delicately carved **pulpit** and a hideous wax statue of St Theophilus, patron of the town, on his deathbed. The saint's birthplace – behind the church in place Théophile – is marked by the **Oratoire St-Théophile**, a large arcaded building which commands a magnificent view across the gorges of Tavignano and Restonica. Born in 1676, Blaise de Signori took the name of Theophilus upon entering the Franciscan brotherhood, and went on to study in Rome and Naples, then to found numerous hermitages in Italy. In 1730 he returned to Corsica, where, after a few years' activity in the fight for independence, he died on May 9, 1740. He was canonized in 1930, the only Corsican to achieve sainthood, and on the anniversary of his death a commemorative Mass takes place in the oratory, followed by a procession from the Chapelle Ste-Croix, carrying a huge figure of Christ.

For the best view of the citadel, follow the signs uphill to the viewing platform, aptly named the **Belvédère**, which faces the medieval tower, suspended high above the town on its pinnacle of rock and dwarfed by the immense crags behind. From here you can also admire the vista of the converging rivers and encircling forest – a summer bar adds to the attraction.

In **place du Poilu**, the forecourt to the citadel, is the house of the di Casanova family, where Napoléon's father – a friend of the Casanovas – lived in 1768, employed as secretary to Pascal Paoli. When the patriots were defeated by the French, Carlo and his wife Letizia were forced to flee, escaping across the mountains to Ajaccio on muleback.

At the gates to the citadel stands the **Palais Nationale**, a great, solid block of a mansion that's the sole example of Genoese civic architecture in Corte. Having served as the seat of Paoli's government for a while, it became the **Università di Corsica** in 1765. Run by Franciscan monks, it offered free education to all (Napoléon's father studied here), and the enlightened monks taught the contemporary social thought of philosophers such as Rousseau and Montesquieu as well as traditional subjects such as theology, mathematics and law. The university closed in 1769 when the French took over the island after the Treaty of Versailles, not to be resurrected until 1981. Today several modern buildings have been added and it houses the Institut Universitaire d'Études Corses, dedicated to the study of Corsican history and culture.

Tickets for the **Citadelle** (daily April–Oct 9am–7pm; 10F) are sold at a signposted hatch just below the Belvédère, where you can get a free map. The only such fortress in the interior of the island, it served as a base for the Foreign Legion from 1962 until 1984, but now houses a rather feeble exhibition of nineteenth-century photographs. When this book was researched, work on the long-awaited museum of Corsican history was well underway in the citadel. However, the project is some two years behind schedule, and probably won't be open to the public until the summer of 1998.

The citadel proper is reached by a huge staircase of Restonica marble, which leads to the medieval tower known as the **Nid d'Aigle** (Eagle's Nest) situated at its highest point. The fortress, of which the tower is the only original part, was built by Vincentello d'Istria in 1420, and the barracks added during the reign of Louis Philippe. These were later converted into a prison, in use as recently as World War II, when the Italian occupiers incarcerated Corsican resistance fighters in the tiny cells. Adjacent to the cells is the **échauguette**, a former watchtower which, at the time of Paoli's government, was inhabited by the hangman. This was a job no Corsican would take – accustomed to killing with guns and knives, they found the practice of hanging someone to death too demeaning and dishonourable. A Sicilian duly volunteered, and in 1766 James Boswell visited the poor wretch: "a more dirty rueful spectacle I never beheld," he wrote of the despised man he found cowering in the turret, with a "miserable bed and a little bit of fire" as his only comfort.

To complete a tour of the *ville haute*, take the steps to the left as you leave the citadel, crossing rue Colonel-Feracci to arrive at the **Fontaine des Quatre-Canons**, once the water supply for all the

houses in the vicinity. From here you can either descend to the *cours*
or carry on down rue Colonel-Feracci for a look at the sixteenth-century **Chapelle Ste-Croix**, notable for its lavish Baroque interior and
its floor of Restonica marble.

Eating and drinking

Corte has a fair number of **restaurants** and more casual eating
places, with the usual sprinkling of pizzerias and crêperies, nearly all
of them on cours Paoli. Place Gaffori is the only place in the *ville
haute* with restaurants, most of which are locked in stiff competition, offering bargain 55F menus to pull in the punters. Local specialities are **trout** and **lasagna with wild-boar sauce**, but if you just
want a snack you could go to the pizza van parked opposite *Café de
France* in place Padoue. The **bars** of cours Paoli are strictly for pos-
ing; place Paoli has three cafés – it is more touristy but at least you
can sit and drink in comfort. Students favour the bar of the **cinema**,
the white building on the road to Restonica just outside the centre of
town, next to the entrance to the *Alivetu* campsite.

Cafés and bars

Bip's, on the square behind cours Paoli, facing av Xavier-Luciani. Cavernous
bar with a small stage that hosts live music most nights, starting at 10.30pm.
The bands are very ordinary rock cover outfits, and there's a stiff 30F cover
charge, but this is as lively as Corte gets.

Café de France, junction of cours Paoli and place Padoue. Pleasant café with
leafy forecourt.

De la Place, place Paoli. On the shady side of the main square, this is the most
popular spot for crowd-watching, and a late-night watering hole for the locals.

Restaurants

A Cantina, 20m south of place Gaffori, towards the Belvédère. Artisanal charcuterie and cheeses served in an attractive stone cellar, with a tasting counter
and shop upstairs. Pricy, but unbeatable quality.

Le Gaffory, place Gaffori. Among the least expensive places in town, with 55F
menus and loads of omelettes, salads and spaghetti.

U Museu, rampe Ribanelle in the *ville haute*, at the foot of the citadel, 30m
down the rue Col-Feracci. Congenial, efficient and well situated, with plenty of
choice on its mixed set menus. Try the 75F *menu corse*, featuring lasagna in
wild-boar sauce, trout, and *tripettes* (imaginatively translated as "trips").
Moderate.

Osteria, 20m from the place Gaffori, off rue Col-Feracci. A cosy little bistro
whose particularly good value economy menu includes *cannelloni al brocciu*,
served in a cavernous room with a vaulted stone ceiling, or on a sociable terrace.

Relais du Lac, Pont de Tagone, Vallée de la Restonica, 10km southwest of
Corte (☎04 95 46 16 85). A good way out of town, but this is a wonderful spot
to round off a day's hiking, with tables beside a rushing stream and topnotch

local cuisine, served alfresco, or inside the wooden cabin. Book ahead in summer.

U **Spuntinu**, rue des Deux-Villas. Filling portions of tasty, traditional and inexpensive Corsican cooking, such as fresh pasta and meat grilled over a wood fire. Evenings only, from 8pm.

Listings

Banks and exchange All the main banks are on cours Paoli; the Société Générale stands midway along, and changes French Franc travellers' cheques free of charge.

Bookshop Maison de la Presse, 22 cours Paoli. Good selection of books about Corsica, and occasional English-language newspapers.

Bus information Ollandini, 2 av Xavier-Luciani (☎04 95 46 02 12).

Car rental Europcar, 9 cours Paoli (☎04 95 46 02 79); Hertz, c/o Cyrnea Tourisme, 9 av Xavier-Luciani (☎04 95 46 24 62).

Hospital av du 9-Septembre (☎04 95 46 05 36).

Mountain- and motorbike rental Scoot'air Location, place Paoli (☎04 95 46 01 85), rents 50cc and 100cc scooters for 200–300F per day (plus a 4000F returnable credit or bankers' card deposit), and mountain bikes for 100F per day.

Pharmacies Several on cours Paoli.

Police 4 av Xavier-Luciani (☎04 95 46 04 81).

Post office av du Baron-Mariani, off place Padoue.

Taxis Taxis Corte (☎04 95 46 07 90 or 04 95 61 01 41).

Train information At the SNCF station (☎04 95 46 00 97).

Travel agents Corte Voyages, 14 cours Paoli, next to the gendarmerie (☎04 95 46 00 35); Cyrnea Tourisme, 9 av Xavier-Luciani (☎04 95 46 24 62).

Around Corte

The **Gorges du Tavignano**, virtually on the town's doorstep, offer an exhilarating hike from Corte but are only accessible on foot. The less energetic can simply drive southwest to the **Vallée de la Restonica**. A torrent of jade-green water punctuated with enormous boulders, the Restonica is followed closely by the road out of Corte, which comes to a stop within striking distance of the stunning **Lac de Melo**, the **Lac de Capitello** and **Monte Rotondo** – a sprawling mountain that may not be much to look at from a distance but is a superb sight close up, with its ring of crags encircling a cluster of blue glacial lakes.

Gorges du Tavignano

A deep cleft of ruddy granite 5km to the west of Corte, the **Gorges du Tavignano** offer one of central Corsica's great walks, marked in yellow paint flashes alongside the broad cascading River Tavignano. You can pick up the trail, a stage of the Mare a Mare Nord long-distance footpath (covered in more detail on p.275), from the bottom of rue Col-Feracci, below the citadel, and follow it as far as the Col de l'Arinella, some 30km west of the town, where it drops into the Niolo valley. There's a **refuge**, *A Sega*, situated 15km along the route, but check first at the tourist office to make sure it's open, as nationalist terrorists blew the place up in 1995.

From the trailhead, an old mule track steadily climbs the steep left bank of the river across a bare hillside scarred with the remains of old farming terraces. Massive rocks, fringed by dense vegetation, border the river below, which you can scramble down to in places for a secluded swim. Some 5km into the walk, the gorge proper begins and the scenery becomes wilder, with bare rock faces surging up on each side and boulders cluttering the path. Passing through patches of dense maquis interspersed with evergreen oak and chestnut trees, you gradually rejoin the river, crossed at the **Passarelle de Rossolino** footbridge after around 2hr 30min. Once you're on the true right bank, the mountainside grows steeper as the path skirts the **Ravin de Bruscu**, then winds gently along the stream to the refuge, reached after 5hr 30min from Corte. From here, you can press on the next day over the **Col de l'Arinella** pass (1592m), which affords one of the best views of Cinto massif and Paglia Orba, or return by the same route to Corte (a 4hr hike). Either way, you should invest in an IGN contour **map** of the area, available at the Parc Naturel Régional office in Corte (see p.298), and at the bookshop mentioned in "Listings", p.303.

The hike from Calacuccia to the Arinella pass is described on p.291.

Vallée de la Restonica

Forming a deep cleft between the barren wastes of the Rotondo massif and the cloud-swept Plateau d'Alzo, the **Vallée de la Restonica** is lined with some of the most spectacular glacier-moulded gorges in the Mediterranean – a riot of twisted granite cliffs lapped by thick Laricio pine forest and a translucent green torrent. Unfortunately, it is also among the few motorable routes into the wild heart of the Corsican watershed, which, along with its proximity to Corte, means the entire 15km stretch from town to the *bergeries* de Grotelle gets hideously congested in high summer. Avoid the area completely between July and early September, or else take it in from the marked forest trail that winds all the way to the *bergeries* along the riverbank.

The **gorges** begin after 6km, just beyond where the route penetrates the **Forêt de la Restonica**, a glorious forest of chestnut, Laricio pine and the tough maritime pine endemic to Corte, recognizable by its conical shape. Not surprisingly, it's a popular place to walk, picnic and bathe – the many pools fed by the cascading torrent of the Restonica River are easily reached by scrambling down the rocky banks.

The **bergeries de Grotelle**, 15km from Corte, mark the end of the road, with an outsize car park that barely accommodates the summer

Hike to Monte Rotondo and the Lac d'Oriente

A jagged topped arc of granite splashed with small blue lakes, **Monte Rotondo** (2622m), Corsica's second-highest mountain, looms southwest of Corte at the head of the Restonica valley. The peak can be scaled from two directions, but the most common approach is from the north, via the beautiful Lac d'Oriente. Though technically straightforward between July and late September, this route is a long hard slog involving 3360m of ascent and descent, much of it across steep and boulder-choked terrain. Don't consider attempting it unless you're in good shape and properly equipped (see p.28), and check the weather forecast carefully before you set off. Of the many hikers that tread the Rotondo trail during the summer, most only aim to reach the lake, a rewarding round trip (4hr 30min) in itself.

The **trailhead** lies 11km up the Restonica valley, 700m beyond the Tagone bridge (where the road crosses from the north to the south side of the gorge) – look for the red spray-painted sign on a rock to the right. From here, a wide forestry track strikes steeply up the side of a stream valley, zigzagging through fragrant pine woods to the **bergeries de Timozzo** (1hr 15min), where it levels out briefly before climbing a long ridge. Follow the red and yellow splashes of paint rather than the cairns (which mark a less well-defined path that gets lost in maquis), crossing the stream near the head of the valley.

Enfolded by the Rotondo massif, the **Lac d'Oriente** (2hr 30min) is a great place to picnic before pressing on to the summit. From here, the trail, which restarts at the south side of the lake, is marked every 10m or so by cairns; as long as you keep close to these, the ascent across the moraine that follows is safe and enjoyable. However, things get a little trickier towards the top, where patches of snow and ice can be hazardous, particularly during early summer (an ice axe or snow stick is recommended if you're attempting this route before August); keep an eye out, too, for loose rocks, as these can be lethal for anyone ascending below you. The last stretch of the climb is a very steep clamber up a narrow corridor; patches of ice are more common on the left side of this, so pick a route up the right (sunnier) side. From the **ridge** (4hr 15min), drop down slightly to the left and follow the cairns to a cleft that leads up the the crow's-nest **summit** (4hr 30min). On a clear day, the views from the top are sublime, taking in all of the island's major peaks, both coasts, the shores of Tuscany and, if you're lucky, the distant Alps. If you have an all-season sleeping bag, it is possible to bivouac in the tiny tin-roofed **Helbronner refuge** just below the summit and enjoy the spectacle at dawn.

Return by the same route, or down the south side of the mountain, via the beautiful **Lac de Bellabone**, to the **Petra Piana refuge**. Note that times given in this account do not take into account rest breaks; allow total of eight hours for the round trip to the top from the Restonica valley and back (5hr 15min ascent and 2hr 45min descent), and aim to start walking by 7am, which will get you to the summit well before the clouds blister up around 2pm.

crowds. From here, a well-worn path winds along the valley floor to a pair of beautiful glacial lakes. The first and largest, **Lac de Melo**, is reached after an easy hour's hike through the rocks. One particularly steep part of the path has been fitted with security chains, and some visitors freeze with vertigo halfway up, causing queues, but the scramble around the side of the passage is perfectly straightforward, and much quicker. Once past Lac de Melo, press on for another forty minutes along the steeper marked trail over a moraine to the second lake, **Lac de Capitello**, the more spectacular of the pair. Hemmed in by vertical cliffs, the deep turquoise-blue pool affords fine views the Rotondo massif on the far side of the valley, and in fine weather you can spend an hour or two exploring the surrounding crags, scoured by rock pipits. Beyond here, the trail climbs higher to meet the GR20, and should only be attempted by experienced and well-equipped mountain walkers.

South of Corte

The main road south of Corte slices into the heart of the Corsican mountains, tracked by the railway through Venaco, Vivario, Vizzavona and Bocognano – a rattling ride that's worth taking even if you have your own vehicle. East from **Vivario** there's an incredible drive through the **Forêt de Rospa-Sorba** to **Vezzani**, while to the southeast lies **Ghisoni**, a mountain base dominated by the peaks of **Kyrie-Eleison** and the craggy **Monte Renoso**. You have a choice of spectacular exits from Ghisoni: east through the **Défilé de l'Inzecca**, a thrilling short cut down to the eastern plain; or south along the zigzagging route to **Col de Verde**, offering incredible views of the peaks. South of the col, **Zicavo** gives access to **Monte Incudine**, the southernmost high peak of the island.

Back on the N193 and the rail line, **Vizzavona** lies at the highest point of the road before its descent to Ajaccio. A beautiful forest lies on one side of this small mountain resort, and the great dome of **Monte d'Oro** looms to the west, but for the best view of this peak you should head down to **Bocognano**, about 7km from the Col de Vizzavona.

Accommodation is very limited in these parts, with the odd hotel at Vezzani, Vivario and Vizzavona.

Corte to Vivario

Immediately south of Corte you ascend into a landscape of lush chestnut forests that lasts as far as the **Col de Bellagranjo** (723m), 9km along the route and just beyond **SANTO PIETRO DI VENACO**. This appealing hamlet has a fine hotel called *Le Torrent* (☎04 95 47 00 18; June–Oct; ③), a stylishly old-fashioned place with a restaurant tucked beneath a tree-shaded terrace by the river. Also in the village is a pleasant **gîte d'étape** (☎04 95 47 07 29; ①–③), a night halt on the Mare a Mare Nord (*variante*) footpath, where you can opt for dorm beds or more comfortable chambre d'hôte accommodation.

A couple of kilometres south of Santo Pietro the road sweeps through **VENACO**, an elegant village of rusty buildings emerging

The Mare a Mare Nord trail and its variant is outlined on p.275.

South of
Corte

Hikes in the Venachese

The mountainous region south of Corte, known as the **Venachese**, was once an important corridor for transhumant pastoralists, who would drive their flocks through here en route between *a piaghja e a muntagna*, "the plains and the mountains". Some of the old trails used by the shepherds have recently been cleared and marked by the Parc Naturel Régional. Six round routes of varying length and difficulty feature in their excellent leaflet *Balades en Corse: Venachese*, which you can pick up at the park office in Corte, and in most tourist offices. For an easy four-hour ramble, try the route from Venaco village to **Pont de Noceta**, which passes a couple of pleasant bathing spots and old dry-stone grain storage huts known as *aghja*. More experienced walkers have a choice of *boucles sportives* (strenuous routes), such as the steep five-hour climb from Venaco to the **Uboli ridge** via the **bergeries de Tatarala**. In settled weather, the park leaflet, which includes a black-and-white contour **map** of the area with the trails marked on it, is adequate for reference as the paths are all regularly marked with splashes of orange paint.

---

from deep-green verdure on the slopes of Monte Padro. You might want to halt here to admire the **vistas** – from the terrace of the Baroque church there's a spectacular view of the lower Vallée du Tavignano in the east – or to **hike** one of the Parc Naturel Régional's waymarked trails mentioned earlier (see box above). Four routes start from, or near, the village, the most challenging being the path straight up the mountain to the Uboli ridge, via the *bergeries* de Tatarellu. Venaco also harbours one of the area's few good **campsites**, the *Camping Peridundellu* – take the D43 towards the Tavignano valley and you'll see it after 4km on your right (☎04 95 47 09 89; April–Oct). It's very cosy, with room for a couple of dozen tents, and **chambre d'hôte** accommodation is available (by reservation only) in the modern farmhouse nearby.

About 5km south of Venaco the road passes the **Pont de Vecchiu**, an arched stone bridge over the River Vecchiu and under the iron bridge designed by Gustave Eiffel in 1888, putting the final touches to the Bastia–Ajaccio rail line. The river's gorge is dominated by **VIVARIO**, a large but innocuous village located 22km south of Corte, at the junction of the routes to the Forêt de Rospa Sorba and the Col de Verde. Straddling a nexus of the area's principal long-distance footpaths, Vivario makes a good base if you're planning to hike in the area. Most visitors arriving by train head straight for the small *Hôtel Macchje e Monti* (☎04 95 47 22 00; ③), but a better place to stay if you have your own vehicle is *U Sambuccu*, 11km further east (for a review of this hotel see p.308).

Vivario's attraction lies in its forest setting, a savage environment that once supported its own **wild man**, dubbed by folk chroniclers as *un Mowgli corse*. In 1800 a 10-year-old boy went missing here after an argument with his parents, and he stayed missing for twenty years, until a group of hunters ensnared him by the Vecchiu. The unfortunate soul was carted off to be reunited with his parents but, unable to adapt to his new life, he perished after a few months. The only traversable spot across the Gorge du Vecchiu, a three-hour walk west of Vivario, is a three-metre jump still known as the **Saut du Sauvage**, or "Wild Man's Leap". Vivario's other claim to fame is as the birthplace of the infamous **Bartolomeo brothers**, who were abducted by pirates here in the sixteenth century, and went on to lead highly eventful lives. Shipwrecked off the coast of Italy, they escaped the clutches of their Saracen captors and swam to safety at Talamona on the Tuscan shore, where they subsequently settled. The elder of the two, later known as Bartolomeo de Talamone, rose to become an admiral in the local navy, and used his position to exact revenge on the pirates who had kidnapped him in his youth, ruthlessly pillaging the Mytilena region of Algeria, home of the Dey of Algiers – the Red Beard, or Barba Rossa, of pirate legends. It is said that the sultan was so incensed at Bartolomeo's behaviour that he attacked Talamona in 1544, only find his adversary dead and buried, whereapon he exhumed the Corsican's corpse and burned and scattered what was left by way of retribution. The other brother, Bartolomeo de Vivario, eventually returned home from Talamona and worked for the Genoese for a while, before defecting to Sampiero Corso's side in the wars of independence, in the course of which he was mortally wounded.

If you feel like a **short walk** from Vivario, head 1km south of the village to the **Fort de Pasciolo**, an evocative ruin beside the N193. Set in a wild site facing a great circle of peaks, and overlooking the deep gorge of the Vecchiu, the fort was built around 1770 by the French, and was transformed into a prison to incarcerate the rebels of Fiumorbo (see p.262).

Vivario to Vezzani

East of Vivario, the D343 follows a tree-lined route around the side of Punta Muru mountain, passing through **MURACCIOLE**, where the view forms a pleasant prelude to the awe-inspiring panorama from the **Col de Morello** (824m), 2km north of the hamlet. From here, a rewarding half-hour walk goes to the **Occhio-Vario**, a rocky eminence providing an even more exceptional viewpoint – a narrow goat track leads north of the col to the point, which is marked by a white granite monument.

After the col the road penetrates the **Forêt de Rospa-Sorba**, a glorious forest of Laricio pines and chestnut trees. Distant snowy peaks most of the year feature all along the meandering road, which swoops in a semicircle towards **VEZZANI**. Fantastically located under the high ridge of Punta di a Ringhella, this mountain village has a couple of **hotels**, of which the best is *U Sambuccu*, 3km south on the Pietrosi road (☎04 95 43 03 38; ③). Set deep in the pine

Monte Renoso

The easiest and most popular ascent of **Monte Renoso** (2352m) is up the
north side, a relatively easy nine-hour circular walk from the Campannelle
refuge. You get to the refuge by following the D69 south of Ghisoni for
about 6km as far as the Pont de Casso, where you turn right onto an exces-
sively windy road that traverses the **Forêt de Ghisoni**, a dense forest of
pines, beech and alders. The refuge – once a shepherd's hut – lies 500m
west of the spot where the road comes to an end, next to a makeshift ski
station that rarely sees enough snow to function.

From here the track is marked with cairns, leading off to the southwest
across the stream beneath the ski lift. Passing the idyllic **Pizzolo springs**,
the track skirts the west shore of the Lac de Bastiani, a grey expanse of
water framed intermittently by snowdrifts, before following the ridge to
the **summit**. Here you'll be treated to one of Corsica's most amazing views
– the panorama embraces the whole of the south of the island, taking in the
Golfe d'Ajaccio and Golfe de Valinco on the west coast, and extending
even as far as Sardinia. If you carry on south along the waymarked track,
past the Punta Orlandino, you'll gain the **Col de Pruno** (2262m) in another thirty minutes or so. From here the path descends to the **bergeries des
Pozzi**, then strikes east to the Plateau de Gialgone, after which it joins the
GR20, which shoulders Monte Renoso around the east side and brings you
back to where you started.

woods, the hotel has comfortable en-suite rooms with views over the
valley and forest, and an excellent **restaurant** where you can enjoy
local mountain cuisine, such as home-made charcuterie, goat stew
and wild boar, at reasonable prices. This is also one of the few places
in the region that stays open all year round.

Vivario to Ghisoni

Just 1km south of Vivario the D69 cuts steeply east to the **Col de
Sorba** (1311m), from where the panorama is stunning: in the foreground rise the needles of Kyrie-Eleison; to the north of the road the
rail line can be made out, winding through the crags to Venaco; and
to the south extend the forests of Pietro Verde and Marmano, with a
towering backdrop formed by Monte d'Oro and the pale grey bulk of
Monte Renoso. Continuing south, the deteriorating and narrowing
route descends through the forest to **GHISONI**, about 7km from the
col. This large village, nestling in a vast hollow on a tributary of the
River Fiumorbo, is dominated by the Renoso massif, and most of the
people than come here do so to climb the peak (see box above). The
only **hotel** is the unsightly mustard-coloured *Kyrié*, close to the centre of the village (☎04 95 57 60 33; ③). It's an unexciting place, but
the rooms are clean (the cheaper ones on the top floor enjoy the best
views of the valley) and there's a cosy, unpretentious little bar-
restaurant. Your only other option for food is *U Sampolu*, a down-
to-earth *ferme-auberge* 8km east across the river (☎04 95 57 60

18; daily except Mon April–Oct), where a full four-course meal will set you back around 100F. Renowned locally for its fresh mountain cuisine, this place does a brisk trade in the summer, in spite of its off-track location, so if you want to eat here phone ahead for a table.

Hugging the sinuous Fium'orbo River, the road running **east from Ghisoni** plunges steeply downhill through the **Défilé des Strette** gorge, affording spectacular views of the two peaks on the far side of the valley: **Kyrie** (1535m) and **Christe Eleison** (1260m). It was at the foot of these mountains that the last group of **Giovanalanis**, devotees of a breakaway Franciscan sect whose rituals were rumoured to include mass orgies, were massacred at the behest of Pope Urban V in 1362. Hounded to this remote spot, they were captured and bound for burning, but just at the point when the wood was to be set alight, an old priest took pity on the heretics and administered their last rites. The assembled crowd is then said to have taken up the last line of the prayer – *Kyrie eleison, Christe eleison* – which echoed through the gorge and across the mountains, giving the peaks the names by which they are known to this day. Further east, the main road skirts the Sampolo reservoir before penetrating the spectacular **Défilé de l'Inzecca**, a sheer trench slicing the coastal range. The gorge forms a little-frequented short cut from the interior to the fertile eastern plains, and after the shattered rock formations, cuttings and tunnels marking the road, the lush orange groves and vineyards around Ghisonaccia come as something of a shock.

For coverage of Aléria and Ghisonaccia, the two east coast settlements nearest the mouth of the Défilé de l'Inzecca, see p.263.

To Zicavo

South of Ghisoni, the narrow D69 wriggles up the slopes of the higher Fiumorbo valley, through the Forêt de Marmano, arriving after 12km at **Col de Verde** (1289m), where the Fiumorbo and Taravo valleys almost meet. An **auberge** at the top provides refreshments, and there is room to park your car if you plan to head off along one of the superb forest **trails** that pass through here. Among the most popular of these, for which you need to be properly equipped and dressed, is the one leading to the **sites des Pozzi**, a string of high-altitude lakes gouged from the slopes of Monte Renoso. A section of the GR20 footpath, the route is marked at regular intervals by splashes of red and white paint. Using the indispensable IGN **map** of the area, follow these west from Col de Verde to **Col de la Flasca**, and thence through the **Vallon de Marmano**, site of some immense pine trees, the largest of which towers to 55m and is thought to be the tallest in Europe. Around an hour and a half from the Col de Verde, you arrive at a clearing, the **Clairière de Gialgone**, where you should turn left off the GR20 and follow the orange waymarks up to the **bergeries des Pozzi**. Beyond here the trail emerges to patches of open marshy ground scattered with lakes and winding water courses interconnecting at different levels. Allow roughly two-and-a-half hours for the

Monte Incudine

The massive four-kilometre-long hump of **Monte Incudine** (2136m) is crenellated by numerous peaks, the highest of which can be climbed in a hard ten-hour round-trip from the **San Petru refuge**, to the southeast of Zicavo. You get to the refuge by turning onto the D428 from the D69 about 10km south of the village, then driving some 5km through the **Forêt du Coscione**, a beautiful expanse of beech trees carpeting the lower slopes of the Punta di Sistaja. From San Petru refuge, where you can leave your car, it's a straightforward climb, following the road south for 7km as far as the Col du Luana (1805m), where the route turns sharply south and you pick up the GR20 trail, waymarked in red and white paint. Three kilometres after the col the route becomes steep and crosses some difficult gullies choked with loose rock, but the view of the Bavella needles from the summit's cross makes the exertion worthwhile. Walkers following the GR20 onto the Col de Bavella might want to make use of the **Asinao refuge**, a short way down the south face of Incudine, above the Asinao stream; after that, the next resting point is the auberge at the col itself (see p.224).

ascent and an hour and a half for the walk back down by the same path.

The road north from Col de Verde is very narrow and crumbling as it heads down through the gorgeous Laricio pines of Forêt de San-Pietro-di-Verde and the adjoining Forêt de St-Antoine to ZICAVO, 20km from the pass. Lined by lofty granite buildings, Zicavo's main street rings with the sound of babbling streams channelled through the village centre to some of the densest chestnut forests on the island, roamed by inordinate numbers of semi-wild pigs. Well off the beaten tourist trail, the unspoilt landscape around Zicavo is riddled with hiking trails, making this an ideal base for excursions into the mountains that ring the valley, among them Monte Incudine (see box above). You've a choice of two **hotels**, both with **restaurants**: the *Tourisme*, in the centre of the village (☎04 95 24 40 06; ③), is a simple, modern and inexpensive place that does good food; and the *Florida*, just north of the village on the Col de Verde road (☎04 95 24 43 11; May–Sept; ③, or ④ per person for half board), has a dozen large en-suite rooms, a popular restaurant and views over the valley.

Vizzavona and around

Monte d'Oro dominates the route south of Vivario to **VIZZAVONA**, about 10km away. Shielded by trees, the village is invisible from the main road, so keep your eyes peeled for a couple of tracks on the right, one of them signposted for the train **station** – the place where the bandit Bellacoscia surrendered to the police at the age of 75 (see p.313). Marking the midway point of the GR20, which here makes a rare descent to road level, Vizzavona gets crowded with hikers during the summer, and those on a modest budget are well catered for with a handful of places offering **gîte d'étape** and chambre d'hôte accommodation. Top of this range is *Le Modern*, near the station (☎04 95 47 21 12; ②), which has a mix of hotel rooms and small dormitories. Directly opposite the station, *Resto-Refuge-Bar "De la Gare"* (☎04 95 47 21 19; ①), one of a handful of simple bar-restaurants, is cheaper and more basic, and very convenient if you're arriving by train. Even in high season, a bed can usually be found a little way out of town at the huge *Monte d'Oro*, situated in the hamlet of LA FOCE, deep in the forest 3km south along the main road (☎04 95 47 21 06; ③). With its period furniture and fittings, *fin-de-siècle* feel and magnificent terrace looking out onto the mountain, this ranks among the most congenial hotels in the area.

For **campers**, there's the small and well-shaded site of *Savaggio*, 4km north of the village on the N193 (☎04 95 47 22 14), which also offers inexpensive gîte d'étape-style dorms. Arriving by train, ask to be dropped at the request stop just before (north of) Vizzavona, which is closer to the site than the main village station.

Forêt de Vizzavona

A glorious forest of beech and Laricio pine, the **Forêt de Vizzavona** is the most popular walking area in Corsica, thanks to the easy access by main road or train. A lot of people come here to tackle the ascent of Monte d'Oro (see box opposite), but there are many less demanding **trails** to follow. One of the most frequented of these is the walk to the **Cascade des Anglais**, which is connected to Vizzavona by a marked trail but is more commonly approached from La Foce, 3km south of the village. Some 200m down the hill from the hamlet, you turn left onto a forest road that plunges towards the river. Here the waymarked GR20 leads to a waterfall where the River Agnone crashes into emerald green pools, providing excellent bathing spots.

Less than 1km west of La Foce lies the highest pass on the Ajaccio–Bastia road, the **Col de Vizzavona** (1163m), which is usually jammed with picnickers, most of whom take a postprandial stroll along one of the various short walks laid out from here. Fifteen minutes south of the col along the forest trail you come to a magnificent **viewpoint** over the forested peaks, with the ruins of the Genoese **Fort de Vizzavona** prominent on a rise in the valley below. You can reach the fort itself in just fifteen minutes along a wide path north of the picnic tables. A walk to **La Madonnuccia** – a mound of scrambled rocks that's supposed to look like the Virgin – takes about thirty minutes from the col, following the trail signposted "Bergeries des Pozzi", which branches off southeast. Another marked path from the col takes you to the **Fontaine de Vitulo**, the source of the Foce stream, which joins the River Gravona further down the mountain.

To get the best out of the forest, though, you should walk to **Col de Palmente** (1460m), a relatively strenuous four-hour there-and-back hike along the GR20 from the maison forestière just south of

Monte d'Oro

The fifth-highest peak on Corsica, **Monte d'Oro** (2389m) offers one of the most rewarding hikes on the island, the view from its summit taking in all the island's principal peaks – Cinto, Rotondo, Renoso and Incudine – as well as Ajaccio to the west and the Tuscan islands beyond the east coast. However, it's a difficult ascent which should on no account be attempted by the inexperienced, and is best tackled during the summer, though you're still likely to encounter snow on the highest slopes.

There are two ways of getting to the summit from Vizzavona. The easier takes about three hours from the **Cascade des Anglais**, following the GR20 along the River Agnone past the bergeries de Portetto **refuge**, then veering off up a steep rocky gradient to the **Col du Porc** (2159m), about 1km west of the main peak. The alternative route, marked with yellow paint flashes, takes four hours from Vizzavona, traversing the ravine of the **Ghilareto** and the **Speloncello valley** before wheeling round up the north face. A narrow corridor known as the *scala* presents a hazardous final approach to the summit.

Vizzavona on the main road. The path winds through magnificent woodland before rising to the col, which affords fantastic views of Monte Renoso and the Forêt de Vizzavona.

Bocognano

From the Col de Vizzavona, the route winds southwards for 6km before reaching the appealing ochre cottages of **BOCOGNANO** (Bucugnanu). Set on a plateau amidst a chestnut forest, the village gives a perfect panorama of Monte d'Oro's pale-grey needles, and is well placed for walks to the **Cascade du Voile de la Mariée**, where the River Gravona crashes from a height of 150m in a series of cascades. The best approach to the falls is 3km along the main road south of Bocognano, just before the Pont de Vitiluccia, from where they're a thirty-minute walk. Another worthwhile stroll from the village is to **La Clue de la Richiusa**, where the stream surges through 60m cliffs, emerging at a chain of beautiful deep pools. Further upstream lies the so-called **Glacier de Busso**, site of what is reputedly Corsica's only eternal snow; avalanches collect and compact so tightly here during the winter that they are able to endure the spring melt. To pick up the trail to the falls, follow the signs for the restored chestnut mill (*moulin*) and cross Gravona via the footbridge near the electricity substation car park.

Bocognano is indissolubly associated with Antoine and Jacques **Bellacoscia**, born here in 1817 and 1832, fathered by a man who earned the family surname – meaning "beautiful thigh" – by also fathering eighteen daughters by three sisters with whom he lived simultaneously. Antoine, the elder son, took to the maquis in 1848, having killed the mayor of the village after an argument over some land. With his brother he went on to commit several more murders in full view of the hapless gendarmes, yet remained at liberty thanks to the support of the local population. In 1871 Jacques and Antoine managed to gain a safe pass into Ajaccio to organize an expedition to fight for the French in the war with Prussia. They returned from the war with their reputations restored, and took up residence in the family home, from where they continued to flaunt the law. In 1888 the police finally succeeded in ousting them from their house, which was converted into a prison. Antoine eventually surrendered at Vizzavona station on June 25, 1892, whereupon he was acquitted and exiled to Marseille in true Corsican tradition. The fate of Jacques is unknown.

Travel details

TRAINS

Bocognano to: Ajaccio (4 daily; 50min); Bastia (4 daily; 3hr); Calvi (2 daily, via Ponte Leccia; 4hr 15min); Corte (4 daily; 1hr 15min); L'Île Rousse (2 daily, via Ponte Leccia; 3hr 45min); Ponte Leccia (4 daily; 1hr 50min); Venaco (4 daily; 1hr); Vivario (4 daily; 40min); Vizzavona (4 daily; 15min).

Corte to: Ajaccio (4 daily; 2hr); Bastia (1hr 45min); Bocognano (4 daily; 1hr 15min); Calvi (2 daily; 3hr); L'Île Rousse (2 daily; 2hr 30min); Ponte Leccia (4 daily; 40min); Venaco (4 daily; 15min); Vivario (4 daily; 30min); Vizzavona (4 daily; 1hr).

Ponte Leccia to: Ajaccio (4 daily; 2hr 40min); Bastia (4 daily; 1hr 10min); Bocognano (4 daily; 50min); Calvi (2 daily; 2hr); Corte (4 daily; 35min); L'Île Rousse (2 daily; 1hr 15min); Venaco (4 daily; 15min); Vivario (4 daily; 35min); Vizzavona (4 daily; 1hr).

Venaco to: Ajaccio (4 daily; 1hr 45min); Bastia (4 daily; 2hr); Bocognano (4 daily; 1hr); Calvi (2 daily; 3hr 20min); Corte (4 daily; 15min); L'Île Rousse (2 daily; 2hr 50min); Ponte Leccia (4 daily; 45min); Vivario (4 daily; 15min); Vizzavona (4 daily; 45min).

Vivario to: Ajaccio (4 daily; 1hr 30min); Bastia (4 daily; 2hr 20min); Bocognano (4 daily; 40min); Calvi (2 daily; 3hr 50min); Corte (4 daily; 40min); L'Île Rousse (2 daily; 3hr); Ponte Leccia (4 daily; 1hr 10min); Venaco (4 daily; 20min); Vizzavona (4 daily; 25min).

Vizzavona to: Ajaccio (4 daily; 1hr); Bastia (4 daily; 2hr 45min); Bocognano (4 daily; 15min); Calvi (2 daily; 4hr); Corte (4 daily; 1hr); L'Île Rousse (2 daily; 3hr 30min); Ponte Leccia (4 daily; 1hr 10min); Venaco (4 daily; 40min); Vivario (4 daily; 20min).

BUSES

Corte to: Ajaccio (2 daily; 2hr); Bastia (2 daily; 2hr); Calacuccia and the Niolo (1 daily; 1hr 10min); Porto (1 daily; 2hr 30min).

Ponte Leccia to: Haut'Asco* (2 daily; 1hr).

*Summer only

Contexts

The Historical Framework

Invasion and resistance are recurring themes throughout Corsica's history. This has always been an island of particular strategic and commercial appeal, with its sheltered harbours and protective mountains, set on the western Mediterranean trade routes within easy reach of several colonizing powers. Greeks, Carthaginians and Romans came in successive waves, landing on the eastern coast, driving native Corsicans into the high interior and battling against new predators in their turn. The Romans were ousted by Vandals, and for the following thirteen centuries the island was attacked, abandoned, settled and sold as nation-states and empires squabbled over Europe's territories, and generations of islanders fought against foreign rule and against each other. In the light of this turbulent past, it seems inevitable that Corsica's early history, unexplored until this century, should have its own pattern of invasion and occupation.

Beginnings

For thousands of years the relics of Corsica's **Stone Age** were simply accepted as an inexplicable aspect of the island's landscape. In 1840 Prosper Mérimée, then Inspector of Historic Monuments, described the simple **menhirs** (from the Celtic maen hir – "long stone") of the southwest and tabulated various primitive stone monuments elsewhere in Corsica, but the origins and functions of these stone slabs and figures

remained unknown until 1954, when French archeologist Roger Grosjean set about excavating and recording the megalithic sites. Only when his excavations started in earnest did a picture emerge of a complex prehistoric society that developed its religious and cultural framework over several millennia.

The First Settlers

It's now believed that Corsica's **original inhabitants** arrived from northern Italy in the **seventh millennium BC**, long before the monument-building era. Making their shelters in caves and under cliffs, they survived by hunting, gathering and fishing. A thousand years later came new settlers with new skills, building villages, planting crops and herding cattle. The practice of **transhumance** – driving sheep to graze on the uplands in summer, then down to coastal pastures in the winter – may have been started in this era, and was followed by Corsican shepherds almost to the present. In the **fourth millennium**, the creators of the island's **megalithic** buildings migrated into the Mediterranean area from Asia Minor and the Aegean. There are numerous interpretations of the stone monuments and tombs that were erected during the next 2000 years, but the most widely held opinion is that they were connected with the veneration of ancestors and the spirits of the dead, and perhaps centred on an Earth Deity or Mother.

At first the dead were buried in underground tombs or **cists**, and were represented, commemorated or maybe guarded by single menhirs placed nearby. Clusters of these tombs and menhirs have been found in the southwestern Sartenais region and near Porto-Vecchio. Cist burial later gave way to the custom of setting stone sarcophagi or **dolmens** (table stones) above ground and covering them with earth; about a hundred of these, measuring about 2m by 2.5m, have been discovered (now exposed after the erosion of the soil), one of the best examples being at **Fontenaccia**. At a later stage the menhirs acquired human forms and features: some were given swords or daggers, some were carved with rudimentary shoulder blades or ribs, and no two statues were the same. The function of these eerie warrior figures, most of which were found at **Filitosa**, can only be imagined. Suggestions range from representations of dead spirits to trophies of war, each one marking a defeated invader.

The Torréens

The culture embodied by these carved menhirs reached its peak towards 1500 BC, when new aggressors – portrayed, perhaps, by the stone warriors – landed in the south and made their first base near Porto-Vecchio. Naming this civilization the **Torréens**, after the dry-wall **torri** (towers) they raised in various parts of the island, Roger Grosjean posited that they were the same people as the sea-going Shardana who are known to have attacked Egypt in the late second millennium BC, and that the bronze weapons with which they subdued the islanders were the weapons depicted on the sword-bearing menhirs of Filitosa.

Their towers, each one built around a central cavity with smaller chambers to the sides, were found to contain remnants of fires, and may have been used to cremate the dead or even sacrifice the living. Fragments of the earlier, Neolithic structures, perhaps destroyed as the Torréens advanced along the island, were incorporated in their walls. Grosjean has traced the invaders' progression to the west, as they drove the megalithic natives further into the interior and finally to the north, where the natives were left to pursue their own beliefs and practices in peace. Stone menhirs were still being created in northern Corsica as the Iron Age got under way, centuries after the Torréen invasion, while in the south of the island – according to Grosjean – rivalry between Torréen settlements precipitated another migration, this time south to the island of Sardinia.

Greeks, Romans and Saracens

In 565 BC Corsica's first major colony was founded at Alalia (Aléria) by Greek refugees from **Phocaea**. For a few decades these settlers made a successful living, planting vines and olive trees and enjoying a brisk trade in metals and cereals, but within thirty years they were fighting off an invading fleet of **Carthaginians** and **Etruscans**. By 535 BC, devastated by their losses in battle, the Greeks had abandoned Alalia to the Etruscans, who in turn were briefly succeeded by Carthaginian settlers in the third century BC.

By now Corsica had attracted the attention of the **Romans**, who sent in troops under the command of Lucius Cornelius Scipio in 259 BC. The indigenous islanders, enslaved or driven into the mountains by each successive invading power, joined forces with the Carthaginians and their leader Hanno to resist Roman occupation. Although the east coast was soon conquered and settled, it took another forty years before Corsica (together with Sardinia) could be brought within Roman administration, and another century of rebellion passed before the island's interior was overpowered.

For over 500 years Corsica remained a province of the Roman Empire. A string of ports was established along the south coast – subsequently flattened by invasion and malaria – and a settlement built at **Mariana**, to the south of present-day Bastia, though Aléria remained the largest settlement. From the third century AD onwards, **Christianity** was introduced to the island and bishoprics were established at Mariana, Aléria, the Nebbio, Sagone and Ajaccio.

This comparatively stable period in Corsican history came to an end as the Roman Empire disintegrated and the **Vandals** started to harass the coast. By 460 AD the Vandals were established on the island, only to be defeated by Belisarius and his Byzantine forces in 534, but absorption into the Byzantine empire did little to protect Corsica from the Ostrogoths and later from the **Lombards**, who managed to annex Corsica in 725 – by which time the coastal settlements were suffering frequent raids by the Saracens (or Moors). In 754 Pépin the Short, King of the Franks, agreed to hand Corsica over to the **papacy** once it was free of the Lombards; when the Lombards were driven out twenty years later, Pépin's son, Charlemagne, honoured the promise.

Within thirty years of its transfer to papal sovereignty, parts of Corsica were being overrun by the **Saracens**. These invaders retained their grip for another two centuries, despite the brief triumph of **Ugo della Colonna**, reputedly a Roman aristocrat sent to "liberate" the island by Pope Stephen IV, but more likely a semi-legendary figure based on Count Boniface of Lucca, who gained a foothold on the island in 825, building the fortress of Bonifacio on its southern tip.

Whatever the facts may be, Ugo della Colonna became a useful point of reference for the local Corsican families, who began to assert their authority as the Moors retreated under pressure from an allied force of Pisans and Genoese at the start of the eleventh century. During the Saracens' rule the native islanders had been confined to the interior, where they had developed a system of administration based on mountain communities, with elected leaders who took every opportunity to make their status hereditary. This period saw the rise of such mighty clans as the **della Rocca** and **Istria** families, the dominant dynasties among the feudal lords known as the **Cinarchesi**, most of whom claimed descent from Ugo della Colonna. As their feuds and rivalries intensified, some swore allegiance to the pope, who in 1077 placed Corsica under Pisan protection; others turned for support to the Genoese, who claimed their own right to the island.

The Pisan Period

In 1133 Pope Innocent II split Corsica's bishoprics between Pisa and Genoa, an action that did nothing to stem the enmity of the two republics. For two centuries, while Corsica remained **officially governed by Pisa**, the Genoese stayed on the offensive, capturing Bonifacio in 1187 and Calvi in 1268. Nevertheless, the Pisans were able to impose a framework of government built around the local parish or *pieve*. A massive programme of church-building got under way, each church providing the focus for its *pieve*, which in turn linked several village communities.

In the meantime, the Corsican nobles continued to flex their muscles. **Sinucello della Rocca**, a vassal of Pisa who held lands in the southwest, took advantage of the running dispute with Genoa and made his own bid for power, taking arms against other Corsican nobles and switching his loyalties between Pisa and Genoa as necessary. He eventually gained control of almost the whole island, drawing up a constitution and earning the name **Giudice** (Judge) for his sense of justice, but his success had made him few friends, and the rival *signori* soon turned against him. When Genoa defeated the Pisan fleet at **Meloria in 1284** and finally took control of the island, della Rocca retreated to his original base in the southwest and was eventually betrayed by his own illegitimate son. Captured by the Genoese, he died in prison in 1306.

The Genoese Period

Despite **Genoa**'s decisive victory at Meloria, the republic's struggle to control Corsica was by no means over. In 1297 the island, along with Sardinia, was handed by Pope Boniface VIII to the **Kingdom of Aragon**, setting off yet another territorial war – one which was to rumble on for two hundred years more. While Genoa held fast against Aragonese attempts to realize their claim to Corsica, the *signori* continued to fight it out among themselves. A people's revolt led by **Sambocuccio d'Alando** drove out the battling nobles of the northeast, and led to a political split between two areas of the island. In the northeast, the area known as *Diqua dai Monti* ('This Side of the Mountains'), the ancestral lands were taken over by village communities to form the **terra di commune**, officially protected by the Genoese, who founded and fortified Bastia in 1380. The southwest – *Dila dai Monti* – remained the **terra dei signori**, ruled in effect by the Cinarchesi, who looked to the more distant power of Aragon for support.

Generations of *signori* kept up a relentless effort to bring the whole island under their rule. Backed by Aragon, **Arrigo della Rocca** gained considerable successes against the Genoese in 1376, and then his nephew, **Vincentello d'Istria**, gained control of most of the island as viceroy of the King of Aragon from 1420 until 1434, when he was captured by Genoese forces and publicly beheaded. In 1453, in a bid to overcome such ambitious nobility, Genoa put Corsica into the hands of the **Bank of Saint George**, a powerful financial corporation with its own army. For ten years the Bank imposed a tough military government, building a series of coastal watchtowers, restoring battered fortifications and containing the fractious warlords.

Sampiero Corso

Events in Europe brought this era to an end: **Henry II of France**, at war with Charles V, struck a blow against the Habsburg emperor's Genoese allies by sending a fleet to capture Corsica. Leading the invasion was mercenary **Sampiero Corso**, who took possession of the entire island except Calvi and Bastia. French rule lasted all of two years, before Corsica was passed back to Genoa under the Treaty of Cateau Cambresis in 1559. Corso, however, was rather less inclined to relinquish his supremacy, and led a successful uprising against the Genoese in 1564, again securing control of most of the island. He was finally defeated by a vicious Corsican custom –

the **vendetta** – according to which any act of violence or dishonour had to be avenged by the victim's relations. Corso was murdered in 1567 by the brothers of his wife Vannina d'Orso, whom he had strangled in the belief that she had betrayed him to his Genoese enemies. His killers were heftily rewarded by the Genoese.

Genoese Consolidation

In the late **sixteenth century** the Corsican population was reeling from years of war, pirate attacks, famine and malaria. The Genoese republic, now governing the island directly, was finally able to impose an administration of sorts. A governor was installed in Bastia to oversee the network of provinces and parishes, leaving local government to the Corsican communities and their assemblies (*consulta*). Attempts were even made to clamp down on the vendetta, but with no success – hundreds of murders were committed each year in the name of honour.

Nevertheless, in comparison with the previous pattern of civil war and invasion, the 170 years of direct Genoese rule were relatively peaceful. Corsicans enjoyed a certain degree of freedom to run their own affairs, and the rural economy developed and prospered – factors that were eventually to undermine the Genoese supremacy. Influential families, beneficiaries of the boom in agricultural trade, formed an articulate and ambitious new class. Excluded from the top ranks of government and resentful of Genoa's trade monopolies and high taxes, they provided the leadership for a Corsican society growing in political maturity and aspirations. Circumstances came to a head in the early eighteenth century, when discontent exploded into armed rebellion.

The Wars of Independence

The hated Genoese taxes were the trigger for **revolt in 1729** when, having suffered a series of failed harvests, one village near Corte refused to pay. Its defiance developed into a full-scale uprising and the reinforcements sent in to suppress it were soon overpowered. Rebellion spread quickly across the island and was formalized in **1731**, when a popular assembly declared **national independence**, adopting a constitution and forming a parliament with a representative from each village. The Genoese, besieged in their coastal fortresses, turned for help to Emperor Charles VI, who responded with six battalions which helped

recapture St-Florent and Algajola from the insurgents. Under pressure from the emperor's troops, the Corsicans agreed to a settlement in 1732, winning several concessions from the Genoese, including access to public office.

The fighting resumed as soon as the emperor's soldiers had withdrawn but the rebels made little progress, being short of resources and blockaded by a Genoese fleet. Salvation arrived in 1736 in the bizarre form of **Theodor von Neuhof**, a Westphalian adventurer brought up in the French royal court, who had spotted in Corsica's chaos an opportunity for glory. Having persuaded Tunisian financiers to back his venture, von Neuhof sailed into Aléria with ample supplies of money, arms and ammunition. The rebels had little choice but to accept his offer of support and they crowned him **King of Corsica**, though his authority was severely restricted by a new constitution, an executive council and an elected legislature. King Theodor's reign lasted eight months, by which time a lack of military success and depleted funds had provoked the hostility of many Corsicans; in November 1736 their monarch left the island, promising to find new allies.

Still the Corsicans and Genoese were in stalemate, each side unable to raise enough funds or forces to influence events decisively – until, in 1738, Genoa appealed to Louis XV of France and received several regiments commanded by the Comte de Boisseux. The following year, after the deployment of a further detachment of French troops, a thousand Corsicans were forced to flee the island. Among the refugees was **Giacinto Paoli**, one of the first leaders of the revolt, who went into exile in Naples with his teenage son Pascal.

The French pulled out of Corsica in 1741 but before long the major European powers were fighting over the island again, hoping for a strategic advantage in the War of the Austrian Succession. A British fleet carrying Austrian and Sardinian troops joined forces with the Corsican patriots, who elected **Gian'Pietru Gaffori** their commander. The 1748 Treaty of Aix-la-Chapelle marked an end to British involvement in the struggle, but the Corsicans continued their campaign, drawing up a new constitution in 1752. Gaffori led a determined drive against the Genoese, eventually capturing their stronghold at Corte, despite the fact that his son had been abducted and held hostage within the city walls. His heroic reputation among the Corsicans was matched by that of his wife, who prevented her household from surrendering to enemy troops by threatening to light a barrel-load of gunpowder and blow them and herself to smithereens.

Paoli's Independent Corsica

The rebels lost their dynamic commander in 1753, when Gaffori was assassinated, and in 1754 **Pascal Paoli**, son of the exiled Corsican leader, was called back to Corsica to take over leadership of the rebellion.

Paoli returned with a keen sense of constitutional theory and a thorough political education. Having been elected leader of the nation in 1755, he introduced a constitution according to which every man over 25 had a vote and every parish could send representatives to the public Assembly, which in turn elected an executive council of state. Paoli himself was in charge of military and foreign matters, but all other policies required the Assembly's agreement. Rapid steps were taken to boost the islanders' flagging morale and pitiful resources: schools were built and a university was founded in Corte; a mint and a printing press were established; mines and an arms factory were put into production. The death penalty was rigorously enforced for vendetta killings, which finally began to decline. Under Paoli's command the Corsican patriots and their enlightened system of government found admirers among the liberals and radicals of Europe. Jean-Jacques Rousseau toyed with the idea of moving to the island and writing its history; James Boswell came to meet Paoli and sang his praises in his journal of the visit, published in 1768.

In the meantime, events were overtaking the Corsicans. French forces occupied five coastal towns in 1764, and in **1768** the **Genoese ceded their rights** to the island, selling their claim to France under the Treaty of Versailles. An invading force landed within a month of the treaty's being signed, taking possession of Cap Corse. Paoli's men – and women – kept up the pressure, hiding out in the maquis and launching guerrilla attacks on the French, but when a new detachment of troops was sent in there was little hope for the Corsicans, who suffered a terrible defeat at the battle of **Ponte-Nuovo** in May 1769. Pascal Paoli was obliged to flee to England.

French Rule to the Twentieth Century

Though sporadic resistance continued even after Paoli's departure, Corsica was brought fairly painlessly within the monarchy as a Pays d'État, with its own biennial gathering of churchmen, nobles and commoners. As part of its programme of assimilation, the French offered Corsica's noble families scholarships to its prestigious military schools. Among the successful applicants was the son of Paoli's ex-secretary – **Napoléon Bonaparte**.

During the twenty years of rule by the French monarchy, the drive for independence gradually subsided, and when the revolutionaries ousted Louis XVI in 1789, Corsica urged the Assembly to make the island a fully integrated part of the French state. The royal ban imposed on political exiles was lifted, and Paoli returned to be elected President of the Corsican Conseil-Général. His authority was at first accepted by the Paris Convention, but soon Paoli fell out of favour after a Paris-instigated campaign to conquer Sardinia ended in failure. When it became known that Paoli was to be arrested, the Corsican Assembly came to his defence, naming him **Father of the Nation**. Paoli's supporters turned on the French and pro-French on the island; the Bonaparte family, who had long since transferred their loyalty to France, left their Ajaccio home to the looters and were hastened to Toulon by Napoléon, by then serving in the French army.

The Anglo-Corsican Interlude

Aware of the superior strength of French forces, Paoli called on his old English allies for help, and in 1794 **Sir Gilbert Elliot** arrived with reinforcements who quickly captured St-Florent, Bastia and Calvi (where Nelson lost an eye). In return for this intervention, Britain demanded a stake in the island's government, and in June **1794** an **Anglo-Corsican kingdom** was proclaimed.

To the bitter disappointment of Paoli and his supporters, Sir Gilbert was made viceroy of the new kingdom, with the power to dissolve parliament, nominate councillors and appoint the highest officers of state. When the Corsican members of parliament responded by electing Paoli their president, Sir Gilbert threatened to pull out his troops, and they were forced to back down. A series of riots followed, and a nervous Sir Gilbert persuaded the king to exile Paoli once again – this time for good. But the damage was already done: Paoli loyalists joined the French in their attacks on British soldiers and in September 1796 Sir Gilbert and his troops sailed away, leaving the island to be retaken by France.

The Napoleonic Era and its Aftermath

Apart from a brief stay in Ajaccio in 1799, **Napoléon** paid scant attention to his homeland during his period of power. A number of uprisings on the island during the 1790s were put down with brutal force, and opposition to Napoleonic rule led to widespread revolt by an alliance of Royalists, Paolists and British supporters in 1799. This, too, was stamped out and its leaders executed. In 1801 the constitution was suspended and Général Morand arrived to administer a harsh military rule. His reign of terror lasted until 1811, when the almost equally unpopular Général César Berthier took his place. In the same year the island was made a single *département* of France (it had been divided into two in 1796), with its capital in Ajaccio. Resistance to the French continued, and in 1814 the citizens of Bastia appealed to Britain to intervene on their behalf. A detachment of British troops was sent, but in April of that year Napoléon abdicated and the soldiers were recalled.

After 1815 and the **restoration of the French monarchy**, the governing state made some attempts to develop the island's economy, opening mines and foundries, setting up a railway, introducing an education act, and building roads and schools. But most of their schemes had little success, and Corsica remained a marginal and largely neglected part of the French economy. For Corsicans, the real opportunities lay in France, and young islanders began to turn away from the old villages, seeking their careers and education on the mainland. The romance and drama that visitors such as Edward Lear and Prosper Mérimée discovered in mid-nineteenth-century Corsica veiled a grim picture of poverty, malaria and violence – the vendetta, though on the decline, was still claiming up to 160 victims a year. In the last half of the century **emigration** surged so dramatically that within sixty years the population had been halved.

The Twentieth Century

In 1909, as a result of a commission set up by Georges Clemenceau, French Minister of the Interior, the French government promised more investment and development for Corsica. This plan was set aside with the outbreak of **World War I**, which itself reduced Corsica's population still further, taking over twenty thousand lives.

During the 1920s and 1930s Mussolini set his sights on Corsica, and World War II brought occupation by eighty thousand Italians and eight thousand German troops – almost half the number of the island's inhabitants. Once more, Corsican rebels took to the maquis, earning worldwide fame for their relentless guerrilla activity against the Axis powers, and lending the name **Maquis** to other resistance movements. In 1943 the Italians surrendered, and in the following year Corsica was the first French *département* to be liberated by the Allied forces. American soldiers moved in and began the process of real change in Corsica's economy, chiefly by using DDT to clear the east coast of malarial mosquitoes.

In the postwar years, Corsica was earmarked by the French government as a target for development, and in 1957 two state-sponsored organizations were set up to exploit its potential: **SOMIVAC** – the Société pour la Mise en Valeur Agricole de la Corse – introduced modern agricultural techniques; **SETCO** – the Société pour l'Équipement Touristique de la Corse – provided funds to build a tourist industry. Both organizations met with considerable distrust, seen as threats to an ancient way of life that had evolved and survived during centuries of hostile occupation. Nevertheless, the development gathered pace and, after 1962, when Algeria gained its independence, the situation was complicated by a massive influx of pieds-noirs refugees from the ex-French colony. Over 15,000 settlers poured into Corsica during the next twenty years, many of them buying up the newly developed land and hotels, adding to Corsican fears of losing control of their resources. Summer **tourists** began to arrive in steadily rising numbers, topping the half-million mark in the early 1970s (and now heading for 1.5 million).

Calls for Autonomy

It was against this background of change and insecurity that demands for greater administrative power were increasingly voiced from the 1960s. Led by the **Simeoni brothers**, Max and Edmond, a party of nationalist students known as L'Action

Régionaliste Corse (**L'ARC**) started to call for decentralized government, for restrictions on the east coast tourist developments, for a Corsican university (Paoli's had been closed by the French), and for compulsory schooling in Corsican language and history. They also mounted campaigns against French plans to install a nuclear power station in Corsica, and against the sale of cheap electricity to neighbouring Sardini, by blowing up pylons.

A number of more radical **autonomist movements**, varying in tactics and demands, entered the political scene, and from the mid-1970s these won substantial support for their manifesto of a national assembly and demand for investment in controlled development and protection of the land. Meanwhile, following the **Aléria siege** of 1975, in which paramilitaries led by Edmond Simeoni occupied a wine cellar on the east coast, a group of activists operating as the **FLNC** (Front de Libération Nationale de la Corse) embarked on a programme of bombing campaigns, targeting the tourist villages and foreign-owned properties that they believed were destroying Corsica's land and culture.

In the early 1980s the autonomists profited from a change of policy in France favouring increased decentralization. A Corsican university was re-established in 1981, providing a channel for the ambitions and political ideas of the younger generation. In the following year, Corsica was the first of the French regions to be granted a national assembly, with limited powers over policy, administration and finance. Nonetheless, benefiting from close links with the IRA, a more ruthless and efficient FLNC intensified its paramilitary activities. Dozens of explosions heralded the **election** of 1984, as allegations of fraud and corruption were levelled against the politicians. Voicing their political messages and demands through nocturnal press conferences in the maquis, known as *nuits bleues*, **terrorists** wearing black balaclavas became symbols of the armed struggle. Money for their campaigns derived increasingly from robberies and racketeering, as the FLNC adopted organized crime as a weapon of war.

In 1986 and 1987, the ruthless summary execution of two Tunisians accused of drug trafficking, followed by another spate of bombings, led to the banning of the separatist party **MCA** (Mouvement Corse pour l'Autodétermination), and a concerted clampdown on the FLNC, mounted by the (then) minister of the interior, **Charles Pasqua**. After infiltration by government spies, dozens of suspected terrorists were arrested, and the activities of known nationalists curtailed, among them the popular Corsican folk-rock band I Muvrini, who were banned from performing in public. Nevertheless, nationalist political parties continued to poll around seventeen percent of the vote in elections, though a crisis was brewing that would inflict considerably more damage to the nationalist movement than any of Pasqua's heavy-handed tactics. Following a period of deepening political divisions, in 1990 the movement split into two opposing factions: **Cuncolta** and their armed wing, the FLNC Canal Historique; and the **MPA**, whose paramilitary group dubbed itself the FLNC Canal Habituel. Soon an all-out blood feud erupted between the two which, by 1996–97, had claimed dozens of lives on both sides. As this book went to press, reports of tit-for-tat killings were still commonplace on the island, and the armed nationalist struggle seems doomed to destroy itself rather than the French political domination that provoked its emergence.

In spite of – or, some would argue, because of – the violence, the past twenty years have seen a slow progression towards a re-evaluation of Corsican culture and the island's attainment of increasing control over its own affairs. A statute passed in 1990 gave a great degree of autonomy to Corsica, and in 1992 the nationalists won 13 of the 61 seats in the regional assembly. Though many young Corsicans still seek jobs and education on the mainland, those who stay can now study the language and customs that once appeared to be dying out, and enjoy a standard of living that has risen markedly since the 1950s, largely as a result of the tourist boom. Parts of the island may seem in danger of becoming bland, international-style holiday resorts, and the abandonment and spoliation of large tracts of agricultural land presents a real problem, but the revival of a strong Corsican identity has led to a reassessment of the island's future – which is guaranteed to be as controversial and unyielding as its past.

Nia Williams

Corsican Wildlife

The **Parc Naturel Régional de la Corse**, established in 1972, now embraces about a third of Corsica, largely down the mountain spine but reaching the sea in the northwest. Managing important sites such as Scandola, the Restonica valley, the Finocchiarola isles in the north and the Lavezzi isles in the south, the park authorities ensure the survival of the mouflon and other endangered species, and increase the accessibility of the wildlife of Corsica, through the publication of excellent books and booklets and through the maintenance of footpaths. The ruggedness of Corsica's heartland naturally restricts intensive exploitation, but even in areas where human intervention has occurred, the island's terrain is extraordinarily rich. The lush chestnut woodland of the Castagniccia, for example, is the result of plantation, and the tangled, headily scented maquis which clothes more than half of Corsica might seem a natural cover, but is in fact what comes in after fire or on abandoned grazing land.

The Habitat Zones

Corsica's landscape has three well-defined **habitat zones**, the lowest of which is the Mediterranean zone, which runs from the sea to an altitude of 1000m. Corsica is noted for its clean seas and varied marine life. At places along the coast you'll find pristine sand dunes, lagoons and estuaries, all three of which are now hard to find elsewhere in the Mediterranean. Trees sometimes grow right at the edge of the beach: the highly resinous **Aleppo pine** prefers rocky ground at this level, while the **stone pine** (or umbrella pine) is often seen growing singly but sometimes in groves – some of the best specimens are at Palombaggia beach near Porto-Vecchio. Stands of tall Australian **eucalyptus** can also be found in many places, planted late last century judging by the size of the trees.

However, the typical indicator of the Mediterranean climate is the **olive tree**. Solitary olive trees can be found everywhere in Corsica's Mediterranean zone (the oldest giant is near the deserted convent below Oletta at the foot of Cap Corse), while the largest groves are in the Balagne and near Propriano. At these lower altitudes erect "funeral" cypresses are often planted alongside family tombs, and three species of oak also identify this zone – the **cork oak** (its trunk dusky red when newly stripped), the evergreen **holm oak** (which has spiny leaves on sucker shoots and is found in both shrub and tree forms) and the **kermes oak** (rarely tree-sized, and with holly-like leaves).

Introduced shrubs and trees which thrive in this Mediterranean climate include **orange** and **lemon** in groves and gardens, red or purple **bougainvillea** in gardens, **palms** in town squares, pink and white **oleanders** and the gigantic cactus-like **Mexican agave** on roadsides.

It's in the Mediterranean zone that the **maquis** comes in after fire or when fields or open grazings are abandoned. Its most easily recognized plants are the shrubs of the **cistus** family, carrying pink or white flowers with crumpled petals which are shed at the end of each day. Some cistus have highly scented gummy stems and leaves – the Montpellier cistus, which likes acid granite soils and has masses of small white flowers, is perhaps the smelliest of all.

Cistus bushes often indicate open, newish maquis, which in time will grow into an all-but-impenetrable scrub, with yellow-flowered **brooms** (some of which are wickedly thorny), the taller **strawberry tree** (the red strawberry-like fruits are edible but pappy), the pungent **mastic** and **myrtle**, **rosemary** and white-flowered **tree heather**, which grows 2m tall or more. In the "tall" maquis, cork, holm oaks and other trees come in, and as their crowns broaden they begin to shade out the shrubs below them, until eventually woodland or forest results.

Towards the top of the Mediterranean zone these trees might be joined by **maritime pine**, which unusually keeps large cones of different ages on its branches, and it keeps those branches even when they are starkly dead – the Restonica valley has many examples. **Sweet chestnut** also makes an appearance (it is most widespread between 500m and 800m), as does bracken. Groves of ancient chestnuts can be found near most of the hill villages, where the production of chestnut flour used to play an important part in the economy. Nowadays the chestnuts are given over to pigs, and many of the trees display dead antler-like branches as a result of attacks of mildew and parasites.

At around 1000m the **mountain zone** succeeds, as oaks and chestnuts give way to forests of the native, tall-trunked **Laricio** (or Corsican) **pine**, maybe mixed with **beeches** and **firs**. The Aitone, Valdo-Niello, Bonifato and Tartagine are among the most magnificent of these forests, featuring centuries-old Laricio pines that are the tallest conifers in Europe, reaching up to 40m.

Above 2000m stretches the **alpine zone** – open and largely rocky, perhaps with scatters of ground-hugging bushy alders, and often with a wonderful variety of flowers.

Wild Flowers

Many Corsican plants are distinctive of the island – of the 2000 species of **wild flowers** found here, eight percent are native to Corsica or shared only by Corsica and Sardinia. Which species you'll see will depend on the soil, the bedrock, the altitude and, of course, the time of year. Spring is glorious, with wild flowers everywhere, and many species celebrate a "second spring" after the summer drought: **cyclamens** and **autumn crocus** appear with the autumn rains, for example, and the handsome **bush spurges** of Cap Corse are in vivid green leaf in winter and spring, but reduced to bare twigs in summer.

Flowers of the Mediterranean Zone

On the seashore in summer, the dramatic **yellow-horned poppy** is worth looking for, with its very long curved seed pods. Colourful **sea stocks** and **sea lavender** grow on shingle and on rocks, where carpets of **stonecrop** – with fleshy red leaves and heads of small blue flowers – also make a handsome showing. The **sea holly**, one of the most beautiful of all wild plants with its grey-green spiny leaves and blue flower heads, sometimes forms low mats a couple of metres across – you'll see it on the open sands at Cargèse, for example. Here and at the back of other sandy beaches you can also find the white **sea daffodil** flowering in August, and almost anywhere you might come across carpets of **Hottentot fig** with its brilliant lilac or yellow-orange flowers.

In spring, various wild flowers brighten the clearings among the colourful **maquis** shrubs. If the maquis is invading old grazing land, or if the open patch is overgrazed and impoverished, there will probably be **asphodel** growing; its delicate white flowers are withered husks by summer, although the tall spikes remain. Many of Corsica's fifty or so species of **wild orchid** flower in the maquis; one of the most handsome is the pink **butterfly orchid**, and there are always a good number of the unmistakable hooded **serapias** group, which are purple or dark red. French **lavender** is common, its small almost black flowers carried below striking purple sails, and in some areas wild **gladiolus** can be seen along the roads or even as a weed in the ploughed fields – it has smaller flowers than the garden hybrids but is easily recognizable.

The verges and rocky cuttings of roads and lanes through the maquis and between the fields are home to **wild pinks** (some of the mountain pinks are endemic to the island), **ferns**, **honeysuckle** and **eglantine** (a wild white rose looking rather like cistus). Wild **asparagus** is often found growing around the olive groves, while in spring **tassel hyacinths** and white **Florentine iris**, the original fleur-de-lis, flower on open soil (the iris is also popular in gardens).

Flowers of the Mountain and Alpine Zones

In the chestnut woods and amongst the pines of the mountain zone grow the handsome green tufts of the **Corsican hellebore**, a poisonous species endemic to Corsica and Sardinia. **Foxgloves** may be found here, and in spring scatters of **cyclamen** mix with **violets** along the stream-sides, together with hosts of delicate white or lilac **anemones** in some areas. **Autumn crocus** and **squill** also flower here and elsewhere towards the end of the year. Wherever you find beech trees at this height you might look for wild red **peony**.

Although the mountain zone is harsh, there can be a surprising variety of flowers when the snow melts, many of them endemic – indeed, half of those you see might grow only in Corsica and Sardinia, such as a Corsican alpine groundwort and a blue mountain columbine. And many common enough in the Alps are not found here, suggesting that these two islands separated from mainland Europe at a far distant time in the past.

Birds

As a result of the closed breeding of its island populations, Corsica's **birds** often display certain differences from those of mainland Europe. Songbirds such as the blackbird have a song that's distinct from that of related European species, and the birds' normal habitats are in many instances extended in some way. In Corsica the blackbird ranges from coastal maquis to the high mountains, while the explosive "chetti" call of the small brown **Cetti's warbler** is heard not only in the reed beds around the coastal lagoons but also in the maquis up to 500m. The most renowned Corsican example is the elusive **Corsican nuthatch** of the Aitone and other high pine forests. The **treecreeper** is another, while there are also forms of **great spotted woodpecker** and **wren** shared with Sardinia. Corsica is the place to add the **Dartford warbler** to your list – it is a localized and rare resident in the south of Britain; here it is common in the coastal maquis but as a darker, smaller subspecies.

Because of its position, Corsica is probably visited by the majority of trans-Mediterranean **migrants**, many of which make landfalls on the headlands or lagoons. The **spring and autumn** list includes common and curlew sandpiper (the latter the commonest migrant wader here), reed bunting, marsh and Montague's harriers, pied flycatcher, grey heron, black kite and tree pipit. Of the birds that come to **winter** on the island, the sparrow-like dunnock is one of the commonest in the maquis, and amongst the other regulars are snipe, cormorant, common starling, gannet, pochard, tufted duck, teal, black-necked grebe, redwing and song thrush. Others such as the wood pigeon are resident, but numbers swell in

winter when incomers fly in to gorge on the plentiful crops of acorns.

Seabirds and Wetland Species

In general most **coastal birdlife** is centred on remote headlands and islands. Scandola, for example, has osprey, peregrine, rock dove and blue rock thrush (which also nest on bare slopes inland to 1800m). Shearwaters nest in some places, but you'll see fewer **gulls** than you might expect. Herring gulls nest at Scandola and Capo Rosso and other remote sites, and you may spot the Mediterranean gull (black-headed in summer) and the slim-winged Audouin's gull, which nests on several offshore islands. Shags too nest on rocky shores and are often seen flying low over the sea.

Despite widespread drainage for vineyards, fruit and other crops, the string of lagoons off the east coast remain as one of the most extensive wetland units of the whole Mediterranean, attracting great crested and little **grebes**, pochard and mallard, and the water rail with its incredible pig-like cry. Reed, moustached, Cetti's and other **warblers** call from the reed beds while marsh harrier and hobby hunt across them. In winter, Biguglia and the other lagoons are an important station for ducks, grey heron, wintering kingfisher and others.

Maquis Species

The **maquis** in its various forms offers ideal nesting for **warblers** and birds such as red-backed shrike, pipits, buntings and even the highly colourful bee-eater. The **linnet** picks out more open areas, as does the **stonechat** and the red-legged **partridge** (the grey has been introduced for shooting in some places). These birds all follow the maquis as it spreads up the valleys and slopes inland, but where it grows tall and is invaded by holm oak and other trees (as seen in the Fango valley, for example) the scrub warblers such as Dartford and Sardinian warblers leave, while the blackcap and subalpine warbler remain. Being evergreen, the maquis maintains its insect larder in winter, when many of its resident birds are joined by migrant cousins.

Kestrel and buzzards (widespread but nowhere very common) patrol above the maquis, as does red kite, which prefers the lower scrubby maquis to the taller growth. At night the clear bell-like notes of the **Scops owl** and the call of the nightjar echo across the maquis, mingling with the constant croaking of frogs.

The chestnut groves are comparatively empty of birdlife, but look for the endemic **tree creeper** here, and also the **mistle thrush** and the **wryneck**, the last now rare almost everywhere.

Mountain Species

In the **mountain** and alpine levels grey wagtail and dipper forage in the spray of the torrents, where the crag martin is often seen as well. The pine forests have **goldcrest**, **coal tit** and the endemic **nuthatch** – this last, found from the Tartagine in the north to Ospedale in the south, is smaller than its mainland cousins and is more often heard than seen. Sparrowhawk and goshawk have a presence in these pine woods, as does the crossbill.

A feature of some parts of the **high mountains** are *pozzines* – small tablelands of peaty turf cut by meandering streams. Here **lark** and **wheatear** are often seen, with even blackbird and chaffinch if there are scrubby alders for cover. The blue rock thrush, though nesting on the coast at Scandola and elsewhere, can be met as high as 1500m. The central mountains are the domain of the yellow-beaked **alpine chough** and the rare **lammergeier** and **golden eagle**. Bonelli's eagle is reported from the Asco valley, but it is not known if it nests.

Garden Species

Gardens attract many birds, such as blackbird, warblers, hooded crow and turtle dove – these last are widely shot when they fly in in spring, but there are always some to be heard in summer. (The collared dove is a recent colonist and still uncommon.) Gardens also attract the spotted flycatcher – the Corsican form scarcely lives up to its name, with few if any speckles, but it is quickly recognized by its lively flycatching sorties, usually returning to the same post. In the Nebbio and a few other spots the **hoopoe** with its dramatic crest is also seen in gardens at dawn. The towns attract **house martin** and **swifts** – both the familiar Eurasian swift and the similar pallid swift.

Mammals

Woodmouse, shrew, rabbit, brown hare, weasel and hedgehog are as familiar in Corsica as elsewhere in Europe, but there are no squirrels.

Squirrel-like nests in shrubs or low trees may be those of the black rat, while a sighting of a small brownish animal with squirrel-like bushy tail would be the **fat dormouse**, though it is shy and nocturnal. The slimmer **garden**, or **oak**, **dormouse**, with white underside to body and tail, is also resident. Both these animals may search houses for a hibernation den in autumn, and you often hear them scratching around in the attic. Bats are common everywhere: in the gorge of the Bonifato forest behind Calvi, for example, they swarm out at sunset.

The fox is seen, and there are reports of a wild cat in remote parts of the island such as the Aitone forest – it may turn out to be a tribe of striped feral cat, domestic stock now living wild. There are similar indecisive reports of pine marten in these forested areas.

Around five hundred **mouflon** – a wild sheep, the males sporting massive curved horns – are found in two main areas, at Asco and at Bavella. They might be the relic of an original wild population which began to be domesticated in Neolithic times, or they may be the descendants of escapees from those first domestic flocks.

The **wild boar** (*sanglier* in French) is found throughout the maquis and in the lower mountains, and has something of a cult status in Corsica. Many villages organize weekly hunts over the winter, culling an estimated 10,000 each year from an average population of 30,000. Even though the males are smaller than their continental cousins (a common island trait this), the Corsican boar can still reach 80kg, and is a formidable animal, being armed with tusks for rooting and grubbing – you'll come across the disturbed ground during walks in the maquis. It is a Corsican habit to let the domestic **pigs** roam free in the chestnut and beech woods on the mountain flanks, so there is certainly interbreeding between boar and pig, yet about forty percent of the wild boar stock remains untainted.

The native **red deer** – the smallest of all red deer – became extinct only a few decades ago, but some Sardinian stock can be seen in a paddock near Quenza in the south.

Offshore, the common and striped **dolphins** and the common **porpoise** patrol, if no longer as regularly or in the numbers that were once seen, and the endangered monk seal of the Mediterranean was last seen in Corsican waters in 1982. The **fin whale**, however, is often seen with young off Cap Corse in Springtime.

Reptiles and Insects

Corsica's hot rocky landscape suits reptiles, and **lizards** are always seen scuttling across walls and rocks. The **Tyrrhenian wall lizard** is a sometimes abundant species found only in Corsica and Sardinia, and the mountain lizard is also endemic, but their variable colouring makes identification of lizard species difficult. Their cousins, the plump but flattened **geckos**, are most often noticed high on room walls and ceilings, which they patrol after sunset, dealing with mosquitoes and other irritations.

There are no poisonous snakes on the island. The **grass snake** is seen in damp places, while the **whip snake** – a slender snake often with a barred pattern – is found on sunny hillsides and other dry habitats. It will attempt to bite if annoyed – its French name is *colereuse*, "quick-tempered one".

Hermann's tortoise is a fairly common sight in some areas, and a centre for tortoise breeding and release has recently been created near Moltifao in the Asco valley. The European pond **terrapin** might be seen in secluded pools and other still waters that have overgrown banks.

Endemic to the island is the **brook salamander**, olive grey and brown and with a clear yellow stripe down its spine, found near running water up to 2000m. The rather larger **fire salamander**, with dramatic black and yellow skin, might also be seen.

Most piercingly vocal are the **edible frog** and the **common tree frog**, which has enormous vocal sacs for its small size. The **green toad**, with spotted green and white skin and shrill warbling call, is also reasonably common.

The frog chorus takes over from the summer daytime chorus of the **cicadas**, especially loud in the vicinity of their favourite umbrella pines. The cicadas are just one of a host of grasshoppers, bushcrickets, beetles, bees and butterflies which make Corsica – and other Mediterranean lands

---

A CHECKLIST OF WILDLIFE SITES

FORESTS

Aitone – magnificent specimens of Laricio pine; in the remoter reaches (towards Monte Cinto), wild boar, eagle and mouflon. See p.151.

Bavella – impressive though fire-damaged hunting reserve; chance of sightings of mouflon and eagle. See p.224.

Bonifato – classic "chaos" of rocks and forest, pines and maquis. See p.134.

Castagniccia – chestnut woods. See p.274.

Ospédale – pines and other trees. See p.253.

Tartagine – bat caves and magnificent pines. See p.131.

Valdo-Niello – the largest of the island's forests, with fine examples of Laricio pine. See p.295.

Vizzavona – some of the finest pines and beech. See p.312.

OTHER WILDLIFE ZONES

Asco valley – possible sightings of mouflon, eagle, lammergeier; Laricio and maritime pines. See p.286.

Biguglia and the east coast lagoons – birdlife. See p.64.

Bonifacio – limestone cliffs with rare flowers. See p.236.

Les Calanche – flowers and coastal birds. See p.146.

Cap Corse – remote maquis, good for birds (maybe eagles attracted by remoteness); nature reserve on Finocchiarola isles. See p.75.

Désert des Agriates – a largish area of thin maquis growing on rocky, impoverished terrain; good for flowers and nesting birds. See p.93

Fango valley – good walking through mix of maquis and forest habitats. See p.136.

Îles Sanguinaires – distinctive island vegetation. See p.175.

Lavezzi isles – nature reserve off Bonifacio. See p.247.

Niolo – alpine choughs and other mountain birds. See p.290.

Restonica – Corsican and maritime pine. See p.304.

Scandola – supreme nature reserve of international importance; classic lava column geology; osprey and other birds; marine life. See p.137.

– so fascinating for anyone with any interest in natural history. Some butterflies will be familiar from northern Europe, such as the migrant painted lady and the red admiral. Of the Mediterranean species, one of the most handsome is the large, strongly flying **two-tailed pasha**, which feeds on the strawberry tree of the maquis. **Hummingbird hawk moths** of various kinds are commonly seen in gardens, hovering in front of the flowers.

Damselflies and mayflies are a common sight dancing over the streams, and the dramatic and fierce **hawker dragonflies** – a birdwatcher's insect if ever there were one – may spend the day hunting across the maquis, far from water.

Geoffrey Young

Books

Very few books about Corsica have been written in English, and the great majority of them are currently out of print, so you'll have to resort to second-hand book shops or libraries if you want to get stuck into the titles listed below. Out-of-print titles are marked "o/p" in the listings below. For those few that are in print, the UK publisher is given first in each listing, followed by the publisher in the US, unless the title is available in one country only, in which case we have specified the country concerned. If the same publisher produces the book in the UK and US, the publisher is simply named once.

For the benefit of fluent French readers, we've also included a handful of French titles which you can buy in any good bookshop in Corsica, or on mainland France.

Travel Books and Journals

James Boswell, *The Journal of a Tour to Corsica* (excerpts published in *Journals of James Boswell*: In Print Publishing/Norwood, o/p). Typically robust and witty account of meetings with a broad cross-section of Corsican people, including absorbing insights into the psychology of local hero Pascal Paoli. Following his eventful trip to the island in 1765, Boswell became famous as an advocate of Corsican independence.

Thomasina Campbell, *Southward Ho!* (o/p). Jolly account of the island as seen through the eyes of a Victorian walker, with plentiful descriptions of wild flowers and scenery – but little on the inhabitants.

Dorothy Carrington, *Granite Island* (Penguin). A fascinating and immensely comprehensive book,

combining the writer's personal experiences with an evocative portrayal of historical figures and events. By far the best study of Corsica ever written in English. Her most recent offering, *The Dream Hunters of Corsica* (Phoenix), covers some of the same ground, but is well worth reading too, focusing on the occult phenomena unique to the island, notably *mazzeri* (see p.235) and the evil eye.

A. Dugmore-Hardie, *Corsica the Beautiful* (o/p). Gushing eulogy of Corsica's landscapes, flora and fauna.

Emma Eleanor Elliot, *The Life and Letters of Sir Gilbert Elliot* (o/p). Observations on Corsica from the British viceroy's office (1794–96), compiled by his granddaughter.

Gustave Flaubert *Voyage dans les Pyrénées et Én Corse* (o/p). Flaubert's parents promised him a trip to Corsica if he passed his baccalaureate, and this book is an account of the trip the young novelist-to-be subsequently made in the summer of 1840. Full of freshness, sensuality and evocative descriptions of the island's landscape and people, it follows the nineteen-year-old's progress across the Pyrenees to the Mediterranean, with a poignant interlude describing his secret love affair with a beautiful Peruvian woman in Marseille.

Edward Lear, *Journal of a Landscape Painter* (Century, UK, o/p). Account of a Corsican visit in the 1860s, augmented by beautifully atmospheric engravings.

John Lowe, *Corsica: A Traveller's Guide* (John Murray, o/p). Rather trite commentary on the Corsican people and their ways, but one of the few English-language books to tackle the present-day island.

Alan Ross, *Time Was Away – A Journey Through Corsica* (Collins Harvill, UK, o/p). Gloomy impressionistic account of a visit to postwar Corsica, with drawings by John Minton.

Geoffrey Wagner, *Elegy for Corsica* (Cassell/Southern Illinois UP, both o/p). Amusing impressions of life in Corsica from an expat's point of view.

Archeology

Roger Grosjean, *La Corse Avant L'Histoire* (o/p). The most influential discussion of the island's prehistoric sites, from the man who excavated most of them. The explanations are clear and precise, and aided by photographs.

Jean Jehasse, *Aléria Grecque et Romaine* (o/p). Heavy-going in-depth study of the Roman site of Aléria.

Genevieve Moracchini-Mazel, *La Corse Romane* (o/p). The island's Pisan Romanesque architecture discussed with drawings and descriptions of building techniques.

Genevieve Moracchini-Mazel, *Les Monuments Préchrétiens de la Corse* (o/p). An important work on Bronze Age Corsica, including an interpretation of the statue-menhirs of Filitosa.

Xavier Poli, *La Corse dans l'Antiquité* (o/p). Rather stuffy but authoritative study of prehistoric Corsica.

History and Society

Philippe Alfonsi, *Les Chemins d'Orgueil* (o/p). The background to the rise of the FLNC, explored through the family history of one of its founder members. Based on solid journalistic research, but written in a fictional style.

Corelli Barnett, *Bonaparte* (Allen & Unwin/Hill & Wong, both o/p). An anti-Napoléon biography with vivid insights into his life in Corsica – good pictures too.

Dorothy Carrington, *Napoleon and his Parents on the Threshold of History* (Viking/Nal-Duhon, both o/p). Lucid study of Napoléon's early years in his native country, from the battle of Ponte-Nuovo until the death of his father in 1785, based on the archives of Prince Napoléon and other previously unconsulted private collections. The most thorough work on this period, with facsimiles of little-known documents and an exhaustive bibliography.

Vincent Cronin, *Napoleon* (Fontana/Harper-Collins). Enthusiastic and accessible biography; you might still find copies of the recently deleted Penguin edition on the shelves.

Peter Geyl, *Napoleon – For and Against* (Penguin, o/p). A compendium of various French scholars' views on Napoléon.

M. Maclaren, *Corsican Boswell* (o/p). Places Boswell's reactions to Corsica within their historical context; an amusing read but difficult to find.

Elie Papadacci, *Les Bandits Corses: Honneur et Dignité* (Éditions Almar, France). The life histories of Corsica's most infamous bandits (see p.215), sympathetically written by the island's top historian.

Valerie Pirie, *His Majesty of Corsica* (o/p). An illuminating biography of Corsica's ephemeral king, Theodor von Neuhof.

Peter Adam Thrasher, *Pasquale Paoli – An Enlightened Hero* (Shoe String, US). A rather laboured biography, but does include some interesting facts about Corsica in the eighteenth century.

Literature

Gabriel Xavier Culioli, *La Terre des Seigneurs* (o/p). Phenomenally successful novel following the evolution of a family through a century in Corsica. A compelling read that's full of fascinating background on island politics and village life.

Alphonse Daudet, *Letters from my Windmill* (Penguin). Tale of a lonely Corsican lighthouse keeper, with colourful description of the Îles Sanguinaires, near Ajaccio.

Alexandre Dumas, *The Corsican Brothers* (Buccaneer, US). Far-fetched tale of two outlaw brothers in nineteenth-century Corsica.

Gustave Flaubert, *Memoires d'un Fou* (o/p). Flaubert romanticizes the bandits, the maquis, the mountains and the sea in letters to his sister.

Guy de Maupassant, *Un Bandit Corse et Autres Contes* (o/p). Maupassant, France's most illustrious short story author, spent two months in Corsica in 1880, and the lively tales in this anthology were all inspired by his visit. The *Bandit Corse* has become a classic, and is said to have been avidly read by the bandits themselves after its publication.

Prosper Mérimée, *Colomba* (o/p). Short novel loosely based on a real-life blood feud which divided the village of Fozzano in the 1830s. A son returns to Corsica and is expected to avenge the death of his father. Though far from historically accurate, the story vividly evokes the violent spirit of the times and was a roaring success for Mérimée, inspiring a mini tourist invasion in Fozzano.

Walking and Climbing

Alan Castle, *The Cosican High Level Route* (Cicerone, UK). Detailed, day-by-day description of the GR20, with plenty of photographs and solid information, but no topo-maps.

Robin G. Collomb, *Corsica Mountains* (West Co, UK). Covers all the principal mountain peaks, with information on different approaches and ascents, backed up with diagrams.

Noel Rochford, *Landscapes of Corsica* (Sunflower, UK). Car tour routes, suggestions for picnic spots and specific walking routes. Good for

ideas for gentle walks, but its directions are sometimes confusing.

Walks in Corsica (in the Robertson McCarta *Footpaths of Europe* series in UK). The cream of Corsica's long-distance hiking trails described in translation from the French Ramblers Association's essential topo-guides, including colour 1:50,000 maps overlaid with the routes. Essential for serious hikers.

Language

familiarize yourself with the information given below before you leave.

The Corsican Language

Corsican, originally a Latin-based language with resemblances to Romanian, developed an Italianate vocabulary and syntax during Pisan and Genoese occupation. Arabic and French influences have added to the complexity of Corsican, which for centuries was predominantly an oral tongue until around two hundred years ago – hence the confusing variety of spellings for placenames, despite attempts at standardization. The commonest variants come about through the transposition of *ll* and *dd* – as in *casteddu* and *castellu*. Buildings and monuments are often labelled in different languages (San Pietro/San Pietru), and on maps you'll find mountain passes, rivers and regions marked in a mixture of Italian, French and Corsican – the *u* ending (pronounced as in English "zoo") is a frequent indicator of Corsican usage. Deep in the country, many old people are still easier with Corsican than French, so a few phrases will be met with surprise and pleasure. Pronunciation is generally as for Italian, but look out for two tricky clusters of consonants – *chj/chi* and *ghj/chi* pronounced "ty" or "dy".

Since 1974 it has been compulsory for schoolchildren to learn Corsican up to the level of the baccalaureate, and at Corte University all students are obliged to study the language. Corsican nationalists use the language for their campaign literature, folk singers always sing in Corsican, and there's a newscast in Corsican on television every evening. Yet the language is struggling to survive in competition with French, a more international language and the official language of the island. French is spoken and understood everywhere in Corsica, where few speak English, even in the tourist offices – so you'd do well to

---

French Pronunciation

One easy rule to remember is that **consonants** at the ends of words are usually silent. *Pas plus tard* (not later) is thus pronounced "pa-plu-tarr". But when the following word begins with a vowel, you run the two together: *pas après* (not after) becomes "pazaprey". **Vowels** are the hardest sounds to get right. Roughly:

a	as in hat	*eu*	like the u in hurt	*ou*	as in food
e	as in get	*i*	as in machine	*u*	as in a pursed-lip
é	between get and gate	*o*	as in hot		version of **u**se
è	between get and gut	*o, au*	as in **o**ver		

More awkward are the **combinations** *in/im*, *en/em*, *an/am*, *on/om*, *un/um* at the ends of words, or followed by consonants other than *n* or *m*. Again, roughly:

in/im	like the **an** in **an**xious	*on/om*	like the **don** in **Don**caster said
an/am	like the **don** in **Don**caster when		by someone with a heavy cold
en/em	said with a nasal accent	*un/um*	like the **u** in **u**nderstand

Consonants are much as in English, except that: *ch* is always "sh", *c* is "s", *h* is silent, *th* is the same as "t", *ll* is like the *y* in "yes", *w* is "v", and *r* is growled (or rolled).

FRENCH WORDS AND PHRASES

Learning Materials

Rough Guide French Phrasebook (Rough Guides). Mini dictionary-style phrasebook with both English–French and French–English sections, along with cultural tips for tricky situations and a menu reader.

Mini French Dictionary (Harrap/Prentice Hall). French–English and English–French, plus a brief grammar and pronunciation guide.

Breakthrough French (Pan; book and two cassettes). Excellent teach-yourself course.

French and English Slang Dictionary (Harrap/Prentice Hall); **Dictionary of Modern**

Colloquial French (Routledge). Both volumes are a bit large to carry, but they are the key to all you ever wanted to understand.

Verbaid (Verbaid, Hawk House, Heath Lane, Farnham, Surrey GU9 0PR). CD-size laminated paper "verb wheel" giving you the tense endings for the regular verbs.

A Vous La France; Franc Extra; Franc-Parler (BBC Publications/EMC Publishing; each has a book and two cassettes). BBC radio courses, running from beginners' level to fairly advanced language.

Basic Words and Phrases

French nouns are divided into masculine and feminine. This causes difficulties with adjectives, whose endings have to change to suit the gender of the nouns they qualify. If you know some grammar, you will know what to do. If not, stick to the masculine form, which is the simplest – it's what we have done in this glossary.

today	*aujourd'hui*	that one	*celà*
yesterday	*hier*	open	*ouvert*
tomorrow	*demain*	closed	*fermé*
in the morning	*le matin*	big	*grand*
in the afternoon	*l'après-midi*	small	*petit*
in the evening	*le soir*	more	*plus*
now	*maintenant*	less	*moins*
later	*plus tard*	a little	*un peu*
at one o'clock	*à une heure*	a lot	*beaucoup*
at three o'clock	*à trois heures*	cheap	*bon marché*
at ten-thirty	*à dix heures et demie*	expensive	*cher*
at midday	*à midi*	good	*bon*
man	*un homme*	bad	*mauvais*
woman	*une femme*	hot	*chaud*
here	*ici*	cold	*froid*
there	*là*	with	*avec*
this one	*ceci*	without	*sans*

Numbers

1	*un*	12	*douze*	30	*trente*	95	*quatre-vingt-*
2	*deux*	13	*treize*	40	*quarante*		*quinze*
3	*trois*	14	*quatorze*	50	*cinquante*	100	*cent*
4	*quatre*	15	*quinze*	60	*soixante*	101	*cent-et-un*
5	*cinq*	16	*seize*	70	*soixante-dix*	200	*deux cents*
6	*six*	17	*dix-sept*	75	*soixante-*	300	*trois cents*
7	*sept*	18	*dix-huit*		*quinze*	500	*cinq cents*
8	*huit*	19	*dix-neuf*	80	*quatre-vingts*	1000	*mille*
9	*neuf*	20	*vingt*	90	*quatre-vingt-*	2000	*deux milles*
10	*dix*	21	*vingt-et-un*		*dix*	5000	*cinq milles*
11	*onze*	22	*vingt-deux*			1,000,000	*un million*

Days and Dates

January	*janvier*	November	*novembre*	August 1	*le premier*
February	*février*	December	*décembre*		*août*
March	*mars*			March 2	*le deux mars*
April	*avril*	Sunday	*dimanche*	July 14	*le quatorze*
May	*mai*	Monday	*lundi*		*juillet*
June	*juin*	Tuesday	*mardi*	November 23	*le vingt-trois*
July	*juillet*	Wednesday	*mercredi*		*novembre*
August	*août*	Thursday	*jeudi*	1997	*dix-neuf-cent-*
September	*septembre*	Friday	*vendredi*		*quatre-vingt-*
October	*octobre*	Saturday	*samedi*		*dix-sept*

Talking to People

When addressing people you should always use *Monsieur* for a man, *Madame* for a woman, *Mademoiselle* for a girl. Plain *bonjour* by itself is not enough. This isn't as formal as it seems, and it has its uses when you've forgotten someone's name or want to attract someone's attention.

Excuse me	*Pardon*	please	*s'il vous plaît*
Do you speak English?	*Vous parlez anglais?*	thank you	*merci*
How do you say it in French?	*Comment ça se dit en Français?*	hello	*bonjour*
		goodbye	*au revoir*
What's your name?	*Comment vous appelez-vous?*	good morning/ afternoon	*bonjour*
My name is . . .	*Je m'appelle . . .*	good evening	*bonsoir*
I'm English/ Irish/Scottish/ Welsh/American/ Australian/ Canadian/ a New Zealander	*Je suis anglais[e]// irlandais[e]/écossais[e]// gallois[e]/américain[e]// australien[ne]// canadien[ne]// néo-zélandais[e]*	good night	*bonne nuit*
		How are you?	*Comment allez-vous?/ Ça va?*
		Fine, thanks	*Très bien, merci*
		I don't know	*Je ne sais pas*
		Let's go	*Allons-y*
yes	*oui*	See you tomorrow	*A demain*
no	*non*	See you soon	*A bientôt*
I understand	*Je comprends*	Sorry	*Pardon, Madame/*
I don't understand	*Je ne comprends pas*		*Je m'excuse*
Can you speak slower please?	*S'il vous plaît, parlez moins vite*	Leave me alone (aggressive)	*Fichez-moi la paix!*
OK/agreed	*d'accord*	Please help me	*Aidez-moi, s'il vous plaît*

Finding the Way

bus	*autobus/bus/car*	hitchhiking	*autostop*
bus station	*gare routière*	on foot	*à pied*
bus stop	*arrêt*	Where are you going?	*Vous allez où?*
car	*voiture*	I'm going to . . .	*Je vais à . . .*
train/taxi/ferry	*train/taxi/ferry*	I want to get off	*Je voudrais descendre*
boat	*bâteau*	at . . .	*à . . .*
plane	*avion*	the road to . . .	*la route pour . . .*
train station	*gare (SNCF)*	near	*près/pas loin*
platform	*quai*	far	*loin*
What time does it leave?	*Il part à quelle heure?*	left	*à gauche*
		right	*à droite*

. . . continues overleaf

. . . continued from overleaf

What time does it arrive?	*Il arrive à quelle heure?*	straight on	*tout droit*
a ticket to . . .	*un billet pour . . .*	on the other side of	*à l'autre côté de*
single ticket	*aller simple*	on the corner of	*à l'angle de*
return ticket	*aller retour*	next to	*à côté de*
validate your ticket	*compostez votre billet*	behind	*derrière*
valid for	*valable pour*	in front of	*devant*
ticket office	*vente de billets*	before	*avant*
how many kilometres?	*combien de kilomètres?*	after	*après*
		under	*sous*
how many hours?	*combien d'heures?*	to cross	*traverser*
		bridge	*pont*

Questions and Requests

The simplest way of asking a question is to start with s'il vous plaît (please), then name the thing you want in an interrogative tone of voice. For example:

Where is there a bakery?	*S'il vous plaît, la boulangerie?*
Which way is it to the Eiffel Tower?	*S'il vous plaît, la route pour la Tour Eiffel?*

Similarly with requests:

We'd like a room for two.	*S'il vous plaît, une chambre pour deux.*
Can I have a kilo of oranges?	*S'il vous plaît, un kilo d'oranges.*

Question words

where?	*où?*	when?	*quand?*
how?	*comment?*	why?	*pourquoi?*
how many/how much?	*combien?*	at what time?	*à quelle heure?*
		what is/which is?	*quel est?*

Accommodation

a room for one/two people	*une chambre pour une/deux personnes*	do laundry	*faire la lessive*
a double bed	*un lit double*	sheets	*draps*
a room with a shower	*une chambre avec douche*	blankets	*couvertures*
		quiet	*calme*
a room with a bath	*une chambre avec salle de bain*	noisy	*bruyant*
for one/two/three nights	*pour une/deux/trois nuits*	hot water	*eau chaude*
		cold water	*eau froide*
Can I see it?	*Je peux la voir?*	Is breakfast included?	*Est-ce que le petit déjeuner est compris?*
a room on the courtyard	*une chambre sur la cour*	I would like breakfast	*Je voudrais prendre le petit déjeuner*
a room over the street	*une chambre sur la rue*	I don't want breakfast	*Je ne veux pas de petit déjeuner*
first floor	*premier étage*	Can we camp here?	*On peut camper ici?*
second floor	*deuxième étage*	campsite	*un camping/terrain de camping*
with a view	*avec vue*		
key	*clef*	tent	*une tente*
to iron	*repasser*	tent space	*un emplacement*
		youth hostel	*auberge de jeunesse*

Cars

service station	*garage*	to put air in the tyres	*gonfler les pneus*
service	*service*	battery	*batterie*
to park the car	*garer la voiture*	the battery is dead	*la batterie est morte*
car park	*un parking*	plugs	*bougies*
no parking	*défense de stationner/ stationnement interdit*	to break down	*tomber en panne*
		gas can	*bidon*
		insurance	*assurance*
gas station	*poste d'essence*	green card	*carte verte*
fuel	*essence*	traffic lights	*feux*
(to) fill it up	*faire le plein*	red light	*feu rouge*
oil	*huile*	green light	*feu vert*
air line	*ligne à air*		

Health Matters

doctor	*médecin*	stomach ache	*mal à l'estomac*
I don't feel well	*Je ne me sens pas bien*	period	*règles*
		pain	*douleur*
medicines	*médicaments*	it hurts	*ça fait mal*
prescription	*ordonnance*	chemist	*pharmacie*
I feel sick	*Je suis malade*	hospital	*hôpital*
I have a headache	*J'ai mal à la tête*		

Other Needs

bakery	*boulangerie*	bank	*banque*
food shop	*alimentation*	money	*argent*
supermarket	*supermarché*	toilets	*toilettes*
to eat	*manger*	police	*police*
to drink	*boire*	telephone	*téléphone*
camping gas	*camping gaz*	cinema	*cinéma*
tobacconist	*tabac*	theatre	*théâtre*
stamps	*timbres*	to reserve/book	*réserver*

CORSICAN WORDS AND PHRASES
Basics

yes, no, OK	*iè, nò, và bé*	cheap, expensive	*bonu mercatu, cara*
please, thank you	*fate u piacè, a' ringraziavvi*	hot, cold	*caldu, fredda*
		more, less	*piu, menu*
where, when	*induve, quandu*	today, tomorrow	*oghje, dumane*
what, how much	*chi, quantu*	day	*ghjurnu*
here, there	*custì, custà*	week	*simana*
this, that	*quellu/quella, quessu/quessa*	month	*meze*
		yesterday	*ieri*
now, later	*ora, dopu*	day before yesterday	*avant'ieri*
open, closed	*apertu, chiusu*		
with, without	*cù, senza*	next week	*simana'dopu*
good, bad	*bonu, male*	next month	*meze'dopu*
big, small	*grande/maio, piccola/chjucu*	nothing	*nulla/nunda/nudda*

. . . continues overleaf

. . . continued from overleaf

morning	*a mane*	girl, boy	*zitella, zitellu*
evening	*a sera*	it's good	*he bonu*
night	*a notte*	something	*qualcosa*
car	*a vittura*	I want	*vogliu*

Greetings and Responses

hello, goodbye	*bonghjornu, a'vedeci*	I (don't) understand	*(nò) capiscu*
good evening	*bona sera*	Do you speak English?	*Parla inglese?*
goodnight	*bona notte*	My name is . . .	*Me chjamanu. . .*
sorry	*me dispiace*	What's your name?	*Cumu a chjamanu*
excuse me	*scusame*	I am English	*Sò Inglese*
How are you?	*Comu sì?*	Let's go	*Andemu*

Questions and Requests

Do you have?	*Avetene?*	. . . with shower/bath	*. . .cùilla*
Give me	*Datemi*		*duscia/bag narola*
(one like that)		It's for one person/	*Ci ne vole una/*
That's enough	*Basta*	two people	*duie persona*
What would you	*Chi vulete beie?*	How long are	*quantu ci avete da*
like to drink?		you staying?	*stà?*
I'd like a lemonade/	*A me una*	for one night/	*. . . pé una notte/*
coffee	*limnata/caffè*	one week	*una semana*
How much?	*Quantu costanu?*	It's fine –	*Và bé quantu*
Is there?	*C'he?*		*costanu?*
. . . a room	*. . . una camera*	how much is it?	
. . . with two beds/double	*. . . cù duie letti*	It's too expensive	*He troppu caru*

Directions

Where is . . ?	*Induv'é?*	How long will it	*Quantu ci vole à*
It's near	*He vicinu*	take to get to	*ghjunghje*
It's far	*He lontana*	Ponte Leccia?	*à u Ponte à a Leccia?*
left, right,	*sinistra, dritta,*	What's the time ?	*Chi ora he?*
straight on	*sempredrittu*	It's three o'clock	*Sò trè ore*

Months and Seasons

January	*Ghjennaghju*	July	*Ghjugliu*	winter	*imbernu/*
February	*Febbraghju*	August	*Aostu*		*Ingnernu*
March	*Marzu*	September	*Sittembre*	spring	*veranu*
April	*Aprile*	October	*Ottobre*	summer	*estate*
May	*Maghjiu*	November	*Novembre*	autumn	*auturnu*
June	*Ghjiugnu*	December	*Dicembre*		

Numbers and Days

1	*unu (una)*	7	*sette*	13	*tredeci*
2	*dui (duie)*	8	*ottu*	14	*quattordeci*
3	*trè*	9	*nove*	15	*quindeci*
4	*quattru*	10	*dece*	16	*sedeci*
5	*cinque*	11	*ondeci*	17	*dicessette*
6	*sei*	12	*dodeci*	18	*diciottu*

19	*dicennove*	60	*sessanta*	Monday	*luni*
20	*vinti*	70	*settanta*	Tuesday	*marti*
21	*vintunu*	80	*ottanta*	Wednesday	*mercuri*
22	*vintidui*	90	*novanta*	Thursday	*ghjovi*
30	*trenta*	100	*centu*	Friday	*venneri*
40	*quaranta*	101	*cent'e unu*	Saturday	*sabatu*
50	*cinquanta*	102	*cent'e dui*	Sunday	*dumenica*

Words of the countryside

bird	*acellu*	plateau	*pianu*
mountain	*montane*	cliff	*scuglialu*
mountain pass	*bocca, foce*	bridge	*ponte*
mountain peak,	*capu, cima,*	river	*fiume*
summit	*monte, punta*	tree	*arburu*
forest, wood	*furesta, valdu*	beach	*a marina*
lake	*lavu*	village	*u paese*

Index

direct orders from

Amsterdam	1-85828-086-9	£7.99	US$13.95	CAN$16.99
Andalucia	1-85828-094-X	8.99	14.95	18.99
Australia	1-85828-141-5	12.99	19.95	25.99
Bali	1-85828-134-2	8.99	14.95	19.99
Barcelona	1-85828-221-7	8.99	14.95	19.99
Berlin	1-85828-129-6	8.99	14.95	19.99
Brazil	1-85828-102-4	9.99	15.95	19.99
Britain	1-85828-208-X	12.99	19.95	25.99
Brittany & Normandy	1-85828-224-1	9.99	16.95	22.99
Bulgaria	1-85828-183-0	9.99	16.95	22.99
California	1-85828-181-4	10.99	16.95	22.99
Canada	1-85828-130-X	10.99	14.95	19.99
China	1-85828-225-X	15.99	24.95	32.95
Corsica	1-85828-089-3	8.99	14.95	18.99
Costa Rica	1-85828-136-9	9.99	15.95	21.99
Crete	1-85828-132-6	8.99	14.95	18.99
Cyprus	1-85828-182-2	9.99	16.95	22.99
Czech & Slovak Republics	1-85828-121-0	9.99	16.95	22.99
Egypt	1-85828-188-1	10.99	17.95	23.99
Europe	1-85828-159-8	14.99	19.95	25.99
England	1-85828-160-1	10.99	17.95	23.99
First Time Europe	1-85828-270-5	7.99	9.95	12.99
Florida	1-85828-184-4	10.99	16.95	22.99
France	1-85828-124-5	10.99	16.95	21.99
Germany	1-85828-128-8	11.99	17.95	23.99
Goa	1-85828-156-3	8.99	14.95	19.99
Greece	1-85828-131-8	9.99	16.95	20.99
Greek Islands	1-85828-163-6	8.99	14.95	19.99
Guatemala	1-85828-189-X	10.99	16.95	22.99
Hawaii: Big Island	1-85828-158-X	8.99	12.95	16.99
Hawaii	1-85828-206-3	10.99	16.95	22.99
Holland, Belgium & Luxembourg	1-85828-087-7	9.99	15.95	20.99
Hong Kong	1-85828-187-3	8.99	14.95	19.99
Hungary	1-85828-123-7	8.99	14.95	19.99
India	1-85828-200-4	14.99	23.95	31.99
Ireland	1-85828-179-2	10.99	17.95	23.99
Italy	1-85828-167-9	12.99	19.95	25.99
Kenya	1-85828-192-X	11.99	18.95	24.99
London	1-85828-231-4	9.99	15.95	21.99
Mallorca & Menorca	1-85828-165-2	8.99	14.95	19.99
Malaysia, Singapore & Brunei	1-85828-103-2	9.99	16.95	20.99
Mexico	1-85828-044-3	10.99	16.95	22.99
Morocco	1-85828-040-0	9.99	16.95	21.99
Moscow	1-85828-118-0	8.99	14.95	19.99
Nepal	1-85828-190-3	10.99	17.95	23.99
New York	1-85828-171-7	9.99	15.95	21.99
Pacific Northwest	1-85828-092-3	9.99	14.95	19.99
Paris	1-85828-235-7	8.99	14.95	19.99

In the UK, Rough Guides are available from all good bookstores, but can be obtained from Penguin by contacting: Penguin Direct, Penguin Books Ltd, Bath Road, Harmondsworth, West Drayton, Middlesex UB7 0DA; or telephone the credit line on 0181-899 4036 (9am–5pm) and ask for Penguin Direct. Visa, Access and Amex accepted. Delivery will normally be within 14 working days. Penguin Direct ordering facilities are only available in the UK and the USA. The availability and published prices quoted are correct at the time of going to press but are subject to alteration without prior notice.

around the world

Poland	1-85828-168-7	10.99	17.95	23.99
Portugal	1-85828-180-6	9.99	16.95	22.99
Prague	1-85828-122-9	8.99	14.95	19.99
Provence	1-85828-127-X	9.99	16.95	22.99
Pyrenees	1-85828-093-1	8.99	15.95	19.99
Rhodes & the Dodecanese	1-85828-120-2	8.99	14.95	19.99
Romania	1-85828-097-4	9.99	15.95	21.99
San Francisco	1-85828-185-7	8.99	14.95	19.99
Scandinavia	1-85828-039-7	10.99	16.99	21.99
Scotland	1-85828-166-0	9.99	16.95	22.99
Sicily	1-85828-178-4	9.99	16.95	22.99
Singapore	1-85828-135-0	8.99	14.95	19.99
Spain	1-85828-240-3	11.99	18.95	24.99
St Petersburg	1-85828-133-4	8.99	14.95	19.99
Thailand	1-85828-140-7	10.99	17.95	24.99
Tunisia	1-85828-139-3	10.99	17.95	24.99
Turkey	1-85828-242-X	12.99	19.95	25.99
Tuscany & Umbria	1-85828-243-8	10.99	17.95	23.99
USA	1-85828-161-X	14.99	19.95	25.99
Venice	1-85828-170-9	8.99	14.95	19.99
Vietnam	1-85828-191-1	9.99	15.95	21.99
Wales	1-85828-245-4	10.99	17.95	23.99
Washington DC	1-85828-246-2	8.99	14.95	19.99
West Africa	1-85828-101-6	15.99	24.95	34.99
More Women Travel	1-85828-098-2	9.99	14.95	19.99
Zimbabwe & Botswana	1-85828-186-5	11.99	18.95	24.99

Phrasebooks

Czech	1-85828-148-2	3.50	5.00	7.00
French	1-85828-144-X	3.50	5.00	7.00
German	1-85828-146-6	3.50	5.00	7.00
Greek	1-85828-145-8	3.50	5.00	7.00
Italian	1-85828-143-1	3.50	5.00	7.00
Mexican	1-85828-176-8	3.50	5.00	7.00
Portuguese	1-85828-175-X	3.50	5.00	7.00
Polish	1-85828-174-1	3.50	5.00	7.00
Spanish	1-85828-147-4	3.50	5.00	7.00
Thai	1-85828-177-6	3.50	5.00	7.00
Turkish	1-85828-173-3	3.50	5.00	7.00
Vietnamese	1-85828-172-5	3.50	5.00	7.00

Reference

Classical Music	1-85828-113-X	12.99	19.95	25.99
Internet	1-85828-198-9	5.00	8.00	10.00
Jazz	1-85828-137-7	16.99	24.95	34.99
Opera	1-85828-138-5	16.99	24.95	34.99
Reggae	1-85828-247-0	12.99	19.95	25.99
Rock	1-85828-201-2	17.99	26.95	35.00
World Music	1-85828-017-6	16.99	22.95	29.99

In the USA, or for international orders, charge your order by Master Card or Visa (US$15.00 minimum order): call 1-800-253-6476; or send orders, with complete name, address and zip code, and list price, plus $2.00 shipping and handling per order to: Consumer Sales, Penguin USA, PO Box 999 – Dept #17109, Bergenfield, NJ 07621. No COD. Prepay foreign orders by international money order, a cheque drawn on a US bank, or US currency. No postage stamps are accepted. All orders are subject to stock availability at the time they are processed. Refunds will be made for books not available at that time. Please allow a minimum of four weeks for delivery.

Stay in touch with us!

ROUGH*NEWS* is Rough Guides' free newsletter.
In three issues a year we give you news, travel
issues, music reviews, readers' letters and the
latest dispatches from authors on the road.

I would like to receive ROUGH*NEWS*: please put me on your free mailing list.

NAME . . . .

ADDRESS . . . .

Please clip or photocopy and send to: Rough Guides, 1 Mercer Street, London WC2H 9QJ, England
or Rough Guides, 375 Hudson Street, New York, NY 10014, USA.

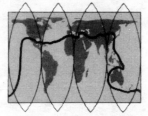

the perfect getaway vehicle

low-price holiday car rental.

rent a car from holiday autos and you'll give yourself real freedom to explore your holiday destination. with great-value, fully-inclusive rates in over 4,000 locations worldwide, wherever you're escaping to, we're there to make sure you get excellent prices and superb service.

what's more, you can book now with complete confidence. our £5 undercut* ensures that you are guaranteed the best value for money in holiday destinations right around the globe.

drive away with a great deal, call holiday autos now on **0990 300 400** and quote ref RG.

holiday autos miles ahead

*in the unlikely event that you should see a cheaper like for like pre-paid rental rate offered by any other independent uk car rental company before or after booking but prior to departure, holiday autos will undercut that price by a full £5. we truly believe we cannot be beaten on price.